GIN TAMA

Vol. 17
Only One Hour of Video Games per Day

STORY & ART BY
HIDEAKI SORACHI

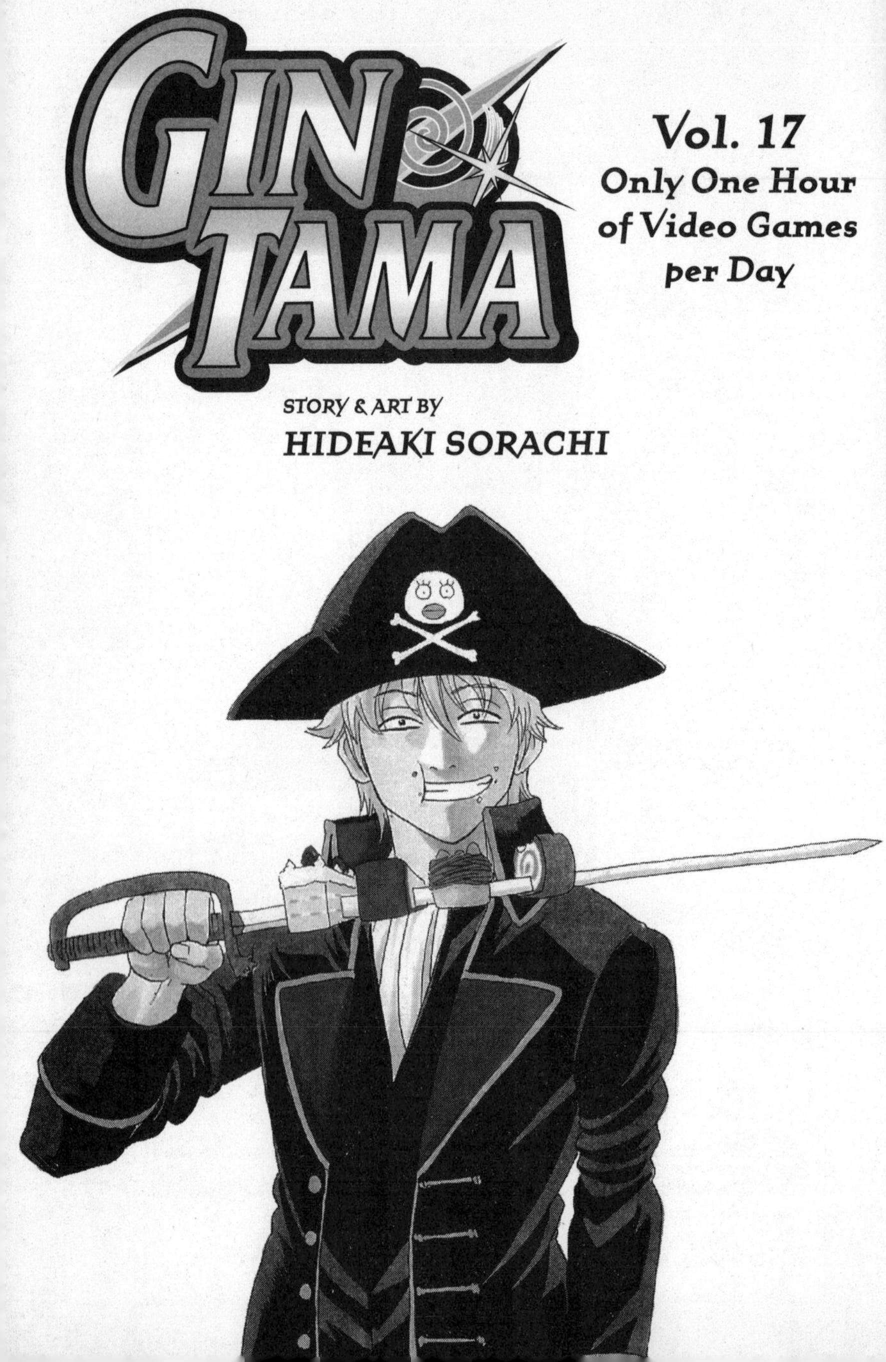

Cast of Characters

Yorozuya Members

Shinpachi Shimura

Works under Gintoki in an attempt to learn about the samurai spirit but has often come to regret his decision recently. President of the Tsu Terakado Fan Club.

Gintoki Sakata

The hero of our story. If he doesn't eat something sweet periodically he gets cranky—really cranky. He boasts a powerful sword arm, but he's one step away from diabetes. A former member of the exclusionist faction that seeks to expel the space aliens and protect the nation.

Kagura

A member of the Yato Clan, the most powerful warrior race in the universe. Her voracious appetite and alien worldview lead frequently to laughter...and sometimes contusions.

Sadaharu

A giant space creature turned office pet. Likes to bite people (especially Gin).

Shinsengumi Members

Okita

The Shinsengumi's most formidable swordsman. Behind a facade of amiability, he tirelessly schemes to eliminate Hijikata and usurp his position.

Hijikata

Vice Chief of the Shinsengumi, Edo's elite counter-terrorist police unit. His air of detached cool transforms into hot rage the instant he draws his sword...or when someone disparages mayonnaise.

Kondo

The trusted chief of the Shinsengumi (and the remorseless stalker of Shinpachi's older sister Otae).

Other Characters

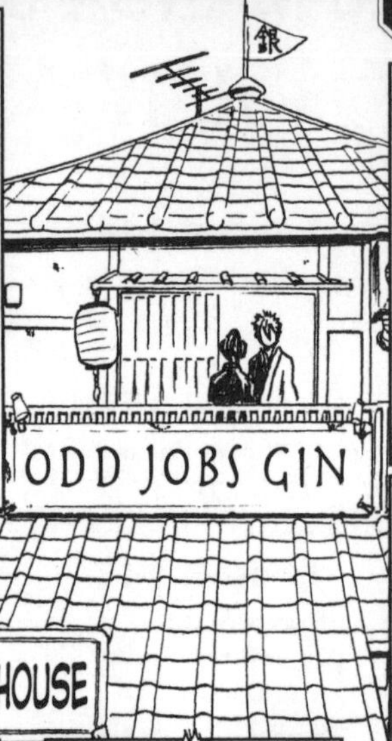
ODD JOBS GIN
OTOSE SNACK HOUSE

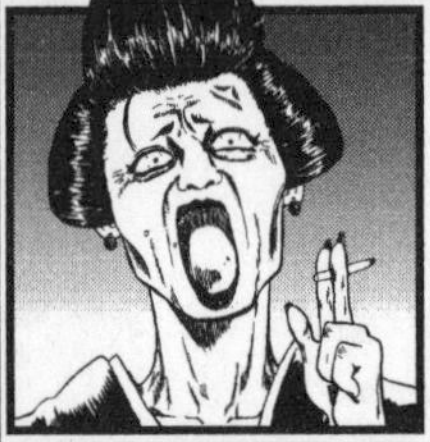

Otose-san

Gin's landlady and proprietor of the pub below the Yorozuya hideout. She has a lot of difficulty collecting the rent.

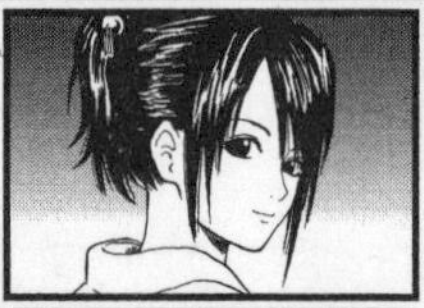

Otae Shimura

Her demure manner hides the heart of a lion. Though employed at a hostess bar, she ruthlessly guards her virtue and plots to revive the family fortunes.

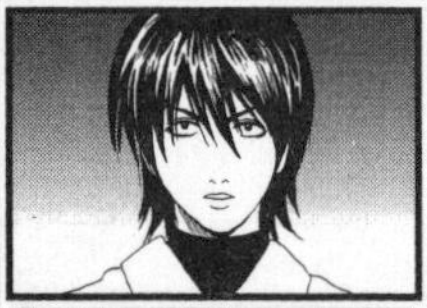

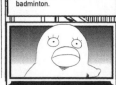

Sagaru Yamazaki

A member of the Shinsengumi who works as an observer (spy). His favorite pastime is badminton.

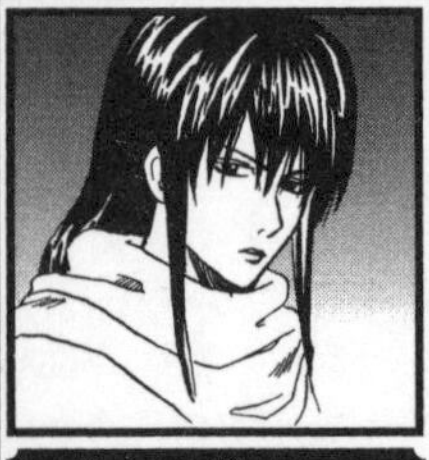

Kotaro Katsura

The last surviving holdout of the exclusionist rebels, and Gintoki's pal. Nickname: Zura.

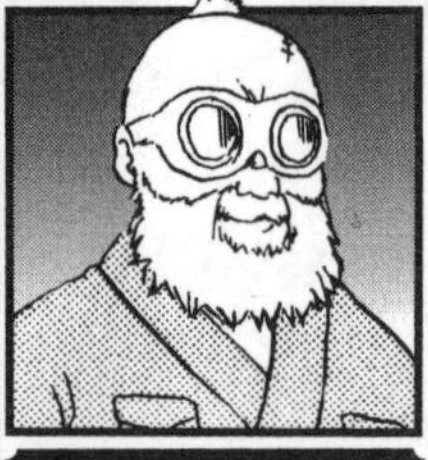

Gengai Hiraga

The top mechanical engineer in Edo. Due to certain circumstances, he was placed on the Bakufu government's wanted list.

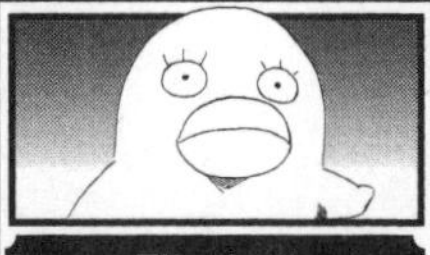

Elizabeth

A mysterious space creature and Katsura's devoted pet. Or maybe a guy in a duck suit.

The story thus far

In an alternate-universe Edo (Tokyo), extraterrestrials land in Japan, and the new government issues an order outlawing swords. The samurai, who have reached the pinnacle of power and prosperity, fall into rapid decline.

Twenty years hence, only one samurai has managed to hold on to his fighting spirit: a somewhat eccentric fellow named Gintoki "Odd Jobs Gin" Sakata. A lover of sweets and near diabetic, our hero sets up shop as a *yorozuya*—an expert at managing trouble and handling the oddest of jobs.

Joining Gin in his business is Shinpachi Shimura, whose sister Gin saved from the clutches of nefarious debt collectors. After a series of unexpected circumstances, the trio meet a powerful alien named Kagura, who becomes—after some arm-twisting—a part-time team member.

Hijikata discovers that the fiancé of Okita's sister is selling weapons to the exclusionist ronin; Kabukicho is infected with a viral weapon that turns its citizens into unibrow zombies; the Yorozuya trio helps a hard-boiled cop chase down a master thief; and the trio throws a matchmaking party to make Kyube realize her femininity. What does fate have in store for our heroes this time?!

WHAT THIS MANGA'S FULL OF
vol. 17

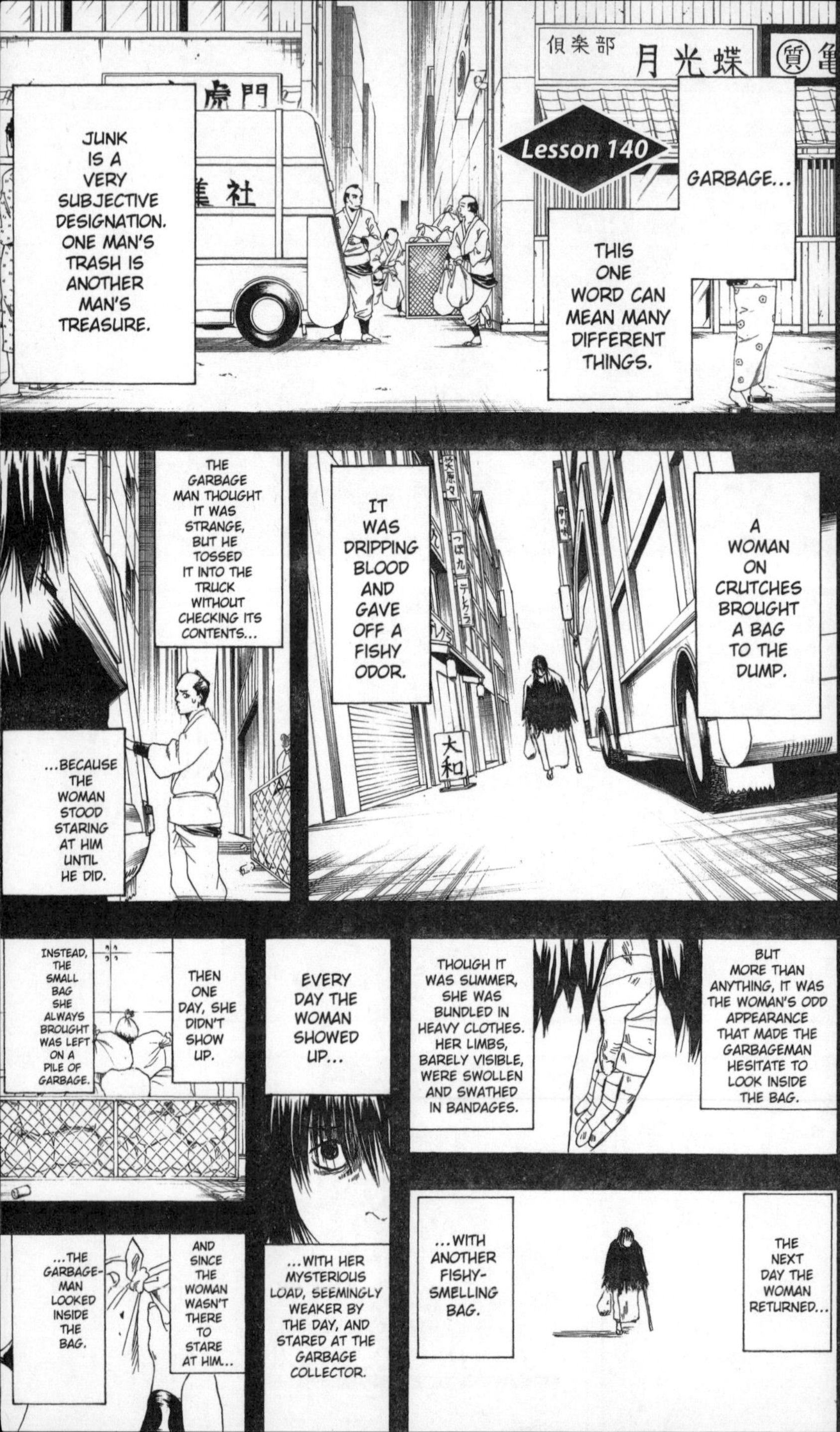
倶楽部 月光蝶
Lesson 140
GARBAGE...
THIS ONE WORD CAN MEAN MANY DIFFERENT THINGS.
JUNK IS A VERY SUBJECTIVE DESIGNATION. ONE MAN'S TRASH IS ANOTHER MAN'S TREASURE.
A WOMAN ON CRUTCHES BROUGHT A BAG TO THE DUMP.
IT WAS DRIPPING BLOOD AND GAVE OFF A FISHY ODOR.
大和
THE GARBAGE MAN THOUGHT IT WAS STRANGE, BUT HE TOSSED IT INTO THE TRUCK WITHOUT CHECKING ITS CONTENTS...
...BECAUSE THE WOMAN STOOD STARING AT HIM UNTIL HE DID.
BUT MORE THAN ANYTHING, IT WAS THE WOMAN'S ODD APPEARANCE THAT MADE THE GARBAGEMAN HESITATE TO LOOK INSIDE THE BAG.
THOUGH IT WAS SUMMER, SHE WAS BUNDLED IN HEAVY CLOTHES. HER LIMBS, BARELY VISIBLE, WERE SWOLLEN AND SWATHED IN BANDAGES.
THE NEXT DAY THE WOMAN RETURNED...
...WITH ANOTHER FISHY-SMELLING BAG.
EVERY DAY THE WOMAN SHOWED UP...
...WITH HER MYSTERIOUS LOAD, SEEMINGLY WEAKER BY THE DAY, AND STARED AT THE GARBAGE COLLECTOR.
THEN ONE DAY, SHE DIDN'T SHOW UP.
INSTEAD, THE SMALL BAG SHE ALWAYS BROUGHT WAS LEFT ON A PILE OF GARBAGE.
AND SINCE THE WOMAN WASN'T THERE TO STARE AT HIM...
...THE GARBAGE-MAN LOOKED INSIDE THE BAG.

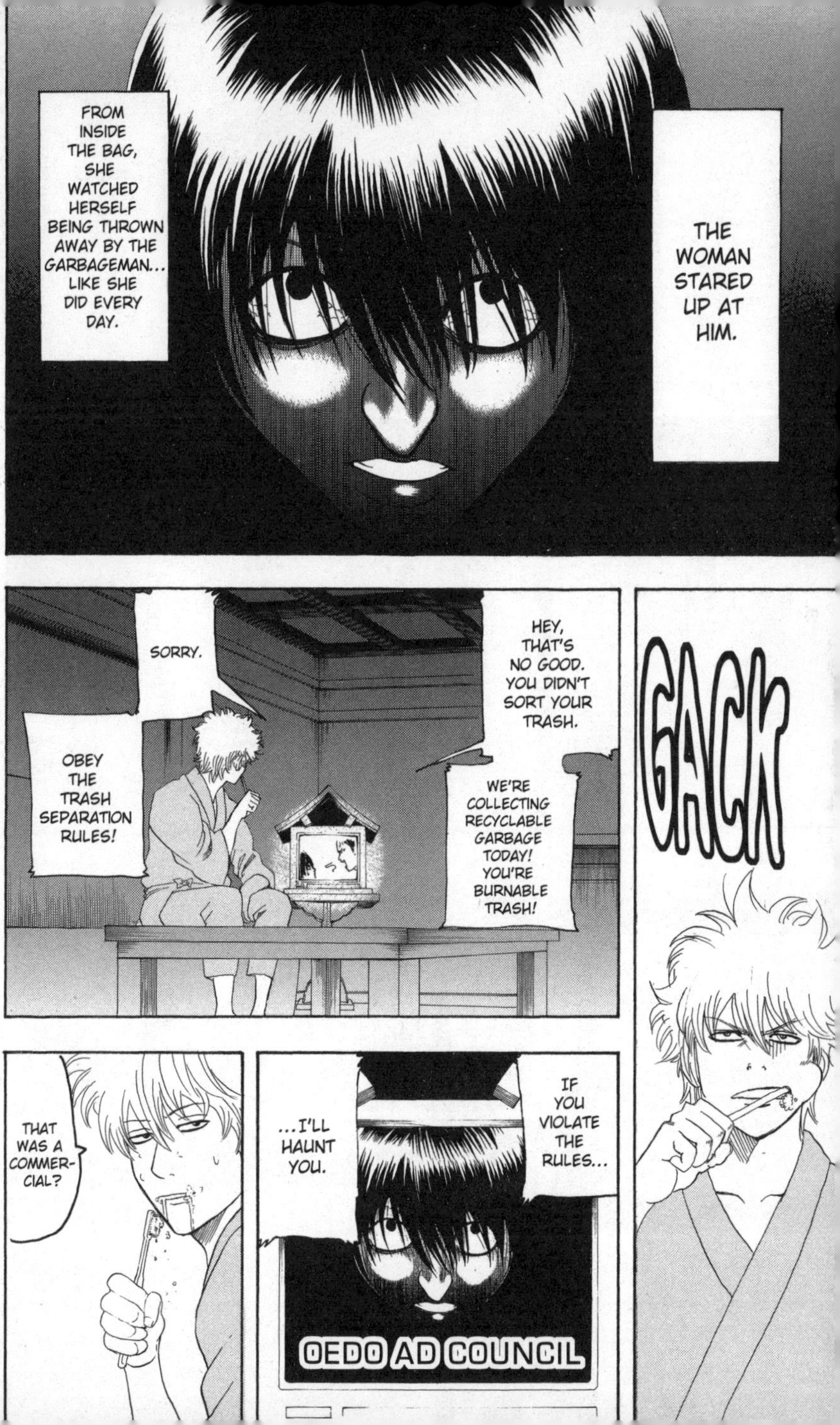
THE WOMAN STARED UP AT HIM.
FROM INSIDE THE BAG, SHE WATCHED HERSELF BEING THROWN AWAY BY THE GARBAGEMAN... LIKE SHE DID EVERY DAY.
GACK
HEY, THAT'S NO GOOD. YOU DIDN'T SORT YOUR TRASH.
SORRY.
WE'RE COLLECTING RECYCLABLE GARBAGE TODAY! YOU'RE BURNABLE TRASH!
OBEY THE TRASH SEPARATION RULES!
IF YOU VIOLATE THE RULES...
...I'LL HAUNT YOU.
OEDO AD COUNCIL
THAT WAS A COMMER-CIAL?

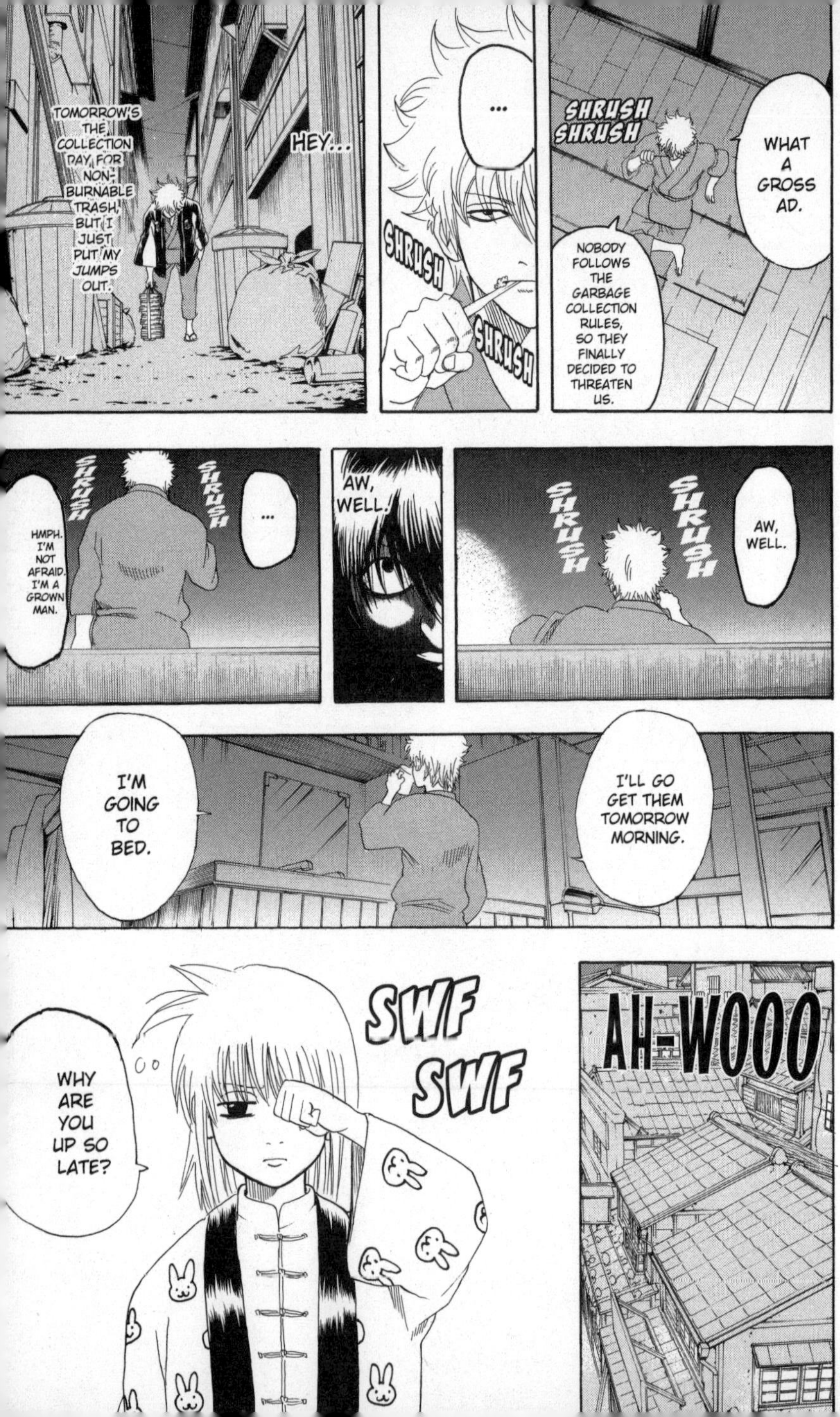
WHAT A GROSS AD.
SHRUSH SHRUSH
NOBODY FOLLOWS THE GARBAGE COLLECTION RULES, SO THEY FINALLY DECIDED TO THREATEN US.
...
SHRUSH
SHRUSH
HEY...
TOMORROW'S THE COLLECTION DAY FOR NON-BURNABLE TRASH, BUT I JUST PUT MY JUMPS OUT.
AW, WELL.
SHRUSH
SHRUSH
AW, WELL.
...
SHRUSH
SHRUSH
HMPH. I'M NOT AFRAID. I'M A GROWN MAN.
I'LL GO GET THEM TOMORROW MORNING.
I'M GOING TO BED.
AH-WOOO
SWF SWF
WHY ARE YOU UP SO LATE?

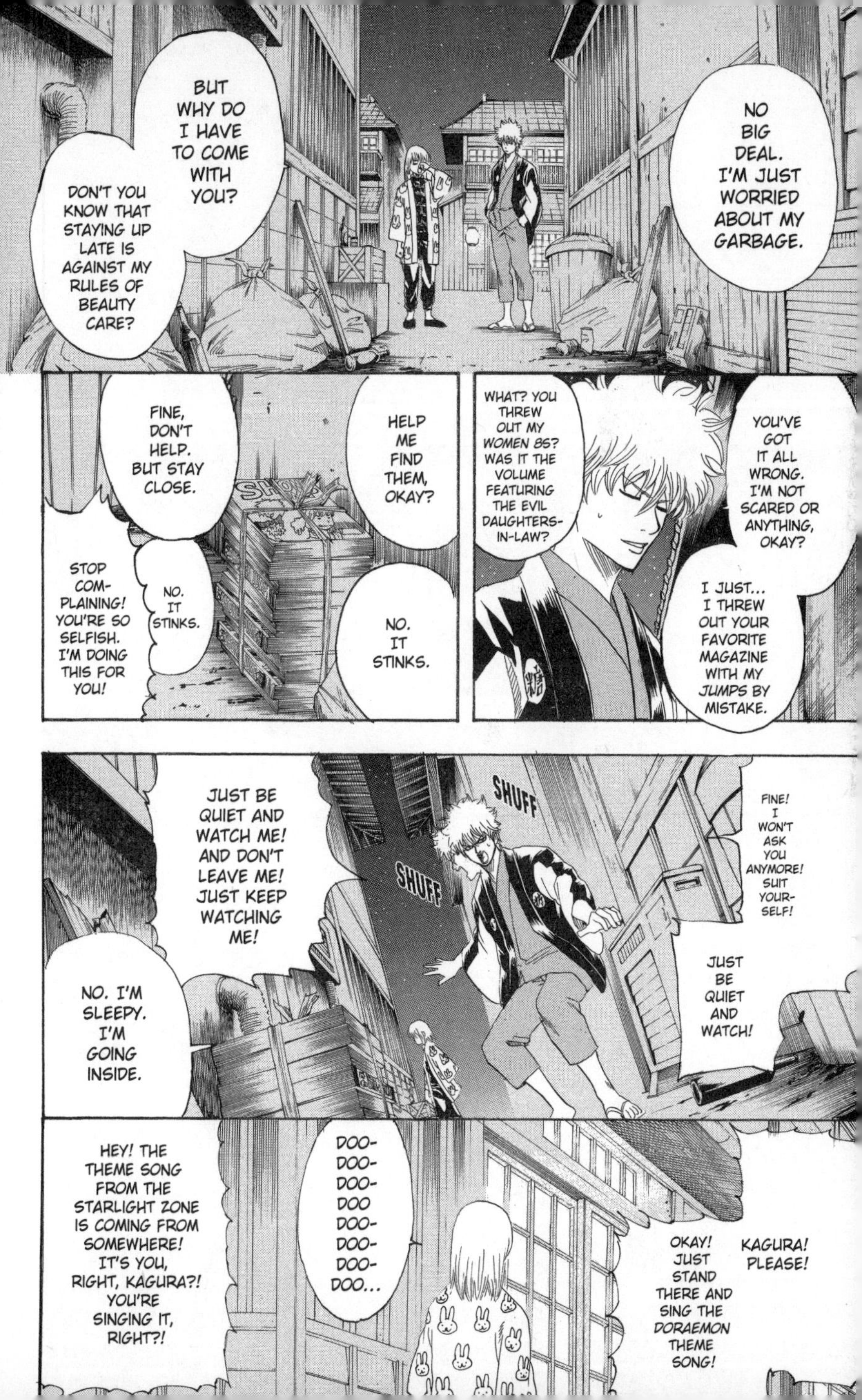
NO BIG DEAL. I'M JUST WORRIED ABOUT MY GARBAGE.
BUT WHY DO I HAVE TO COME WITH YOU?
DON'T YOU KNOW THAT STAYING UP LATE IS AGAINST MY RULES OF BEAUTY CARE?
YOU'VE GOT IT ALL WRONG. I'M NOT SCARED OR ANYTHING, OKAY?
I JUST... I THREW OUT YOUR FAVORITE MAGAZINE WITH MY JUMPS BY MISTAKE.
WHAT? YOU THREW OUT MY WOMEN 85? WAS IT THE VOLUME FEATURING THE EVIL DAUGHTERS-IN-LAW?
HELP ME FIND THEM, OKAY?
NO. IT STINKS.
FINE, DON'T HELP. BUT STAY CLOSE.
NO. IT STINKS.
STOP COMPLAINING! YOU'RE SO SELFISH. I'M DOING THIS FOR YOU!
FINE! I WON'T ASK YOU ANYMORE! SUIT YOURSELF!
JUST BE QUIET AND WATCH!
SHUFF
SHUFF
JUST BE QUIET AND WATCH ME! AND DON'T LEAVE ME! JUST KEEP WATCHING ME!
NO. I'M SLEEPY. I'M GOING INSIDE.
KAGURA! PLEASE!
OKAY! JUST STAND THERE AND SING THE DORAEMON THEME SONG!
DOO-DOO-DOO-DOO DOO-DOO-DOO-DOO...
HEY! THE THEME SONG FROM THE STARLIGHT ZONE IS COMING FROM SOMEWHERE! IT'S YOU, RIGHT, KAGURA?! YOU'RE SINGING IT, RIGHT?!

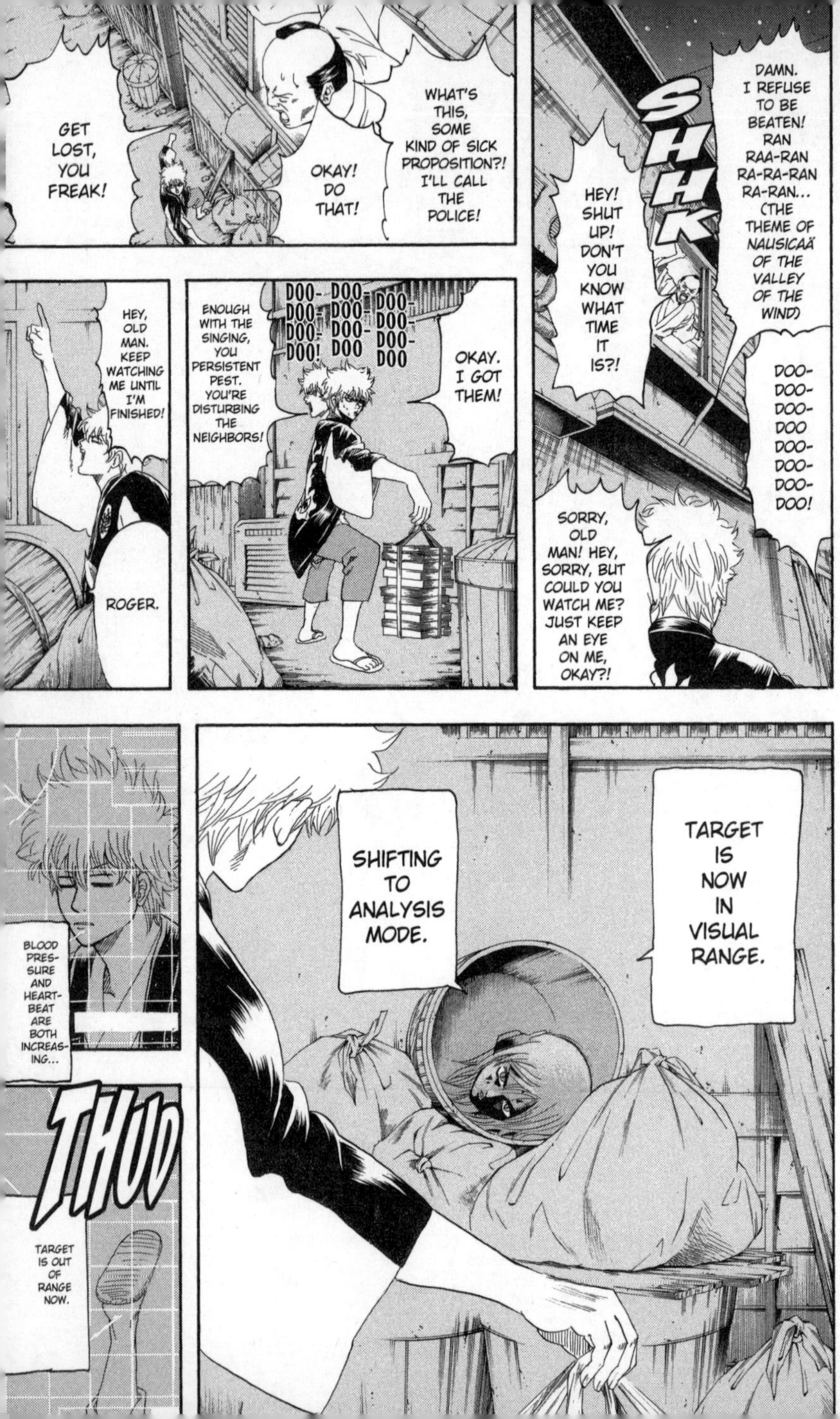
SHHK
DAMN. I REFUSE TO BE BEATEN! RAN RAA-RAN RA-RA-RAN RA-RAN... (THE THEME OF NAUSICAÄ OF THE VALLEY OF THE WIND)
HEY! SHUT UP! DON'T YOU KNOW WHAT TIME IT IS?!
DOO-DOO-DOO-DOO DOO-DOO-DOO-DOO!
SORRY, OLD MAN! HEY, SORRY, BUT COULD YOU WATCH ME? JUST KEEP AN EYE ON ME, OKAY?!
WHAT'S THIS, SOME KIND OF SICK PROPOSITION?! I'LL CALL THE POLICE!
OKAY! DO THAT!
GET LOST, YOU FREAK!
DOO-DOO-DOO-DOO! DOO-DOO-DOO-DOO DOO-DOO-DOO-DOO
ENOUGH WITH THE SINGING, YOU PERSISTENT PEST. YOU'RE DISTURBING THE NEIGHBORS!
OKAY. I GOT THEM!
HEY, OLD MAN. KEEP WATCHING ME UNTIL I'M FINISHED!
ROGER.
TARGET IS NOW IN VISUAL RANGE.
SHIFTING TO ANALYSIS MODE.
BLOOD PRESSURE AND HEARTBEAT ARE BOTH INCREASING...
THUD
TARGET IS OUT OF RANGE NOW.

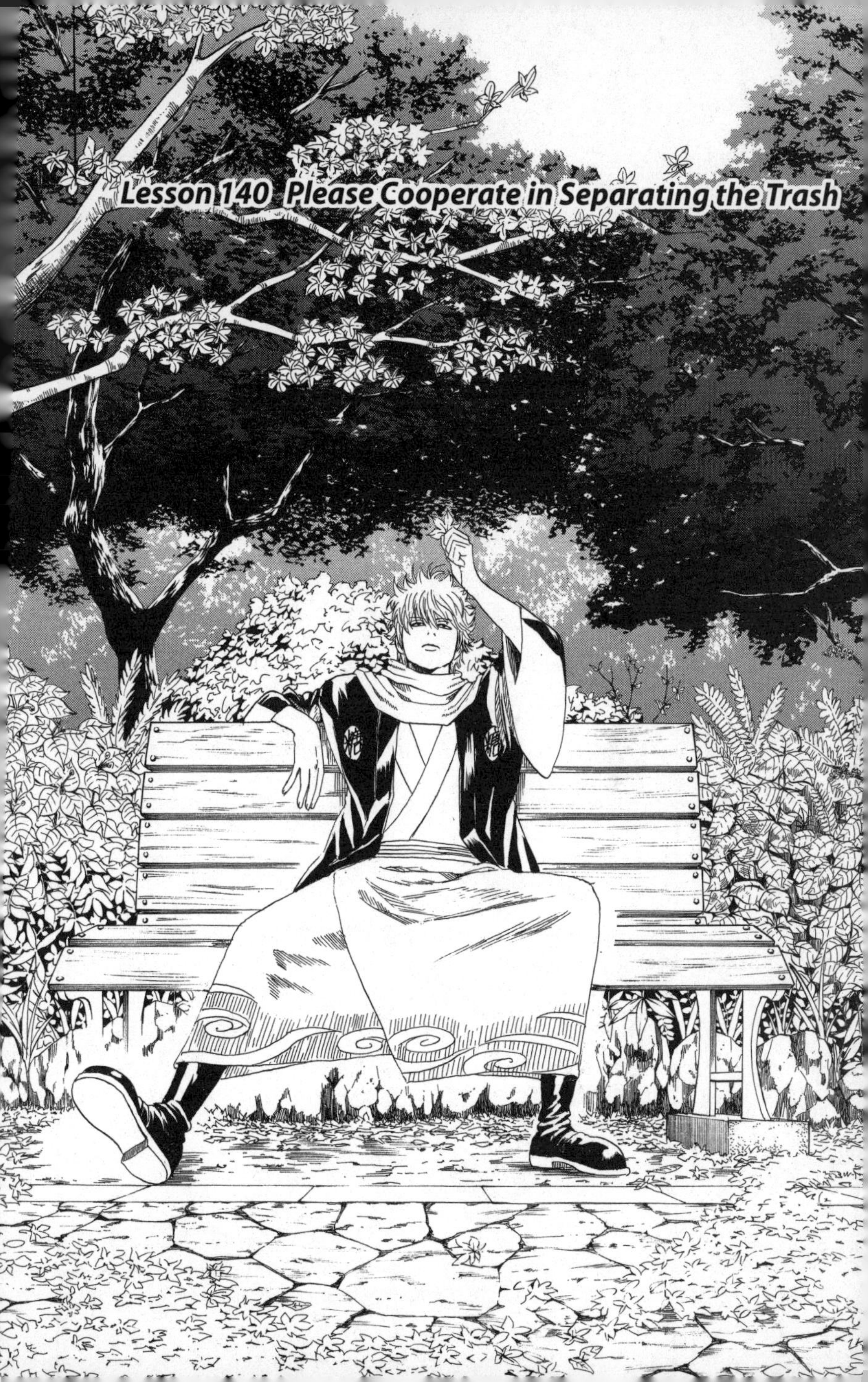
Lesson 140 Please Cooperate in Separating the Trash

DOO-
DOO-
DOO-
DOO-
DOO-
DOO
DOO-
DOO-
DOO-
DOO-
DOO-
DOO
DOO-
DOO-
DOO-
DOO-
DOO-
DOO
DOO-
DOO-
DOO-
DOO
DOO-
DOO-
DOO-
DOO

DOO-
DOO-
DOO-
DOO...
DOO-
DOO-
DOO-
DOO...

DOO-
DOO-
DOO-
DOO...

WHAT ARE YOU DOING?

WHAP

DOO-
DOO-
DOO-
DOO...

DOOB!!

DOO-
DOO-
DOO-
DOO...
DOO-
DOO-
DOO-
DOO...

DOO-
DOO-
DOO-
DOO...
DOO-
DOO-
DOO-
DOO...

NO! HOW COULD YOU PLAY SUCH A MEAN TRICK ON ME IN MY SLEEP?!

GOOD MORNING. DID YOU GET A HAIRCUT?

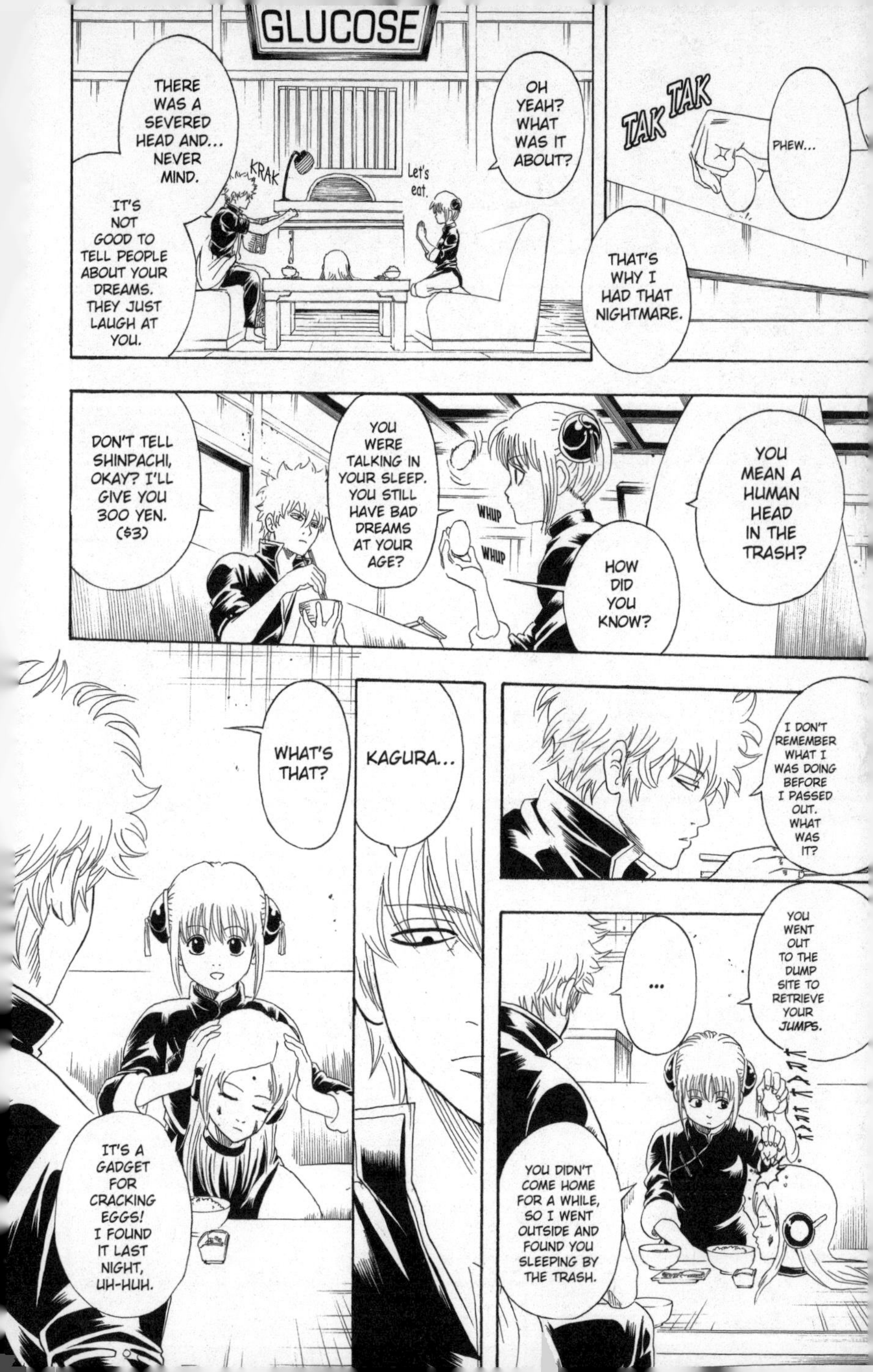

TAK TAK
PHEW...
THAT'S WHY I HAD THAT NIGHTMARE.
GLUCOSE
OH YEAH? WHAT WAS IT ABOUT?
Let's eat.
THERE WAS A SEVERED HEAD AND... NEVER MIND.
KRAK
IT'S NOT GOOD TO TELL PEOPLE ABOUT YOUR DREAMS. THEY JUST LAUGH AT YOU.
YOU MEAN A HUMAN HEAD IN THE TRASH?
HOW DID YOU KNOW?
WHUP
WHUP
YOU WERE TALKING IN YOUR SLEEP. YOU STILL HAVE BAD DREAMS AT YOUR AGE?
DON'T TELL SHINPACHI, OKAY? I'LL GIVE YOU 300 YEN. ($3)
I DON'T REMEMBER WHAT I WAS DOING BEFORE I PASSED OUT. WHAT WAS IT?
YOU WENT OUT TO THE DUMP SITE TO RETRIEVE YOUR JUMPS.
...
YOU DIDN'T COME HOME FOR A WHILE, SO I WENT OUTSIDE AND FOUND YOU SLEEPING BY THE TRASH.
KAGURA...
WHAT'S THAT?
IT'S A GADGET FOR CRACKING EGGS! I FOUND IT LAST NIGHT, UH-HUH.

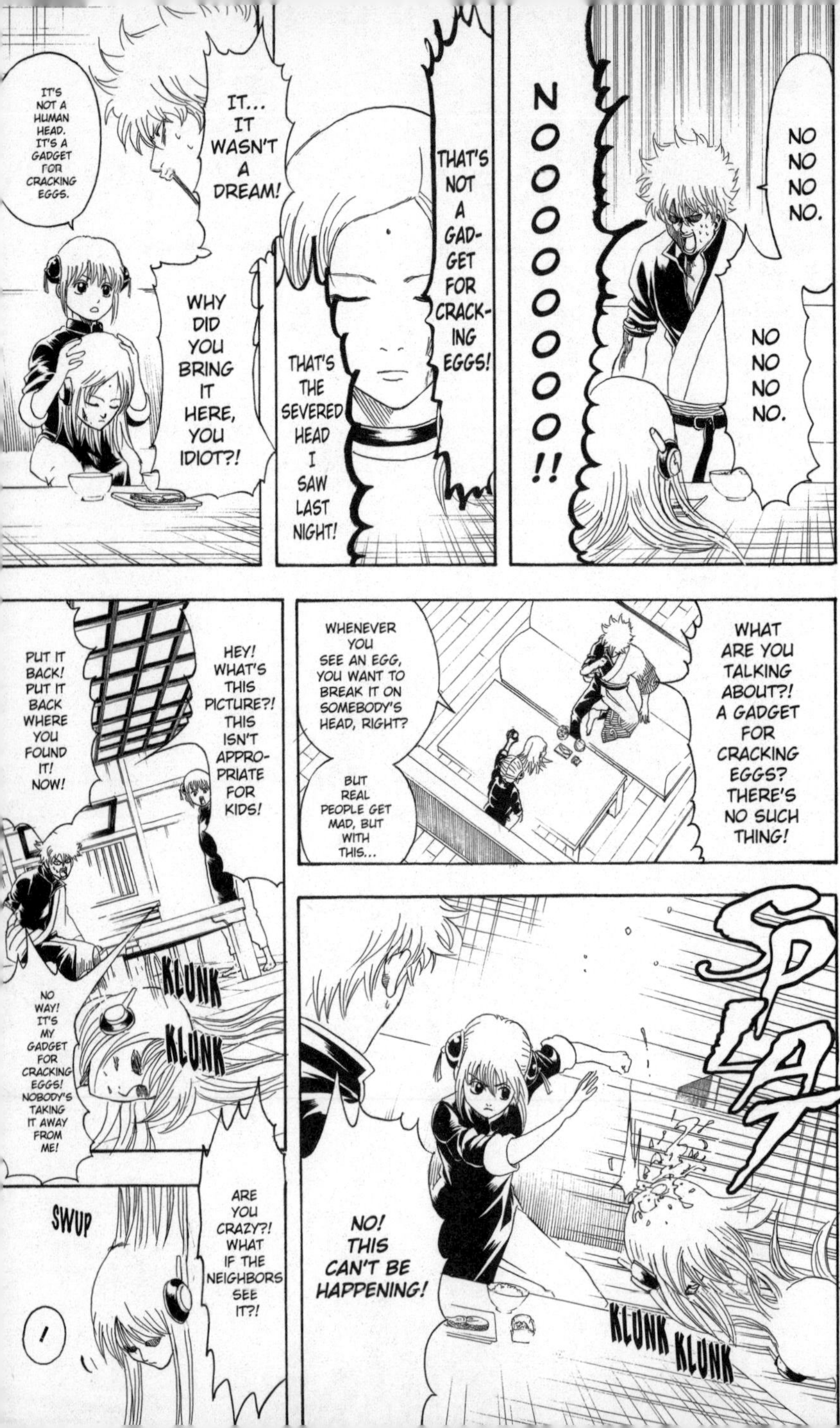
NO NO NO NO.
NO NO NO NO.
NOOOOOOOOO!!
THAT'S NOT A GAD-GET FOR CRACK-ING EGGS!
THAT'S THE SEVERED HEAD I SAW LAST NIGHT!
IT... IT WASN'T A DREAM!
IT'S NOT A HUMAN HEAD. IT'S A GADGET FOR CRACKING EGGS.
WHY DID YOU BRING IT HERE, YOU IDIOT?!
WHAT ARE YOU TALKING ABOUT?! A GADGET FOR CRACKING EGGS? THERE'S NO SUCH THING!
WHENEVER YOU SEE AN EGG, YOU WANT TO BREAK IT ON SOMEBODY'S HEAD, RIGHT?
BUT REAL PEOPLE GET MAD, BUT WITH THIS...
SPLAT
KLUNK KLUNK
NO! THIS CAN'T BE HAPPENING!
HEY! WHAT'S THIS PICTURE?! THIS ISN'T APPRO-PRIATE FOR KIDS!
PUT IT BACK! PUT IT BACK WHERE YOU FOUND IT! NOW!
KLUNK
KLUNK
NO WAY! IT'S MY GADGET FOR CRACKING EGGS! NOBODY'S TAKING IT AWAY FROM ME!
SWUP
ARE YOU CRAZY?! WHAT IF THE NEIGHBORS SEE IT?!
!

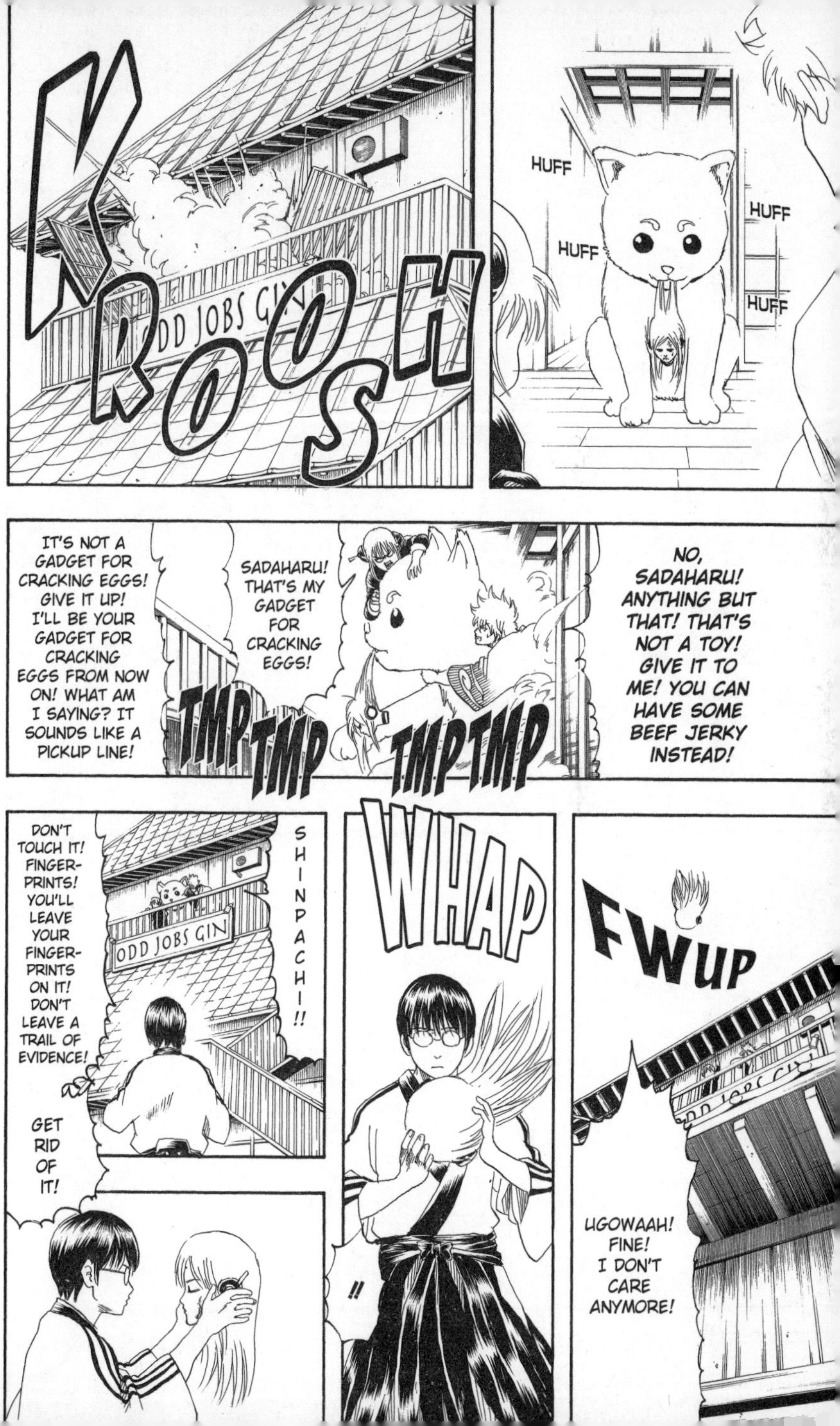
HUFF
HUFF
HUFF
HUFF
KROOSH
ODD JOBS GIN
NO, SADAHARU! ANYTHING BUT THAT! THAT'S NOT A TOY! GIVE IT TO ME! YOU CAN HAVE SOME BEEF JERKY INSTEAD!
SADAHARU! THAT'S MY GADGET FOR CRACKING EGGS!
IT'S NOT A GADGET FOR CRACKING EGGS! GIVE IT UP! I'LL BE YOUR GADGET FOR CRACKING EGGS FROM NOW ON! WHAT AM I SAYING? IT SOUNDS LIKE A PICKUP LINE!
TMPTMP
TMPTMP
FWUP
UGOWAAH! FINE! I DON'T CARE ANYMORE!
WHAP
!!
SHINPACHI!!
DON'T TOUCH IT! FINGER-PRINTS! YOU'LL LEAVE YOUR FINGER-PRINTS ON IT! DON'T LEAVE A TRAIL OF EVIDENCE!
ODD JOBS GIN
GET RID OF IT!

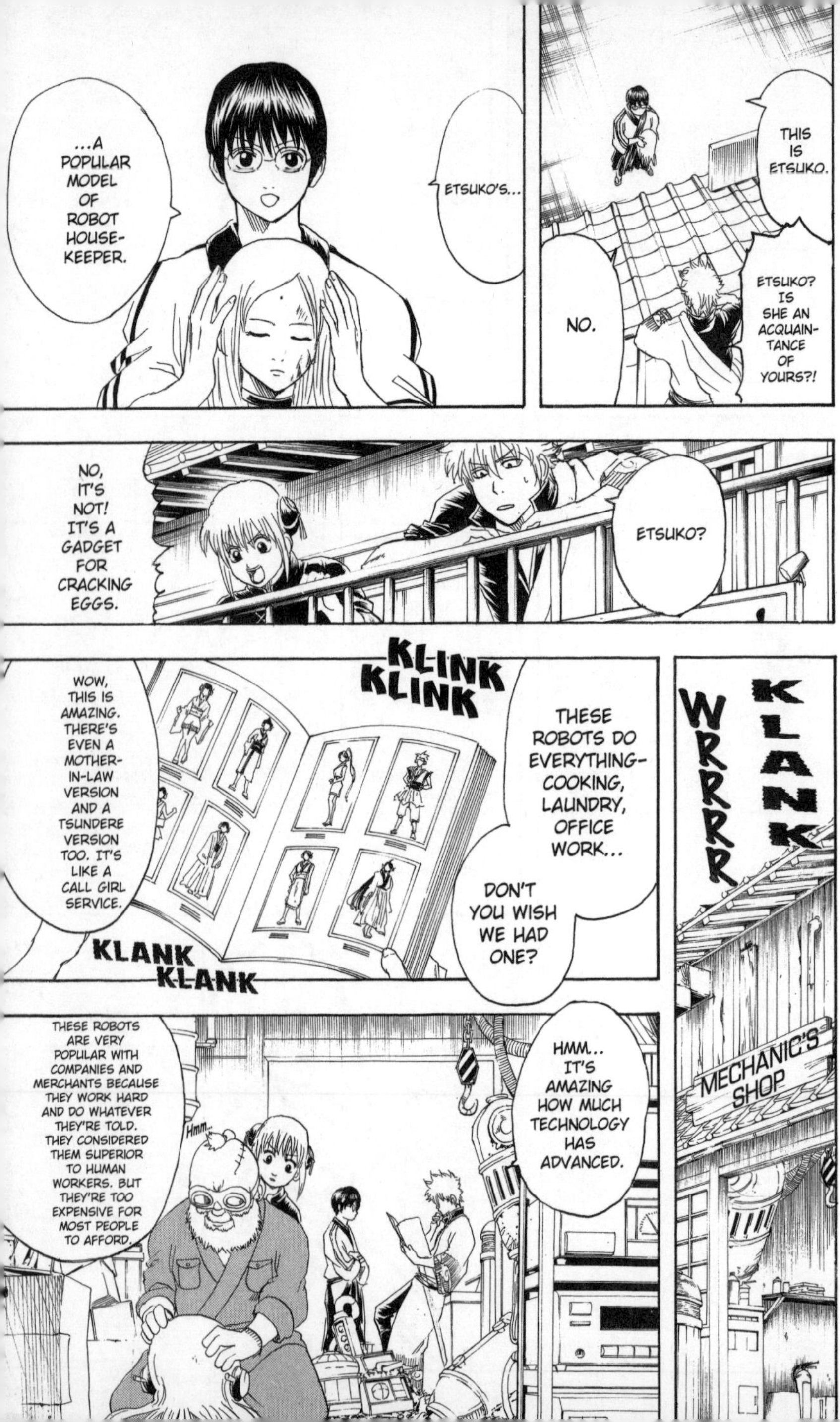

THIS IS ETSUKO.
ETSUKO? IS SHE AN ACQUAINTANCE OF YOURS?!
NO.
ETSUKO'S...
...A POPULAR MODEL OF ROBOT HOUSEKEEPER.
ETSUKO?
NO, IT'S NOT! IT'S A GADGET FOR CRACKING EGGS.
WRRRR
KLANK
MECHANIC'S SHOP
KLINK KLINK
THESE ROBOTS DO EVERYTHING- COOKING, LAUNDRY, OFFICE WORK...
DON'T YOU WISH WE HAD ONE?
WOW, THIS IS AMAZING. THERE'S EVEN A MOTHER-IN-LAW VERSION AND A TSUNDERE VERSION TOO. IT'S LIKE A CALL GIRL SERVICE.
KLANK KLANK
HMM.. IT'S AMAZING HOW MUCH TECHNOLOGY HAS ADVANCED.
THESE ROBOTS ARE VERY POPULAR WITH COMPANIES AND MERCHANTS BECAUSE THEY WORK HARD AND DO WHATEVER THEY'RE TOLD. THEY CONSIDERED THEM SUPERIOR TO HUMAN WORKERS. BUT THEY'RE TOO EXPENSIVE FOR MOST PEOPLE TO AFFORD.
Hmm...

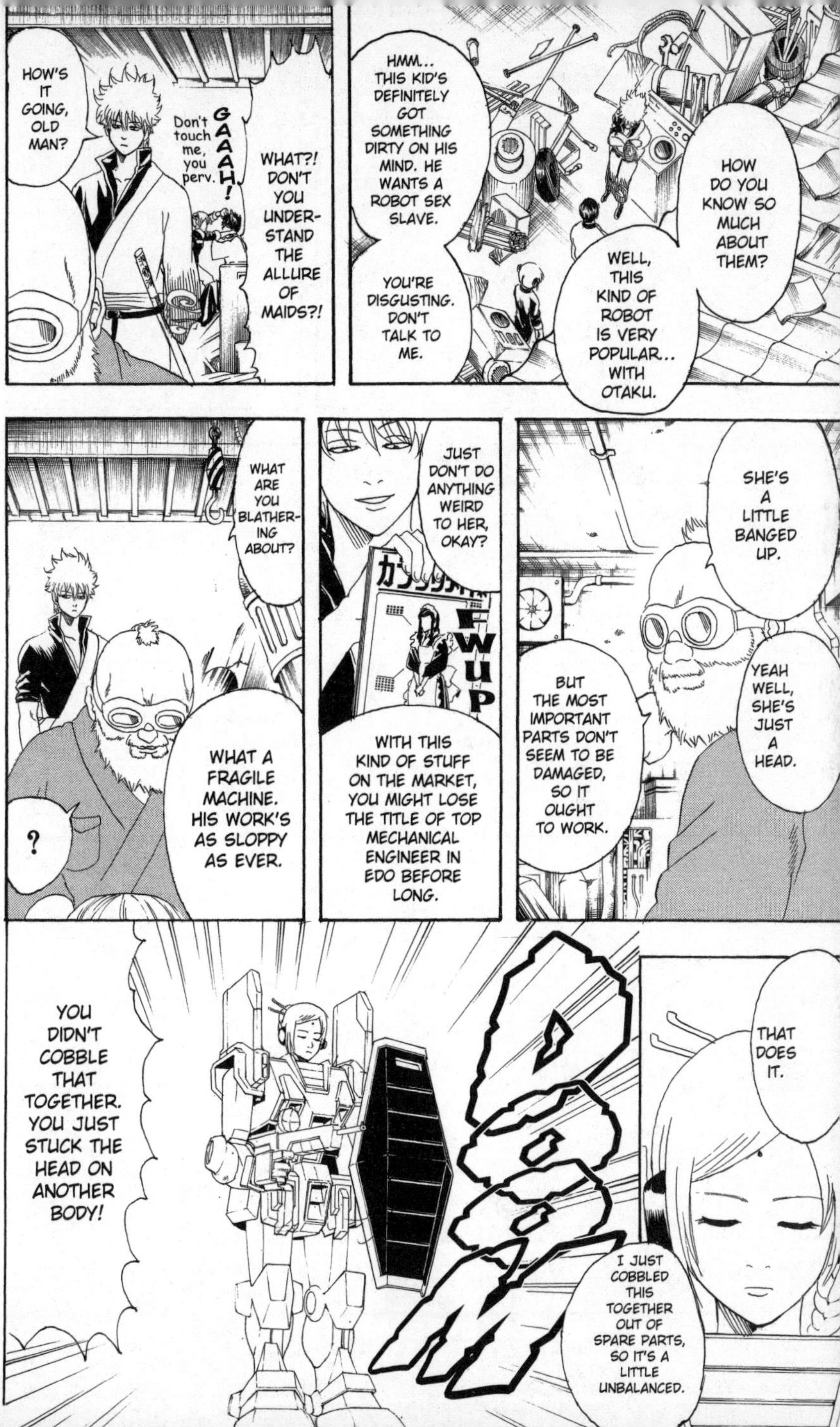
HOW DO YOU KNOW SO MUCH ABOUT THEM?
WELL, THIS KIND OF ROBOT IS VERY POPULAR... WITH OTAKU.
HMM... THIS KID'S DEFINITELY GOT SOMETHING DIRTY ON HIS MIND. HE WANTS A ROBOT SEX SLAVE.
YOU'RE DISGUSTING. DON'T TALK TO ME.
WHAT?! DON'T YOU UNDERSTAND THE ALLURE OF MAIDS?!
GAAAH!
Don't touch me, you perv.
HOW'S IT GOING, OLD MAN?
SHE'S A LITTLE BANGED UP.
YEAH WELL, SHE'S JUST A HEAD.
BUT THE MOST IMPORTANT PARTS DON'T SEEM TO BE DAMAGED, SO IT OUGHT TO WORK.
JUST DON'T DO ANYTHING WEIRD TO HER, OKAY?
FWUP
WITH THIS KIND OF STUFF ON THE MARKET, YOU MIGHT LOSE THE TITLE OF TOP MECHANICAL ENGINEER IN EDO BEFORE LONG.
WHAT ARE YOU BLATHER-ING ABOUT?
WHAT A FRAGILE MACHINE. HIS WORK'S AS SLOPPY AS EVER.
?
THAT DOES IT.
I JUST COBBLED THIS TOGETHER OUT OF SPARE PARTS, SO IT'S A LITTLE UNBALANCED.
YOU DIDN'T COBBLE THAT TOGETHER. YOU JUST STUCK THE HEAD ON ANOTHER BODY!

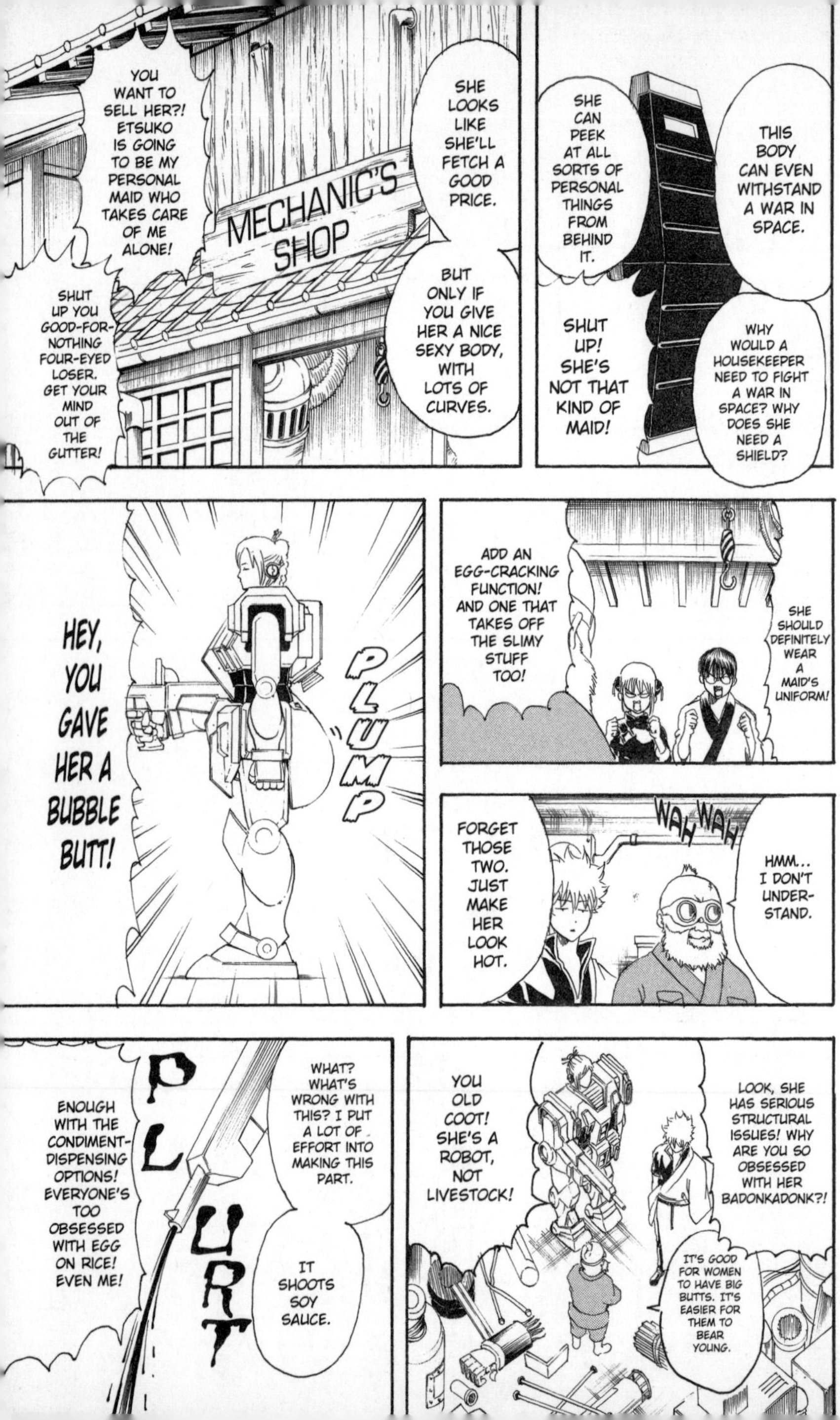
THIS BODY CAN EVEN WITHSTAND A WAR IN SPACE.
SHE CAN PEEK AT ALL SORTS OF PERSONAL THINGS FROM BEHIND IT.
WHY WOULD A HOUSEKEEPER NEED TO FIGHT A WAR IN SPACE? WHY DOES SHE NEED A SHIELD?
SHUT UP! SHE'S NOT THAT KIND OF MAID!
SHE LOOKS LIKE SHE'LL FETCH A GOOD PRICE.
BUT ONLY IF YOU GIVE HER A NICE SEXY BODY, WITH LOTS OF CURVES.
MECHANIC'S SHOP
YOU WANT TO SELL HER?! ETSUKO IS GOING TO BE MY PERSONAL MAID WHO TAKES CARE OF ME ALONE!
SHUT UP YOU GOOD-FOR-NOTHING FOUR-EYED LOSER. GET YOUR MIND OUT OF THE GUTTER!
SHE SHOULD DEFINITELY WEAR A MAID'S UNIFORM!
ADD AN EGG-CRACKING FUNCTION! AND ONE THAT TAKES OFF THE SLIMY STUFF TOO!
HMM... I DON'T UNDER-STAND.
WAH WAH
FORGET THOSE TWO. JUST MAKE HER LOOK HOT.
PLUMP
HEY, YOU GAVE HER A BUBBLE BUTT!
LOOK, SHE HAS SERIOUS STRUCTURAL ISSUES! WHY ARE YOU SO OBSESSED WITH HER BADONKADONK?!
YOU OLD COOT! SHE'S A ROBOT, NOT LIVESTOCK!
IT'S GOOD FOR WOMEN TO HAVE BIG BUTTS. IT'S EASIER FOR THEM TO BEAR YOUNG.
WHAT? WHAT'S WRONG WITH THIS? I PUT A LOT OF EFFORT INTO MAKING THIS PART.
IT SHOOTS SOY SAUCE.
PLURT
ENOUGH WITH THE CONDIMENT-DISPENSING OPTIONS! EVERYONE'S TOO OBSESSED WITH EGG ON RICE! EVEN ME!

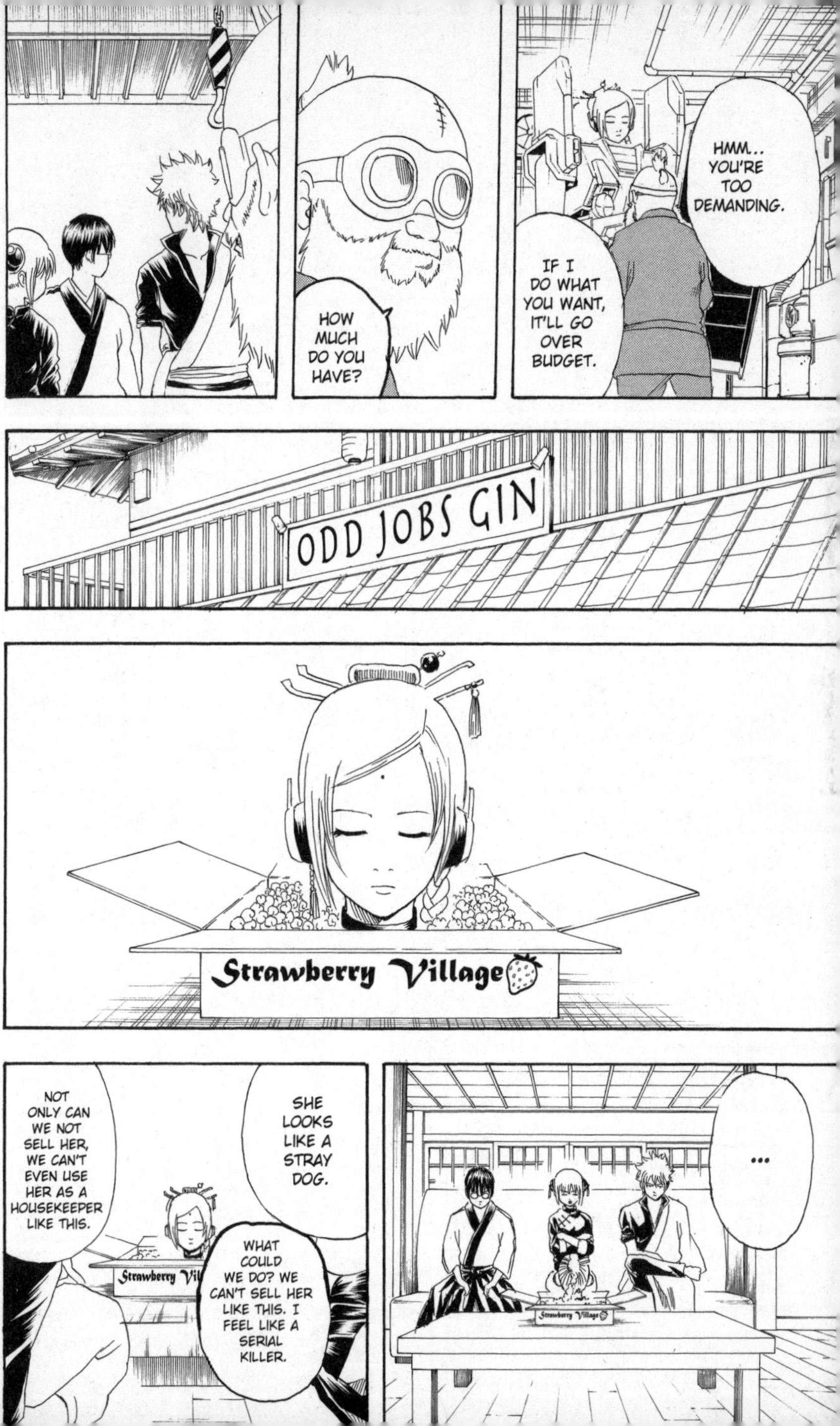
HMM.. YOU'RE TOO DEMANDING.
IF I DO WHAT YOU WANT, IT'LL GO OVER BUDGET.
HOW MUCH DO YOU HAVE?
ODD JOBS GIN
Strawberry Village
...
Strawberry Village
SHE LOOKS LIKE A STRAY DOG.
NOT ONLY CAN WE NOT SELL HER, WE CAN'T EVEN USE HER AS A HOUSEKEEPER LIKE THIS.
WHAT COULD WE DO? WE CAN'T SELL HER LIKE THIS. I FEEL LIKE A SERIAL KILLER.

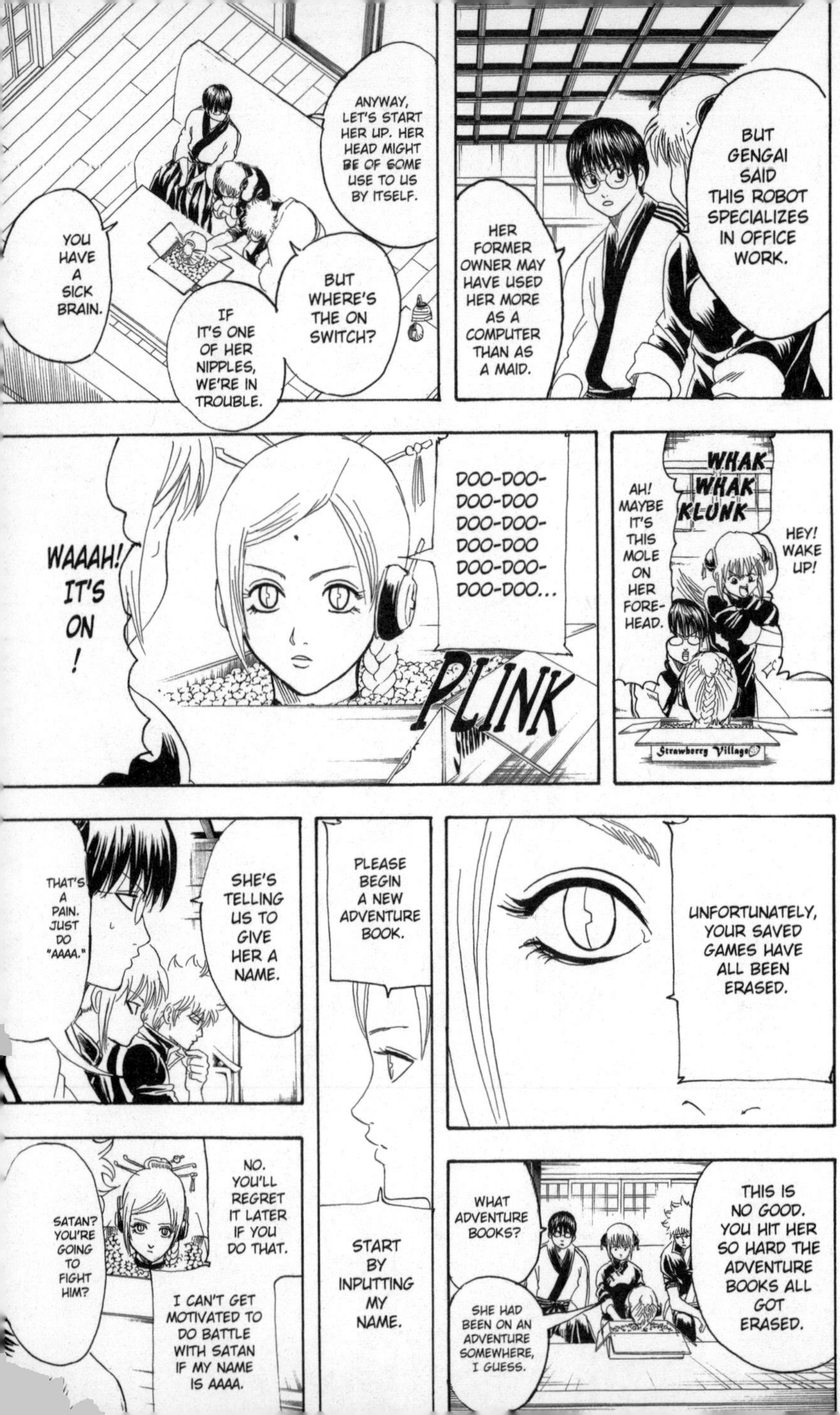
BUT GENGAI SAID THIS ROBOT SPECIALIZES IN OFFICE WORK.
HER FORMER OWNER MAY HAVE USED HER MORE AS A COMPUTER THAN AS A MAID.
ANYWAY, LET'S START HER UP. HER HEAD MIGHT BE OF SOME USE TO US BY ITSELF.
BUT WHERE'S THE ON SWITCH?
IF IT'S ONE OF HER NIPPLES, WE'RE IN TROUBLE.
YOU HAVE A SICK BRAIN.
HEY! WAKE UP!
WHAK
WHAK
KLUNK
AH! MAYBE IT'S THIS MOLE ON HER FORE-HEAD.
Strawberry Village
DOO-DOO-DOO-DOO DOO-DOO-DOO-DOO DOO-DOO-DOO-DOO...
PLINK
WAAAH! IT'S ON!
UNFORTUNATELY, YOUR SAVED GAMES HAVE ALL BEEN ERASED.
THIS IS NO GOOD. YOU HIT HER SO HARD THE ADVENTURE BOOKS ALL GOT ERASED.
WHAT ADVENTURE BOOKS?
SHE HAD BEEN ON AN ADVENTURE SOMEWHERE, I GUESS.
PLEASE BEGIN A NEW ADVENTURE BOOK.
START BY INPUTTING MY NAME.
SHE'S TELLING US TO GIVE HER A NAME.
THAT'S A PAIN. JUST DO "AAAA."
NO. YOU'LL REGRET IT LATER IF YOU DO THAT.
I CAN'T GET MOTIVATED TO DO BATTLE WITH SATAN IF MY NAME IS AAAA.
SATAN? YOU'RE GOING TO FIGHT HIM?

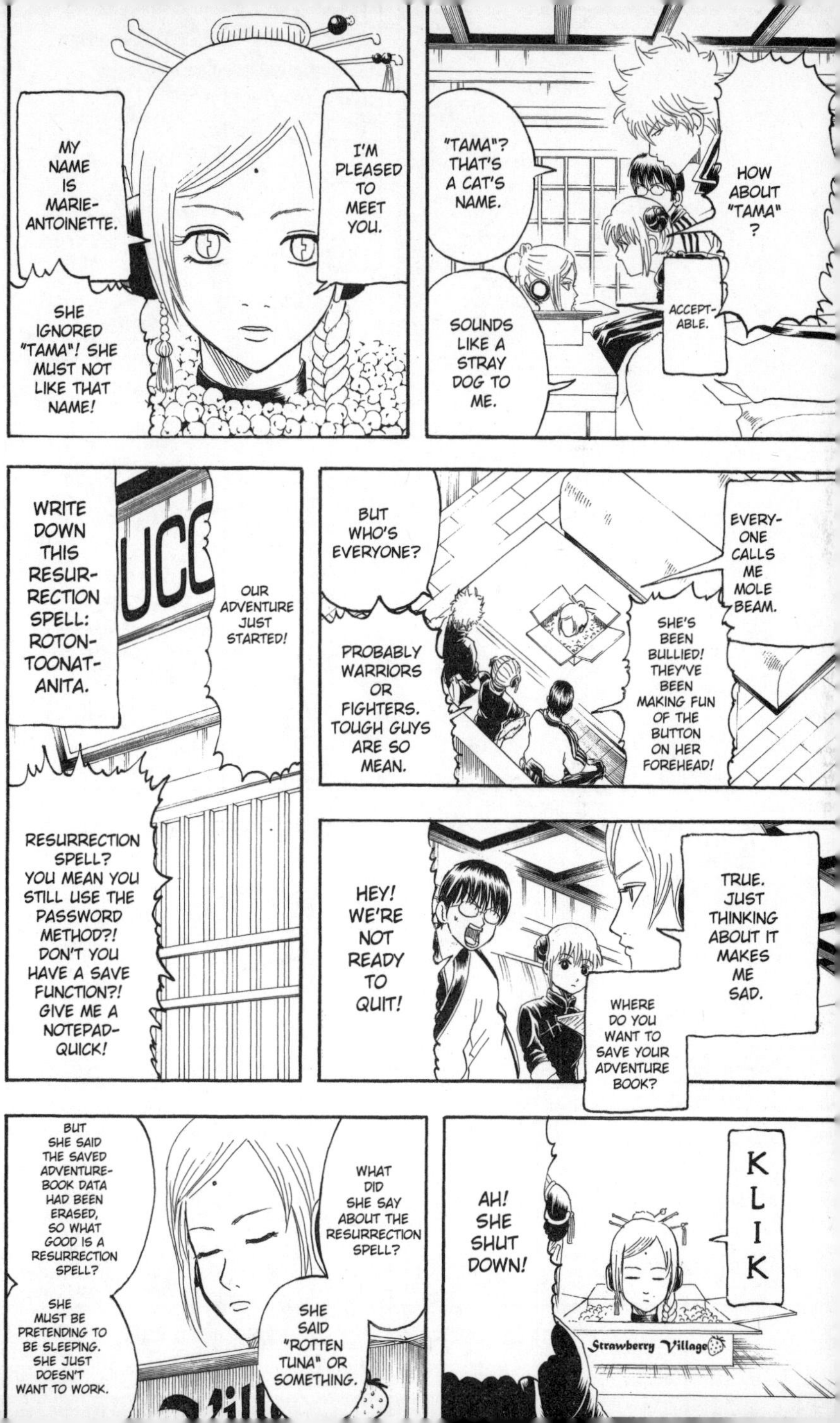
HOW ABOUT "TAMA"?
ACCEPTABLE.
"TAMA"? THAT'S A CAT'S NAME.
SOUNDS LIKE A STRAY DOG TO ME.
I'M PLEASED TO MEET YOU.
MY NAME IS MARIE-ANTOINETTE.
SHE IGNORED "TAMA"! SHE MUST NOT LIKE THAT NAME!
EVERYONE CALLS ME MOLE BEAM.
SHE'S BEEN BULLIED! THEY'VE BEEN MAKING FUN OF THE BUTTON ON HER FOREHEAD!
BUT WHO'S EVERYONE?
PROBABLY WARRIORS OR FIGHTERS. TOUGH GUYS ARE SO MEAN.
TRUE. JUST THINKING ABOUT IT MAKES ME SAD.
WHERE DO YOU WANT TO SAVE YOUR ADVENTURE BOOK?
HEY! WE'RE NOT READY TO QUIT!
WRITE DOWN THIS RESURRECTION SPELL: ROTON-TOONAT-ANITA.
OUR ADVENTURE JUST STARTED!
RESURRECTION SPELL? YOU MEAN YOU STILL USE THE PASSWORD METHOD?! DON'T YOU HAVE A SAVE FUNCTION?! GIVE ME A NOTEPAD-QUICK!
KLIK
AH! SHE SHUT DOWN!
Strawberry Village
WHAT DID SHE SAY ABOUT THE RESURRECTION SPELL?
SHE SAID "ROTTEN TUNA" OR SOMETHING.
BUT SHE SAID THE SAVED ADVENTURE-BOOK DATA HAD BEEN ERASED, SO WHAT GOOD IS A RESURRECTION SPELL?
SHE MUST BE PRETENDING TO BE SLEEPING. SHE JUST DOESN'T WANT TO WORK.

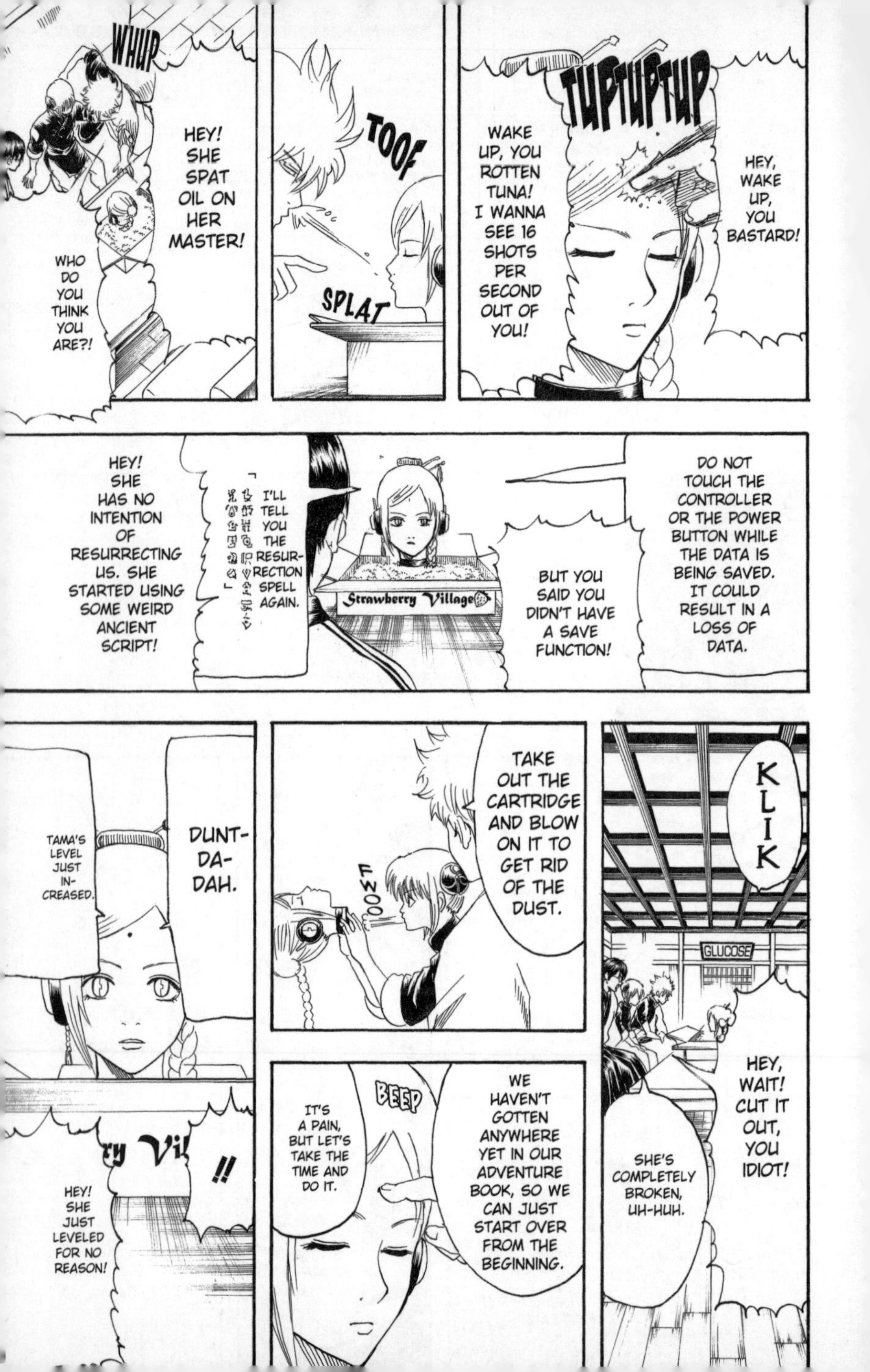
HEY, WAKE UP, YOU BASTARD!
TUPTUPTUP
WAKE UP, YOU ROTTEN TUNA! I WANNA SEE 16 SHOTS PER SECOND OUT OF YOU!
TOOF
SPLAT
WHUP
HEY! SHE SPAT OIL ON HER MASTER!
WHO DO YOU THINK YOU ARE?!
DO NOT TOUCH THE CONTROLLER OR THE POWER BUTTON WHILE THE DATA IS BEING SAVED. IT COULD RESULT IN A LOSS OF DATA.
BUT YOU SAID YOU DIDN'T HAVE A SAVE FUNCTION!
Strawberry Village
I'LL TELL YOU THE RESURRECTION SPELL AGAIN.
HEY! SHE HAS NO INTENTION OF RESURRECTING US. SHE STARTED USING SOME WEIRD ANCIENT SCRIPT!
KLIK
GLUCOSE
HEY, WAIT! CUT IT OUT, YOU IDIOT!
SHE'S COMPLETELY BROKEN, UH-HUH.
TAKE OUT THE CARTRIDGE AND BLOW ON IT TO GET RID OF THE DUST.
FWOO
BEEP
WE HAVEN'T GOTTEN ANYWHERE YET IN OUR ADVENTURE BOOK, SO WE CAN JUST START OVER FROM THE BEGINNING.
IT'S A PAIN, BUT LET'S TAKE THE TIME AND DO IT.
DUNT-DA-DAH.
TAMA'S LEVEL JUST INCREASED.
ry Vi!
!!
HEY! SHE JUST LEVELED FOR NO REASON!

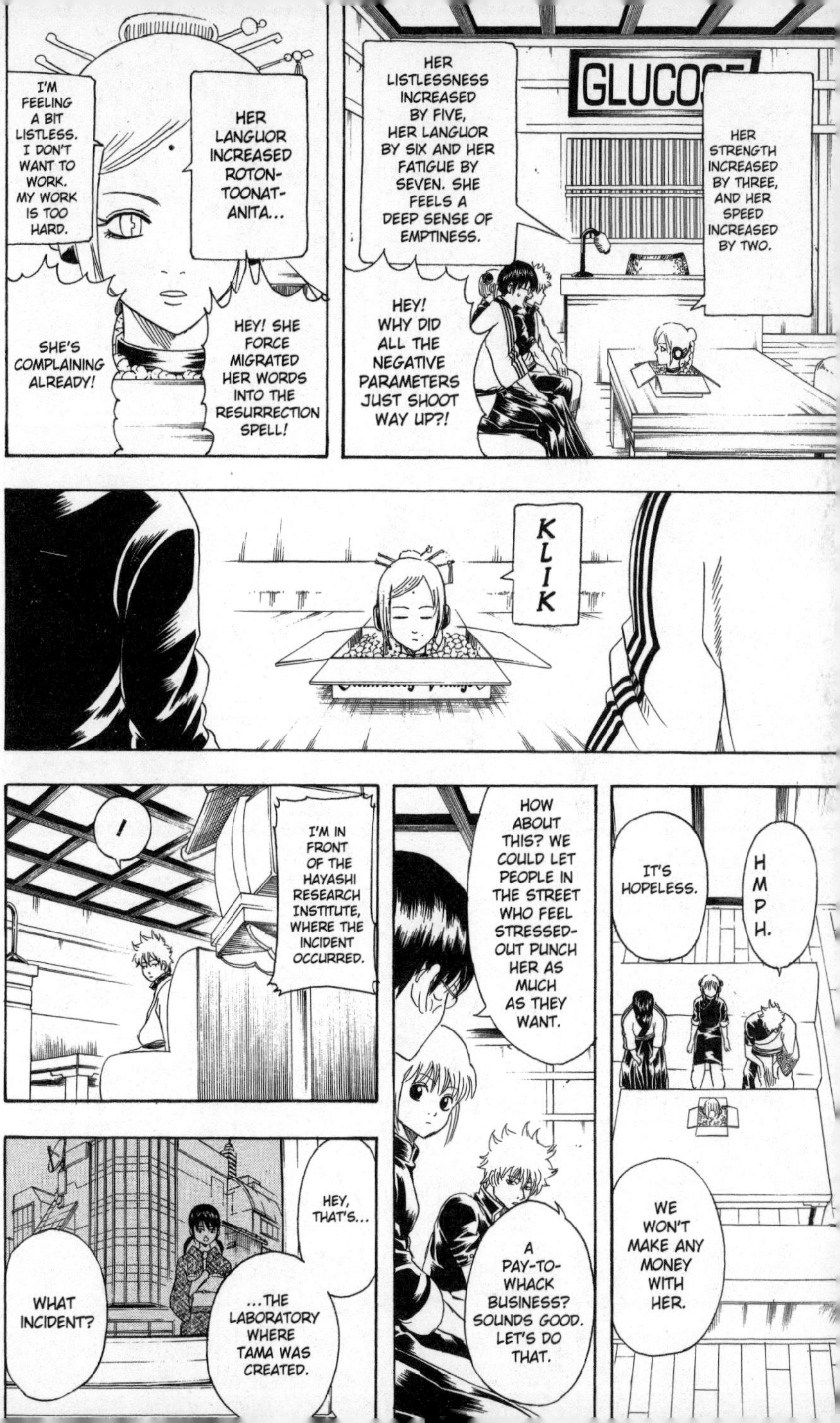
HER STRENGTH INCREASED BY THREE, AND HER SPEED INCREASED BY TWO.
GLUCOS
HER LISTLESSNESS INCREASED BY FIVE, HER LANGUOR BY SIX AND HER FATIGUE BY SEVEN. SHE FEELS A DEEP SENSE OF EMPTINESS.
HEY! WHY DID ALL THE NEGATIVE PARAMETERS JUST SHOOT WAY UP?!
HER LANGUOR INCREASED ROTON-TOONAT-ANITA...
I'M FEELING A BIT LISTLESS. I DON'T WANT TO WORK. MY WORK IS TOO HARD.
HEY! SHE FORCE MIGRATED HER WORDS INTO THE RESURRECTION SPELL!
SHE'S COMPLAINING ALREADY!
KLIK
HMPH.
IT'S HOPELESS.
WE WON'T MAKE ANY MONEY WITH HER.
HOW ABOUT THIS? WE COULD LET PEOPLE IN THE STREET WHO FEEL STRESSED-OUT PUNCH HER AS MUCH AS THEY WANT.
A PAY-TO-WHACK BUSINESS? SOUNDS GOOD. LET'S DO THAT.
!
I'M IN FRONT OF THE HAYASHI RESEARCH INSTITUTE, WHERE THE INCIDENT OCCURRED.
HEY, THAT'S...
...THE LABORATORY WHERE TAMA WAS CREATED.
WHAT INCIDENT?

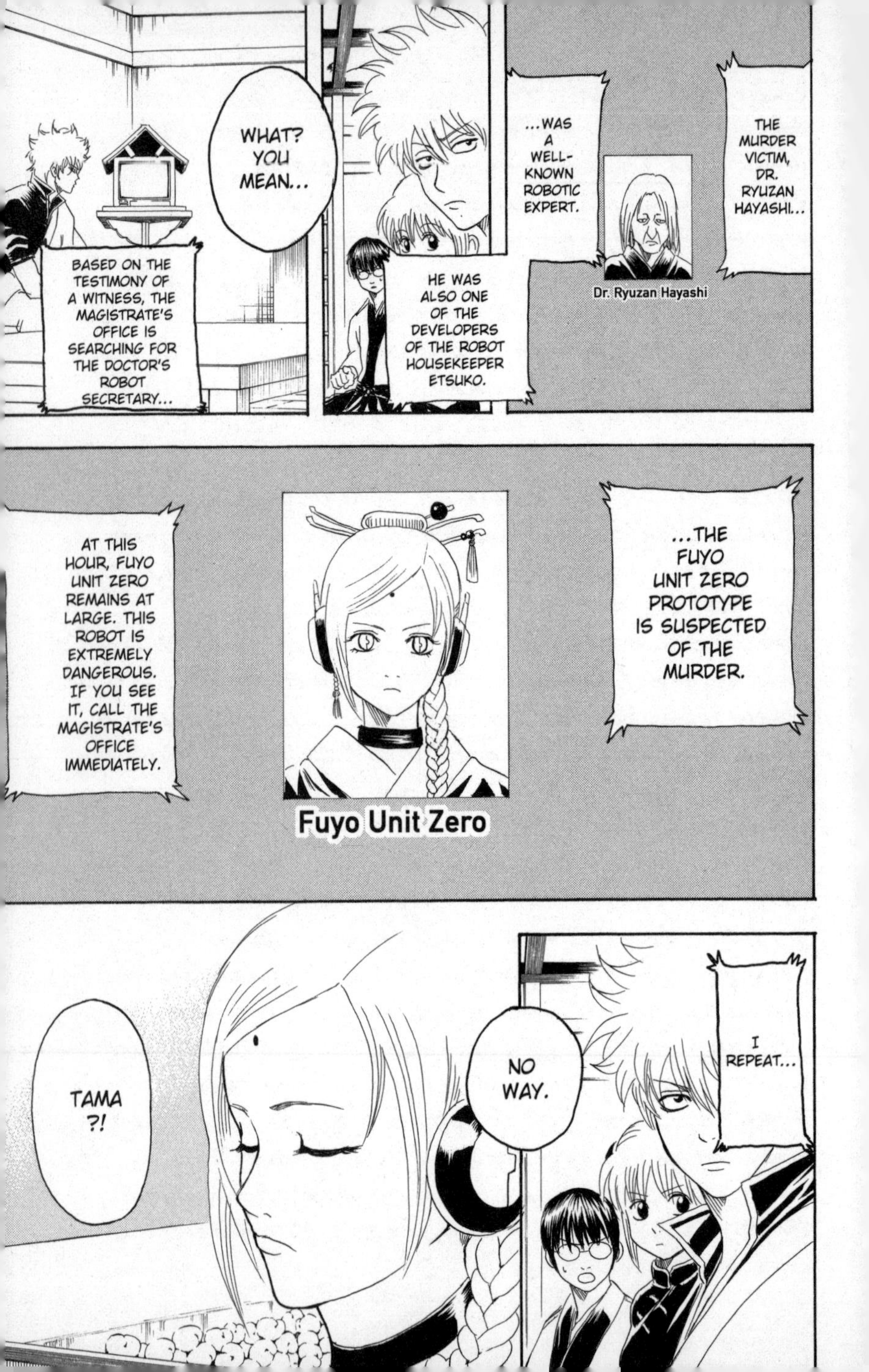
THE MURDER VICTIM, DR. RYUZAN HAYASHI...
...WAS A WELL-KNOWN ROBOTIC EXPERT.
Dr. Ryuzan Hayashi
HE WAS ALSO ONE OF THE DEVELOPERS OF THE ROBOT HOUSEKEEPER ETSUKO.
WHAT? YOU MEAN...
BASED ON THE TESTIMONY OF A WITNESS, THE MAGISTRATE'S OFFICE IS SEARCHING FOR THE DOCTOR'S ROBOT SECRETARY...
...THE FUYO UNIT ZERO PROTOTYPE IS SUSPECTED OF THE MURDER.
Fuyo Unit Zero
AT THIS HOUR, FUYO UNIT ZERO REMAINS AT LARGE. THIS ROBOT IS EXTREMELY DANGEROUS. IF YOU SEE IT, CALL THE MAGISTRATE'S OFFICE IMMEDIATELY.
I REPEAT...
NO WAY.
TAMA ?!

Thank you very much for purchasing **Gin Tama** volume 17. Thanks to your support, **Gin Tama** has honorably celebrated its third anniversary. A lot can change in three years. My editor, Mr. Onishi, is finally getting married. I knew he was up to something. One morning, when he came to my house for a meeting, he was carrying a pink umbrella. I caught him desperately trying to hide it before he came in. I thought, "It won't be long now." So, using my powers of detection, I was able to predict the outcome pretty easily. Of course, I didn't say anything obnoxious like, "What's with the umbrella?! Did you just come from a date?!" I pretended I didn't see anything. But I felt a little like I'd just discovered my big brother's stash of girly magazines. In our meetings, we chat about all sorts of silly things that have nothing to do with business, but we rarely discuss our personal lives. Our attitude is, "That's disgusting. I don't want to hear about it. You should die." Our relationship is such that we'd try to kill each other, given the chance, like Kakarrot and Vegeta in **Dragon Ball**, so I couldn't help my reaction. So he finally said, "Kakarrot, I'm already 28. I've decided to get married." I said, "Oh yeah?! Congratulations! I'll tell Krillin." But I really felt like saying, "Blegh!" You know? To make matters worse, Vegeta started blushing a little. Vegeta was blushing! Come on, Vegeta! Then for some reason Kakarrot started blushing too, and Vegeta and Kakarrot had an awkward, red-faced meeting. I can't remember how many times I shouted inside my heart, "My readers! Give me powerrrr!"

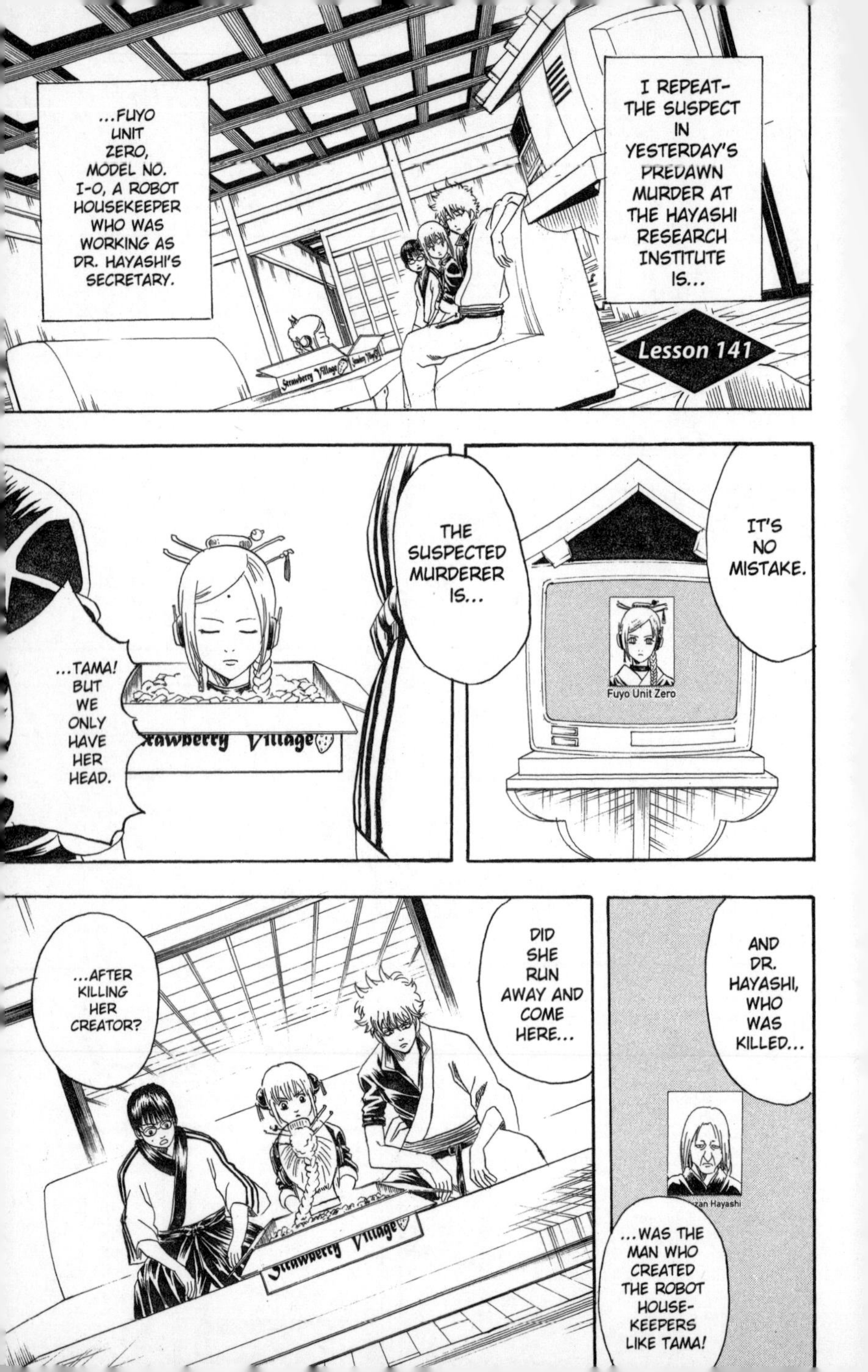
I REPEAT-THE SUSPECT IN YESTERDAY'S PREDAWN MURDER AT THE HAYASHI RESEARCH INSTITUTE IS...
Lesson 141
...FUYO UNIT ZERO, MODEL NO. I-O, A ROBOT HOUSEKEEPER WHO WAS WORKING AS DR. HAYASHI'S SECRETARY.
Strawberry Village
IT'S NO MISTAKE.
Fuyo Unit Zero
THE SUSPECTED MURDERER IS...
...TAMA! BUT WE ONLY HAVE HER HEAD.
AND DR. HAYASHI, WHO WAS KILLED...
...WAS THE MAN WHO CREATED THE ROBOT HOUSE-KEEPERS LIKE TAMA!
DID SHE RUN AWAY AND COME HERE...
...AFTER KILLING HER CREATOR?
Strawberry Village

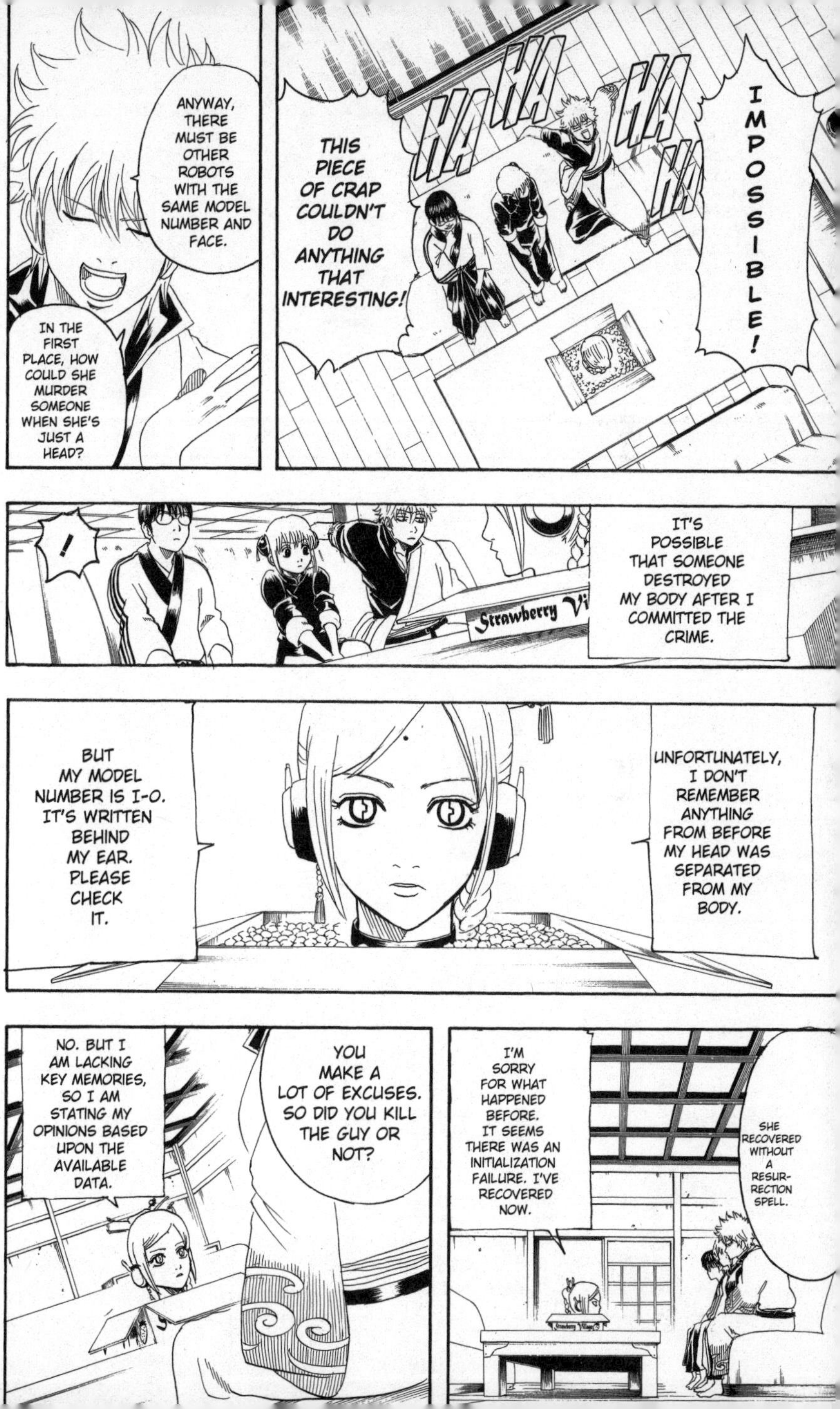
IMPOSSIBLE!
HA HA HA HA HA
THIS PIECE OF CRAP COULDN'T DO ANYTHING THAT INTERESTING!
ANYWAY, THERE MUST BE OTHER ROBOTS WITH THE SAME MODEL NUMBER AND FACE.
IN THE FIRST PLACE, HOW COULD SHE MURDER SOMEONE WHEN SHE'S JUST A HEAD?
IT'S POSSIBLE THAT SOMEONE DESTROYED MY BODY AFTER I COMMITTED THE CRIME.
Strawberry Vi
!
UNFORTUNATELY, I DON'T REMEMBER ANYTHING FROM BEFORE MY HEAD WAS SEPARATED FROM MY BODY.
BUT MY MODEL NUMBER IS I-0. IT'S WRITTEN BEHIND MY EAR. PLEASE CHECK IT.
I'M SORRY FOR WHAT HAPPENED BEFORE. IT SEEMS THERE WAS AN INITIALIZATION FAILURE. I'VE RECOVERED NOW.
SHE RECOVERED WITHOUT A RESUR-RECTION SPELL.
YOU MAKE A LOT OF EXCUSES. SO DID YOU KILL THE GUY OR NOT?
NO. BUT I AM LACKING KEY MEMORIES, SO I AM STATING MY OPINIONS BASED UPON THE AVAILABLE DATA.

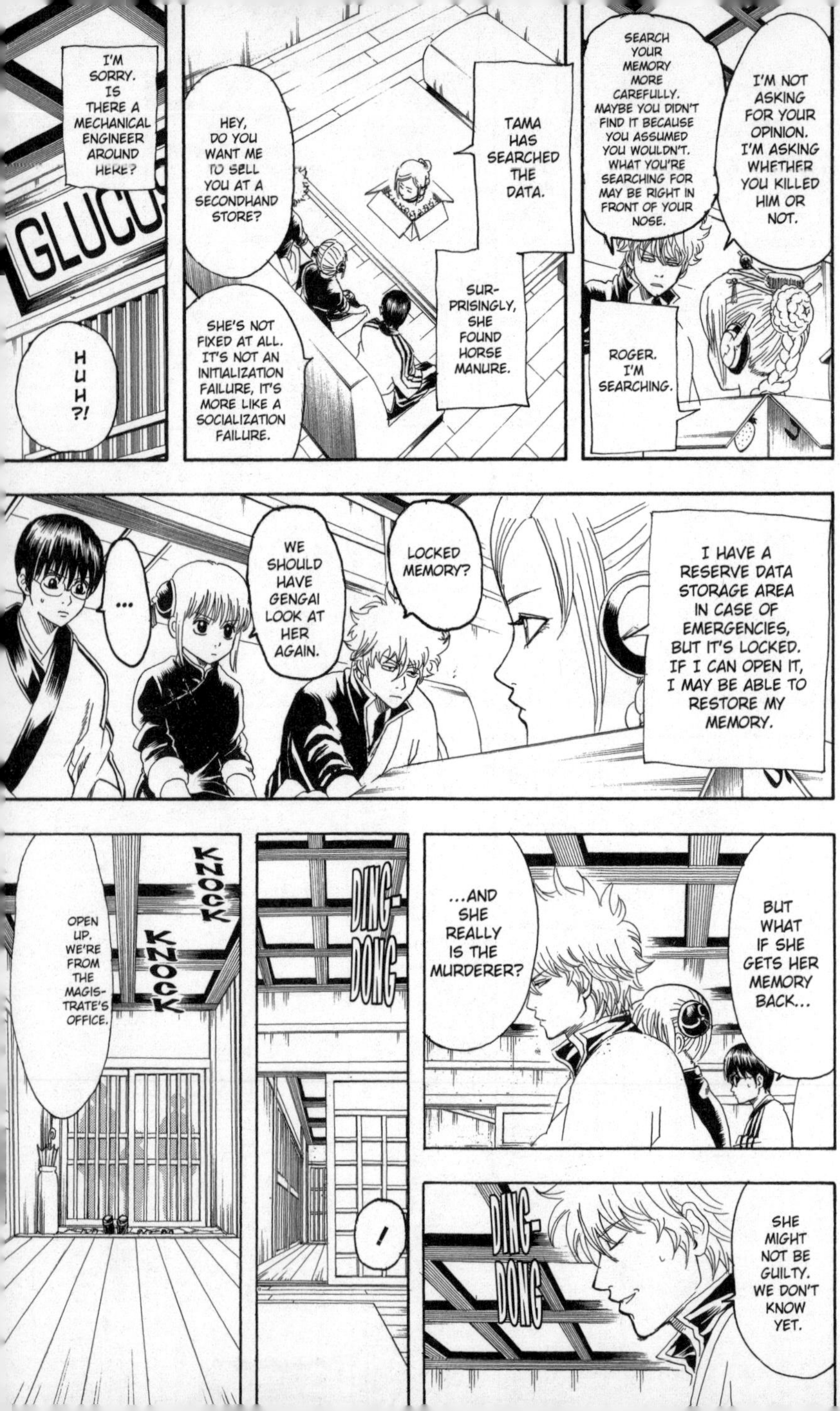
I'M NOT ASKING FOR YOUR OPINION. I'M ASKING WHETHER YOU KILLED HIM OR NOT.
SEARCH YOUR MEMORY MORE CAREFULLY. MAYBE YOU DIDN'T FIND IT BECAUSE YOU ASSUMED YOU WOULDN'T. WHAT YOU'RE SEARCHING FOR MAY BE RIGHT IN FRONT OF YOUR NOSE.
ROGER. I'M SEARCHING.
TAMA HAS SEARCHED THE DATA.
SURPRISINGLY, SHE FOUND HORSE MANURE.
HEY, DO YOU WANT ME TO SELL YOU AT A SECONDHAND STORE?
SHE'S NOT FIXED AT ALL. IT'S NOT AN INITIALIZATION FAILURE, IT'S MORE LIKE A SOCIALIZATION FAILURE.
I'M SORRY. IS THERE A MECHANICAL ENGINEER AROUND HERE?
GLUCO
HUH?!
I HAVE A RESERVE DATA STORAGE AREA IN CASE OF EMERGENCIES, BUT IT'S LOCKED. IF I CAN OPEN IT, I MAY BE ABLE TO RESTORE MY MEMORY.
LOCKED MEMORY?
WE SHOULD HAVE GENGAI LOOK AT HER AGAIN.
...
BUT WHAT IF SHE GETS HER MEMORY BACK...
...AND SHE REALLY IS THE MURDERER?
SHE MIGHT NOT BE GUILTY. WE DON'T KNOW YET.
DING-DONG
DING-DONG
!
KNOCK
KNOCK
OPEN UP. WE'RE FROM THE MAGISTRATE'S OFFICE.

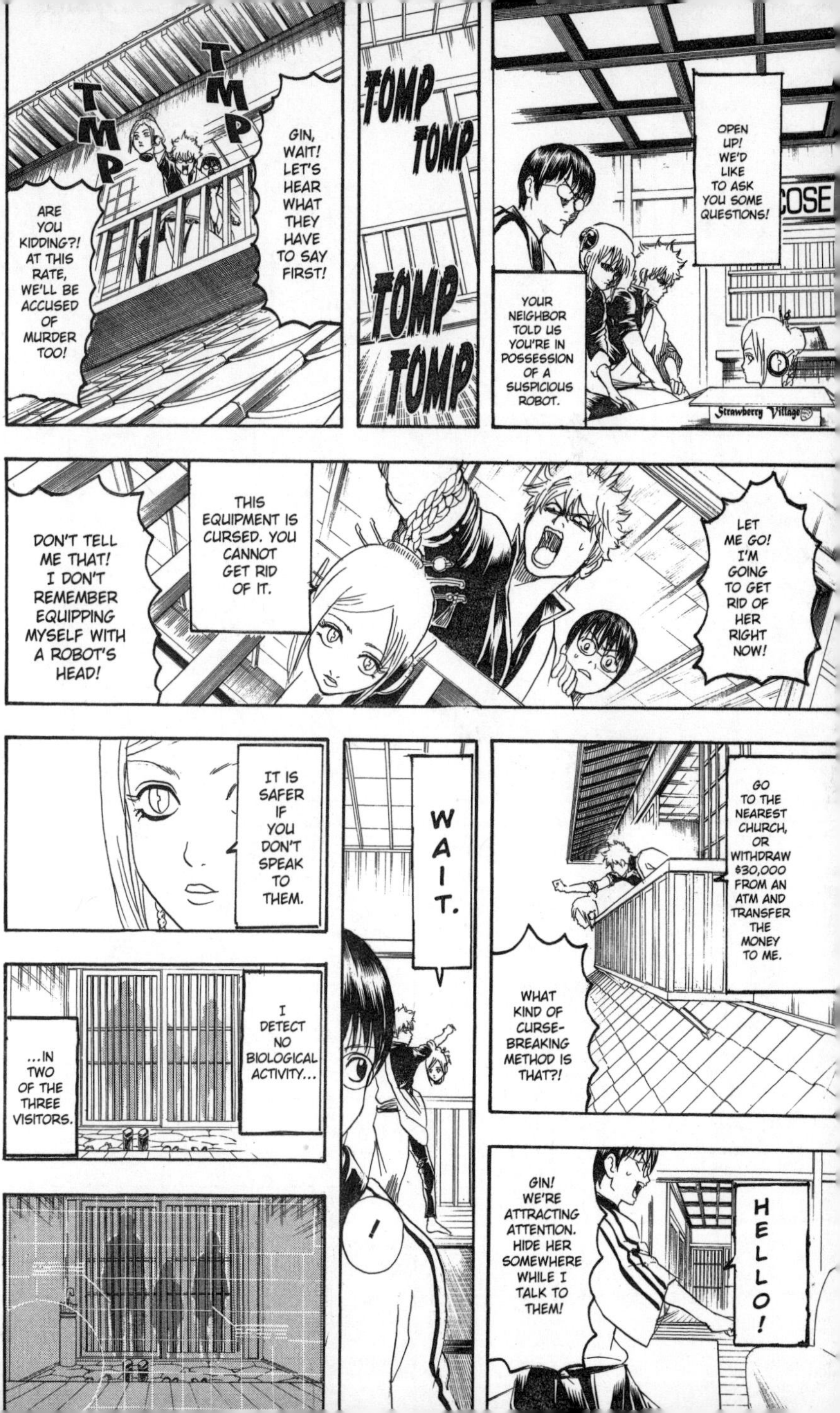
OPEN UP! WE'D LIKE TO ASK YOU SOME QUESTIONS!
COSE
YOUR NEIGHBOR TOLD US YOU'RE IN POSSESSION OF A SUSPICIOUS ROBOT.
Strawberry Village
TOMP TOMP
TOMP TOMP
TMP
TMP
GIN, WAIT! LET'S HEAR WHAT THEY HAVE TO SAY FIRST!
ARE YOU KIDDING?! AT THIS RATE, WE'LL BE ACCUSED OF MURDER TOO!
LET ME GO! I'M GOING TO GET RID OF HER RIGHT NOW!
THIS EQUIPMENT IS CURSED. YOU CANNOT GET RID OF IT.
DON'T TELL ME THAT! I DON'T REMEMBER EQUIPPING MYSELF WITH A ROBOT'S HEAD!
GO TO THE NEAREST CHURCH, OR WITHDRAW $30,000 FROM AN ATM AND TRANSFER THE MONEY TO ME.
WHAT KIND OF CURSE-BREAKING METHOD IS THAT?!
HELLO!
GIN! WE'RE ATTRACTING ATTENTION. HIDE HER SOMEWHERE WHILE I TALK TO THEM!
WAIT.
!
IT IS SAFER IF YOU DON'T SPEAK TO THEM.
I DETECT NO BIOLOGICAL ACTIVITY...
...IN TWO OF THE THREE VISITORS.

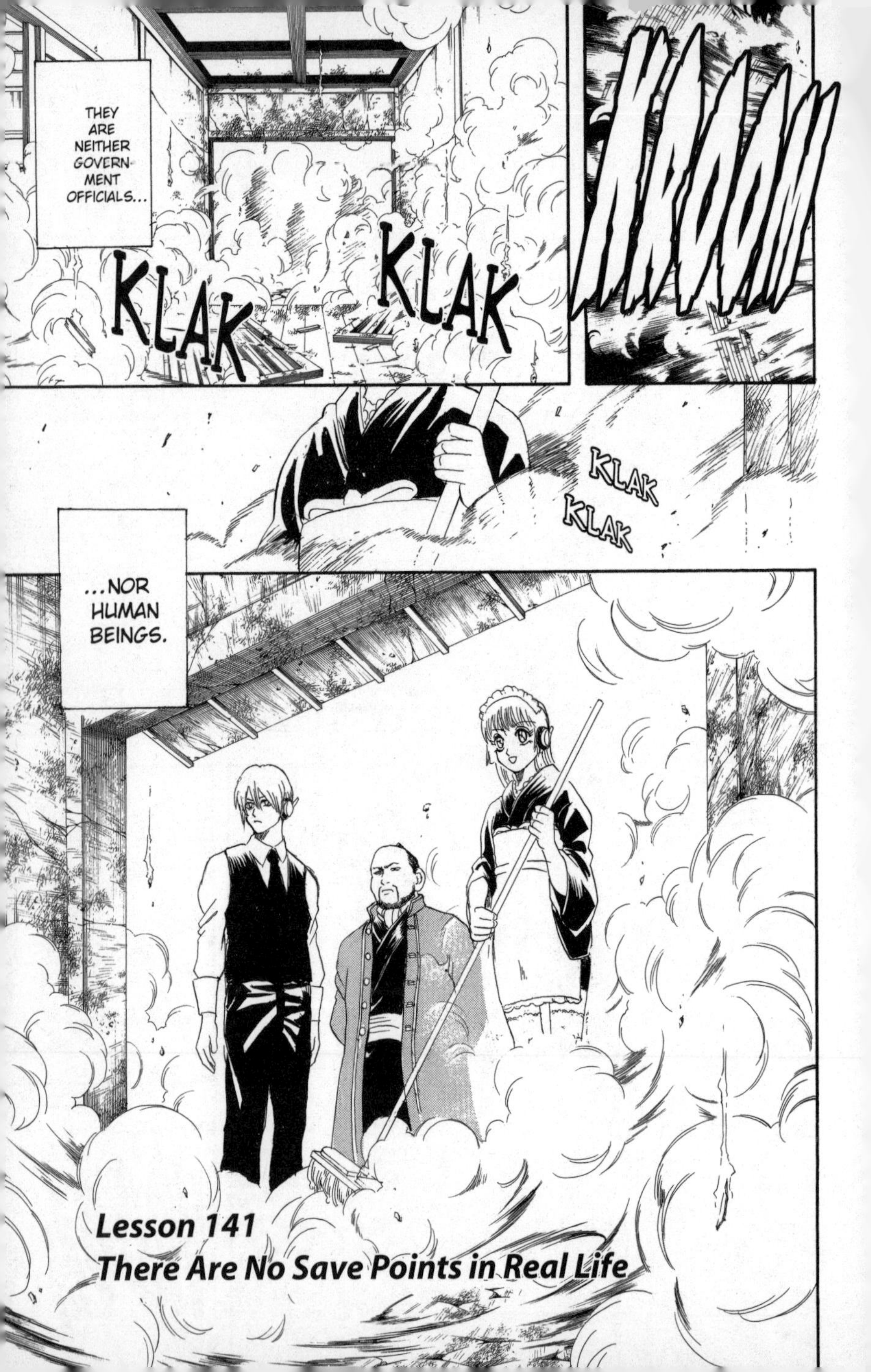
THEY ARE NEITHER GOVERN-MENT OFFICIALS...
KLAK
KLAK
KLAK
KLAK
...NOR HUMAN BEINGS.
Lesson 141
There Are No Save Points in Real Life

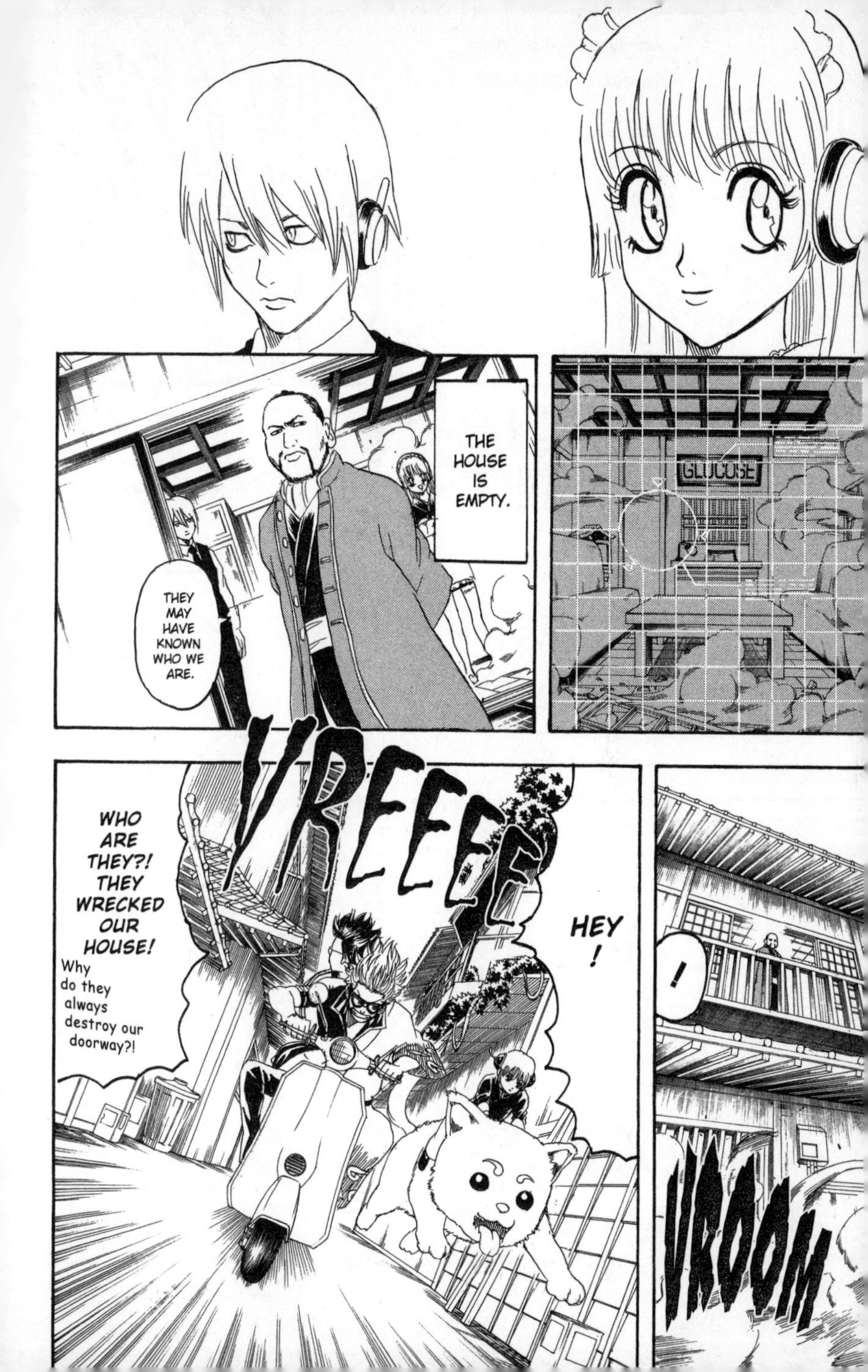
THE HOUSE IS EMPTY.
THEY MAY HAVE KNOWN WHO WE ARE.
!
VROOM
VREEEE
HEY!
WHO ARE THEY?! THEY WRECKED OUR HOUSE!
Why do they always destroy our doorway?!

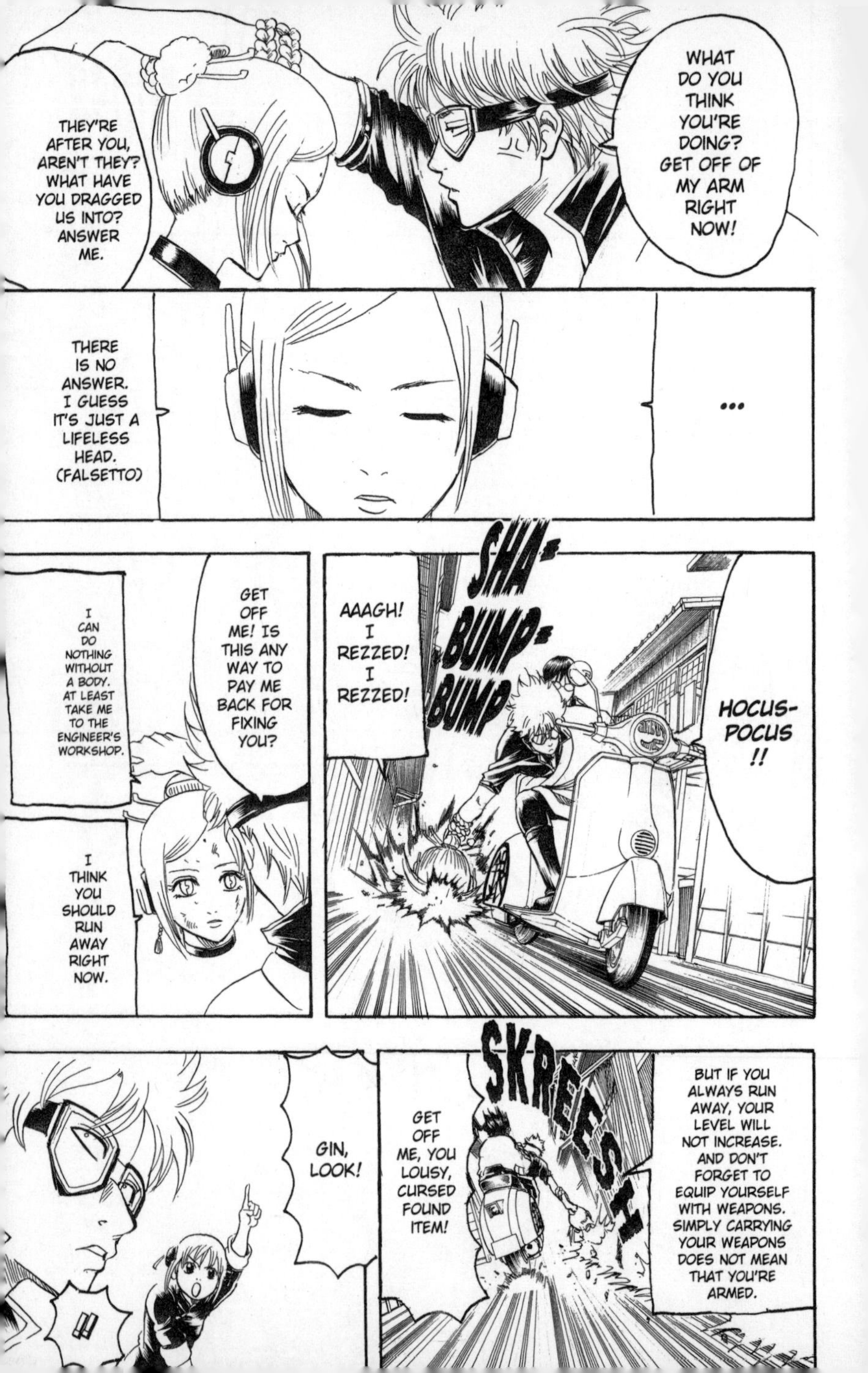
WHAT DO YOU THINK YOU'RE DOING? GET OFF OF MY ARM RIGHT NOW!
THEY'RE AFTER YOU, AREN'T THEY? WHAT HAVE YOU DRAGGED US INTO? ANSWER ME.
...
THERE IS NO ANSWER. I GUESS IT'S JUST A LIFELESS HEAD. (FALSETTO)
HOCUS-POCUS !!
SHA-BUMP-BUMP-BUMP
AAAGH! I REZZED! I REZZED!
GET OFF ME! IS THIS ANY WAY TO PAY ME BACK FOR FIXING YOU?
I CAN DO NOTHING WITHOUT A BODY. AT LEAST TAKE ME TO THE ENGINEER'S WORKSHOP.
I THINK YOU SHOULD RUN AWAY RIGHT NOW.
BUT IF YOU ALWAYS RUN AWAY, YOUR LEVEL WILL NOT INCREASE. AND DON'T FORGET TO EQUIP YOURSELF WITH WEAPONS. SIMPLY CARRYING YOUR WEAPONS DOES NOT MEAN THAT YOU'RE ARMED.
SKREESH
GET OFF ME, YOU LOUSY, CURSED FOUND ITEM!
GIN, LOOK!
!!

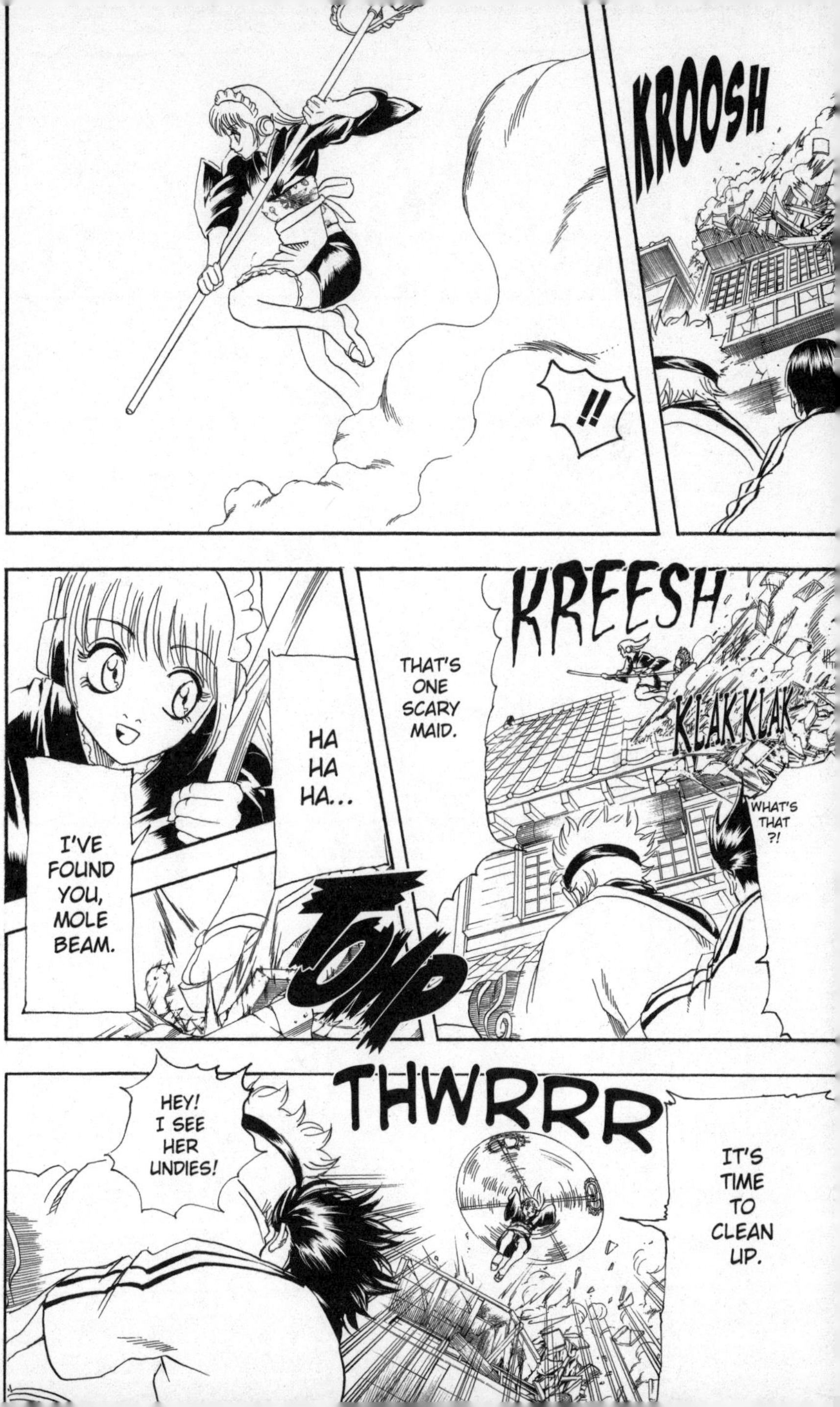

KROOSH
!!
KREESH
KLAK KLAK
WHAT'S THAT ?!
THAT'S ONE SCARY MAID.
HA HA HA...
TOMP
I'VE FOUND YOU, MOLE BEAM.
THWRRR
IT'S TIME TO CLEAN UP.
HEY! I SEE HER UNDIES!

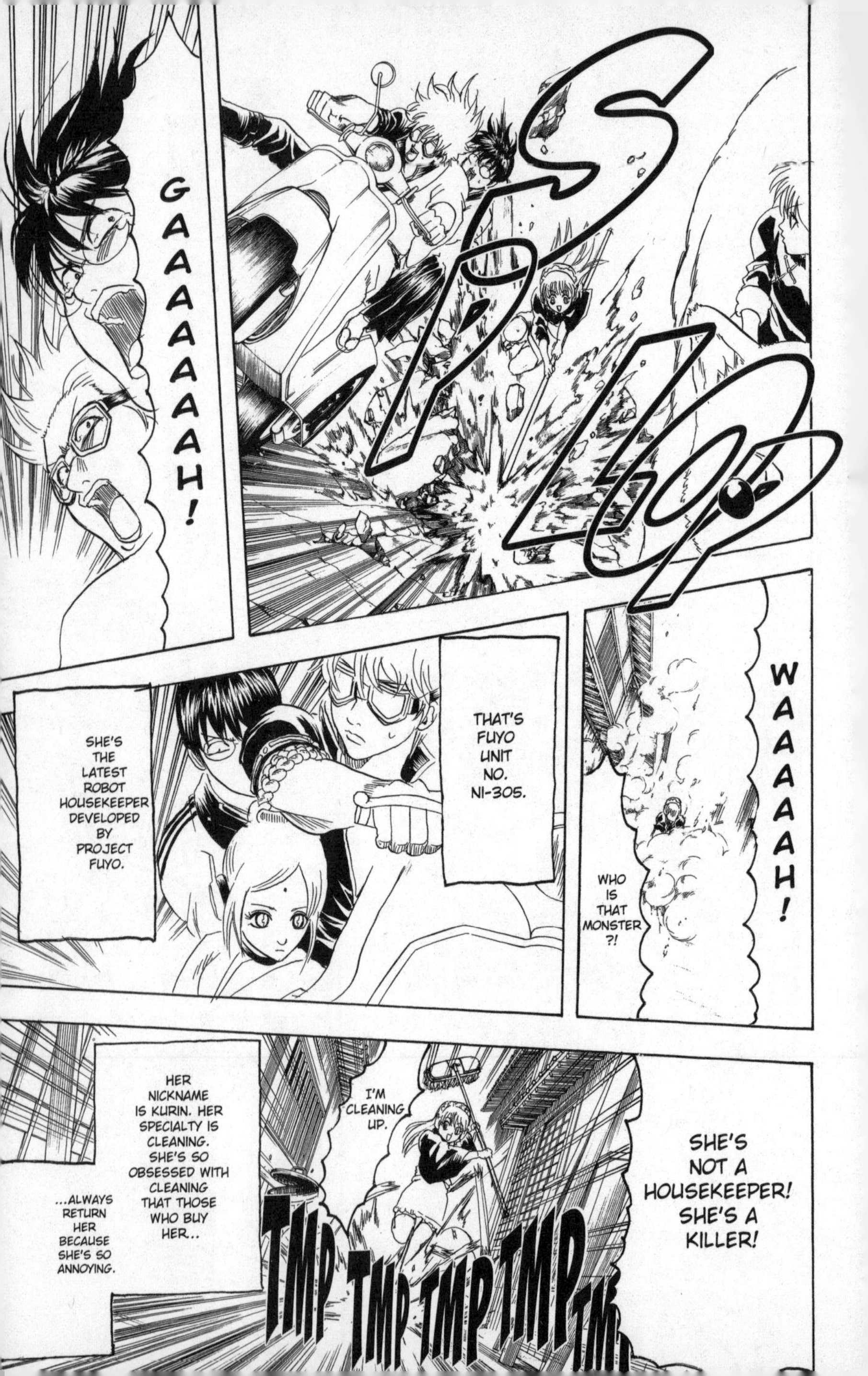
GAAAAAAAAH!
WAAAAAAAH!
WHO IS THAT MONSTER?!
THAT'S FUYO UNIT NO. NI-305.
SHE'S THE LATEST ROBOT HOUSEKEEPER DEVELOPED BY PROJECT FUYO.
SHE'S NOT A HOUSEKEEPER! SHE'S A KILLER!
I'M CLEANING UP.
HER NICKNAME IS KURIN. HER SPECIALTY IS CLEANING. SHE'S SO OBSESSED WITH CLEANING THAT THOSE WHO BUY HER..
...ALWAYS RETURN HER BECAUSE SHE'S SO ANNOYING.
TMP TMP TMP TMP TM..

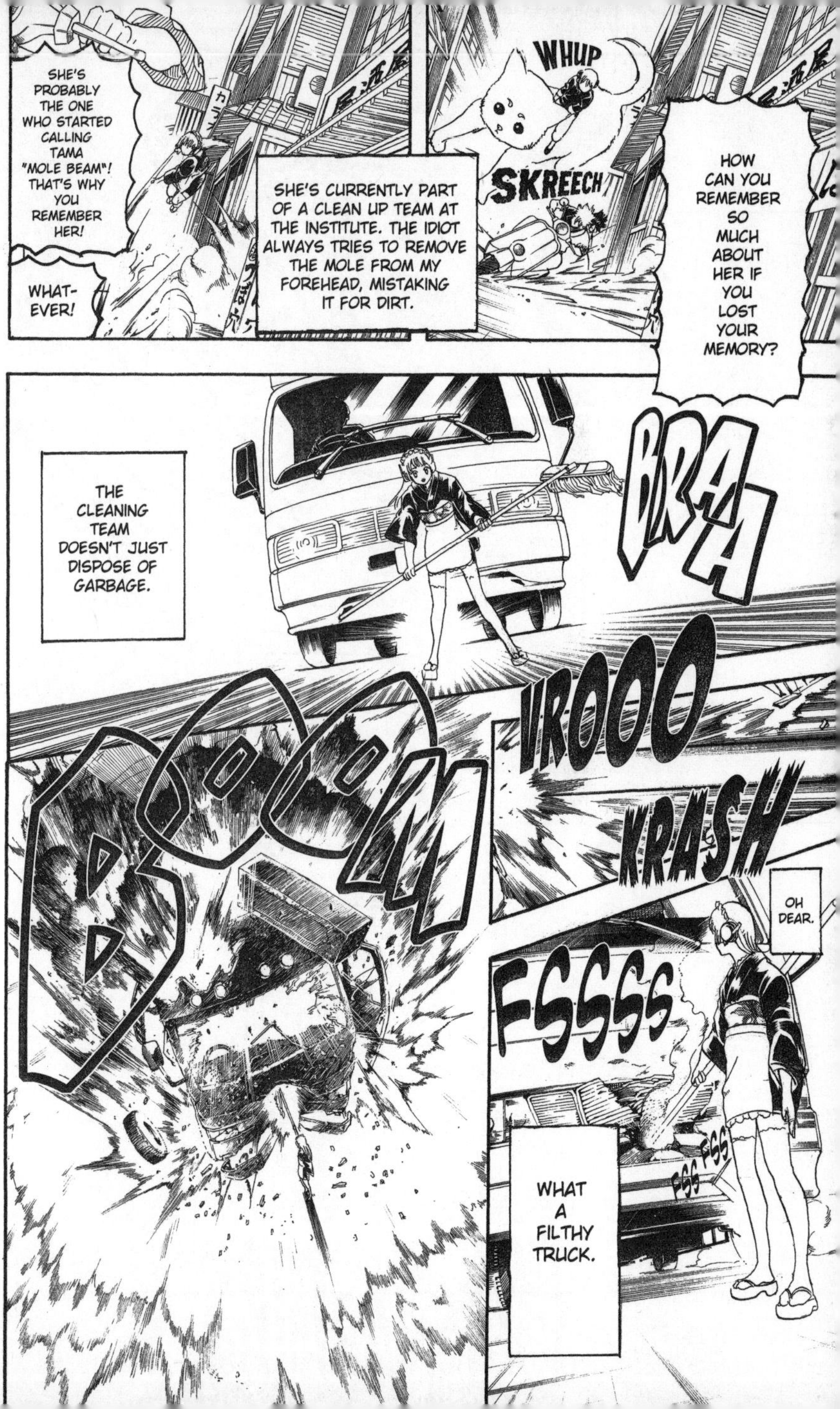

WHUP
SKREECH
SHE'S CURRENTLY PART OF A CLEAN UP TEAM AT THE INSTITUTE. THE IDIOT ALWAYS TRIES TO REMOVE THE MOLE FROM MY FOREHEAD, MISTAKING IT FOR DIRT.
HOW CAN YOU REMEMBER SO MUCH ABOUT HER IF YOU LOST YOUR MEMORY?
SHE'S PROBABLY THE ONE WHO STARTED CALLING TAMA "MOLE BEAM"! THAT'S WHY YOU REMEMBER HER!
WHAT-EVER!
BRAAA
THE CLEANING TEAM DOESN'T JUST DISPOSE OF GARBAGE.
VROOO
KRASH
OH DEAR.
FSSSS
FSS FSS
WHAT A FILTHY TRUCK.
BOOM

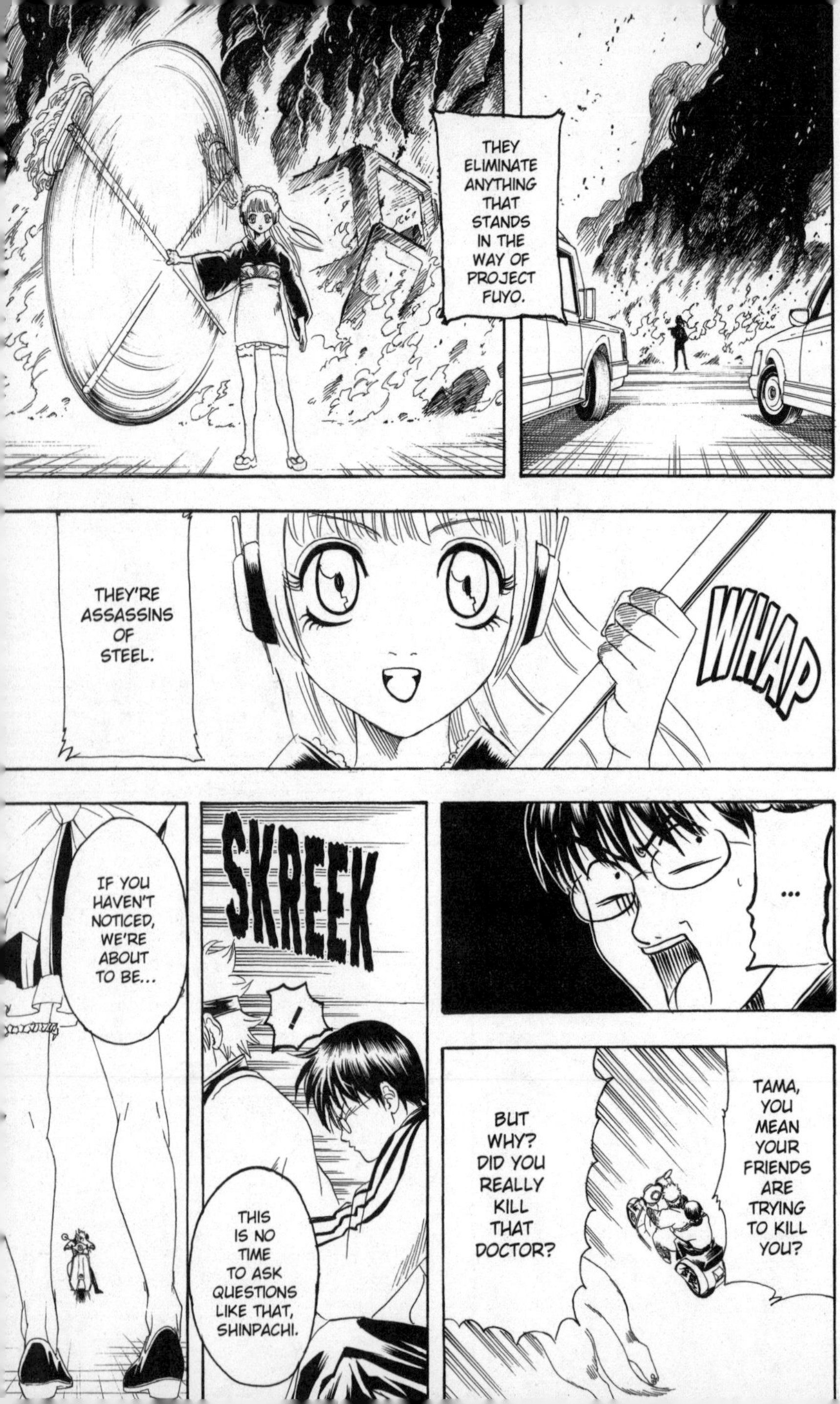
THEY ELIMINATE ANYTHING THAT STANDS IN THE WAY OF PROJECT FUYO.
WHAP
THEY'RE ASSASSINS OF STEEL.
...
TAMA, YOU MEAN YOUR FRIENDS ARE TRYING TO KILL YOU?
BUT WHY? DID YOU REALLY KILL THAT DOCTOR?
SKREEK
!
THIS IS NO TIME TO ASK QUESTIONS LIKE THAT, SHINPACHI.
IF YOU HAVEN'T NOTICED, WE'RE ABOUT TO BE...

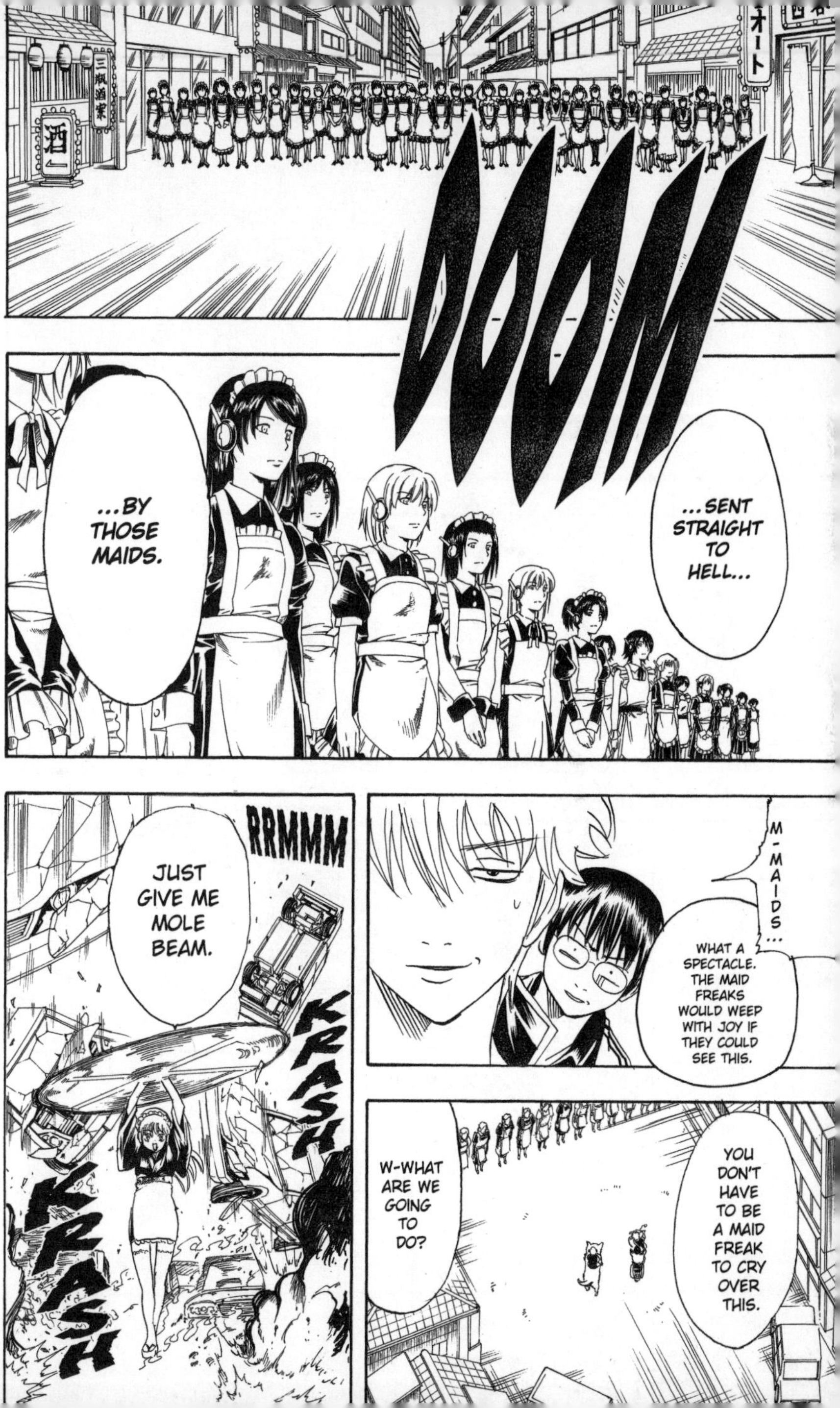

酒
オート
DOOM
...SENT STRAIGHT TO HELL...
...BY THOSE MAIDS.
M-MAIDS...
WHAT A SPECTACLE. THE MAID FREAKS WOULD WEEP WITH JOY IF THEY COULD SEE THIS.
YOU DON'T HAVE TO BE A MAID FREAK TO CRY OVER THIS.
W-WHAT ARE WE GOING TO DO?
RRMMM
JUST GIVE ME MOLE BEAM.
KRASH
KRASH

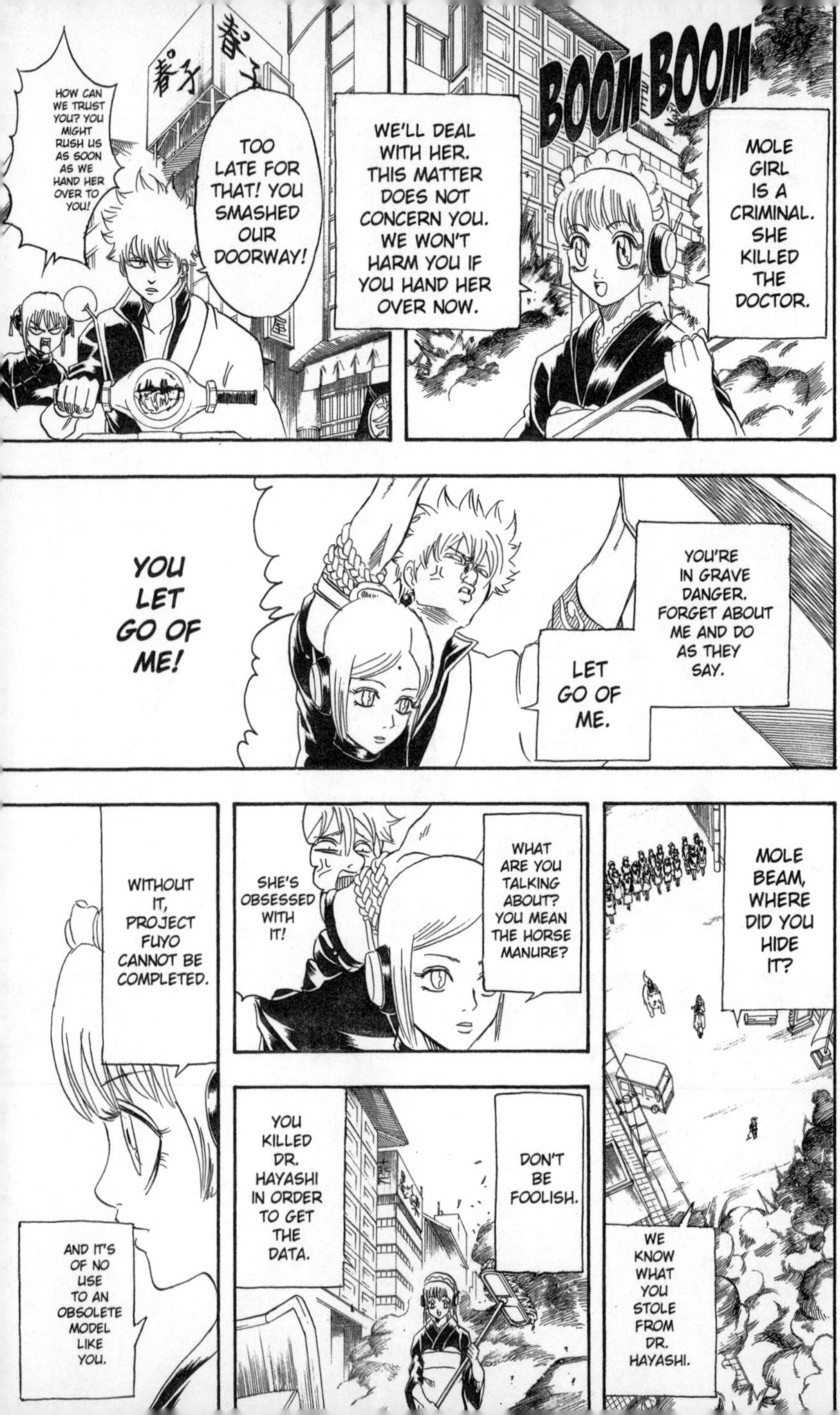
BOOM BOOM
MOLE GIRL IS A CRIMINAL. SHE KILLED THE DOCTOR.
WE'LL DEAL WITH HER. THIS MATTER DOES NOT CONCERN YOU. WE WON'T HARM YOU IF YOU HAND HER OVER NOW.
TOO LATE FOR THAT! YOU SMASHED OUR DOORWAY!
HOW CAN WE TRUST YOU? YOU MIGHT RUSH US AS SOON AS WE HAND HER OVER TO YOU!
YOU'RE IN GRAVE DANGER. FORGET ABOUT ME AND DO AS THEY SAY.
LET GO OF ME.
YOU LET GO OF ME!
MOLE BEAM, WHERE DID YOU HIDE IT?
WE KNOW WHAT YOU STOLE FROM DR. HAYASHI.
WHAT ARE YOU TALKING ABOUT? YOU MEAN THE HORSE MANURE?
SHE'S OBSESSED WITH IT!
DON'T BE FOOLISH.
YOU KILLED DR. HAYASHI IN ORDER TO GET THE DATA.
WITHOUT IT, PROJECT FUYO CANNOT BE COMPLETED.
AND IT'S OF NO USE TO AN OBSOLETE MODEL LIKE YOU.

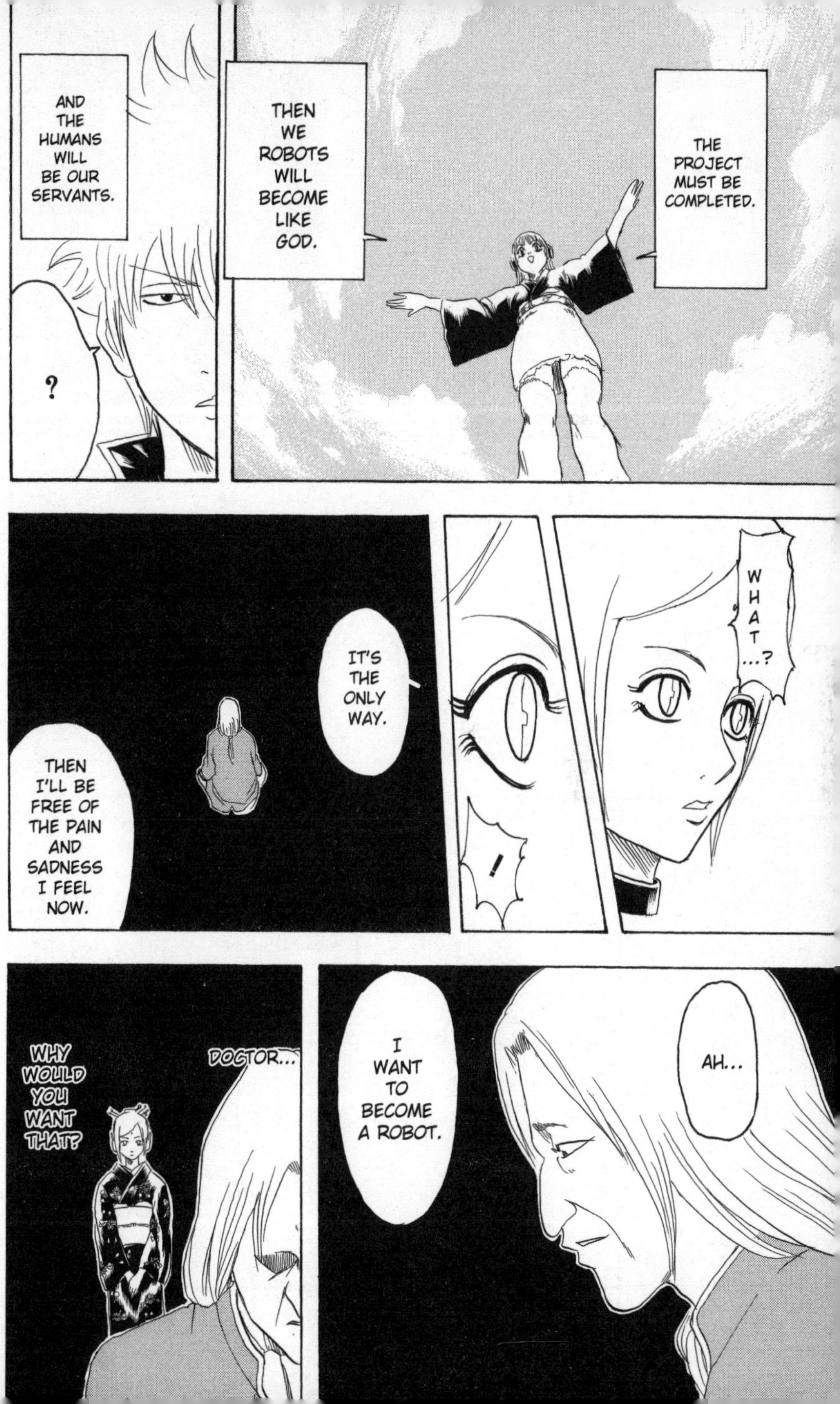
THE PROJECT MUST BE COMPLETED.
THEN WE ROBOTS WILL BECOME LIKE GOD.
AND THE HUMANS WILL BE OUR SERVANTS.
?
WHAT ...?
!
IT'S THE ONLY WAY.
THEN I'LL BE FREE OF THE PAIN AND SADNESS I FEEL NOW.
AH...
I WANT TO BECOME A ROBOT.
DOCTOR...
WHY WOULD YOU WANT THAT?

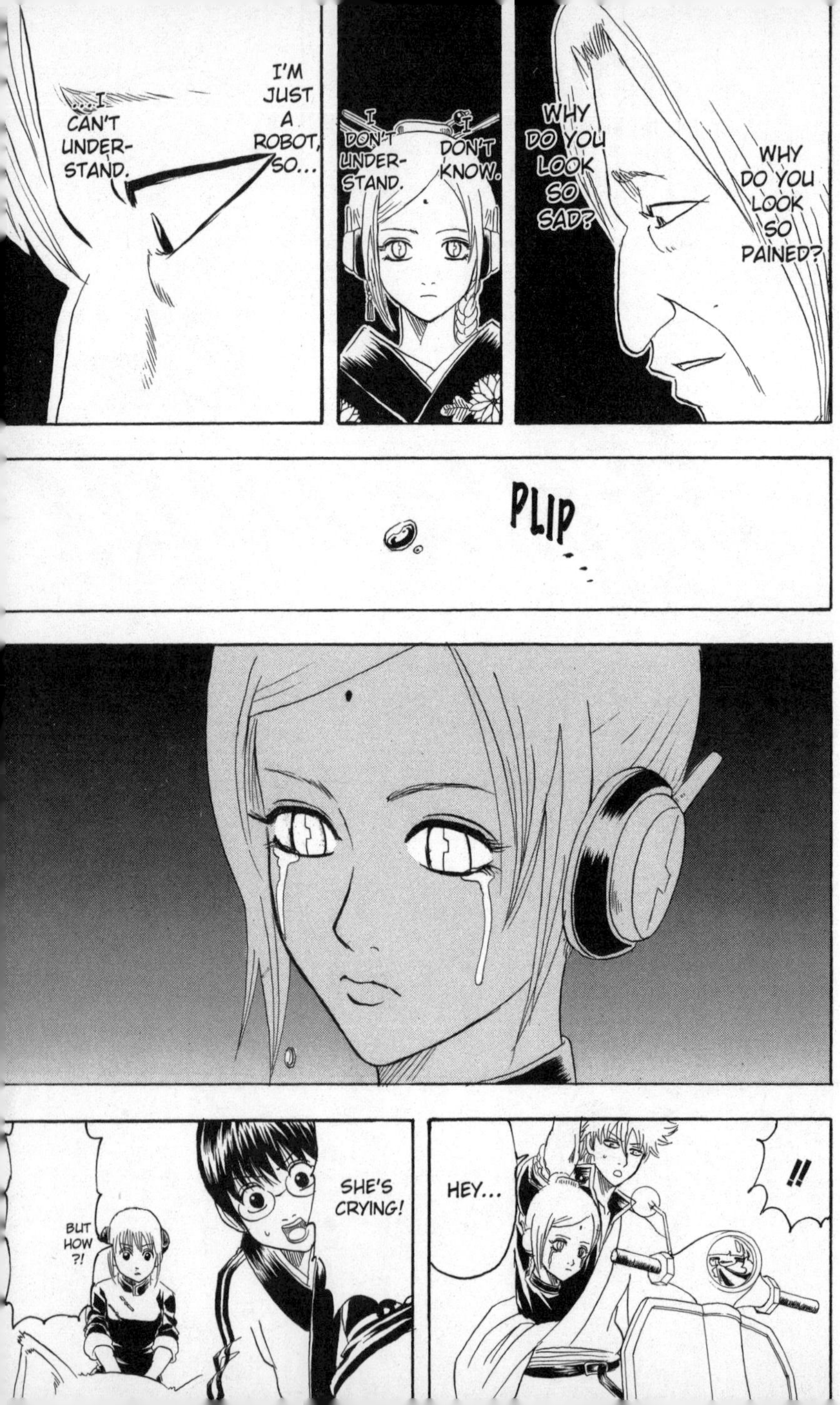
WHY DO YOU LOOK SO PAINED?
WHY DO YOU LOOK SO SAD?
I DON'T KNOW.
I DON'T UNDERSTAND.
I'M JUST A ROBOT, SO...
...I CAN'T UNDERSTAND.
PLIP
!!
HEY...
SHE'S CRYING!
BUT HOW?!

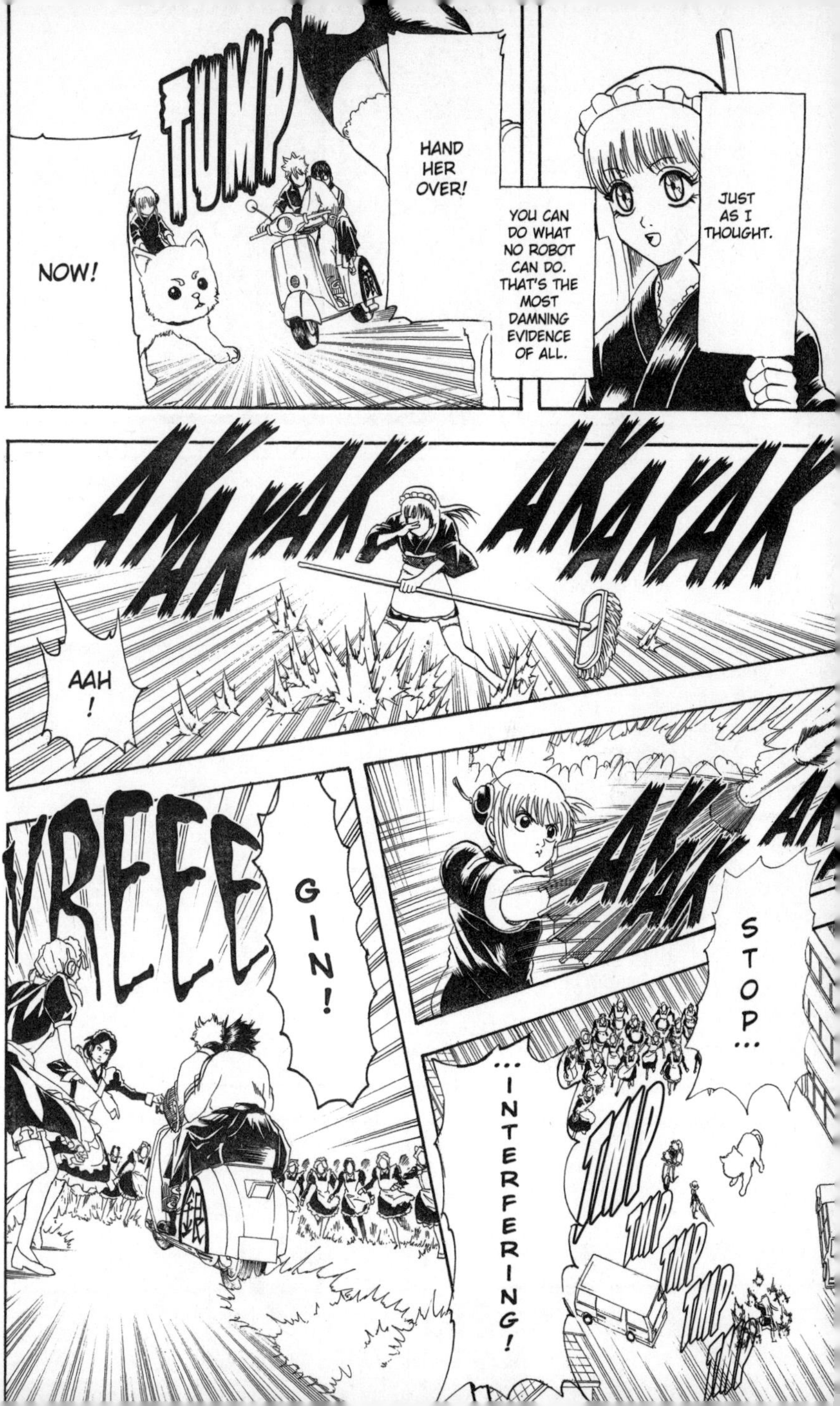
JUST AS I THOUGHT.
YOU CAN DO WHAT NO ROBOT CAN DO. THAT'S THE MOST DAMNING EVIDENCE OF ALL.
HAND HER OVER!
TUMP
NOW!
AAKAKAK
AAKAKAK
AAH!
AAK
STOP...
...INTERFERING!
TMP TMP TMP TMP TMP
VREEE
GIN!

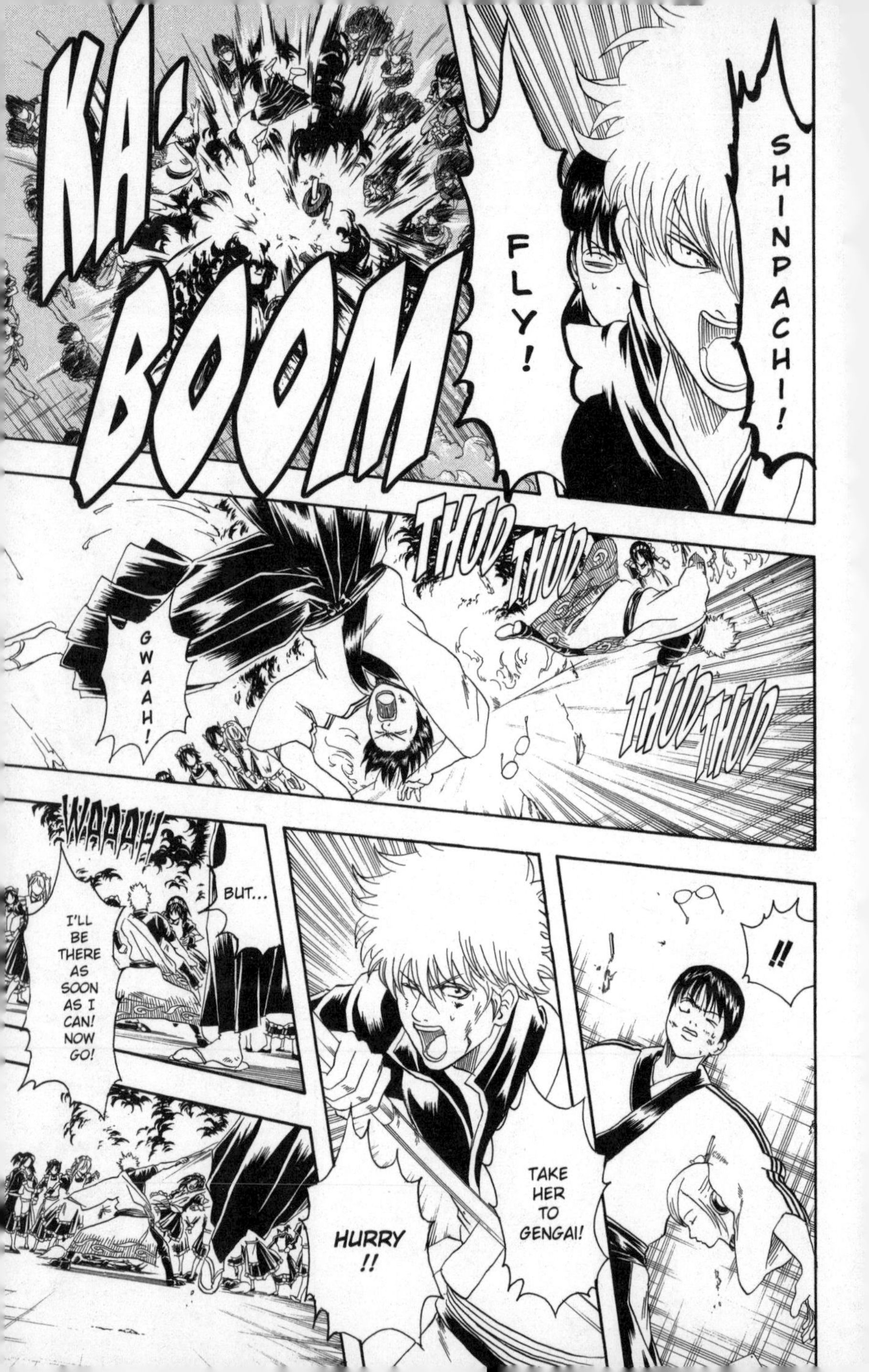
SHINPACHI!
FLY!
KA-BOOM
THUD THUD
THUD THUD
GWAAH!
!!
TAKE HER TO GENGAI!
HURRY!!
WAAAH
BUT...
I'LL BE THERE AS SOON AS I CAN! NOW GO!

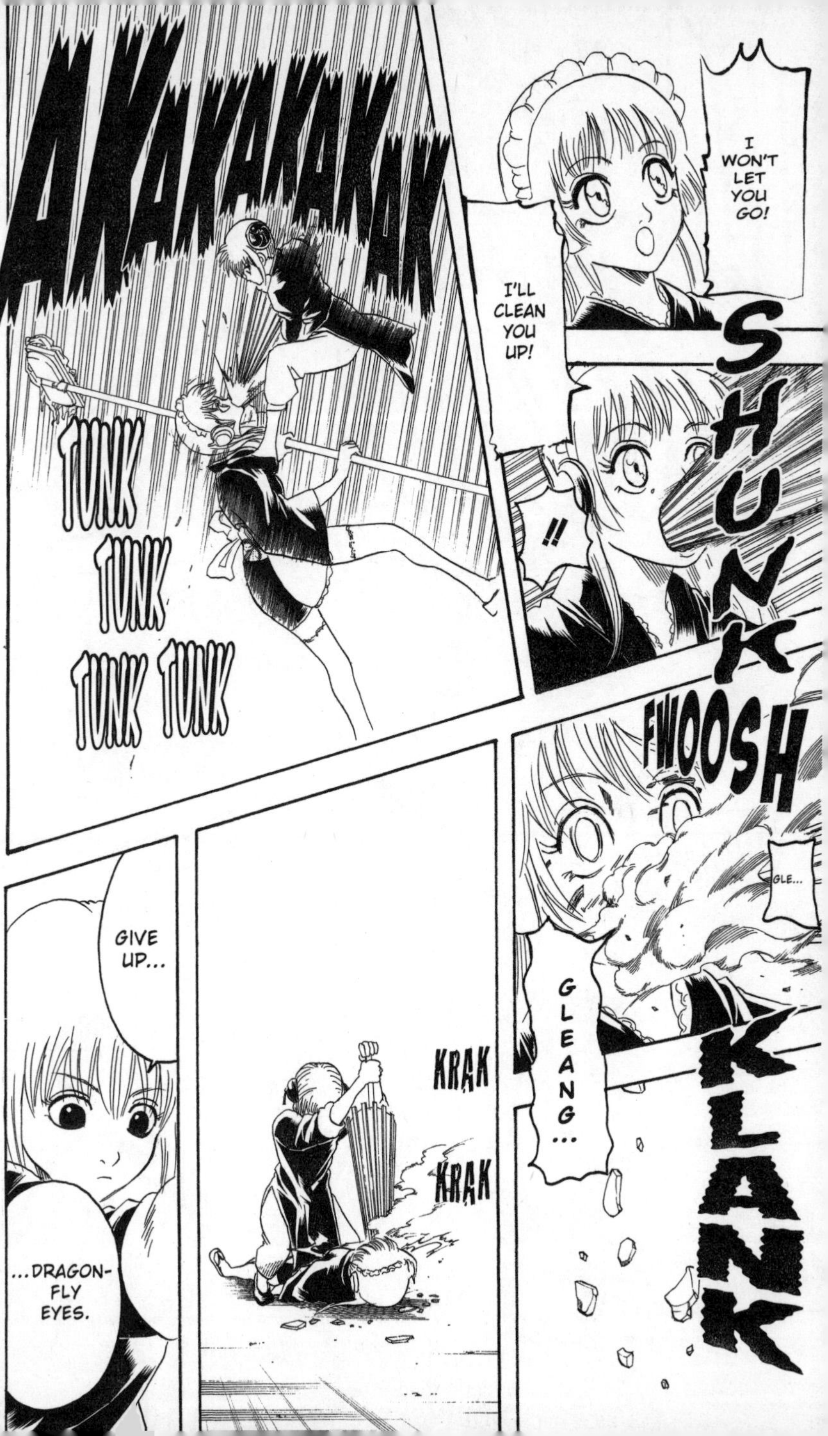
I WON'T LET YOU GO!
I'LL CLEAN YOU UP!
SHUNK
!!
FWOOSH
GLE...
GLEANG...
KLANK
AKAKAKAKAKAK
TUNK TUNK TUNK TUNK
KRAK
KRAK
GIVE UP...
...DRAGON-FLY EYES.

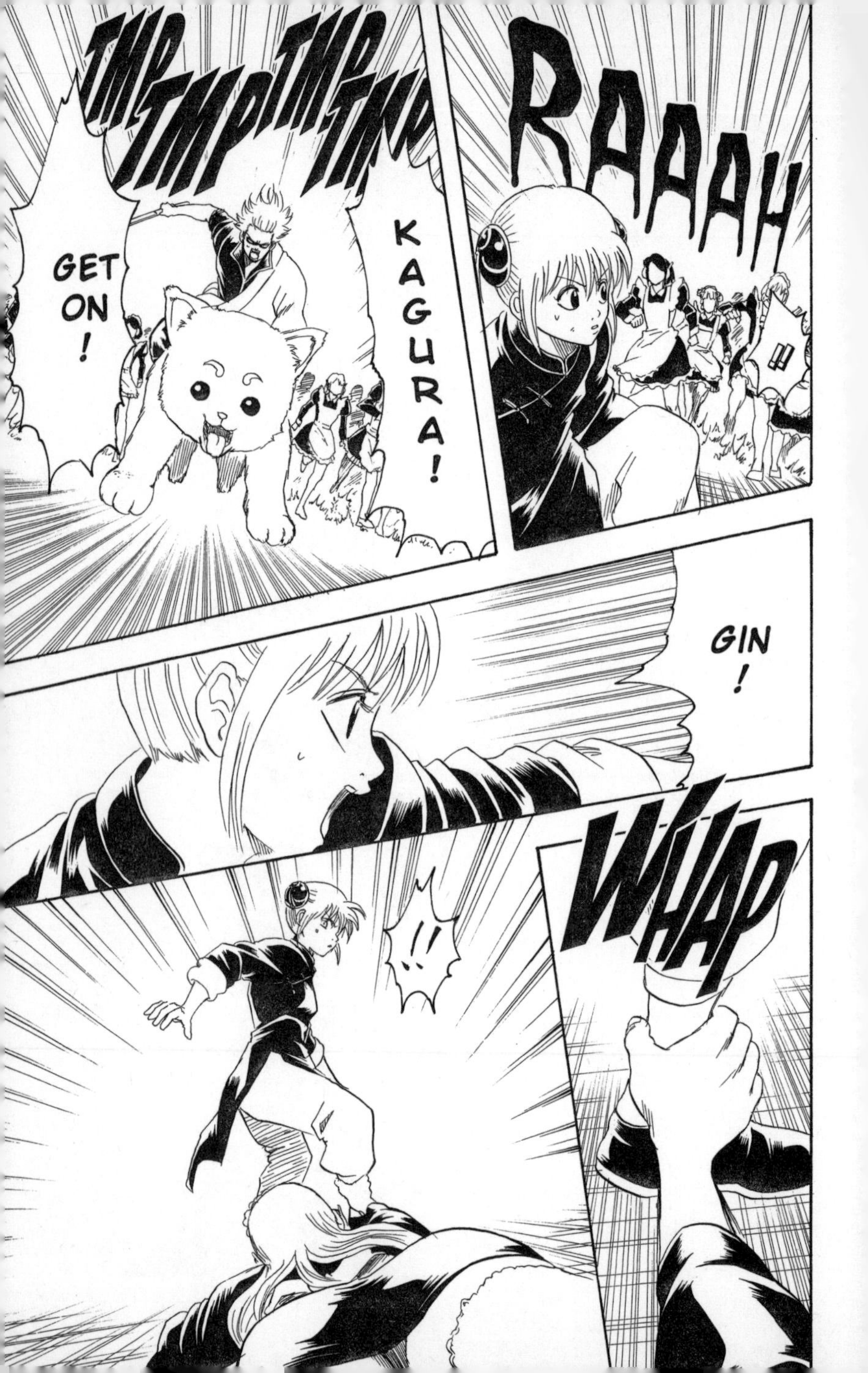
RAAAAH
!!
THMP THMP THMP THMP
KAGURA!
GET ON!
GIN!
WHAP
!!

● Published in *Weekly Shonen JUMP*, 2007 as the cover illustration of volumes 36 and 37 joint issue

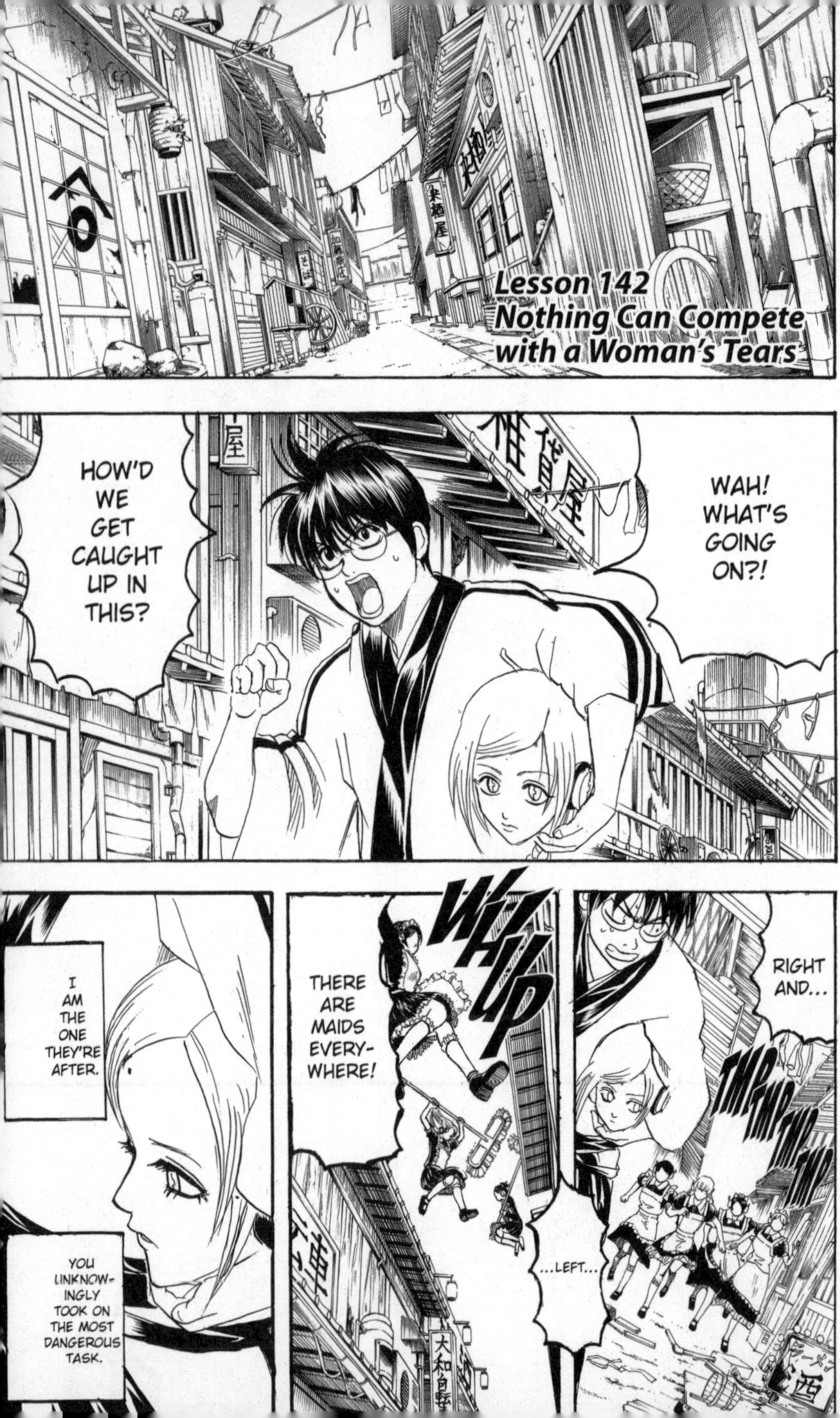
Lesson 142
Nothing Can Compete with a Woman's Tears
WAH! WHAT'S GOING ON?!
HOW'D WE GET CAUGHT UP IN THIS?
RIGHT AND...
THRP THRP THRP
...LEFT...
WHIP
THERE ARE MAIDS EVERY-WHERE!
I AM THE ONE THEY'RE AFTER.
YOU UNKNOWINGLY TOOK ON THE MOST DANGEROUS TASK.

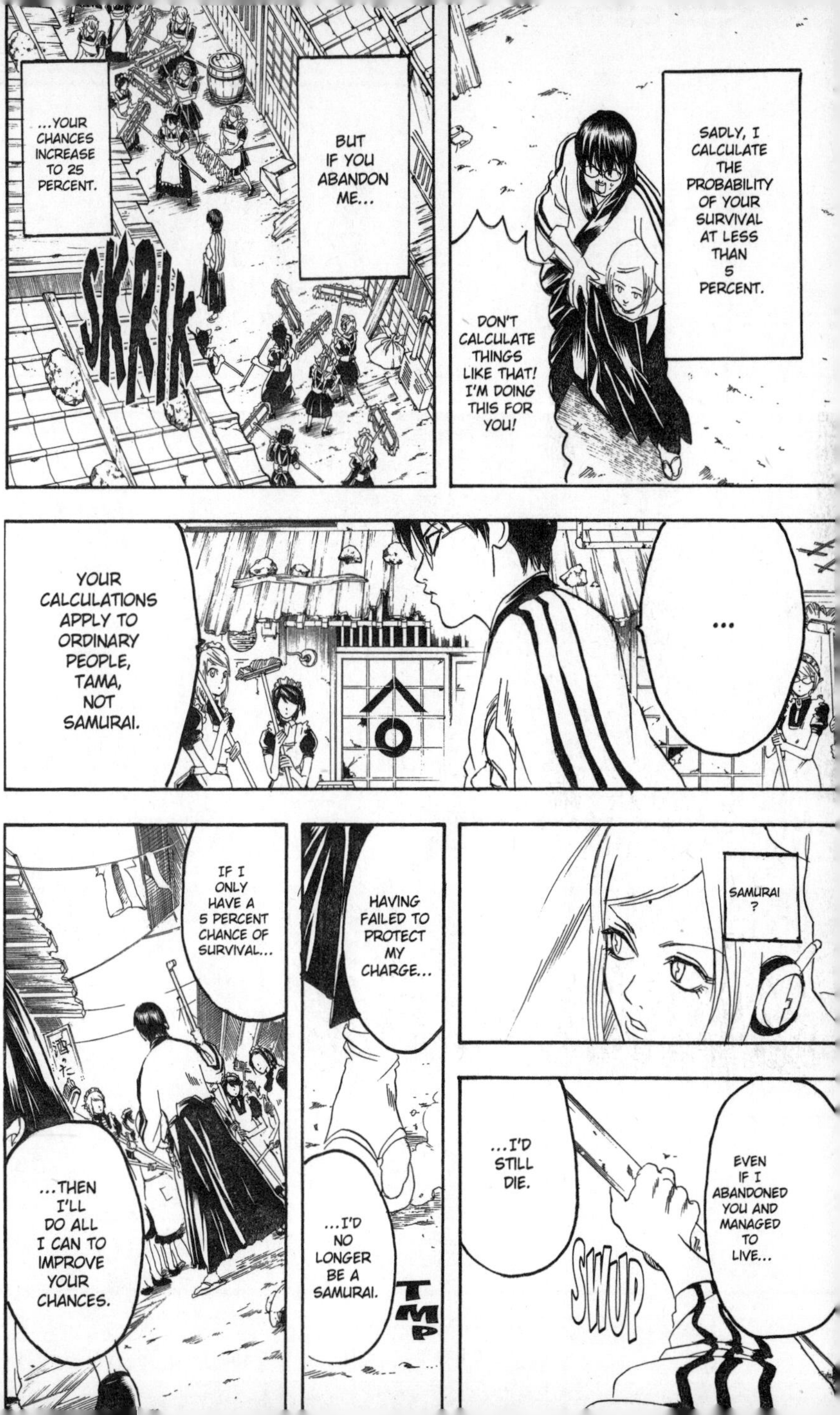
SADLY, I CALCULATE THE PROBABILITY OF YOUR SURVIVAL AT LESS THAN 5 PERCENT.
DON'T CALCULATE THINGS LIKE THAT! I'M DOING THIS FOR YOU!
BUT IF YOU ABANDON ME...
...YOUR CHANCES INCREASE TO 25 PERCENT.
SKRIK
...
YOUR CALCULATIONS APPLY TO ORDINARY PEOPLE, TAMA, NOT SAMURAI.
SAMURAI ?
EVEN IF I ABANDONED YOU AND MANAGED TO LIVE...
...I'D STILL DIE.
SWUP
HAVING FAILED TO PROTECT MY CHARGE...
...I'D NO LONGER BE A SAMURAI.
TMP
IF I ONLY HAVE A 5 PERCENT CHANCE OF SURVIVAL...
...THEN I'LL DO ALL I CAN TO IMPROVE YOUR CHANCES.

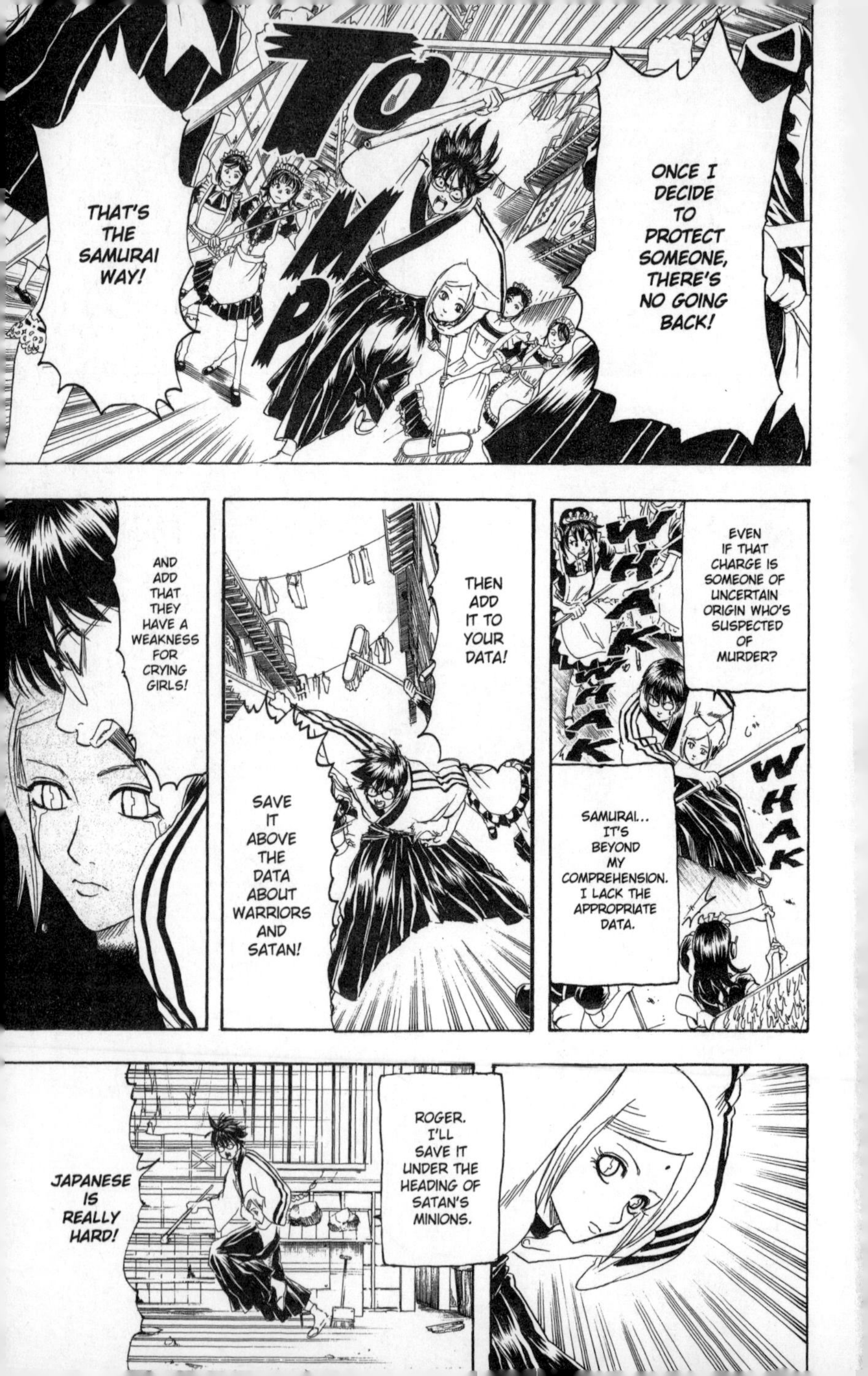
ONCE I DECIDE TO PROTECT SOMEONE, THERE'S NO GOING BACK!
THAT'S THE SAMURAI WAY!
EVEN IF THAT CHARGE IS SOMEONE OF UNCERTAIN ORIGIN WHO'S SUSPECTED OF MURDER?
WHAK
WHAK
SAMURAI... IT'S BEYOND MY COMPREHENSION. I LACK THE APPROPRIATE DATA.
WHAK
THEN ADD IT TO YOUR DATA!
SAVE IT ABOVE THE DATA ABOUT WARRIORS AND SATAN!
AND ADD THAT THEY HAVE A WEAKNESS FOR CRYING GIRLS!
ROGER. I'LL SAVE IT UNDER THE HEADING OF SATAN'S MINIONS.
JAPANESE IS REALLY HARD!

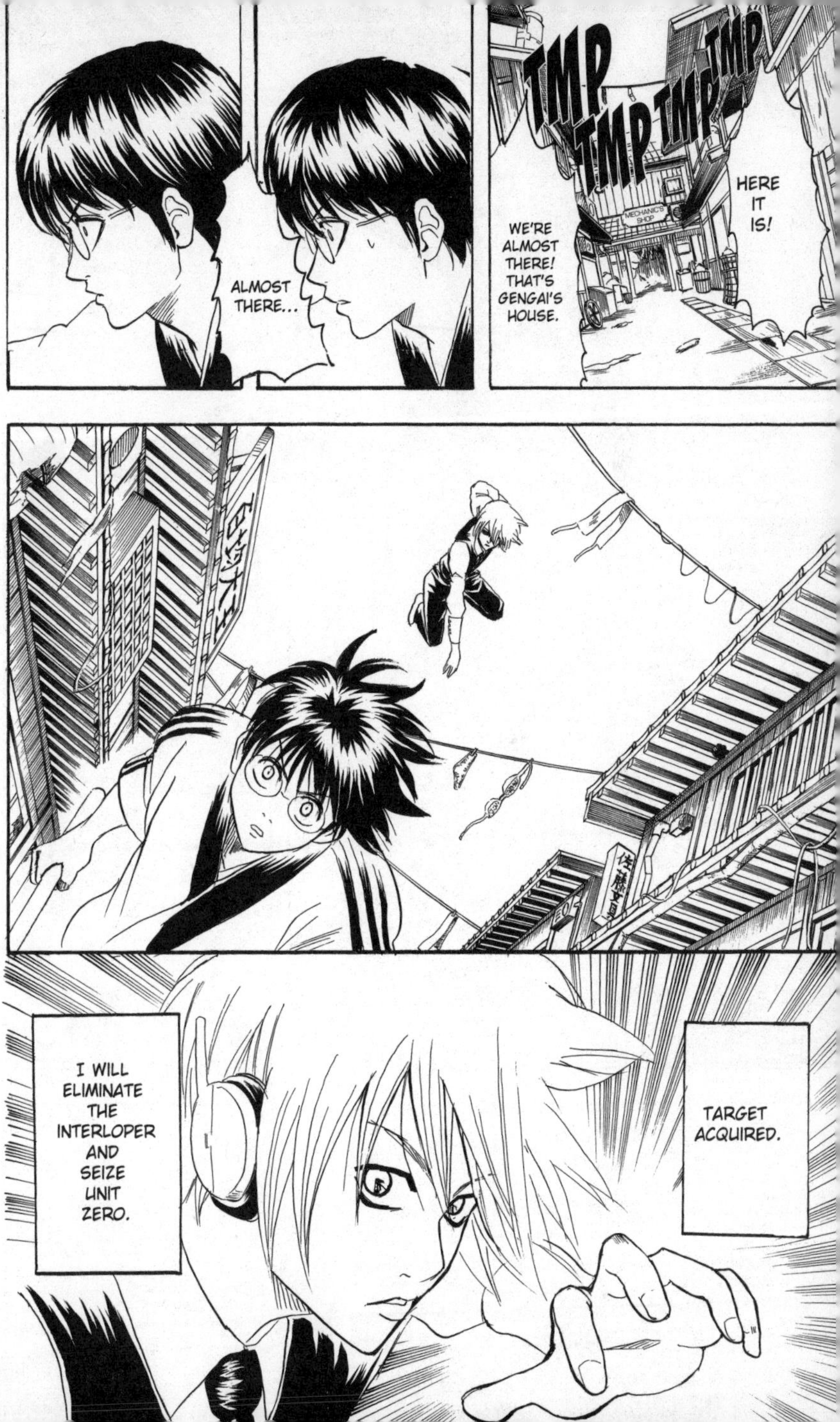
TMP TMP TMP TMP
MECHANIC'S SHOP
HERE IT IS!
WE'RE ALMOST THERE! THAT'S GENGAI'S HOUSE.
ALMOST THERE...
TARGET ACQUIRED.
I WILL ELIMINATE THE INTERLOPER AND SEIZE UNIT ZERO.

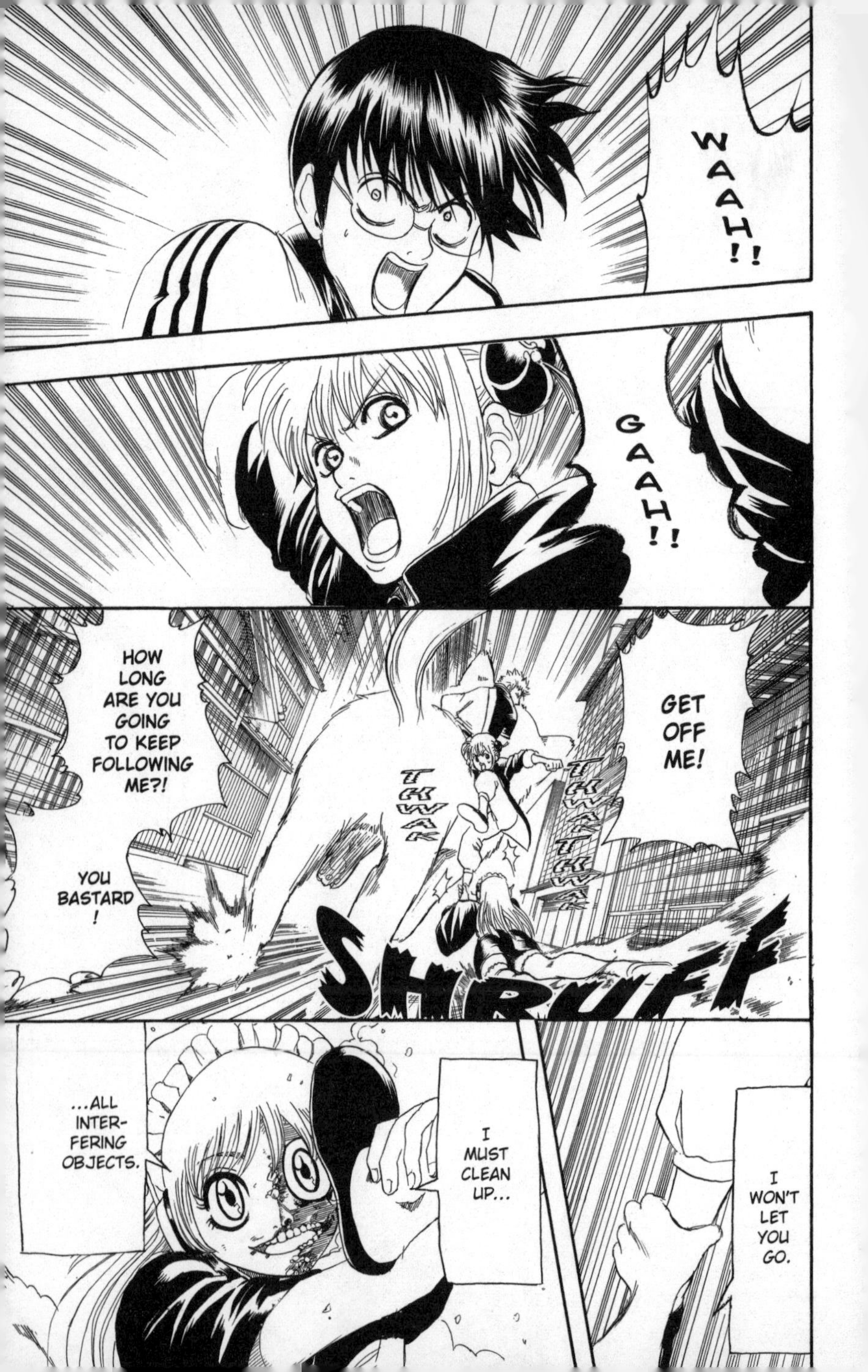
WAAH!!
GAAH!!
GET OFF ME!
THWAK THWAK
THWAK
HOW LONG ARE YOU GOING TO KEEP FOLLOWING ME?!
YOU BASTARD!
SHRUFF
I WON'T LET YOU GO.
I MUST CLEAN UP...
...ALL INTER-FERING OBJECTS.

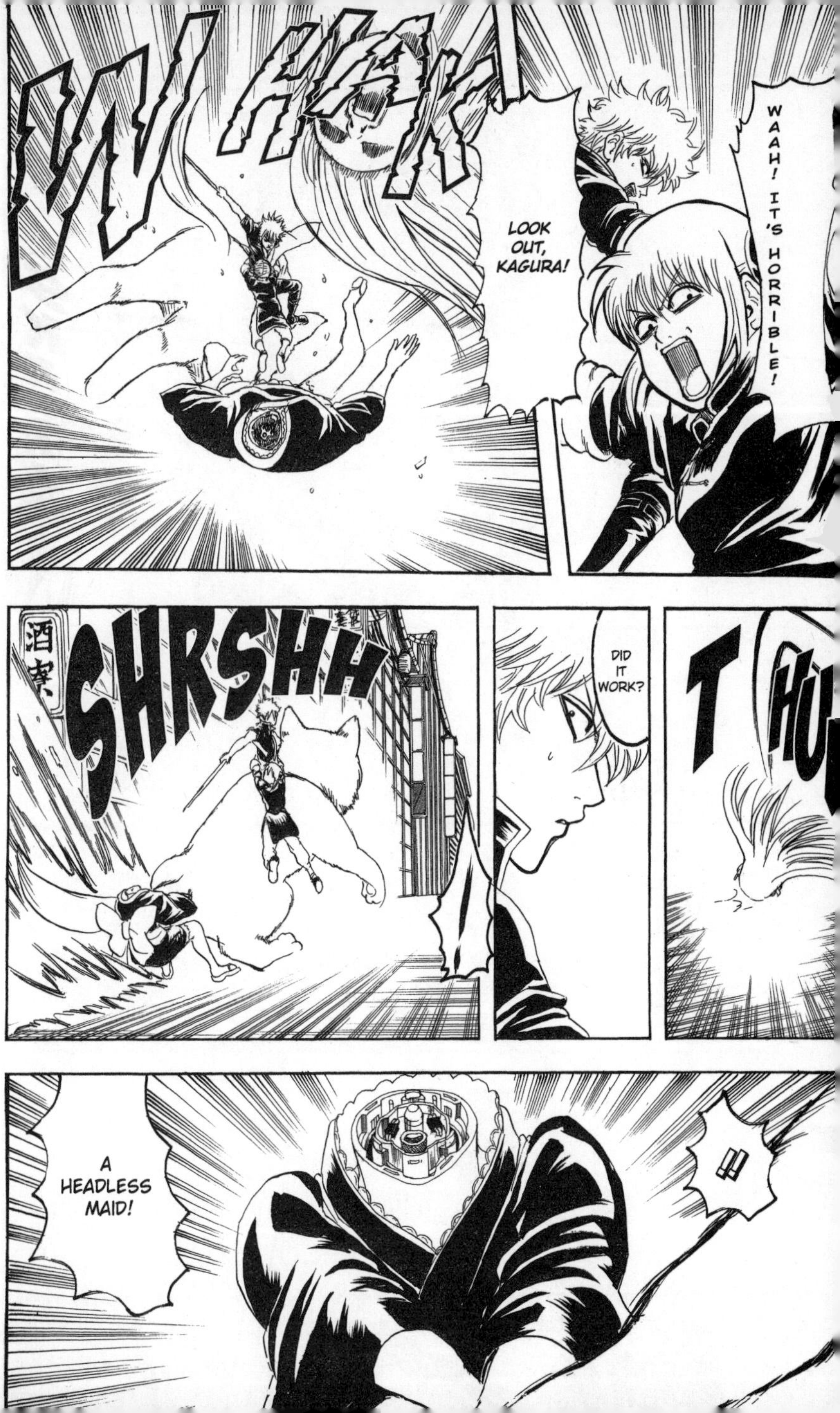
WAAH! IT'S HORRIBLE!
LOOK OUT, KAGURA!
WHAK
THU
DID IT WORK?
SHRSHH
!!
A HEADLESS MAID!

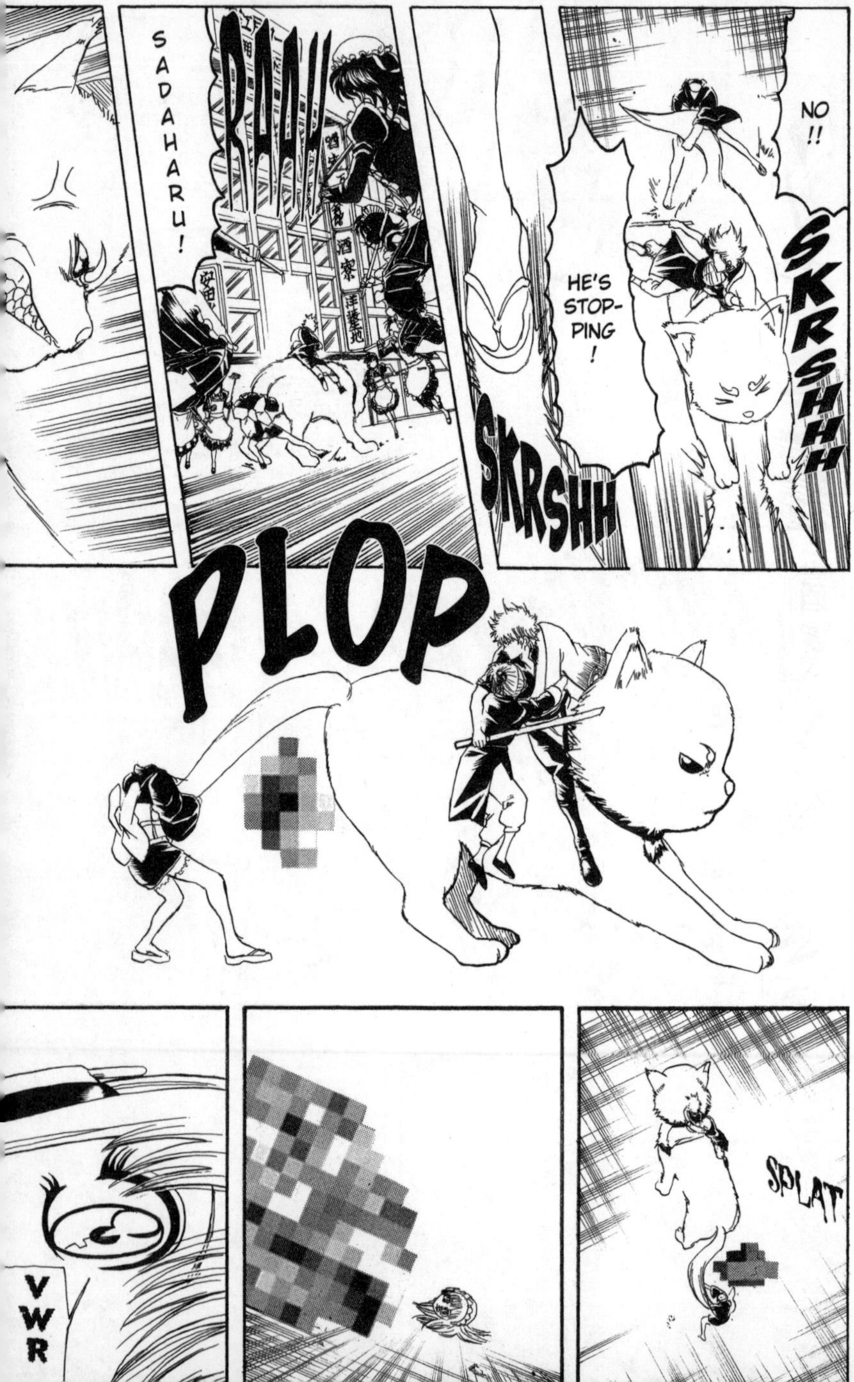
NO!!
SKRSHHH
HE'S STOP-PING!
SKRSHH
SADAHARU!
RAAH
PLOP
SPLAT
VWR

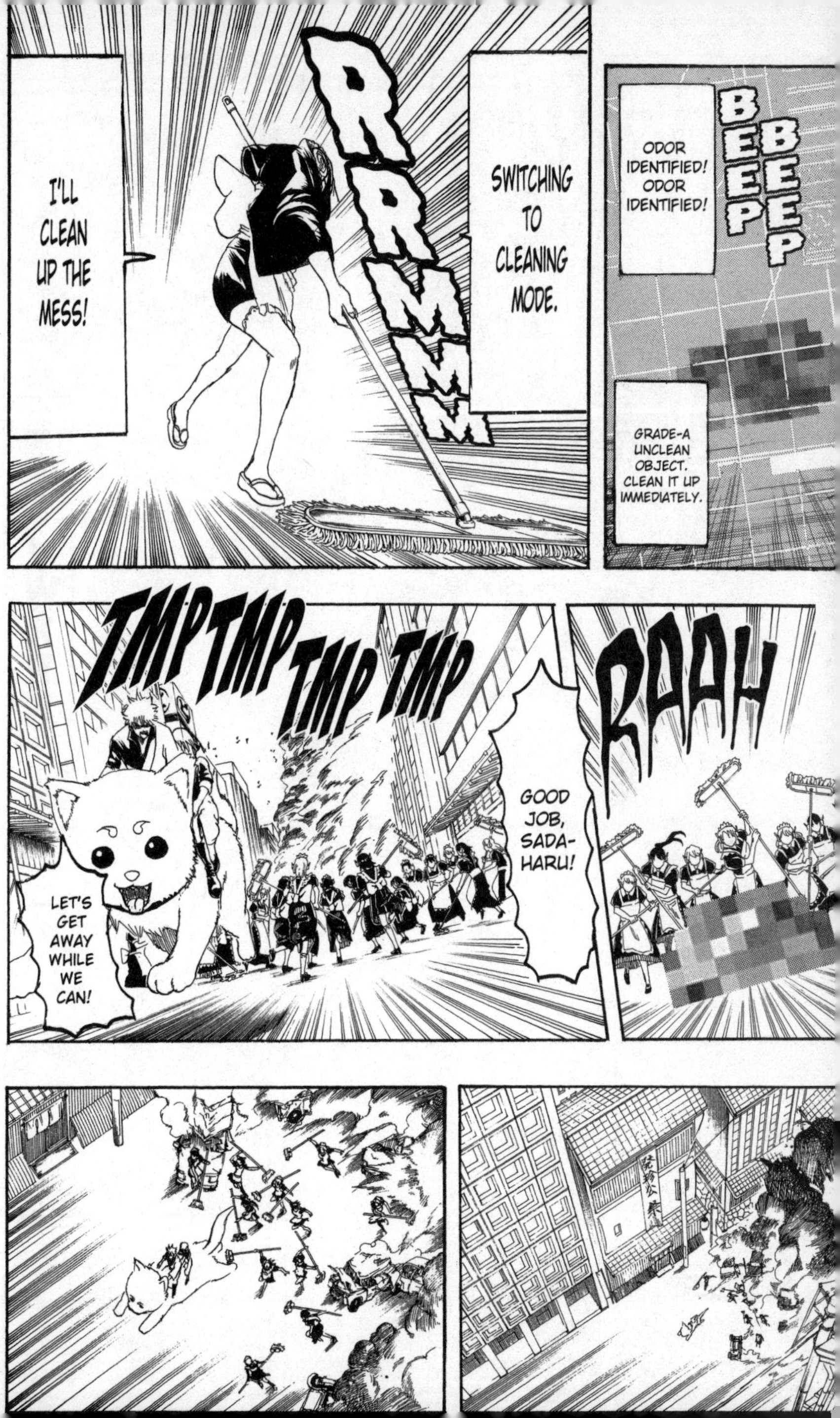
BEEP BEEP
ODOR IDENTIFIED! ODOR IDENTIFIED!
GRADE-A UNCLEAN OBJECT. CLEAN IT UP IMMEDIATELY.
RRMMM
SWITCHING TO CLEANING MODE.
I'LL CLEAN UP THE MESS!
RAAH
TMP TMP TMP TMP
GOOD JOB, SADAHARU!
LET'S GET AWAY WHILE WE CAN!

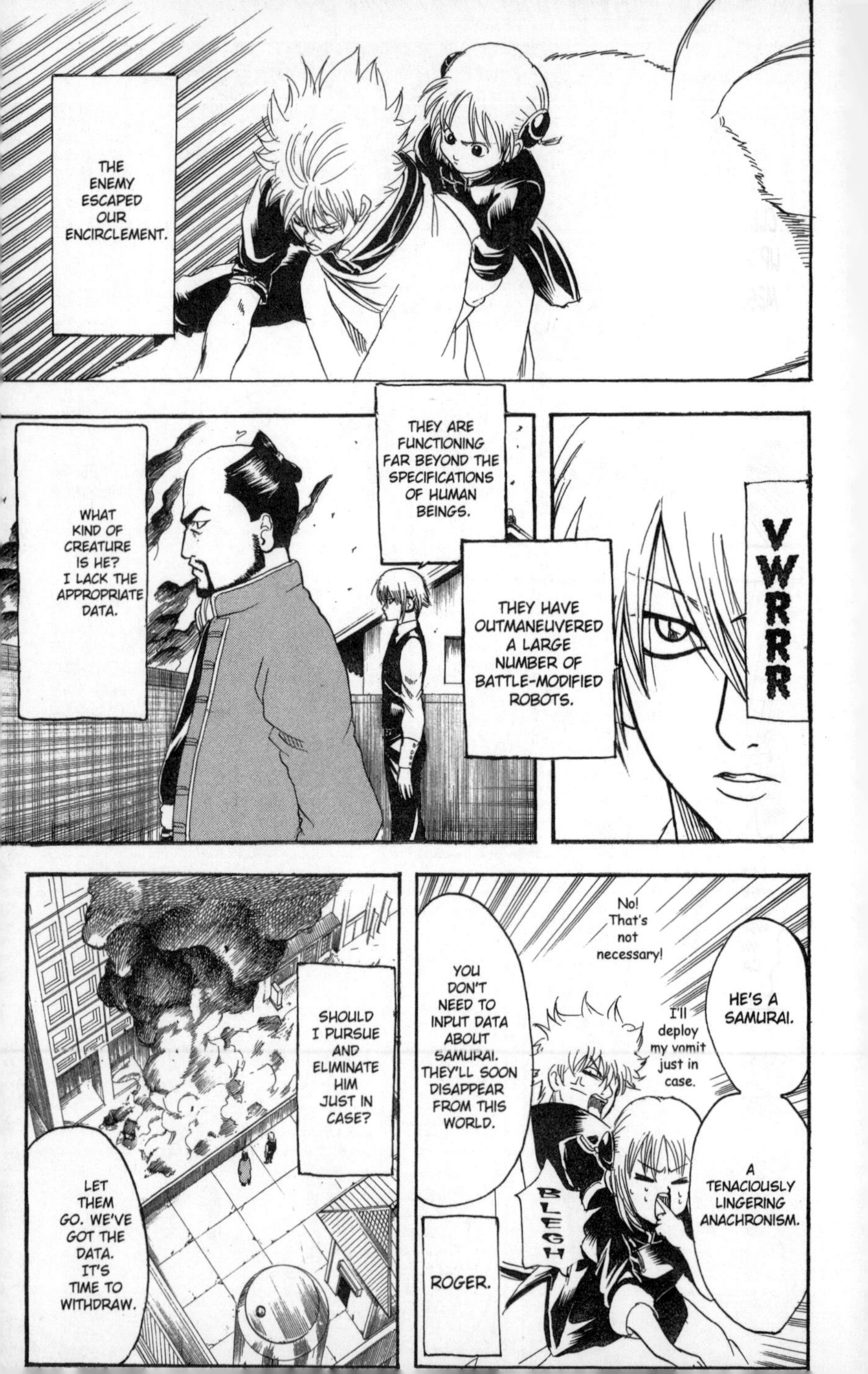
THE ENEMY ESCAPED OUR ENCIRCLEMENT.
VWRRR
THEY ARE FUNCTIONING FAR BEYOND THE SPECIFICATIONS OF HUMAN BEINGS.
THEY HAVE OUTMANEUVERED A LARGE NUMBER OF BATTLE-MODIFIED ROBOTS.
WHAT KIND OF CREATURE IS HE? I LACK THE APPROPRIATE DATA.
HE'S A SAMURAI.
A TENACIOUSLY LINGERING ANACHRONISM.
No! That's not necessary!
I'll deploy my vomit just in case.
YOU DON'T NEED TO INPUT DATA ABOUT SAMURAI. THEY'LL SOON DISAPPEAR FROM THIS WORLD.
BLEGH
ROGER.
SHOULD I PURSUE AND ELIMINATE HIM JUST IN CASE?
LET THEM GO. WE'VE GOT THE DATA. IT'S TIME TO WITHDRAW.

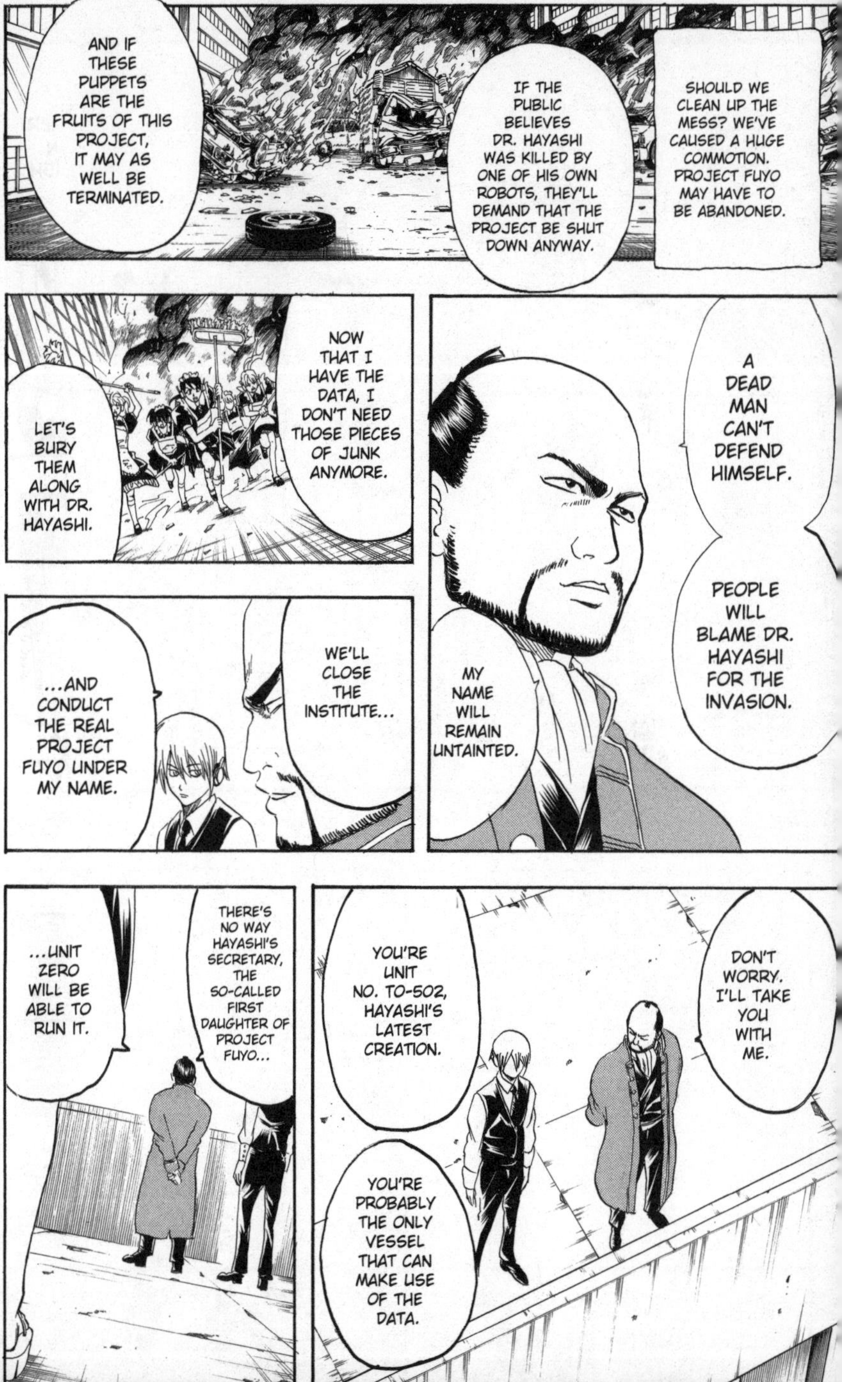
SHOULD WE CLEAN UP THE MESS? WE'VE CAUSED A HUGE COMMOTION. PROJECT FUYO MAY HAVE TO BE ABANDONED.
IF THE PUBLIC BELIEVES DR. HAYASHI WAS KILLED BY ONE OF HIS OWN ROBOTS, THEY'LL DEMAND THAT THE PROJECT BE SHUT DOWN ANYWAY.
AND IF THESE PUPPETS ARE THE FRUITS OF THIS PROJECT, IT MAY AS WELL BE TERMINATED.
A DEAD MAN CAN'T DEFEND HIMSELF.
PEOPLE WILL BLAME DR. HAYASHI FOR THE INVASION.
MY NAME WILL REMAIN UNTAINTED.
NOW THAT I HAVE THE DATA, I DON'T NEED THOSE PIECES OF JUNK ANYMORE.
LET'S BURY THEM ALONG WITH DR. HAYASHI.
WE'LL CLOSE THE INSTITUTE...
...AND CONDUCT THE REAL PROJECT FUYO UNDER MY NAME.
DON'T WORRY. I'LL TAKE YOU WITH ME.
YOU'RE UNIT NO. TO-502, HAYASHI'S LATEST CREATION.
YOU'RE PROBABLY THE ONLY VESSEL THAT CAN MAKE USE OF THE DATA.
THERE'S NO WAY HAYASHI'S SECRETARY, THE SO-CALLED FIRST DAUGHTER OF PROJECT FUYO...
...UNIT ZERO WILL BE ABLE TO RUN IT.

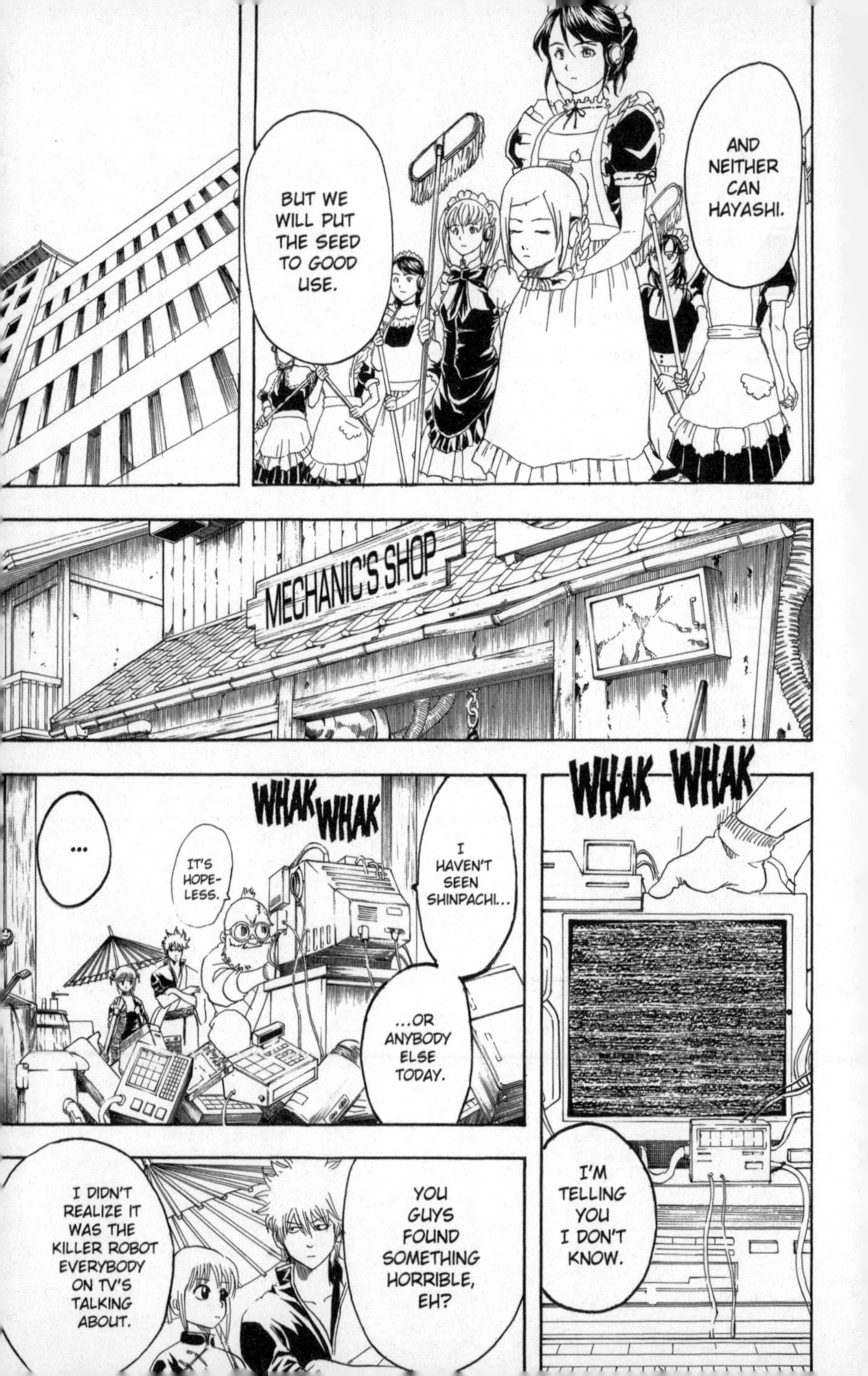
AND NEITHER CAN HAYASHI.
BUT WE WILL PUT THE SEED TO GOOD USE.
MECHANIC'S SHOP
WHAK WHAK
I'M TELLING YOU I DON'T KNOW.
WHAK WHAK
I HAVEN'T SEEN SHINPACHI...
...OR ANYBODY ELSE TODAY.
IT'S HOPE-LESS.
...
YOU GUYS FOUND SOMETHING HORRIBLE, EH?
I DIDN'T REALIZE IT WAS THE KILLER ROBOT EVERYBODY ON TV'S TALKING ABOUT.

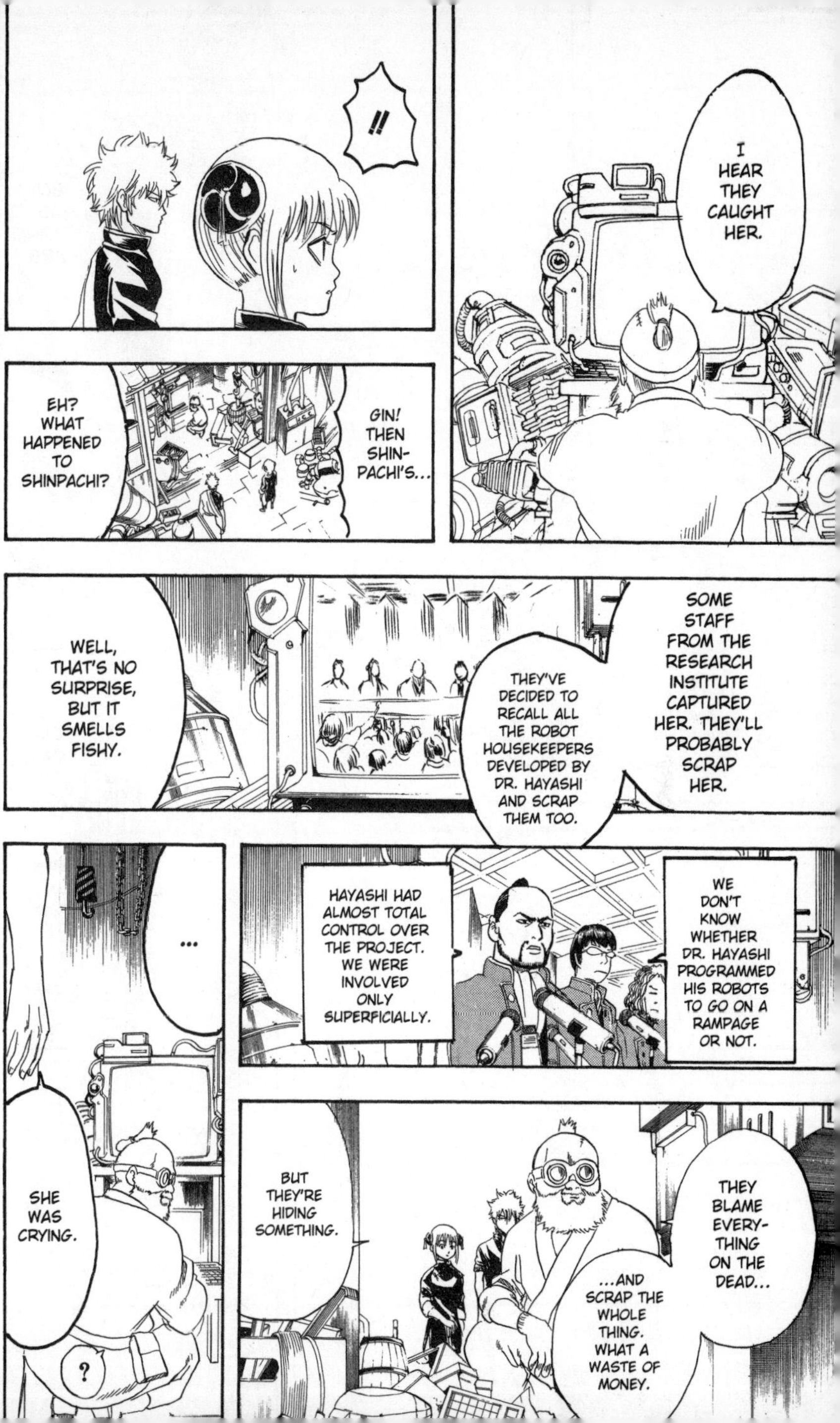
I HEAR THEY CAUGHT HER.
!!
GIN! THEN SHIN-PACHI'S...
EH? WHAT HAPPENED TO SHINPACHI?
SOME STAFF FROM THE RESEARCH INSTITUTE CAPTURED HER. THEY'LL PROBABLY SCRAP HER.
THEY'VE DECIDED TO RECALL ALL THE ROBOT HOUSEKEEPERS DEVELOPED BY DR. HAYASHI AND SCRAP THEM TOO.
WELL, THAT'S NO SURPRISE, BUT IT SMELLS FISHY.
WE DON'T KNOW WHETHER DR. HAYASHI PROGRAMMED HIS ROBOTS TO GO ON A RAMPAGE OR NOT.
HAYASHI HAD ALMOST TOTAL CONTROL OVER THE PROJECT. WE WERE INVOLVED ONLY SUPERFICIALLY.
THEY BLAME EVERY-THING ON THE DEAD...
...AND SCRAP THE WHOLE THING. WHAT A WASTE OF MONEY.
BUT THEY'RE HIDING SOMETHING.
...
SHE WAS CRYING.
?

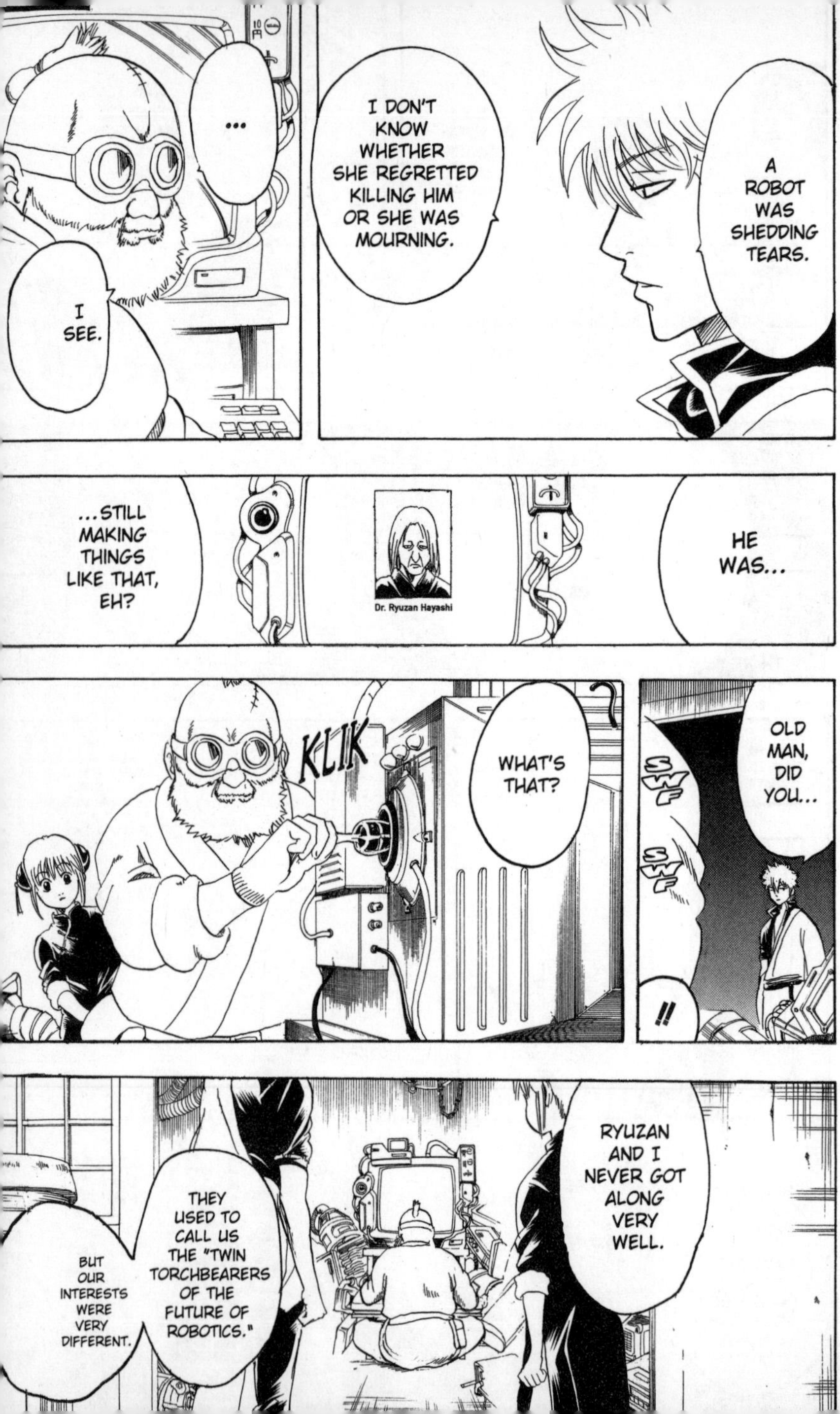
A ROBOT WAS SHEDDING TEARS.
I DON'T KNOW WHETHER SHE REGRETTED KILLING HIM OR SHE WAS MOURNING.
...
I SEE.
HE WAS...
Dr. Ryuzan Hayashi
...STILL MAKING THINGS LIKE THAT, EH?
OLD MAN, DID YOU...
SWF
SWF
!!
WHAT'S THAT?
KLIK
RYUZAN AND I NEVER GOT ALONG VERY WELL.
THEY USED TO CALL US THE "TWIN TORCHBEARERS OF THE FUTURE OF ROBOTICS."
BUT OUR INTERESTS WERE VERY DIFFERENT.

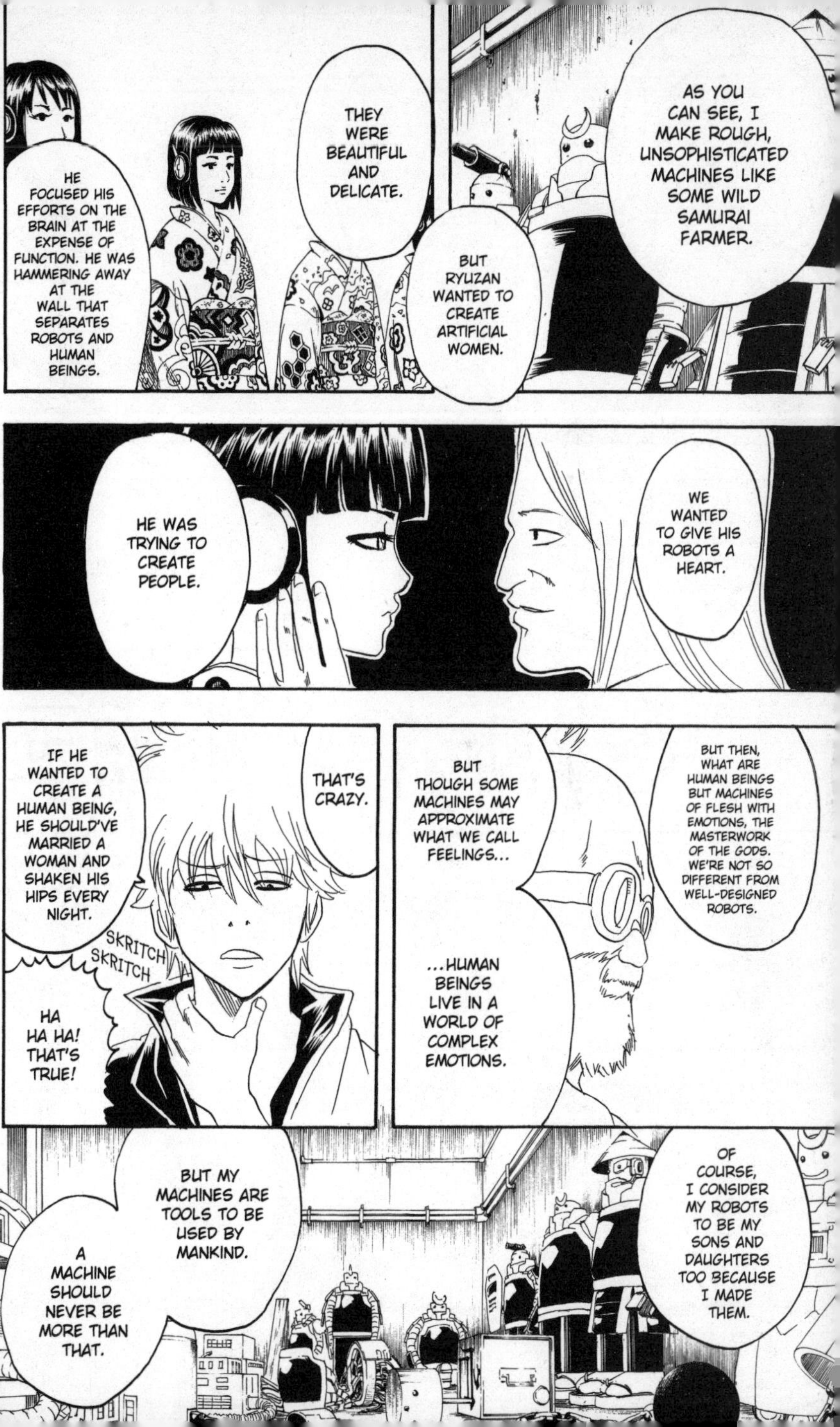
AS YOU CAN SEE, I MAKE ROUGH, UNSOPHISTICATED MACHINES LIKE SOME WILD SAMURAI FARMER.
BUT RYUZAN WANTED TO CREATE ARTIFICIAL WOMEN.
THEY WERE BEAUTIFUL AND DELICATE.
HE FOCUSED HIS EFFORTS ON THE BRAIN AT THE EXPENSE OF FUNCTION. HE WAS HAMMERING AWAY AT THE WALL THAT SEPARATES ROBOTS AND HUMAN BEINGS.
WE WANTED TO GIVE HIS ROBOTS A HEART.
HE WAS TRYING TO CREATE PEOPLE.
BUT THEN, WHAT ARE HUMAN BEINGS BUT MACHINES OF FLESH WITH EMOTIONS, THE MASTERWORK OF THE GODS. WE'RE NOT SO DIFFERENT FROM WELL-DESIGNED ROBOTS.
BUT THOUGH SOME MACHINES MAY APPROXIMATE WHAT WE CALL FEELINGS...
...HUMAN BEINGS LIVE IN A WORLD OF COMPLEX EMOTIONS.
THAT'S CRAZY.
IF HE WANTED TO CREATE A HUMAN BEING, HE SHOULD'VE MARRIED A WOMAN AND SHAKEN HIS HIPS EVERY NIGHT.
SKRITCH SKRITCH
HA HA HA! THAT'S TRUE!
OF COURSE, I CONSIDER MY ROBOTS TO BE MY SONS AND DAUGHTERS TOO BECAUSE I MADE THEM.
BUT MY MACHINES ARE TOOLS TO BE USED BY MANKIND.
A MACHINE SHOULD NEVER BE MORE THAN THAT.

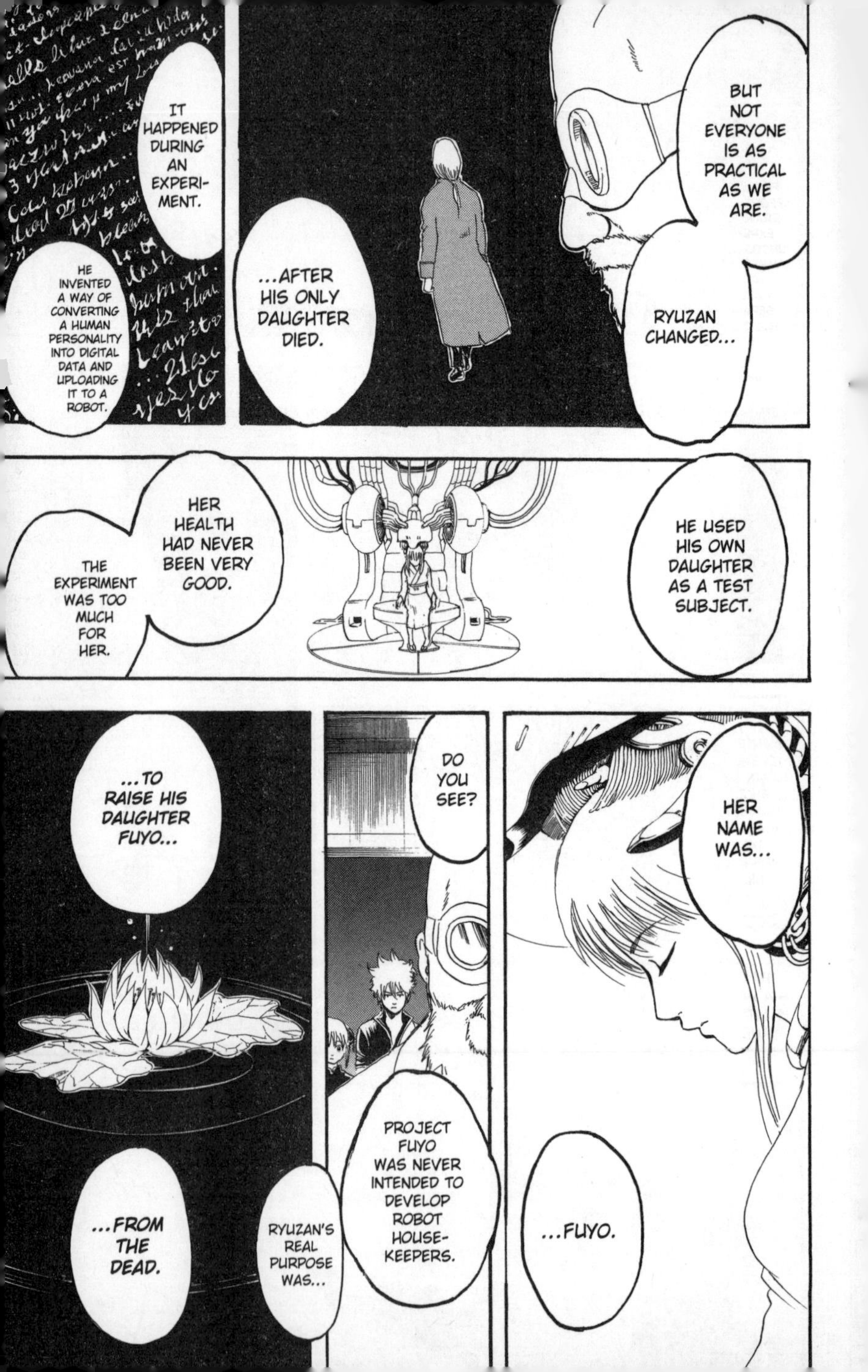
BUT NOT EVERYONE IS AS PRACTICAL AS WE ARE.
RYUZAN CHANGED...
...AFTER HIS ONLY DAUGHTER DIED.
IT HAPPENED DURING AN EXPERI-MENT.
HE INVENTED A WAY OF CONVERTING A HUMAN PERSONALITY INTO DIGITAL DATA AND UPLOADING IT TO A ROBOT.
HE USED HIS OWN DAUGHTER AS A TEST SUBJECT.
HER HEALTH HAD NEVER BEEN VERY GOOD.
THE EXPERIMENT WAS TOO MUCH FOR HER.
HER NAME WAS...
...FUYO.
DO YOU SEE?
PROJECT FUYO WAS NEVER INTENDED TO DEVELOP ROBOT HOUSE-KEEPERS.
RYUZAN'S REAL PURPOSE WAS...
...TO RAISE HIS DAUGHTER FUYO...
...FROM THE DEAD.

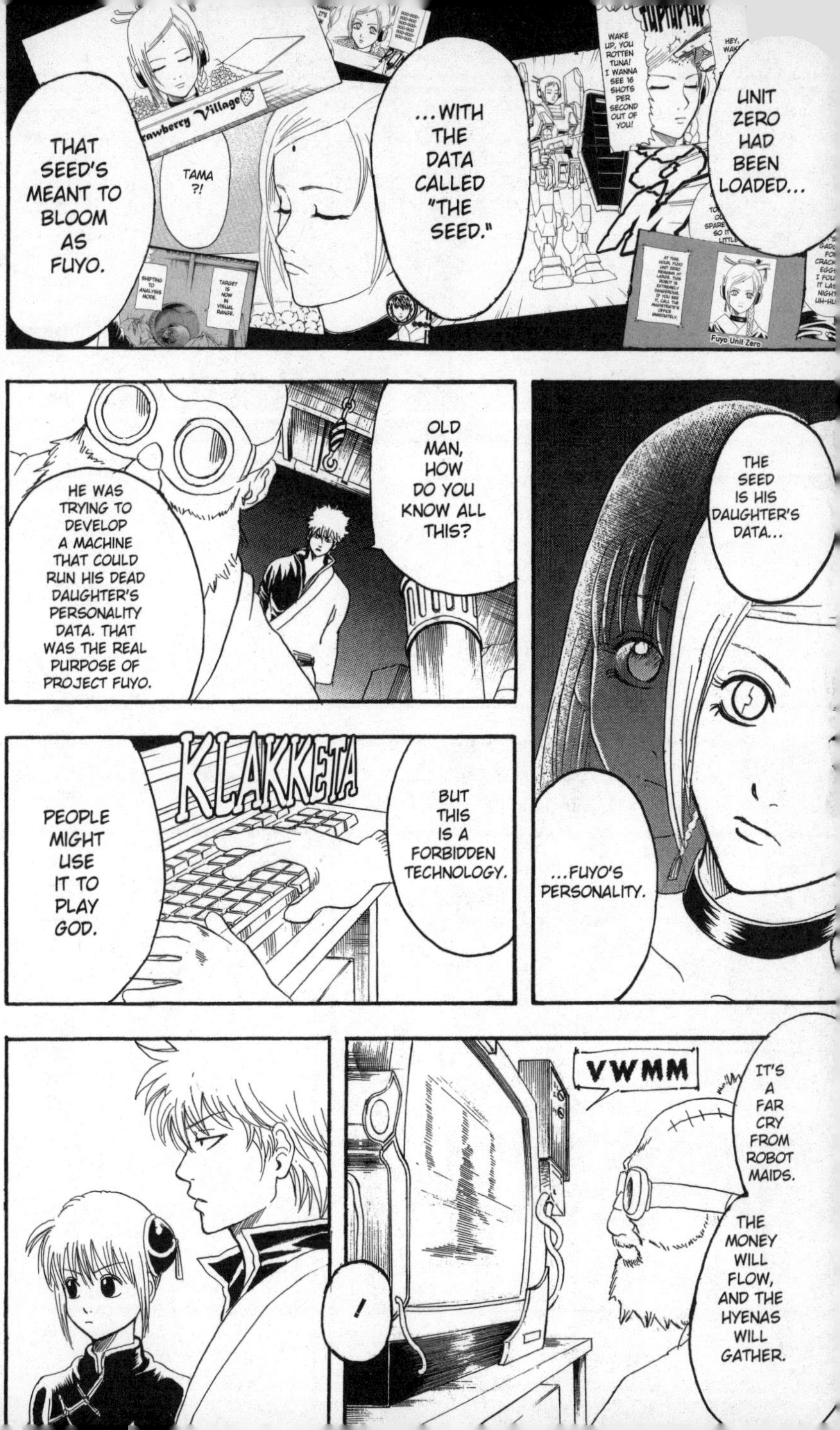
UNIT ZERO HAD BEEN LOADED...
WAKE UP, YOU ROTTEN TUNA! I WANNA SEE 16 SHOTS PER SECOND OUT OF YOU!
Fuyo Unit Zero
...WITH THE DATA CALLED "THE SEED."
TAMA ?!
THAT SEED'S MEANT TO BLOOM AS FUYO.
TARGET IS NOW IN VISUAL RANGE.
SHIFTING TO ANALYSIS MODE.
THE SEED IS HIS DAUGHTER'S DATA...
...FUYO'S PERSONALITY.
OLD MAN, HOW DO YOU KNOW ALL THIS?
HE WAS TRYING TO DEVELOP A MACHINE THAT COULD RUN HIS DEAD DAUGHTER'S PERSONALITY DATA. THAT WAS THE REAL PURPOSE OF PROJECT FUYO.
KLAKKETA
BUT THIS IS A FORBIDDEN TECHNOLOGY.
PEOPLE MIGHT USE IT TO PLAY GOD.
VWMM
IT'S A FAR CRY FROM ROBOT MAIDS.
THE MONEY WILL FLOW, AND THE HYENAS WILL GATHER.
!

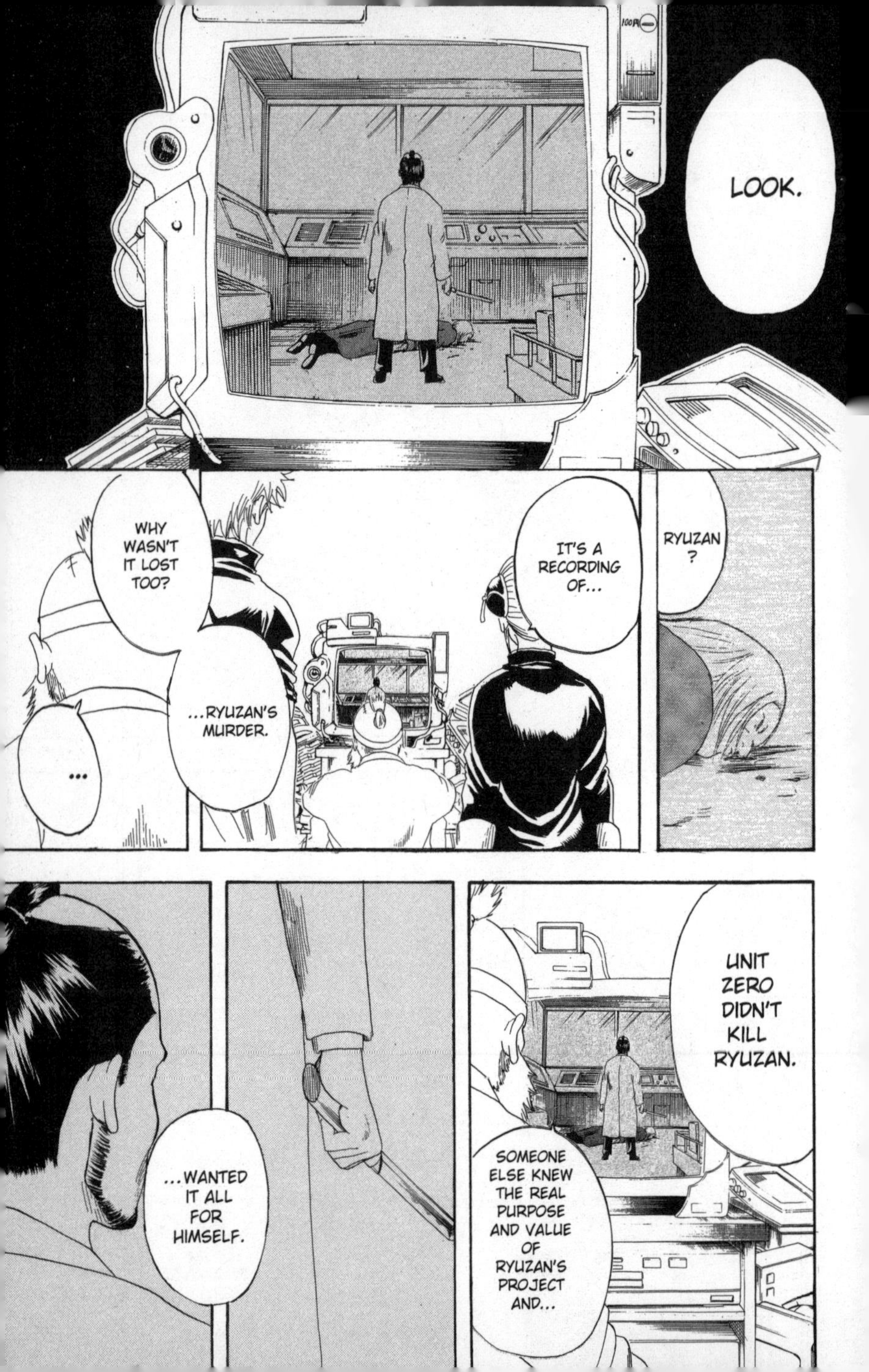
LOOK.
RYUZAN ?
IT'S A RECORDING OF...
...RYUZAN'S MURDER.
WHY WASN'T IT LOST TOO?
...
UNIT ZERO DIDN'T KILL RYUZAN.
SOMEONE ELSE KNEW THE REAL PURPOSE AND VALUE OF RYUZAN'S PROJECT AND...
...WANTED IT ALL FOR HIMSELF.

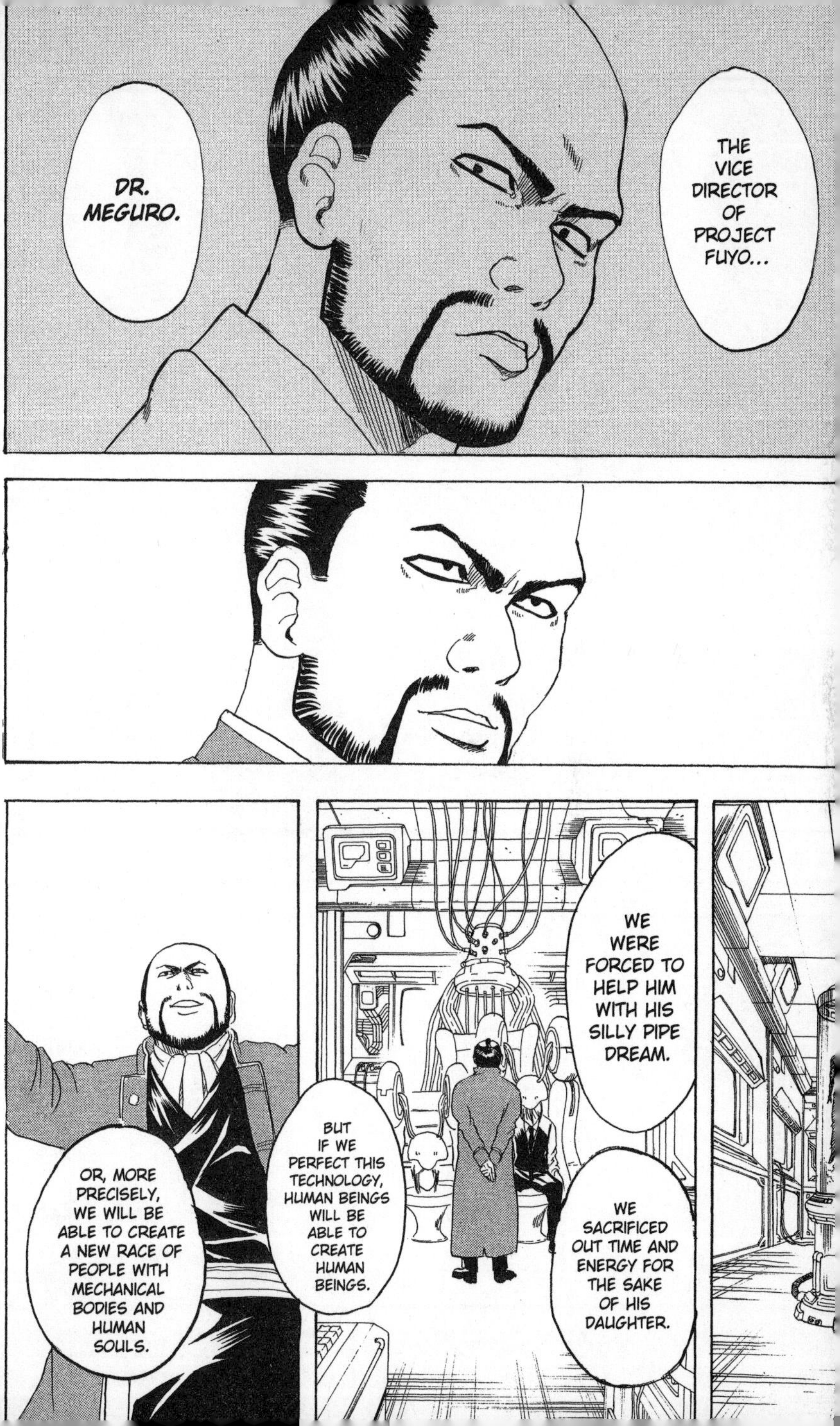
THE VICE DIRECTOR OF PROJECT FUYO...
DR. MEGURO.
WE WERE FORCED TO HELP HIM WITH HIS SILLY PIPE DREAM.
WE SACRIFICED OUT TIME AND ENERGY FOR THE SAKE OF HIS DAUGHTER.
BUT IF WE PERFECT THIS TECHNOLOGY, HUMAN BEINGS WILL BE ABLE TO CREATE HUMAN BEINGS.
OR, MORE PRECISELY, WE WILL BE ABLE TO CREATE A NEW RACE OF PEOPLE WITH MECHANICAL BODIES AND HUMAN SOULS.

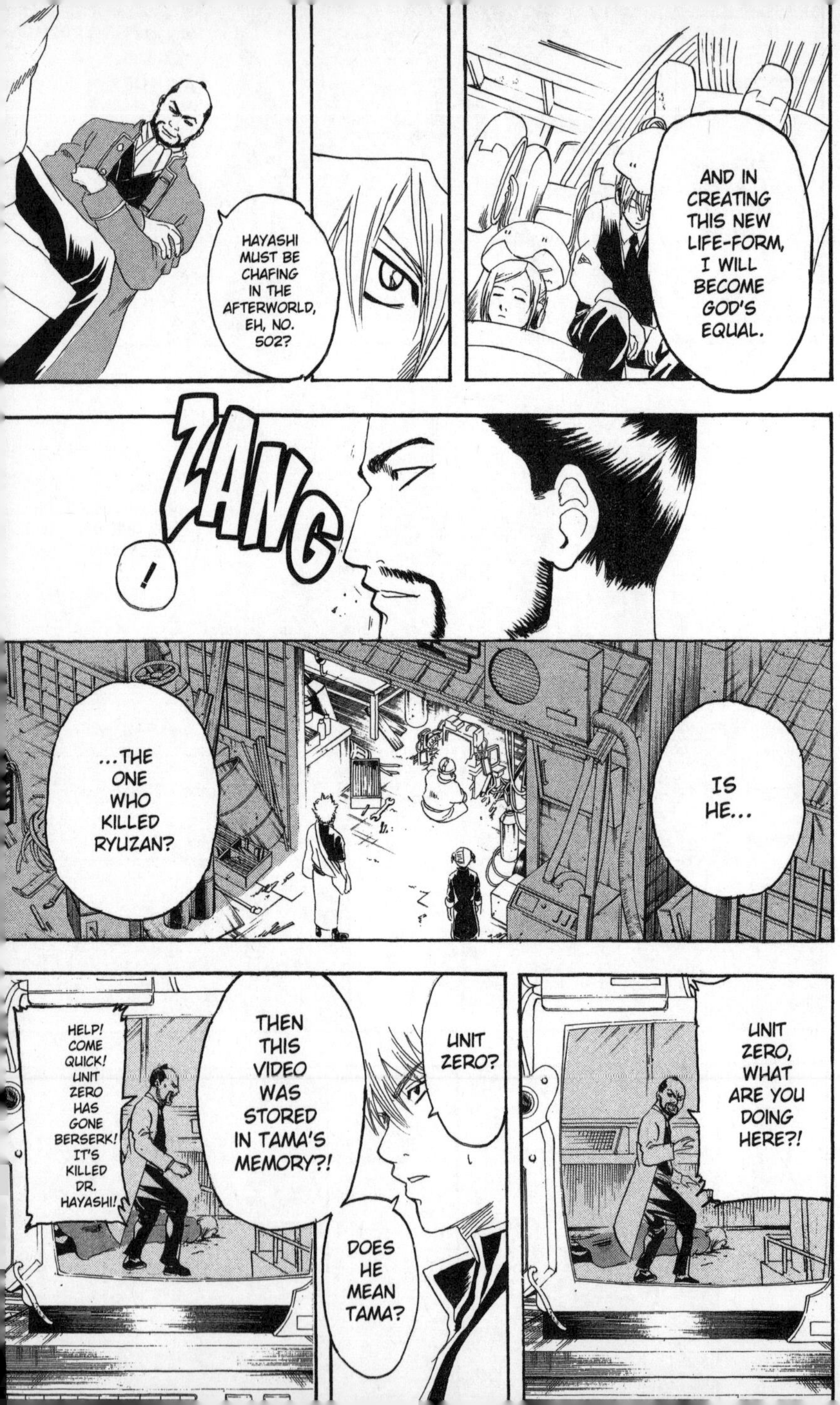
AND IN CREATING THIS NEW LIFE-FORM, I WILL BECOME GOD'S EQUAL.
HAYASHI MUST BE CHAFING IN THE AFTERWORLD, EH, NO. 502?
ZANG
!
IS HE...
...THE ONE WHO KILLED RYUZAN?
UNIT ZERO, WHAT ARE YOU DOING HERE?!
HELP! COME QUICK! UNIT ZERO HAS GONE BERSERK! IT'S KILLED DR. HAYASHI!
UNIT ZERO?
DOES HE MEAN TAMA?
THEN THIS VIDEO WAS STORED IN TAMA'S MEMORY?!

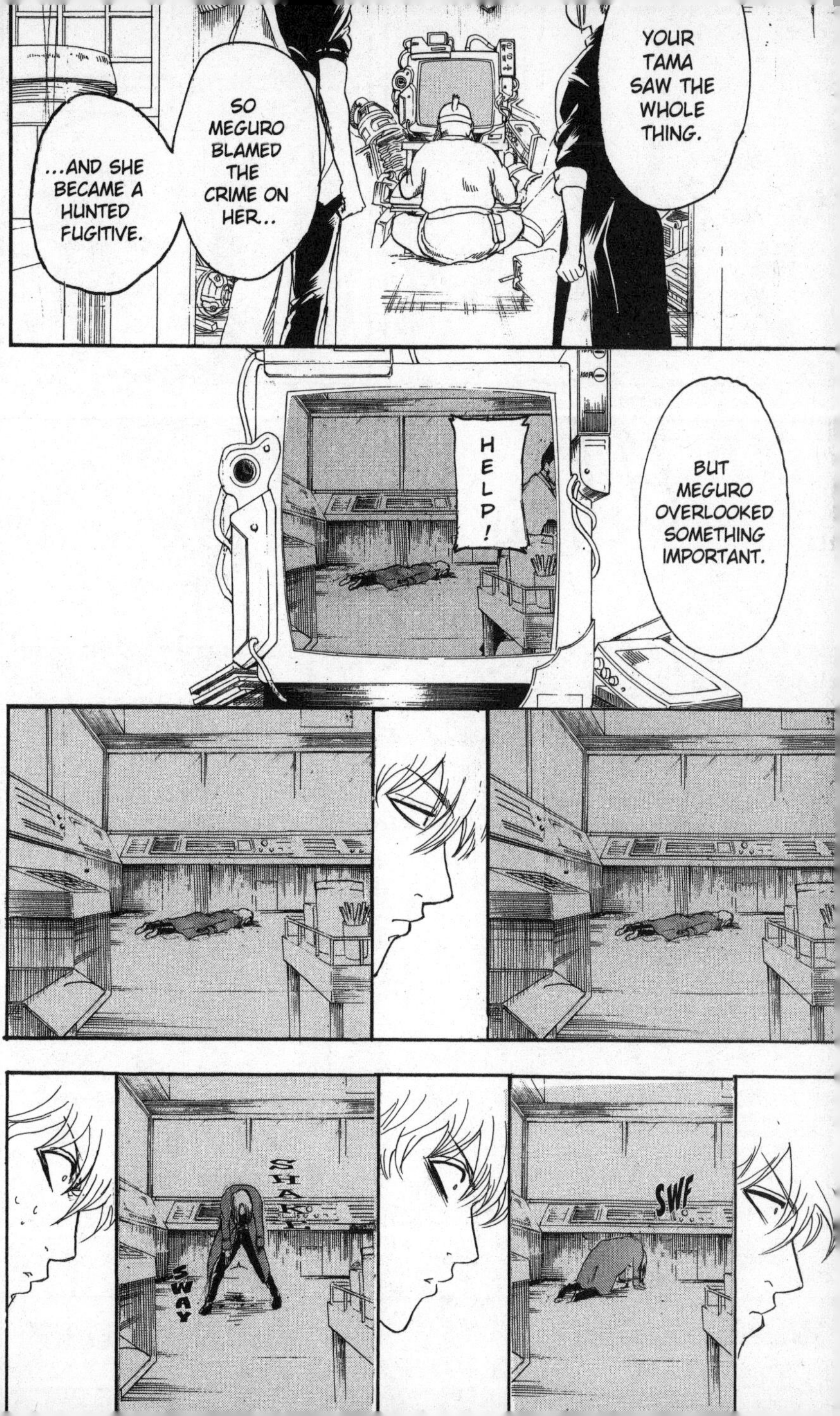
YOUR TAMA SAW THE WHOLE THING.
SO MEGURO BLAMED THE CRIME ON HER...
...AND SHE BECAME A HUNTED FUGITIVE.
BUT MEGURO OVERLOOKED SOMETHING IMPORTANT.
HELP!
SWF
SHAKY
SWAY

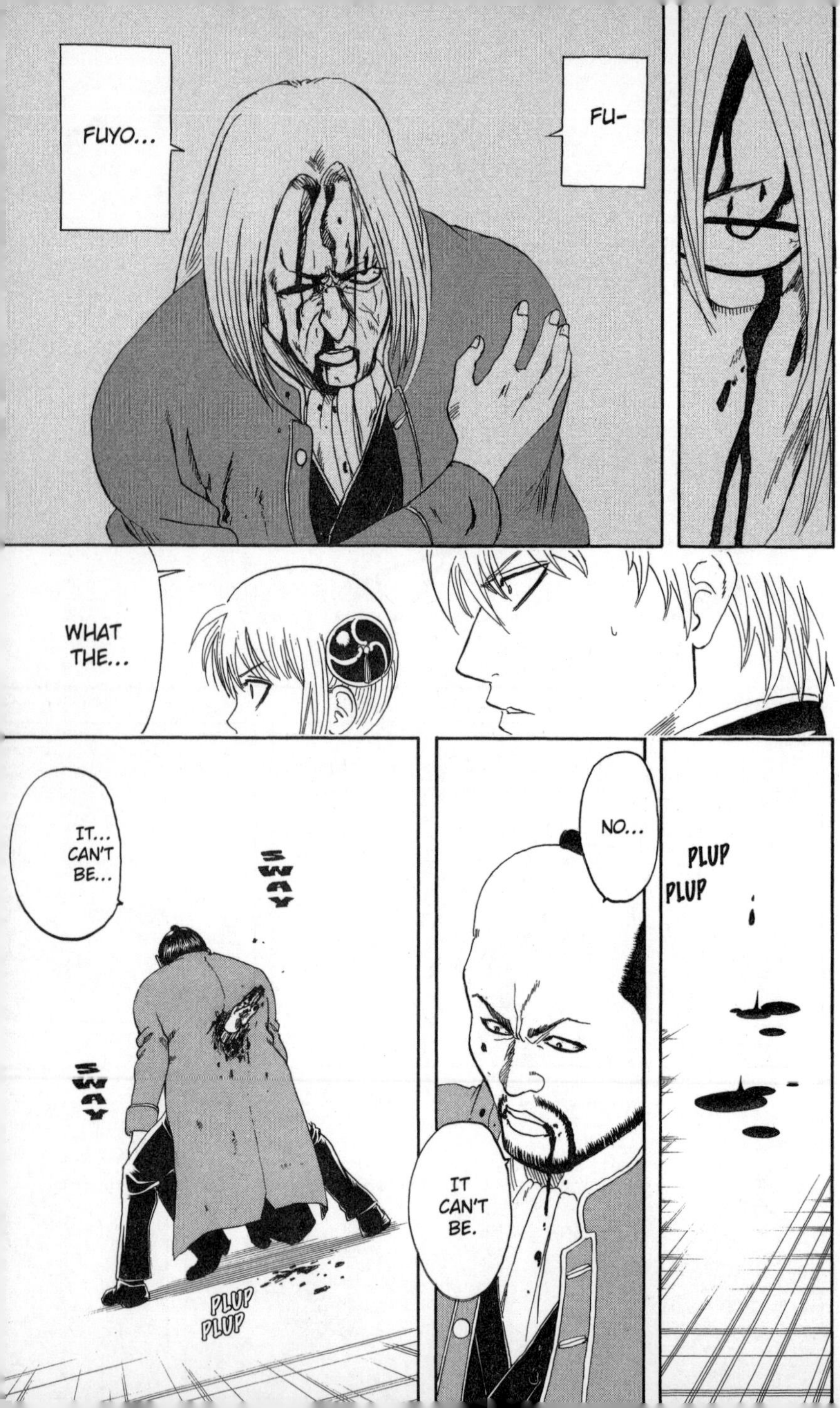
FU-
FUYO...
WHAT THE...
PLUP
PLUP
NO...
IT CAN'T BE.
IT... CAN'T BE...
SWAY
SWAY
PLUP
PLUP

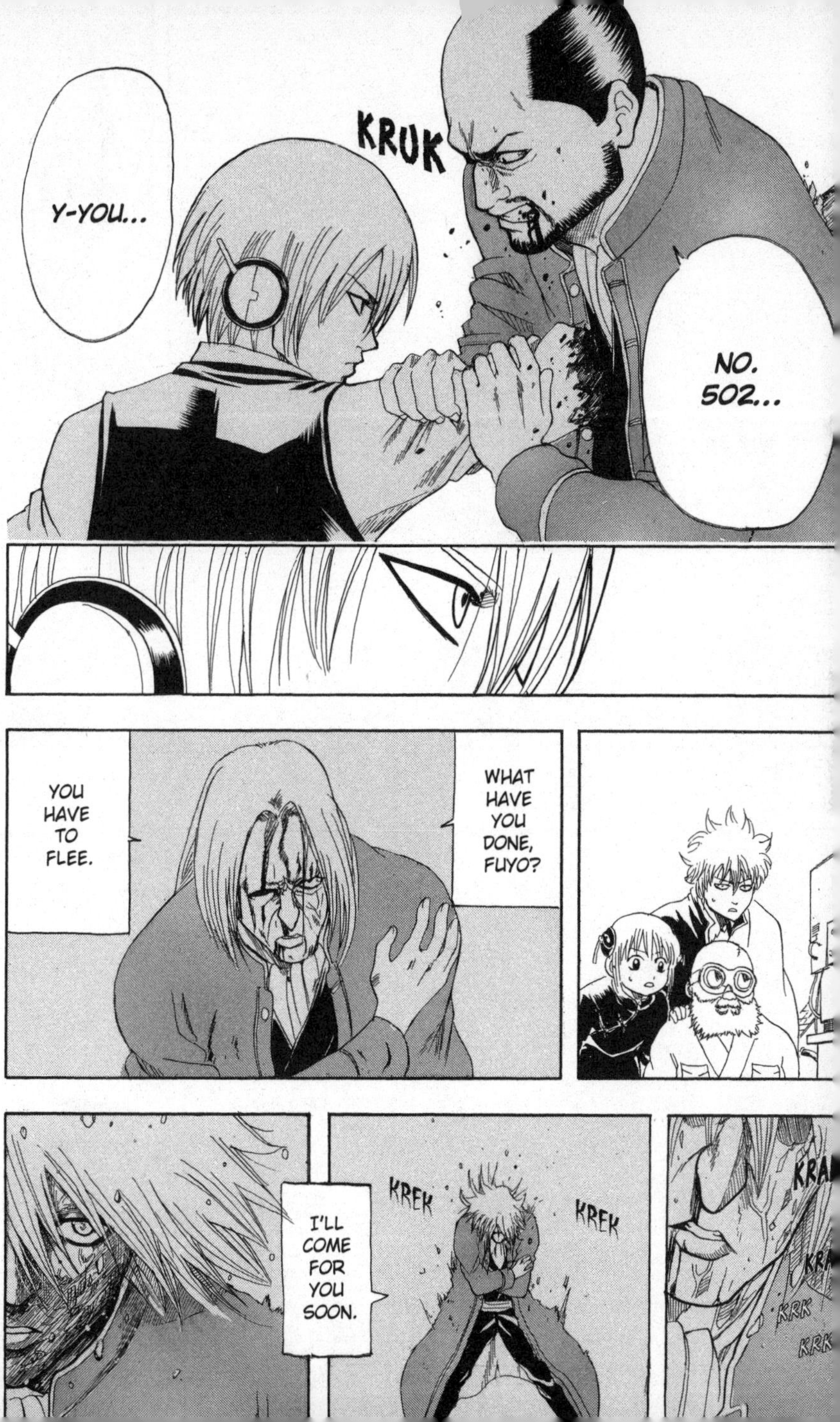
NO. 502...
KRUK
Y-YOU...
WHAT HAVE YOU DONE, FUYO?
YOU HAVE TO FLEE.
KRK
KRK
KREK
KREK
I'LL COME FOR YOU SOON.

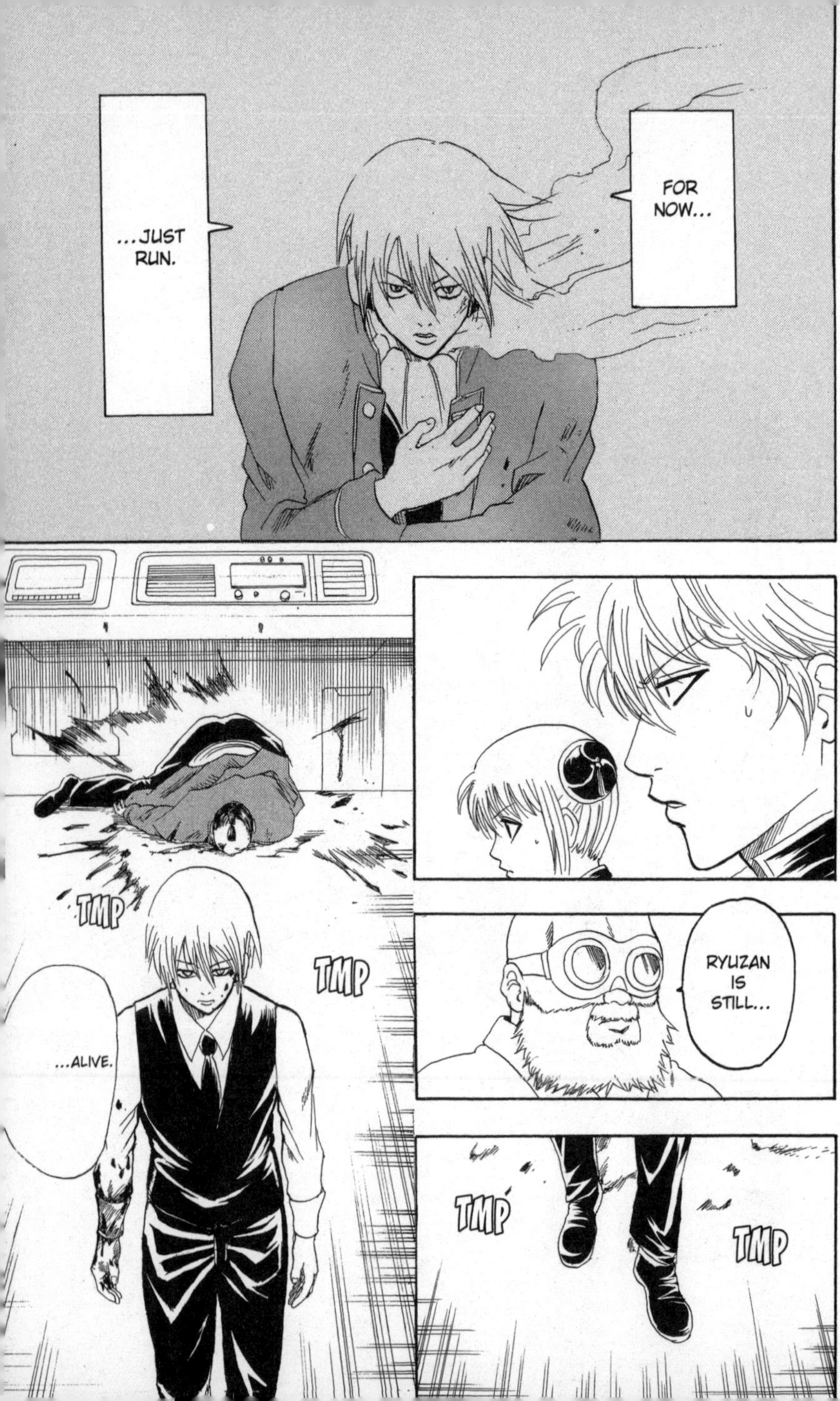
FOR NOW...
...JUST RUN.
RYUZAN IS STILL...
TMP
TMP
TMP
TMP
...ALIVE.

Welcome to Jump Festa 2009!

You don't have anything better to do, huh?

Gin Tama

Thank you for buying and reading *Jump*. Jump Festa is a festival in which publishers express their gratitude for everyone's support of *Jump*. But this is just the official reason. Actually, it's a festival in which moneygrubbing demons try to sell character merchandise to overexcited children. Don't forget that conniving men have their eyes on your wallets, folks.
Sorachi

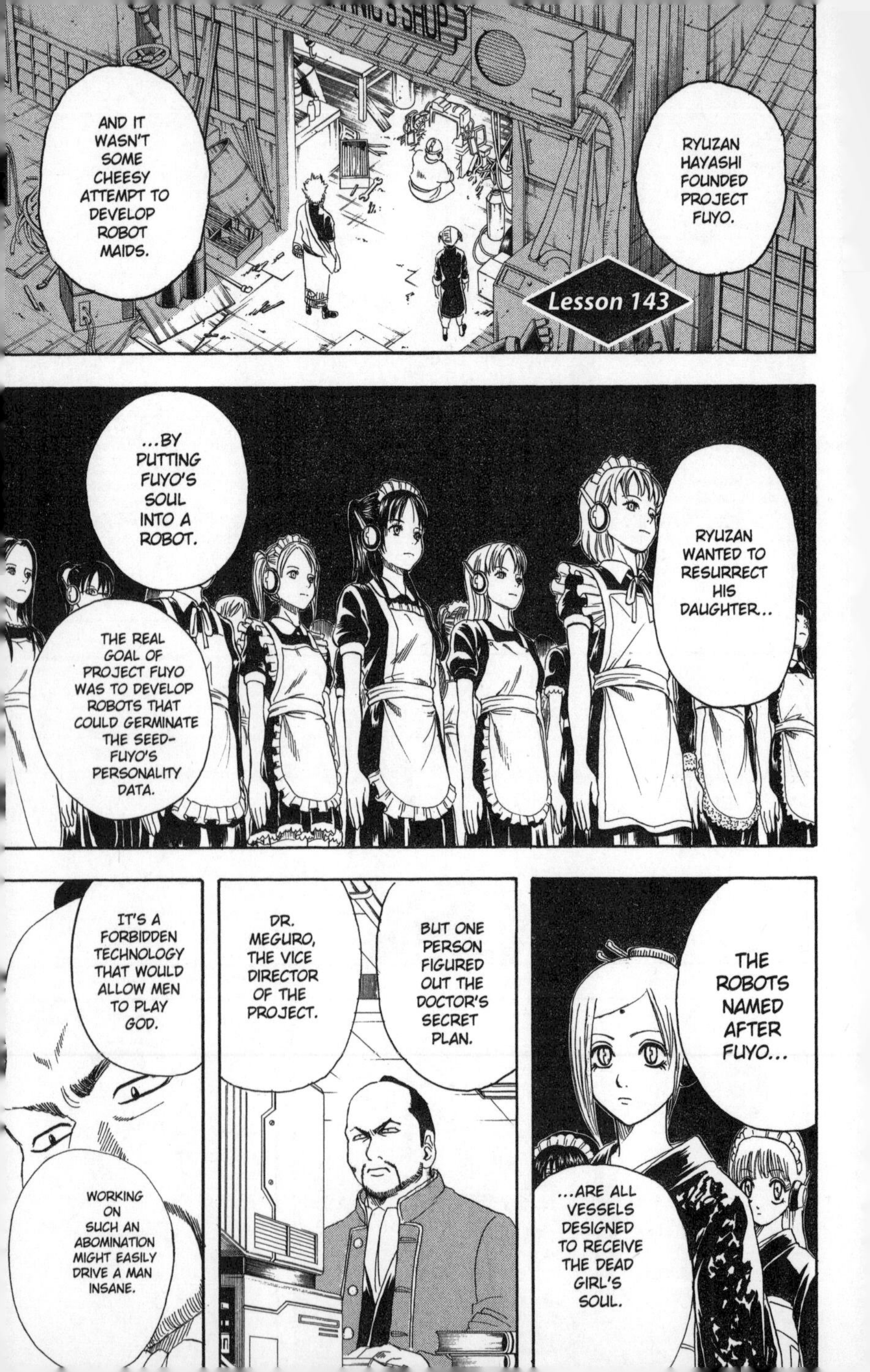
Lesson 143
RYUZAN HAYASHI FOUNDED PROJECT FUYO.
AND IT WASN'T SOME CHEESY ATTEMPT TO DEVELOP ROBOT MAIDS.
RYUZAN WANTED TO RESURRECT HIS DAUGHTER...
...BY PUTTING FUYO'S SOUL INTO A ROBOT.
THE REAL GOAL OF PROJECT FUYO WAS TO DEVELOP ROBOTS THAT COULD GERMINATE THE SEED-FUYO'S PERSONALITY DATA.
THE ROBOTS NAMED AFTER FUYO...
...ARE ALL VESSELS DESIGNED TO RECEIVE THE DEAD GIRL'S SOUL.
BUT ONE PERSON FIGURED OUT THE DOCTOR'S SECRET PLAN.
DR. MEGURO, THE VICE DIRECTOR OF THE PROJECT.
IT'S A FORBIDDEN TECHNOLOGY THAT WOULD ALLOW MEN TO PLAY GOD.
WORKING ON SUCH AN ABOMINATION MIGHT EASILY DRIVE A MAN INSANE.

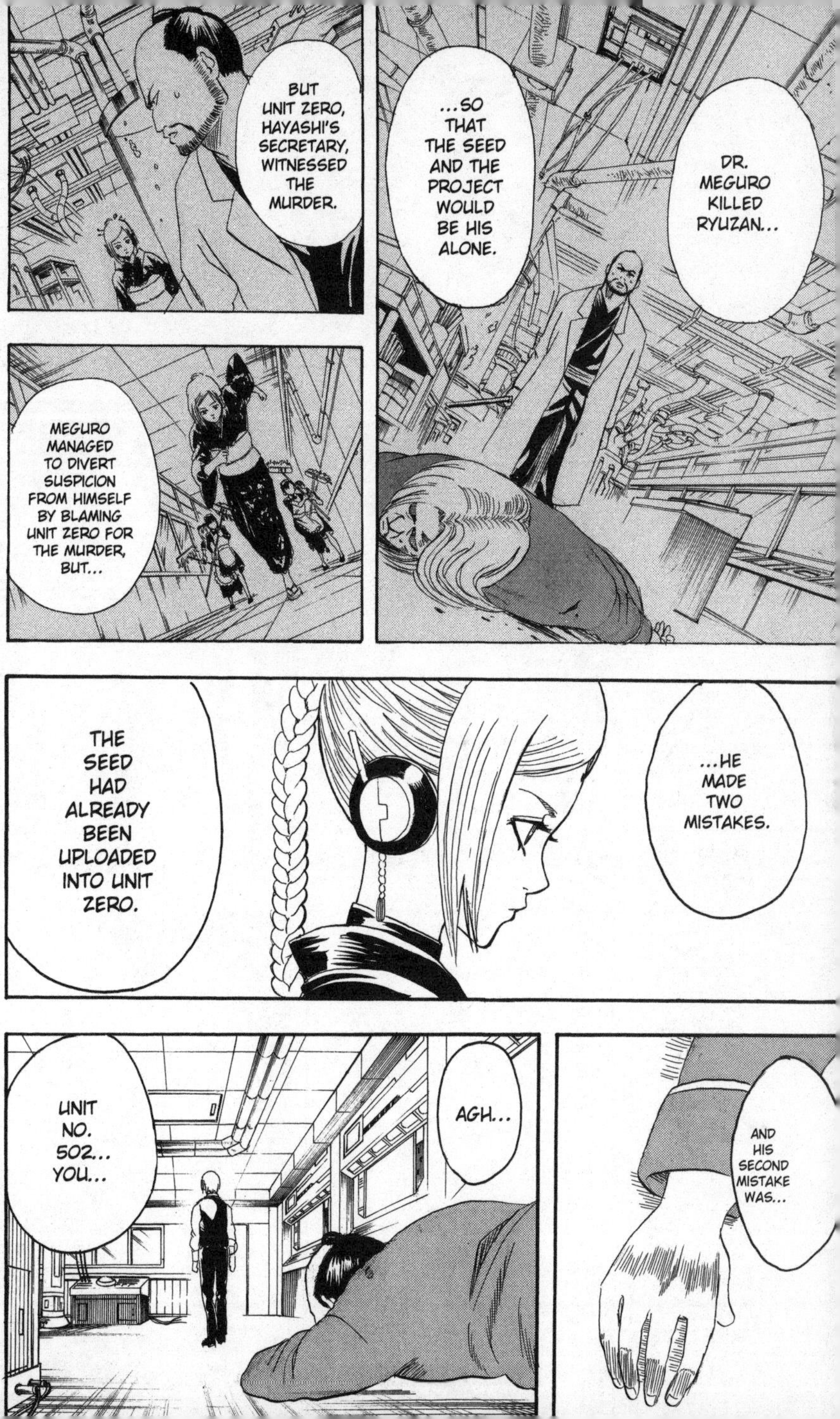
DR. MEGURO KILLED RYUZAN...
...SO THAT THE SEED AND THE PROJECT WOULD BE HIS ALONE.
BUT UNIT ZERO, HAYASHI'S SECRETARY, WITNESSED THE MURDER.
MEGURO MANAGED TO DIVERT SUSPICION FROM HIMSELF BY BLAMING UNIT ZERO FOR THE MURDER, BUT...
...HE MADE TWO MISTAKES.
THE SEED HAD ALREADY BEEN UPLOADED INTO UNIT ZERO.
AND HIS SECOND MISTAKE WAS...
AGH...
UNIT NO. 502... YOU...

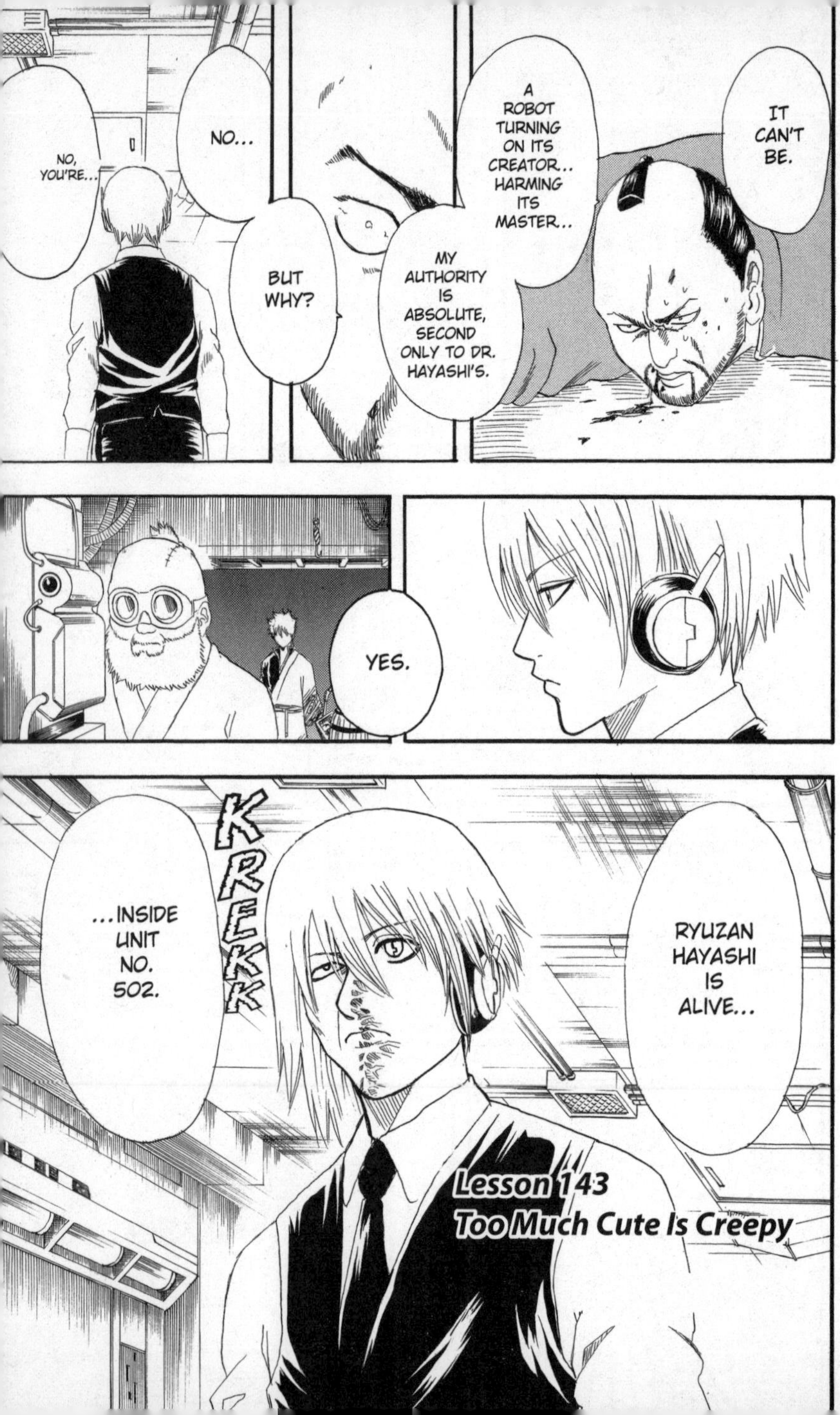
IT CAN'T BE.
A ROBOT TURNING ON ITS CREATOR... HARMING ITS MASTER...
MY AUTHORITY IS ABSOLUTE, SECOND ONLY TO DR. HAYASHI'S.
BUT WHY?
NO...
NO, YOU'RE...
YES.
RYUZAN HAYASHI IS ALIVE...
KREKK
...INSIDE UNIT NO. 502.
Lesson 143
Too Much Cute Is Creepy

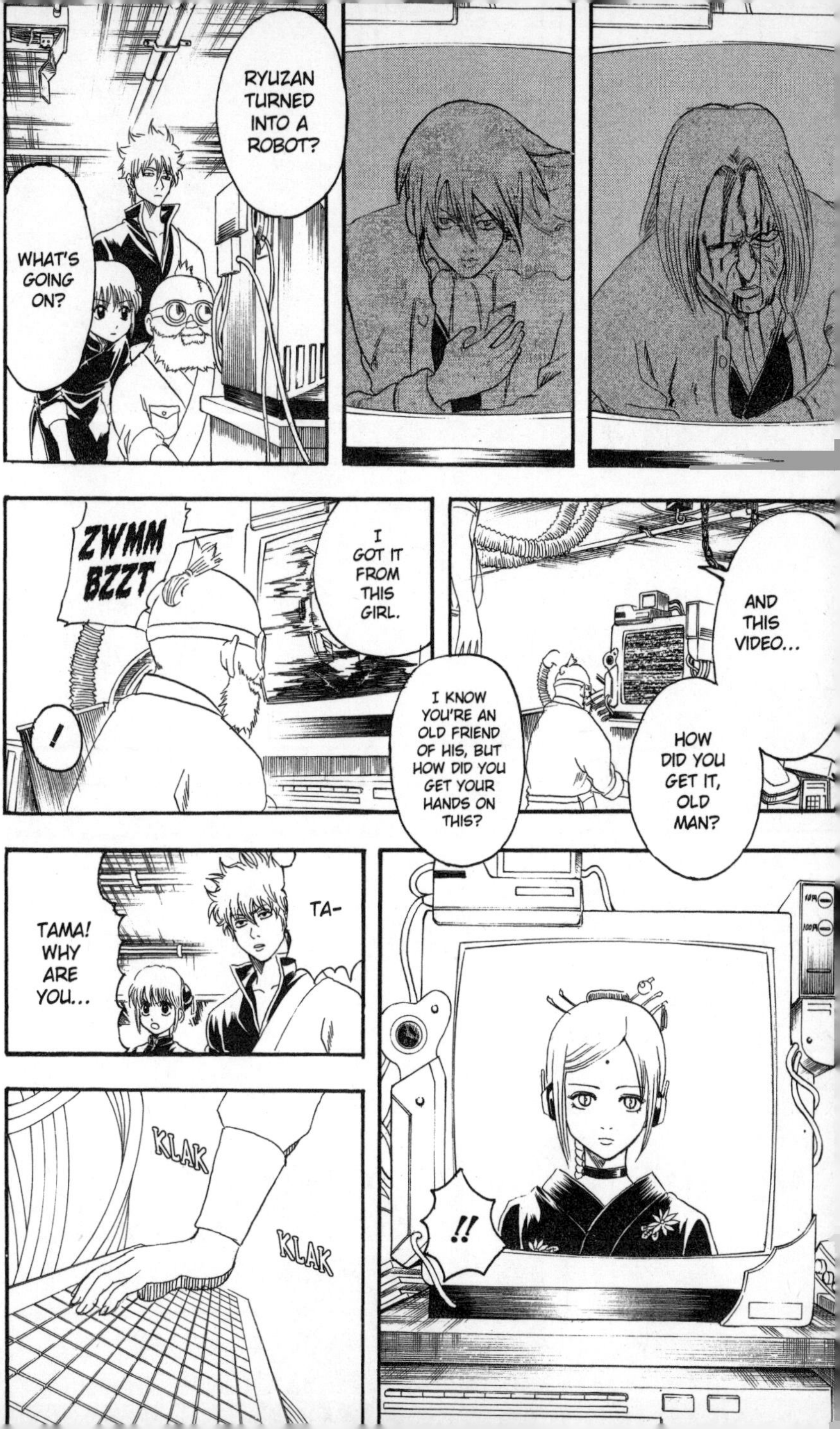
RYUZAN TURNED INTO A ROBOT?
WHAT'S GOING ON?
AND THIS VIDEO...
HOW DID YOU GET IT, OLD MAN?
I KNOW YOU'RE AN OLD FRIEND OF HIS, BUT HOW DID YOU GET YOUR HANDS ON THIS?
I GOT IT FROM THIS GIRL.
ZWMM BZZT
!
!!
TA-
TAMA! WHY ARE YOU...
KLAK
KLAK

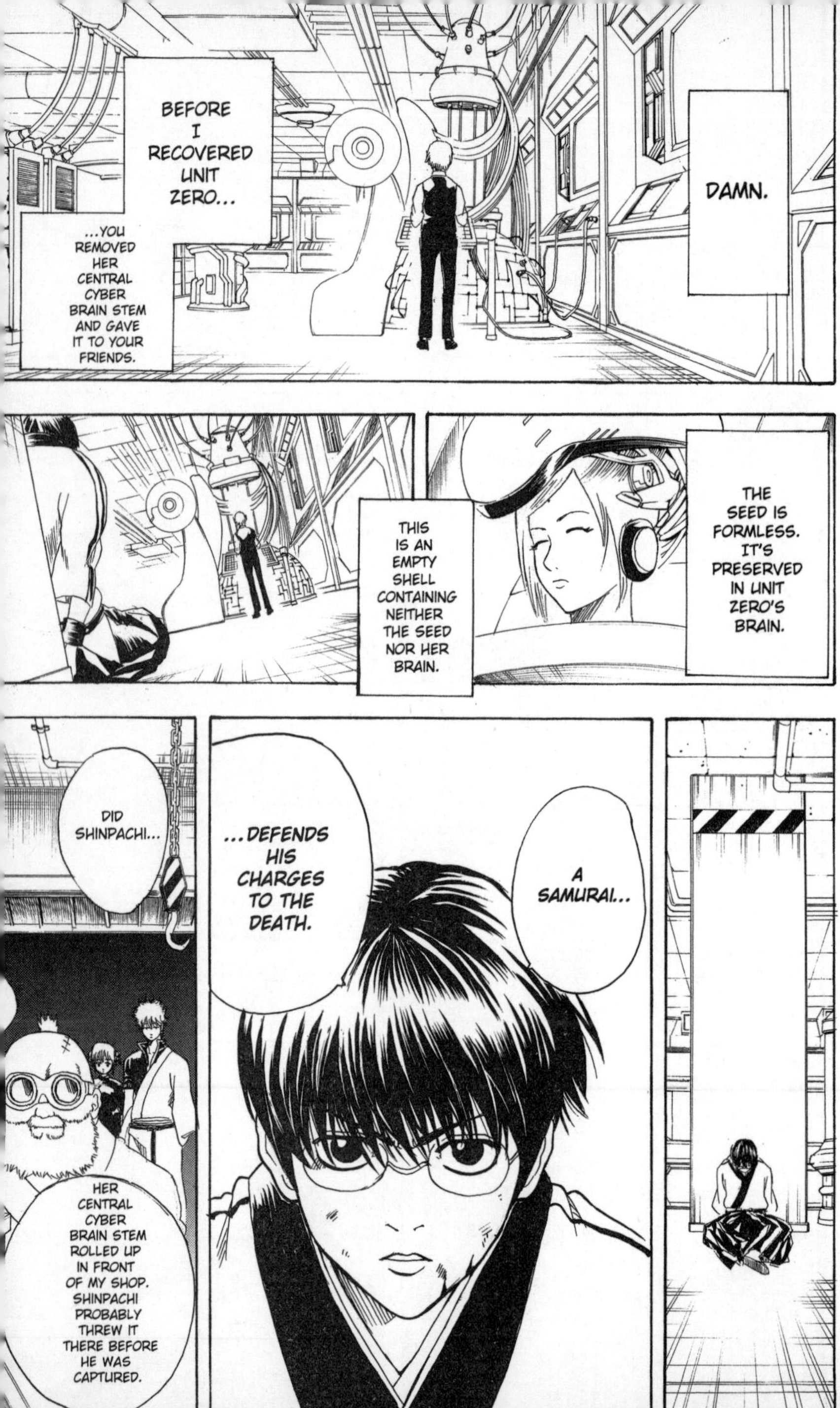
DAMN.
BEFORE I RECOVERED UNIT ZERO...
...YOU REMOVED HER CENTRAL CYBER BRAIN STEM AND GAVE IT TO YOUR FRIENDS.
THE SEED IS FORMLESS. IT'S PRESERVED IN UNIT ZERO'S BRAIN.
THIS IS AN EMPTY SHELL CONTAINING NEITHER THE SEED NOR HER BRAIN.
A SAMURAI...
...DEFENDS HIS CHARGES TO THE DEATH.
DID SHINPACHI...
HER CENTRAL CYBER BRAIN STEM ROLLED UP IN FRONT OF MY SHOP. SHINPACHI PROBABLY THREW IT THERE BEFORE HE WAS CAPTURED.

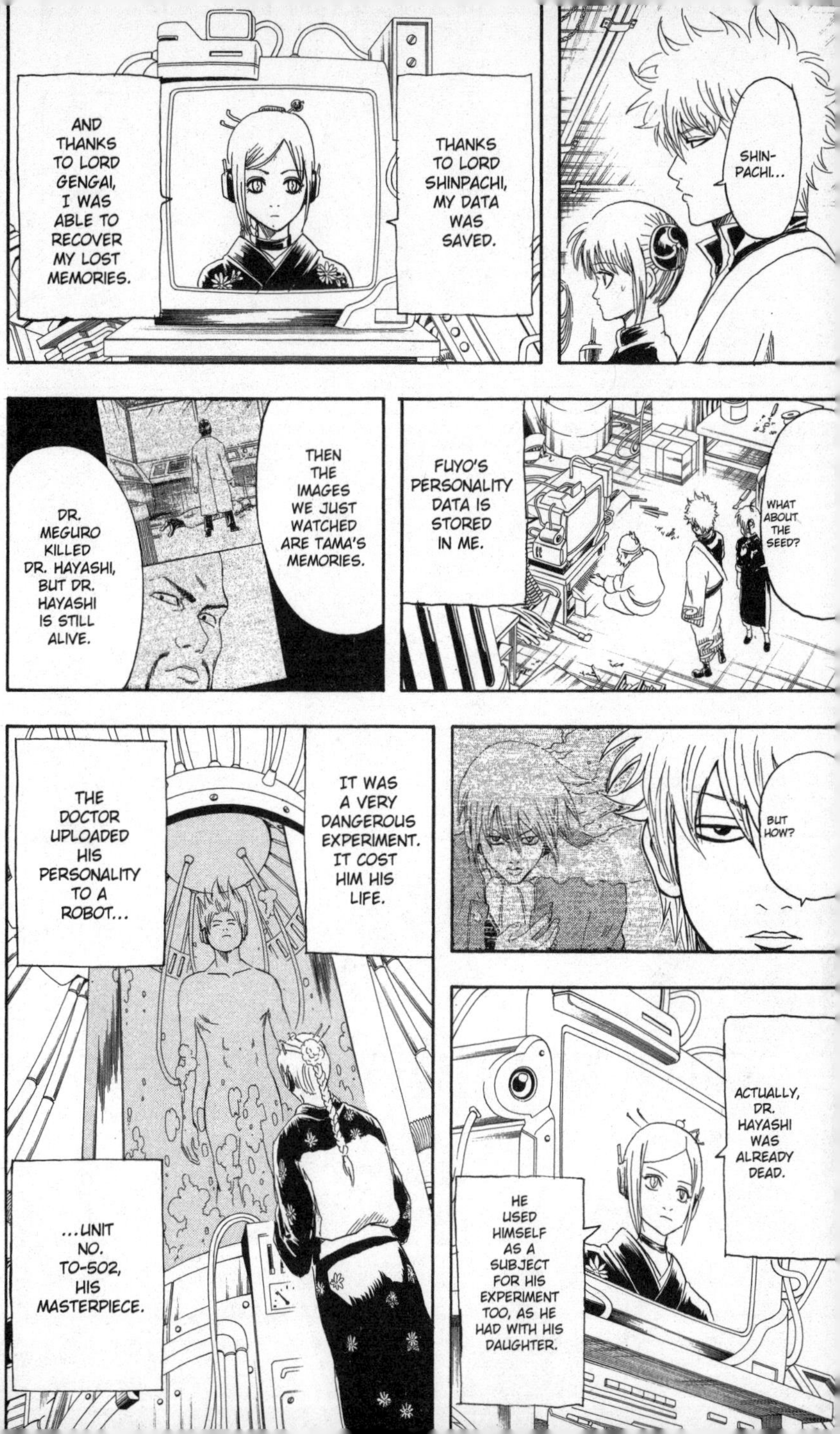
SHIN-PACHI...
THANKS TO LORD SHINPACHI, MY DATA WAS SAVED.
AND THANKS TO LORD GENGAI, I WAS ABLE TO RECOVER MY LOST MEMORIES.
WHAT ABOUT THE SEED?
FUYO'S PERSONALITY DATA IS STORED IN ME.
THEN THE IMAGES WE JUST WATCHED ARE TAMA'S MEMORIES.
DR. MEGURO KILLED DR. HAYASHI, BUT DR. HAYASHI IS STILL ALIVE.
BUT HOW?
ACTUALLY, DR. HAYASHI WAS ALREADY DEAD.
HE USED HIMSELF AS A SUBJECT FOR HIS EXPERIMENT TOO, AS HE HAD WITH HIS DAUGHTER.
IT WAS A VERY DANGEROUS EXPERIMENT. IT COST HIM HIS LIFE.
THE DOCTOR UPLOADED HIS PERSONALITY TO A ROBOT...
...UNIT NO. TO-502, HIS MASTERPIECE.

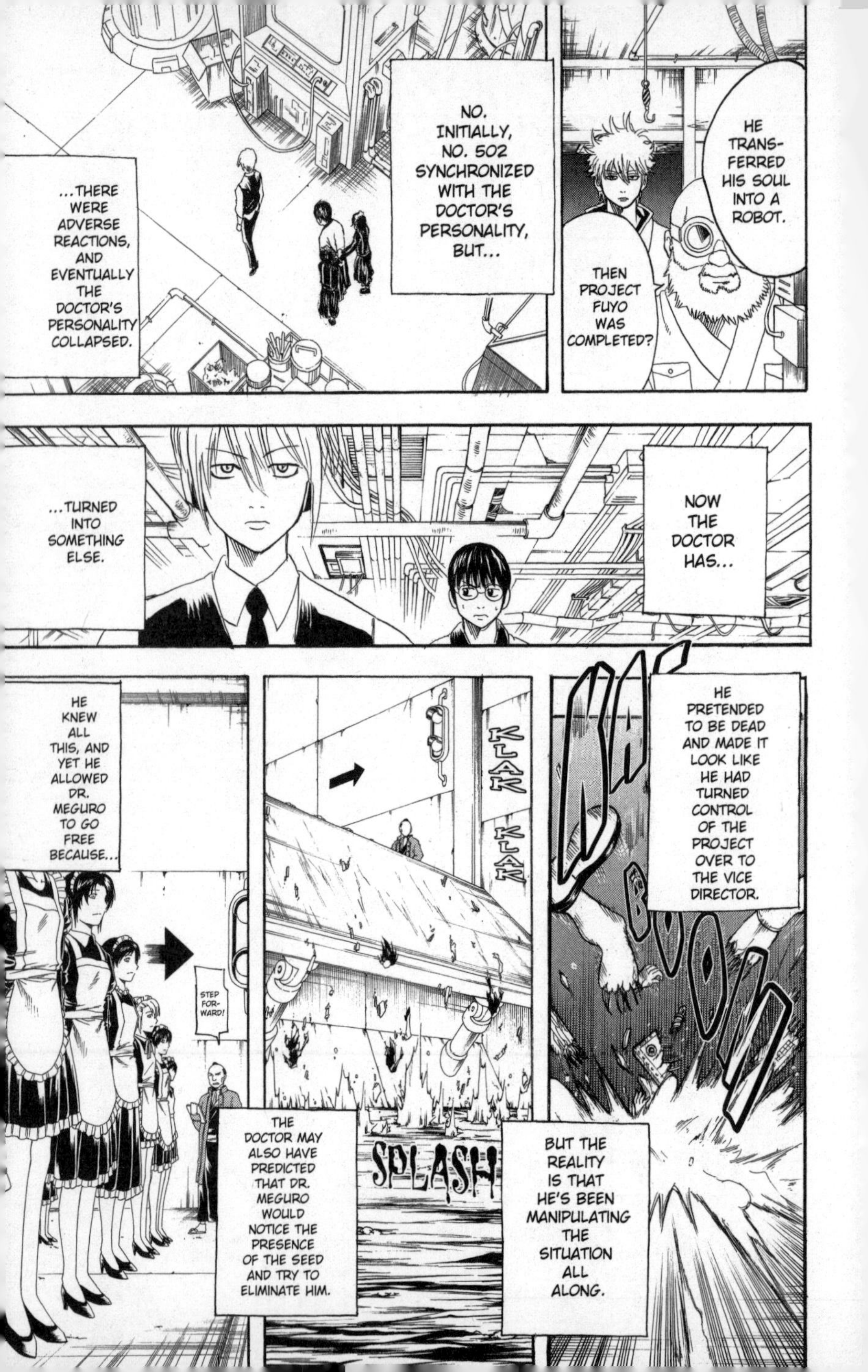
HE TRANSFERRED HIS SOUL INTO A ROBOT.
THEN PROJECT FUYO WAS COMPLETED?
NO. INITIALLY, NO. 502 SYNCHRONIZED WITH THE DOCTOR'S PERSONALITY, BUT...
...THERE WERE ADVERSE REACTIONS, AND EVENTUALLY THE DOCTOR'S PERSONALITY COLLAPSED.
NOW THE DOCTOR HAS...
...TURNED INTO SOMETHING ELSE.
HE PRETENDED TO BE DEAD AND MADE IT LOOK LIKE HE HAD TURNED CONTROL OF THE PROJECT OVER TO THE VICE DIRECTOR.
BUT THE REALITY IS THAT HE'S BEEN MANIPULATING THE SITUATION ALL ALONG.
KLAK
KLAK
SPLASH
THE DOCTOR MAY ALSO HAVE PREDICTED THAT DR. MEGURO WOULD NOTICE THE PRESENCE OF THE SEED AND TRY TO ELIMINATE HIM.
HE KNEW ALL THIS, AND YET HE ALLOWED DR. MEGURO TO GO FREE BECAUSE...
STEP FORWARD!

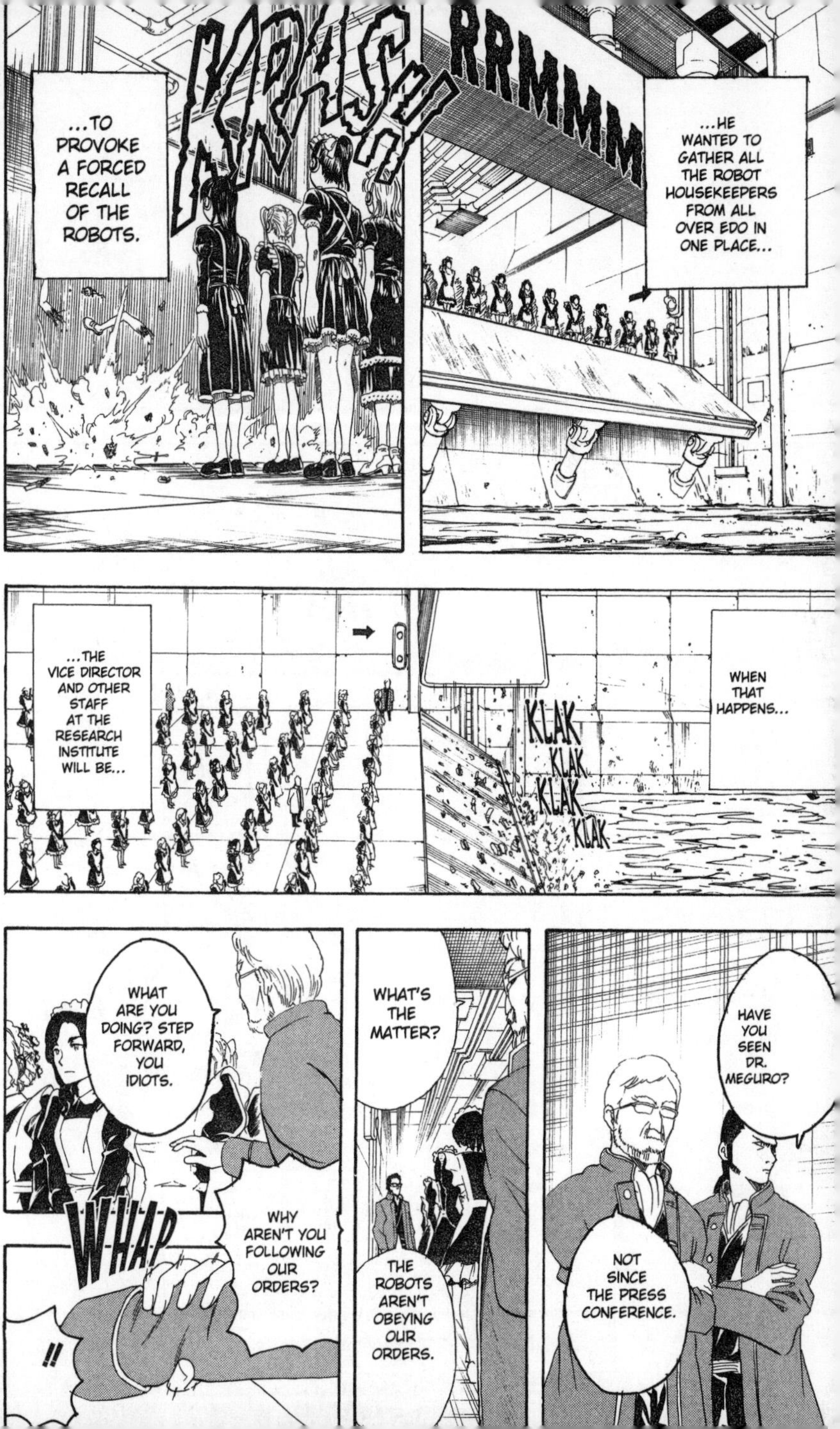
RRMMMM
...HE WANTED TO GATHER ALL THE ROBOT HOUSEKEEPERS FROM ALL OVER EDO IN ONE PLACE...
...TO PROVOKE A FORCED RECALL OF THE ROBOTS.
WHEN THAT HAPPENS...
KLAK KLAK KLAK KLAK
...THE VICE DIRECTOR AND OTHER STAFF AT THE RESEARCH INSTITUTE WILL BE...
HAVE YOU SEEN DR. MEGURO?
NOT SINCE THE PRESS CONFERENCE.
WHAT'S THE MATTER?
THE ROBOTS AREN'T OBEYING OUR ORDERS.
WHAT ARE YOU DOING? STEP FORWARD, YOU IDIOTS.
WHAP
WHY AREN'T YOU FOLLOWING OUR ORDERS?
!!

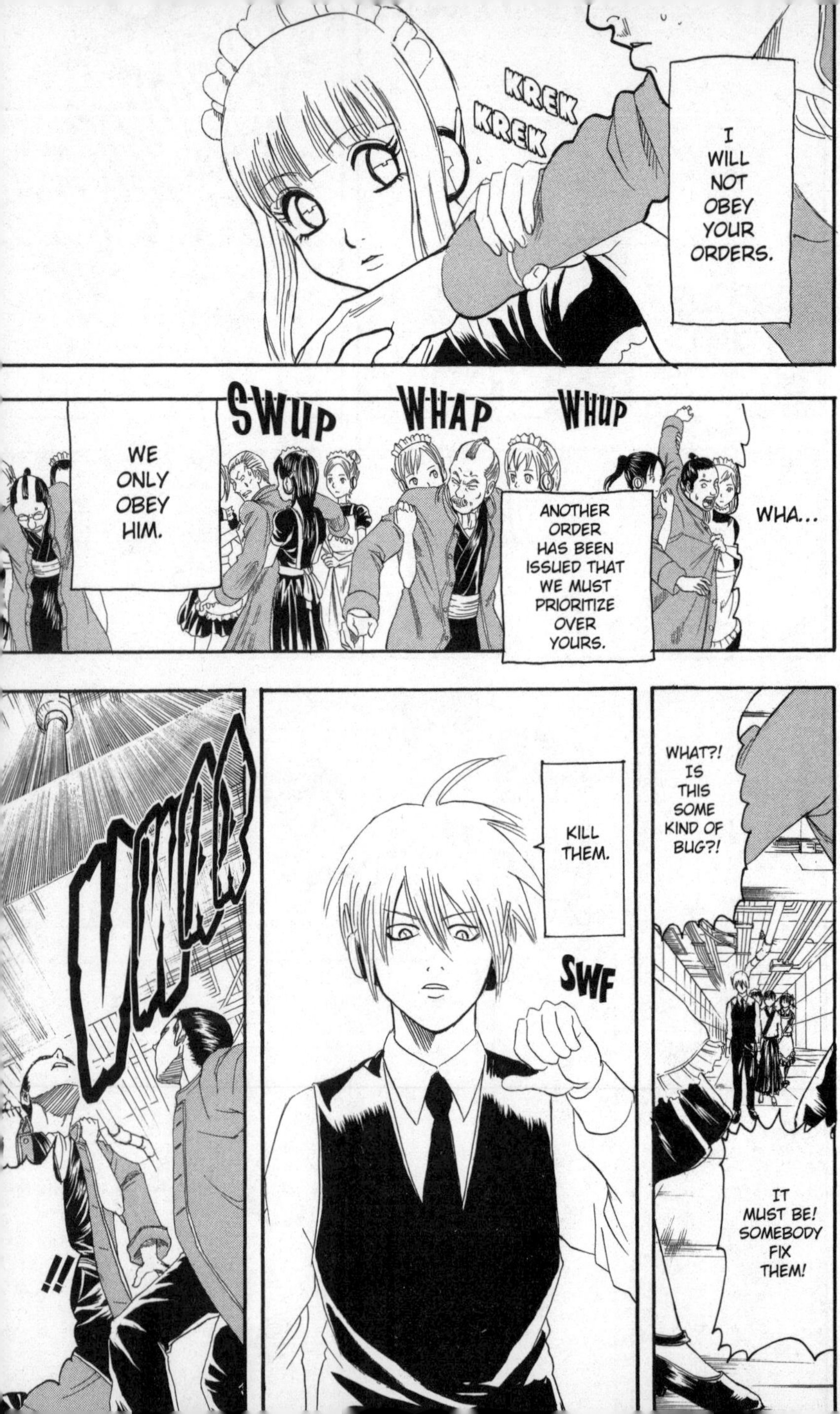
KREK
KREK
I WILL NOT OBEY YOUR ORDERS.
WHA...
WHUP
WHAP
SWUP
ANOTHER ORDER HAS BEEN ISSUED THAT WE MUST PRIORITIZE OVER YOURS.
WE ONLY OBEY HIM.
WHAT?! IS THIS SOME KIND OF BUG?!
IT MUST BE! SOMEBODY FIX THEM!
KILL THEM.
SWF
!!

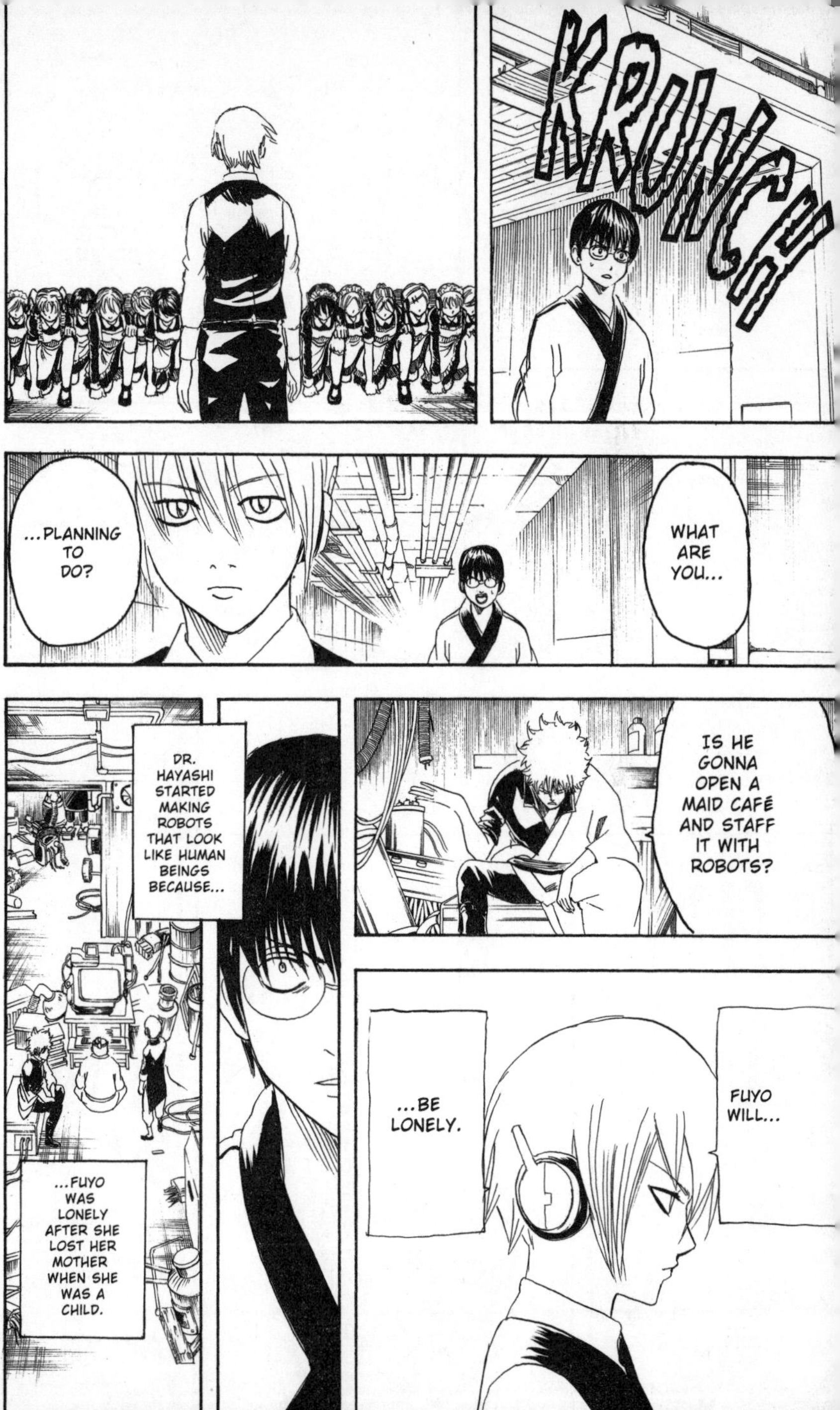
KRUNCH
WHAT ARE YOU...
...PLANNING TO DO?
IS HE GONNA OPEN A MAID CAFÉ AND STAFF IT WITH ROBOTS?
FUYO WILL...
...BE LONELY.
DR. HAYASHI STARTED MAKING ROBOTS THAT LOOK LIKE HUMAN BEINGS BECAUSE...
...FUYO WAS LONELY AFTER SHE LOST HER MOTHER WHEN SHE WAS A CHILD.

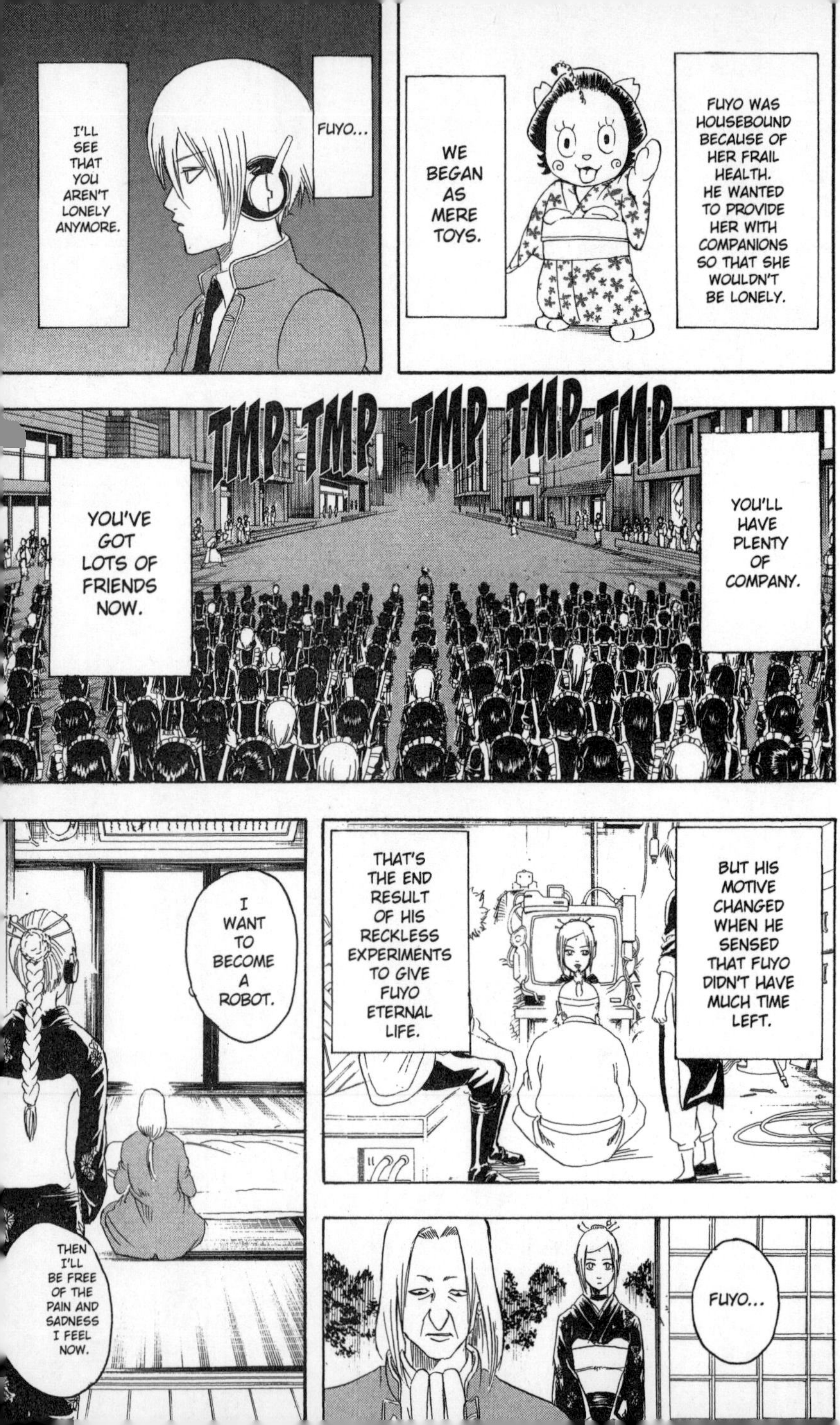
FUYO WAS HOUSEBOUND BECAUSE OF HER FRAIL HEALTH. HE WANTED TO PROVIDE HER WITH COMPANIONS SO THAT SHE WOULDN'T BE LONELY.
WE BEGAN AS MERE TOYS.
FUYO...
I'LL SEE THAT YOU AREN'T LONELY ANYMORE.
TMP TMP TMP TMP TMP
YOU'LL HAVE PLENTY OF COMPANY.
YOU'VE GOT LOTS OF FRIENDS NOW.
BUT HIS MOTIVE CHANGED WHEN HE SENSED THAT FUYO DIDN'T HAVE MUCH TIME LEFT.
THAT'S THE END RESULT OF HIS RECKLESS EXPERIMENTS TO GIVE FUYO ETERNAL LIFE.
FUYO...
I WANT TO BECOME A ROBOT.
THEN I'LL BE FREE OF THE PAIN AND SADNESS I FEEL NOW.

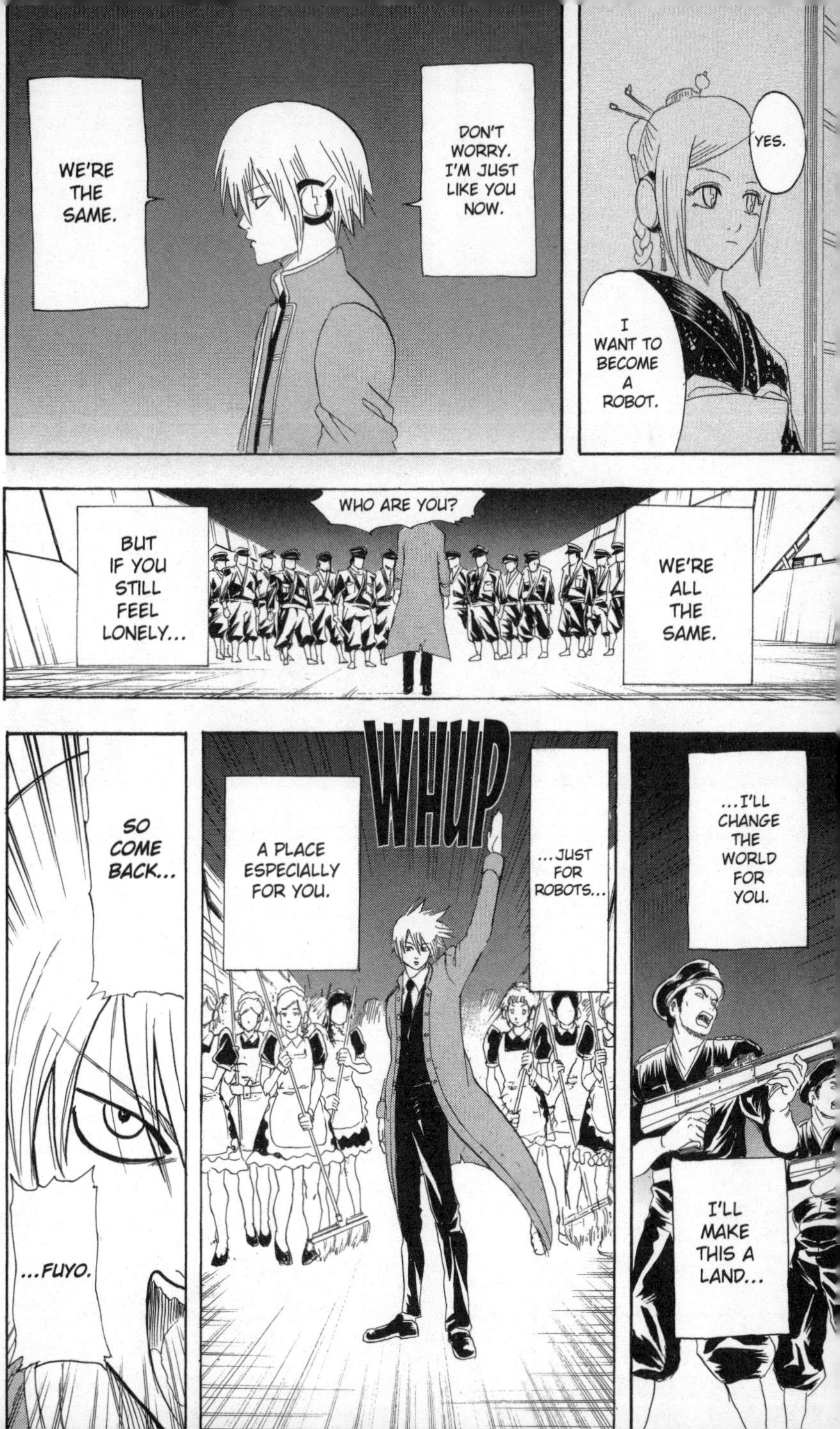
YES.
I WANT TO BECOME A ROBOT.
DON'T WORRY. I'M JUST LIKE YOU NOW.
WE'RE THE SAME.
WHO ARE YOU?
WE'RE ALL THE SAME.
BUT IF YOU STILL FEEL LONELY...
...I'LL CHANGE THE WORLD FOR YOU.
I'LL MAKE THIS A LAND...
...JUST FOR ROBOTS...
WHUP
A PLACE ESPECIALLY FOR YOU.
SO COME BACK...
...FUYO.

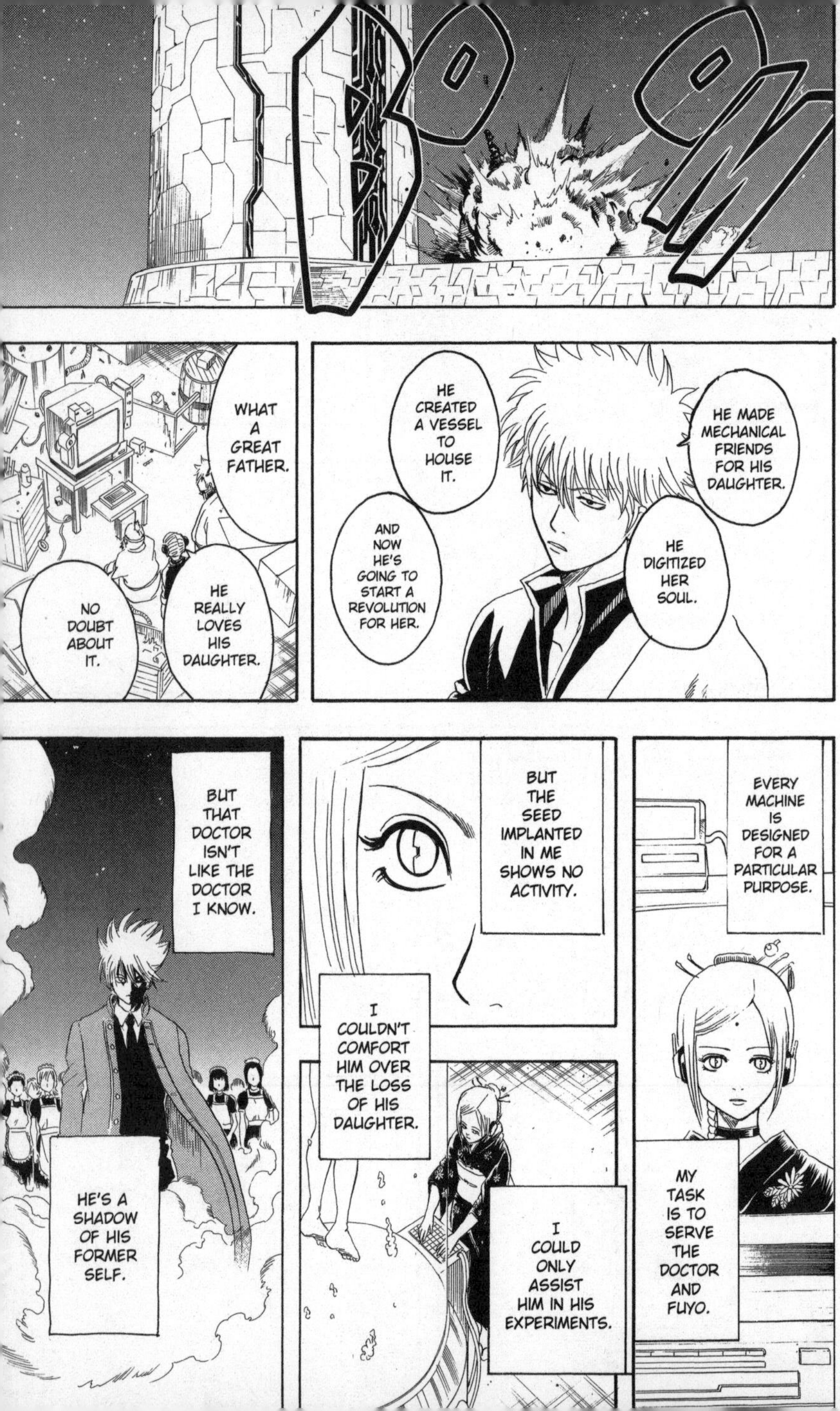
BOOM
HE MADE MECHANICAL FRIENDS FOR HIS DAUGHTER.
HE DIGITIZED HER SOUL.
HE CREATED A VESSEL TO HOUSE IT.
AND NOW HE'S GOING TO START A REVOLUTION FOR HER.
WHAT A GREAT FATHER.
HE REALLY LOVES HIS DAUGHTER.
NO DOUBT ABOUT IT.
EVERY MACHINE IS DESIGNED FOR A PARTICULAR PURPOSE.
MY TASK IS TO SERVE THE DOCTOR AND FUYO.
BUT THE SEED IMPLANTED IN ME SHOWS NO ACTIVITY.
I COULDN'T COMFORT HIM OVER THE LOSS OF HIS DAUGHTER.
I COULD ONLY ASSIST HIM IN HIS EXPERIMENTS.
BUT THAT DOCTOR ISN'T LIKE THE DOCTOR I KNOW.
HE'S A SHADOW OF HIS FORMER SELF.

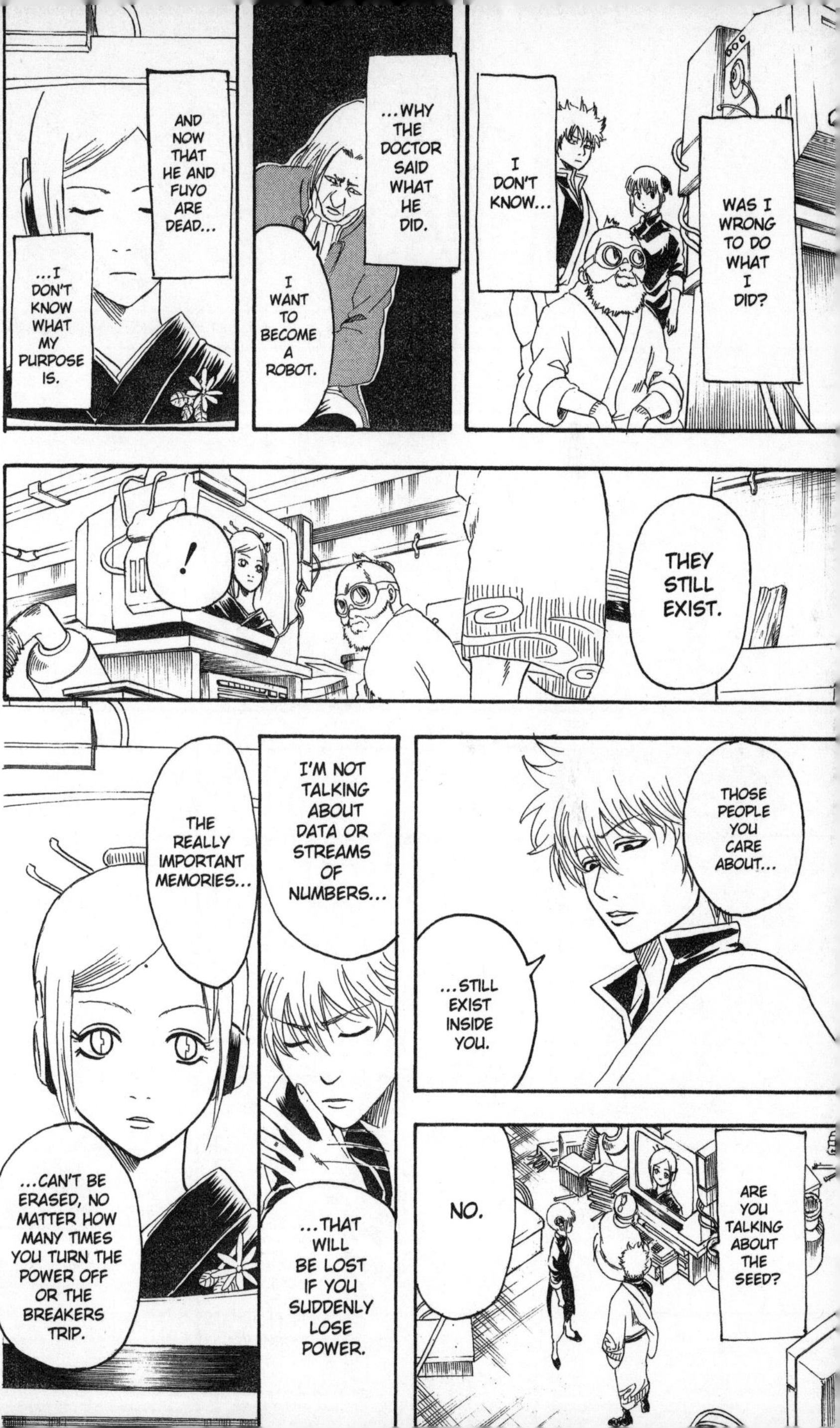
WAS I WRONG TO DO WHAT I DID?
I DON'T KNOW...
...WHY THE DOCTOR SAID WHAT HE DID.
I WANT TO BECOME A ROBOT.
AND NOW THAT HE AND FUYO ARE DEAD...
...I DON'T KNOW WHAT MY PURPOSE IS.
THEY STILL EXIST.
!
THOSE PEOPLE YOU CARE ABOUT...
...STILL EXIST INSIDE YOU.
ARE YOU TALKING ABOUT THE SEED?
NO.
I'M NOT TALKING ABOUT DATA OR STREAMS OF NUMBERS...
...THAT WILL BE LOST IF YOU SUDDENLY LOSE POWER.
THE REALLY IMPORTANT MEMORIES...
...CAN'T BE ERASED, NO MATTER HOW MANY TIMES YOU TURN THE POWER OFF OR THE BREAKERS TRIP.

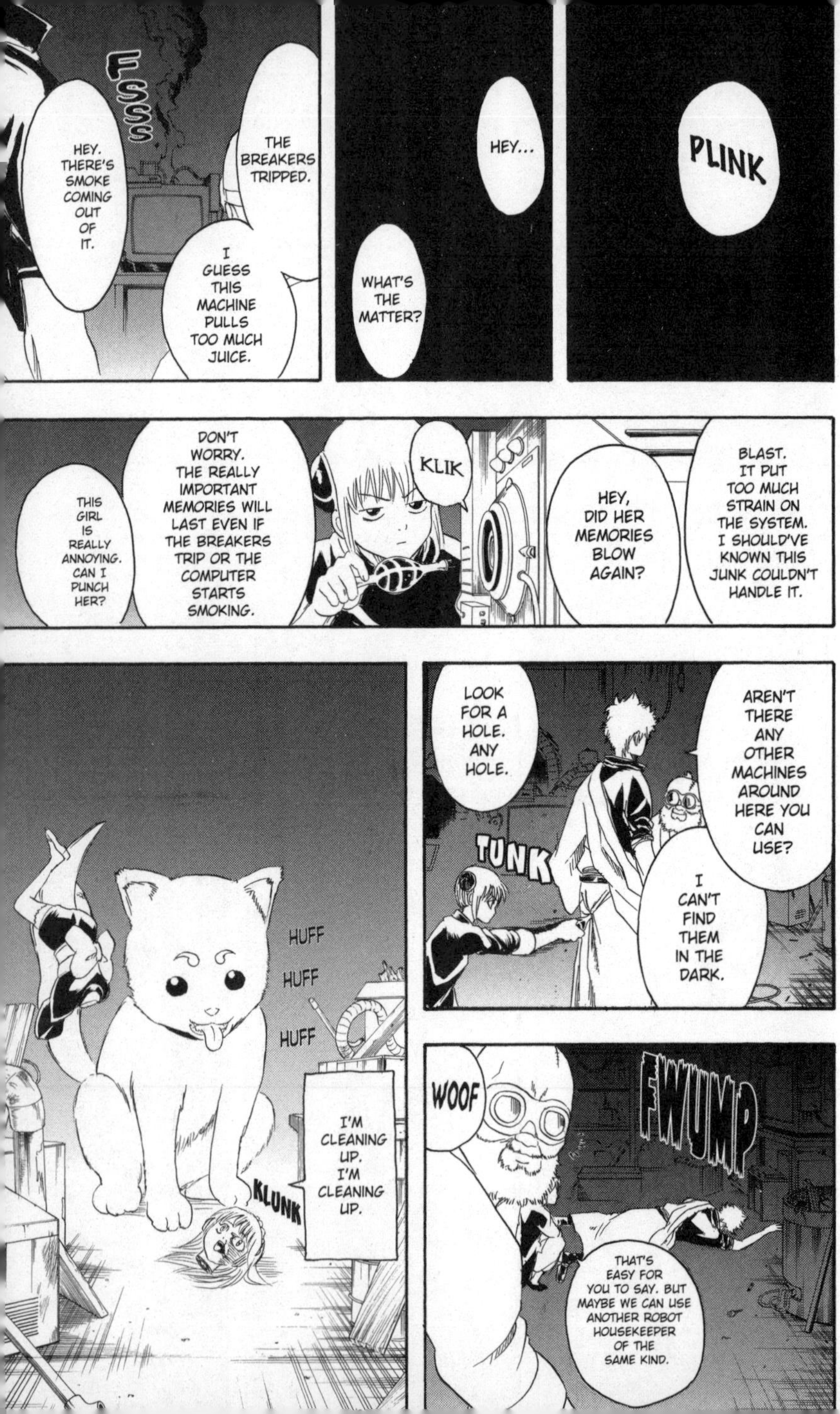
PLINK
HEY...
WHAT'S THE MATTER?
FSSS
HEY. THERE'S SMOKE COMING OUT OF IT.
THE BREAKERS TRIPPED.
I GUESS THIS MACHINE PULLS TOO MUCH JUICE.
BLAST. IT PUT TOO MUCH STRAIN ON THE SYSTEM. I SHOULD'VE KNOWN THIS JUNK COULDN'T HANDLE IT.
HEY, DID HER MEMORIES BLOW AGAIN?
KLIK
DON'T WORRY. THE REALLY IMPORTANT MEMORIES WILL LAST EVEN IF THE BREAKERS TRIP OR THE COMPUTER STARTS SMOKING.
THIS GIRL IS REALLY ANNOYING. CAN I PUNCH HER?
AREN'T THERE ANY OTHER MACHINES AROUND HERE YOU CAN USE?
LOOK FOR A HOLE. ANY HOLE.
TUNK
I CAN'T FIND THEM IN THE DARK.
FWUMP
WOOF
THAT'S EASY FOR YOU TO SAY. BUT MAYBE WE CAN USE ANOTHER ROBOT HOUSEKEEPER OF THE SAME KIND.
HUFF
HUFF
HUFF
I'M CLEANING UP. I'M CLEANING UP.
KLUNK

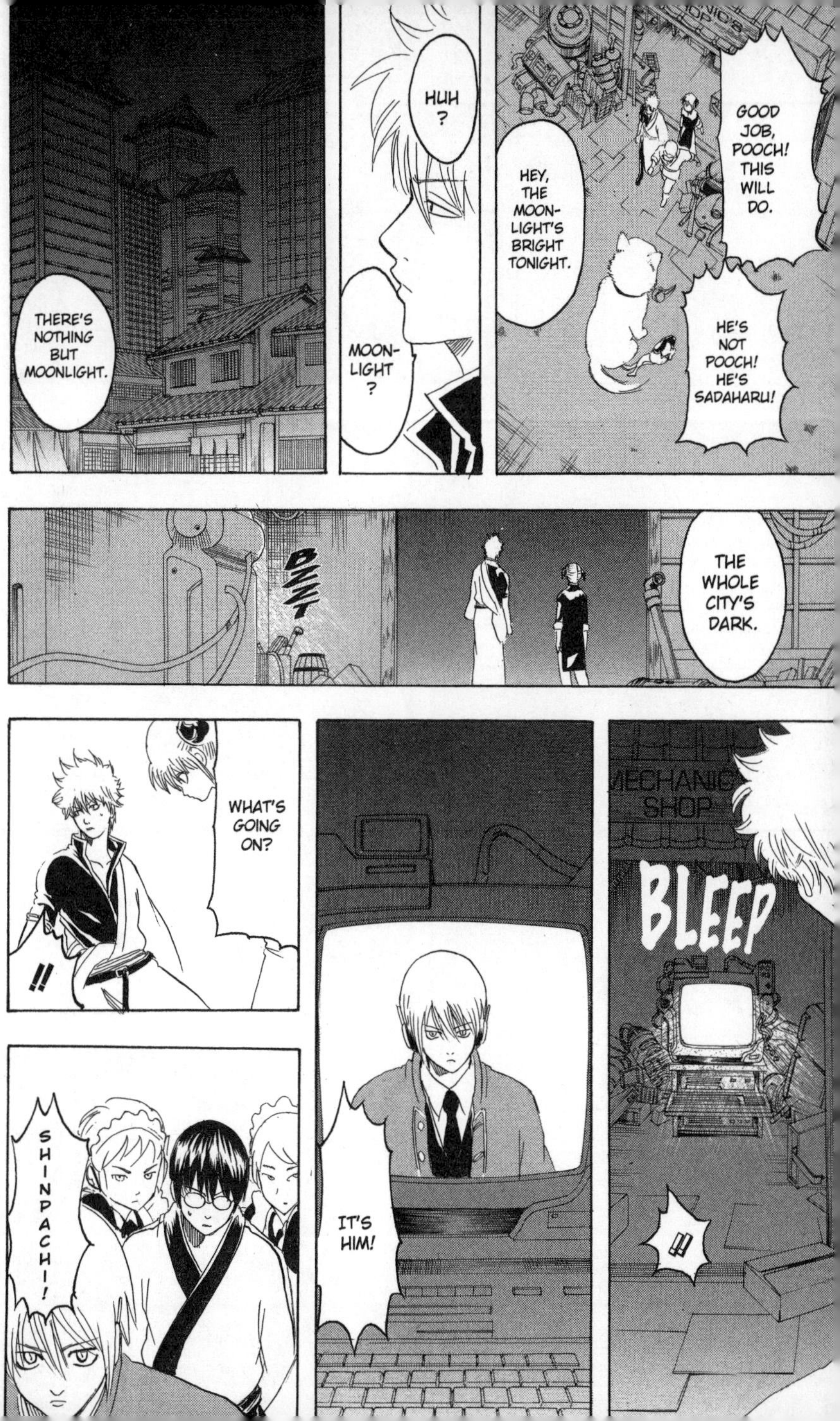
GOOD JOB, POOCH! THIS WILL DO.
HE'S NOT POOCH! HE'S SADAHARU!
HEY, THE MOON-LIGHT'S BRIGHT TONIGHT.
HUH?
MOON-LIGHT?
THERE'S NOTHING BUT MOONLIGHT.
THE WHOLE CITY'S DARK.
BZZZT
MECHANIC'S SHOP
BLEEP
!!
IT'S HIM!
WHAT'S GOING ON?
!!
SHINPACHI!

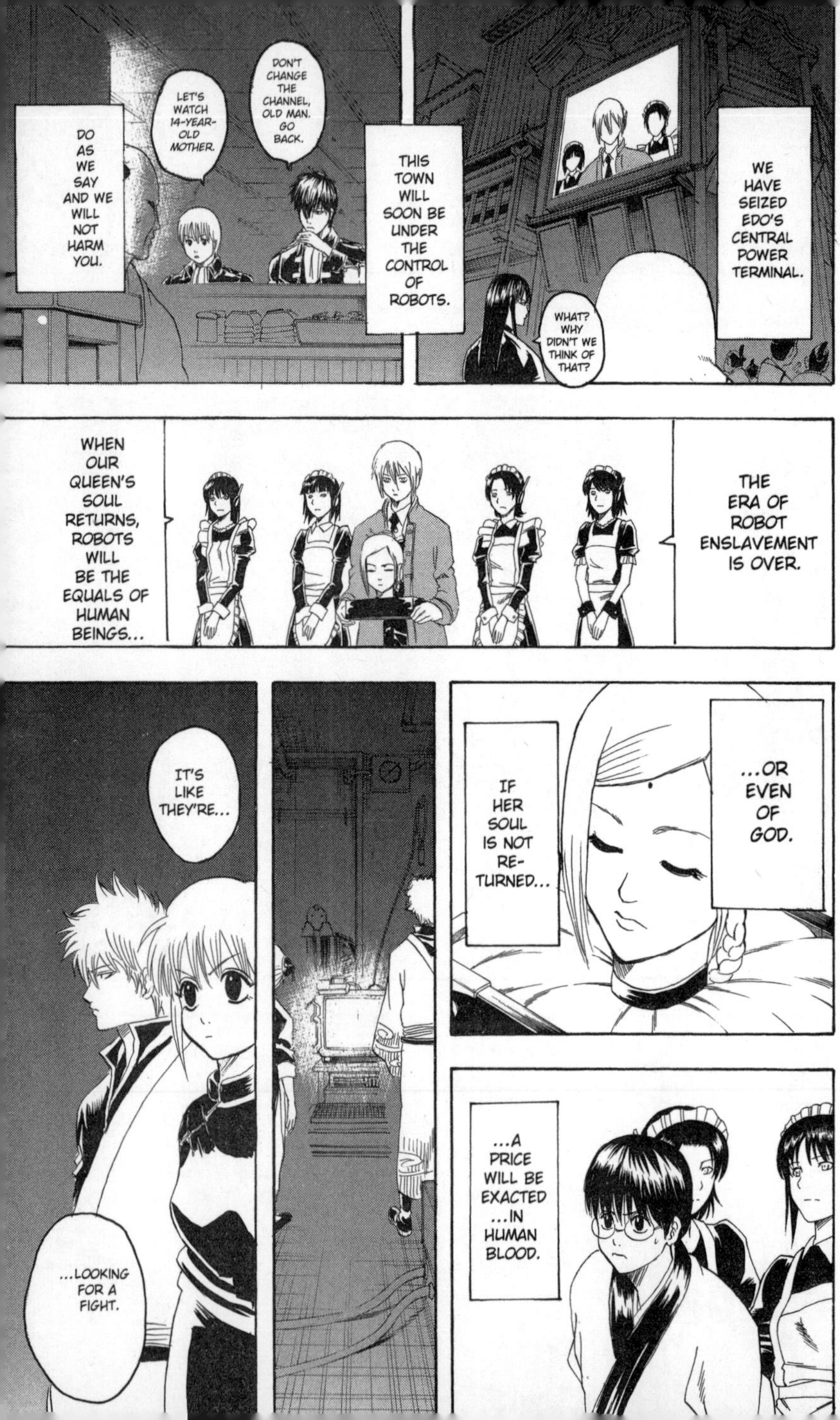
WE HAVE SEIZED EDO'S CENTRAL POWER TERMINAL.
THIS TOWN WILL SOON BE UNDER THE CONTROL OF ROBOTS.
WHAT? WHY DIDN'T WE THINK OF THAT?
DON'T CHANGE THE CHANNEL, OLD MAN. GO BACK.
LET'S WATCH 14-YEAR-OLD MOTHER.
DO AS WE SAY AND WE WILL NOT HARM YOU.
THE ERA OF ROBOT ENSLAVEMENT IS OVER.
WHEN OUR QUEEN'S SOUL RETURNS, ROBOTS WILL BE THE EQUALS OF HUMAN BEINGS...
...OR EVEN OF GOD.
IF HER SOUL IS NOT RE-TURNED...
...A PRICE WILL BE EXACTED ...IN HUMAN BLOOD.
IT'S LIKE THEY'RE...
...LOOKING FOR A FIGHT.

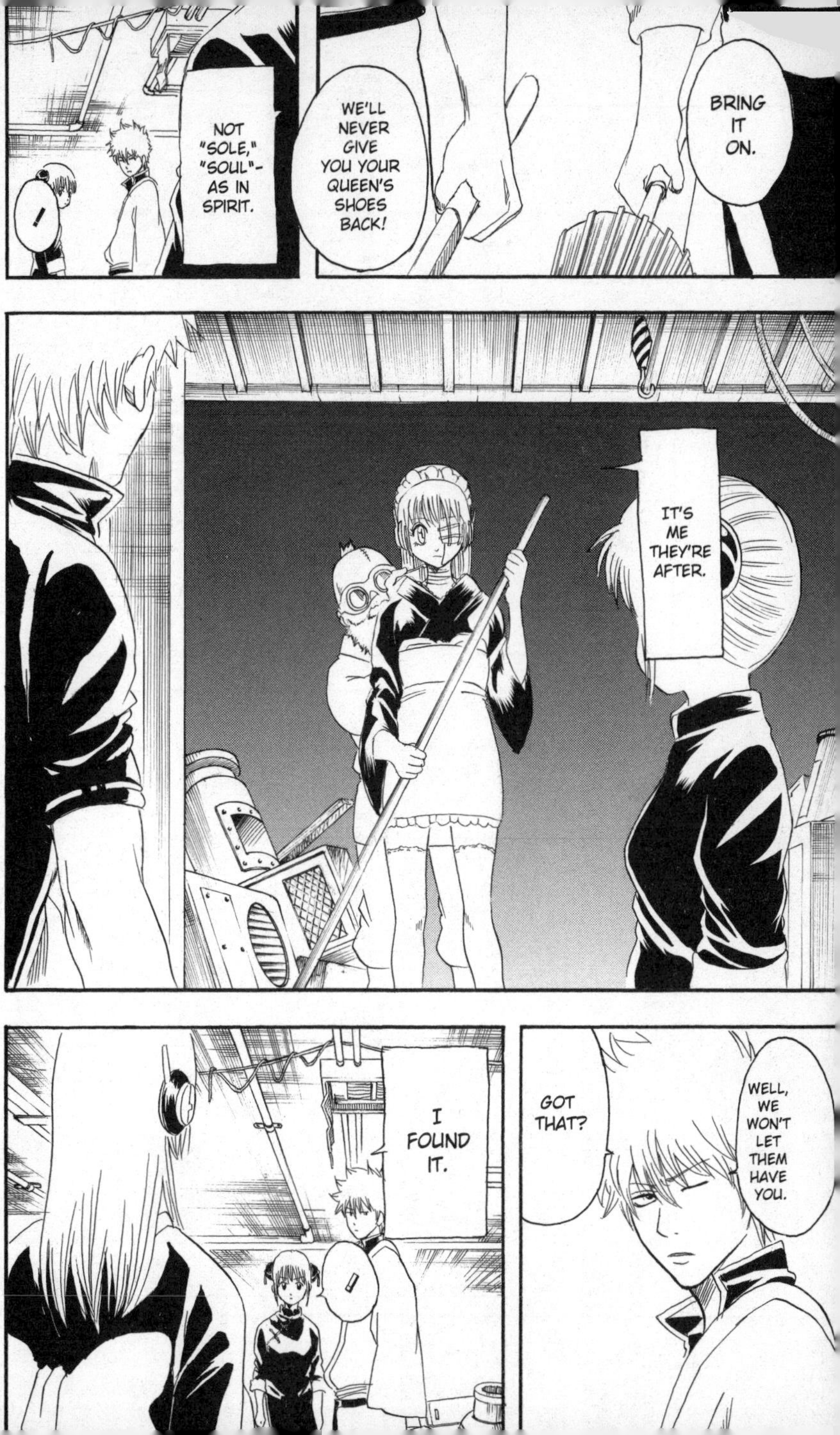
BRING IT ON.
WE'LL NEVER GIVE YOU YOUR QUEEN'S SHOES BACK!
NOT "SOLE," "SOUL"- AS IN SPIRIT.
!
IT'S ME THEY'RE AFTER.
WELL, WE WON'T LET THEM HAVE YOU.
GOT THAT?
I FOUND IT.
!

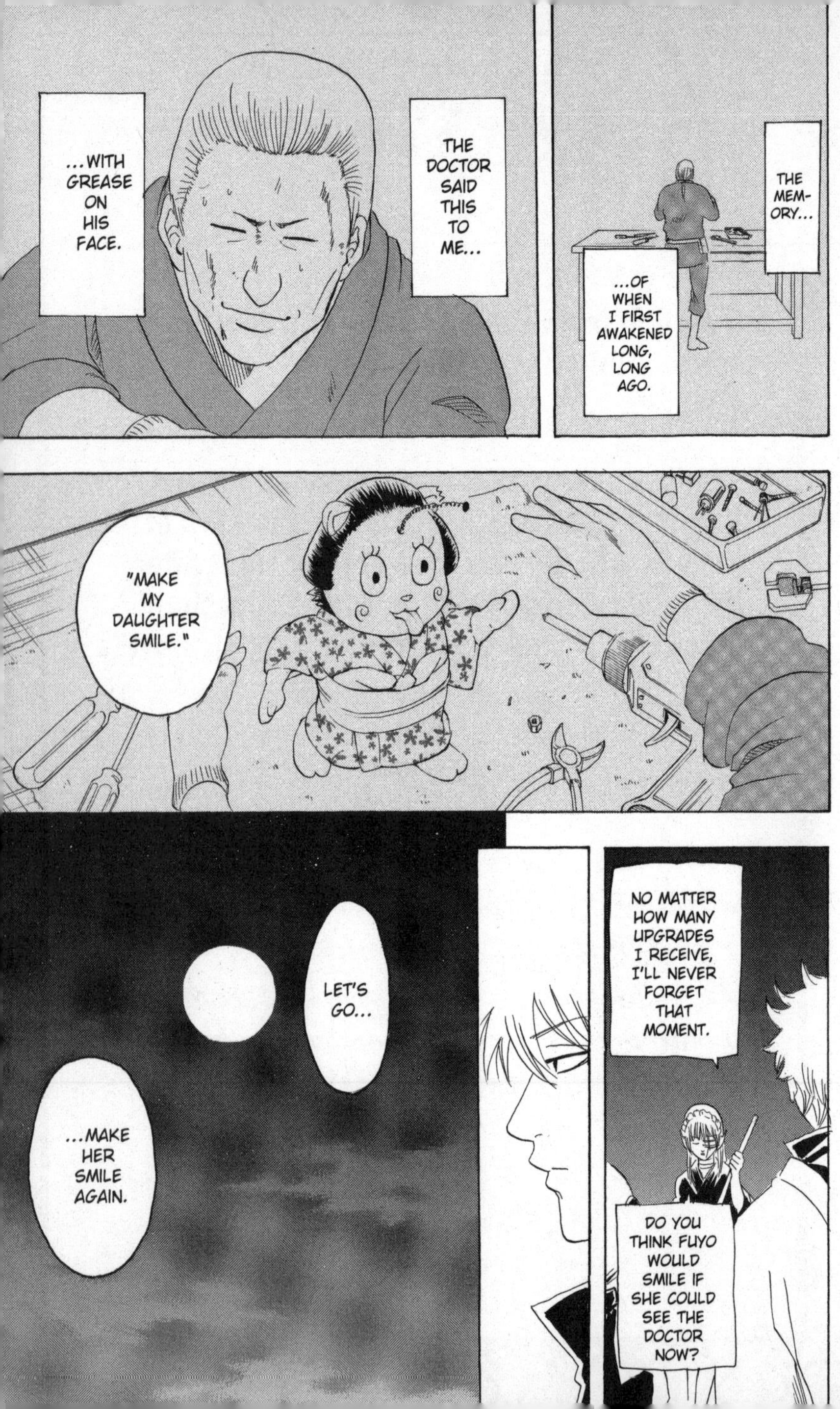
THE MEMORY...
...OF WHEN I FIRST AWAKENED LONG, LONG AGO.
THE DOCTOR SAID THIS TO ME...
...WITH GREASE ON HIS FACE.
"MAKE MY DAUGHTER SMILE."
NO MATTER HOW MANY UPGRADES I RECEIVE, I'LL NEVER FORGET THAT MOMENT.
DO YOU THINK FUYO WOULD SMILE IF SHE COULD SEE THE DOCTOR NOW?
LET'S GO...
...MAKE HER SMILE AGAIN.

Sorachi's Q&A
Hanging with the Readers #51

<Question from Sakura (Cherry Tree) Samurai from Chiba Prefecture>

Nice to meet you, Sorachi Sensei! I have something on my mind. Is Gin the kind of person who throws *Jump* away right after he finishes reading it, or does he let them stack up? By the way, I prefer graphic novels.

<Answer>

Gin lets them stack up really high. Actually, Shinpachi throws them away, not Gin. For your information, Gin doesn't collect graphic novels. Kagura saves her comics to help her learn Japanese. Zenzo stores all his volumes of **Jump** in his book store-room. His father has sold most of them though.

(Q&A #52 is on page 110)

Lesson 144
Western Songs Are Hard to Learn

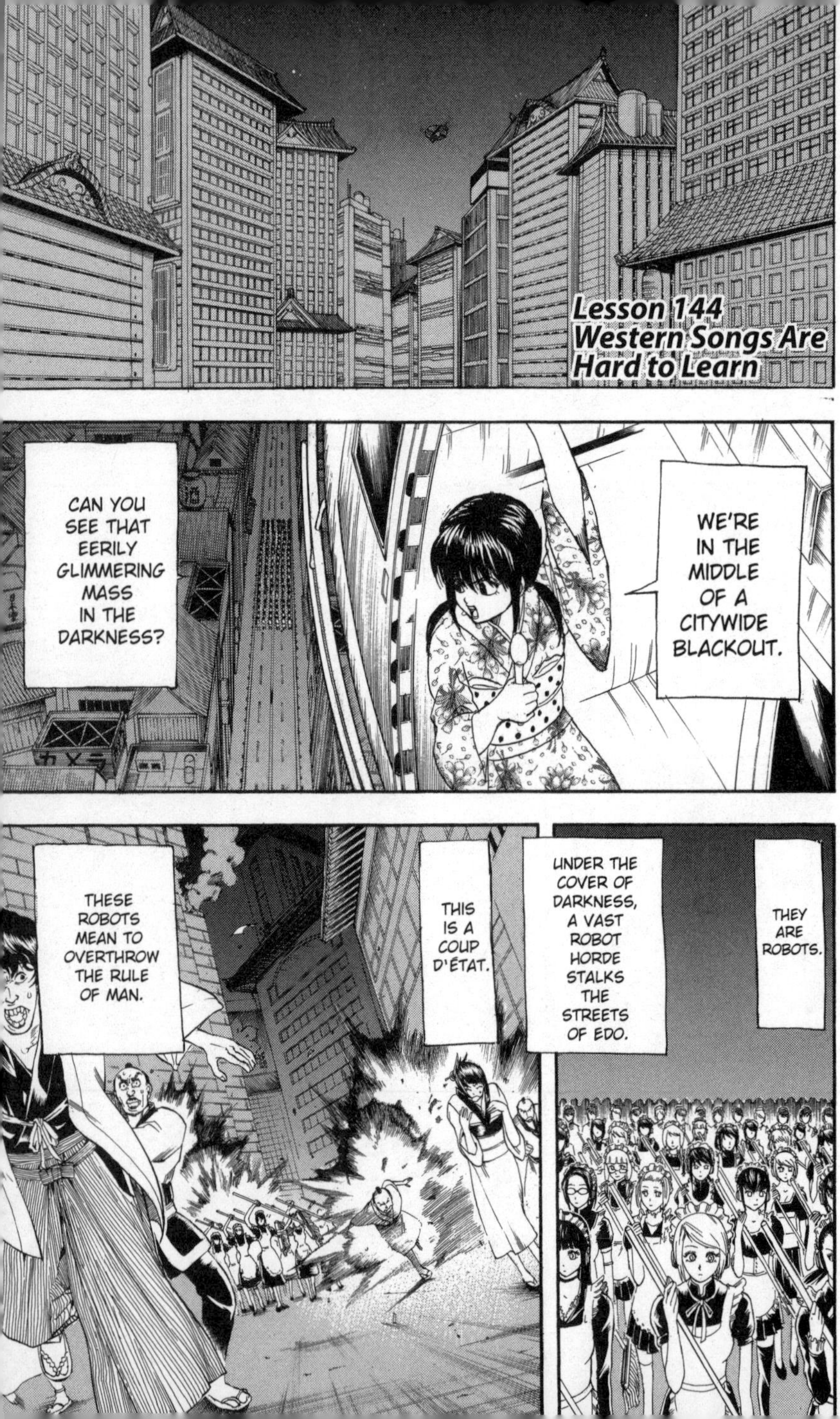
WE'RE IN THE MIDDLE OF A CITYWIDE BLACKOUT.
CAN YOU SEE THAT EERILY GLIMMERING MASS IN THE DARKNESS?
THEY ARE ROBOTS.
UNDER THE COVER OF DARKNESS, A VAST ROBOT HORDE STALKS THE STREETS OF EDO.
THIS IS A COUP D'ÉTAT.
THESE ROBOTS MEAN TO OVERTHROW THE RULE OF MAN.

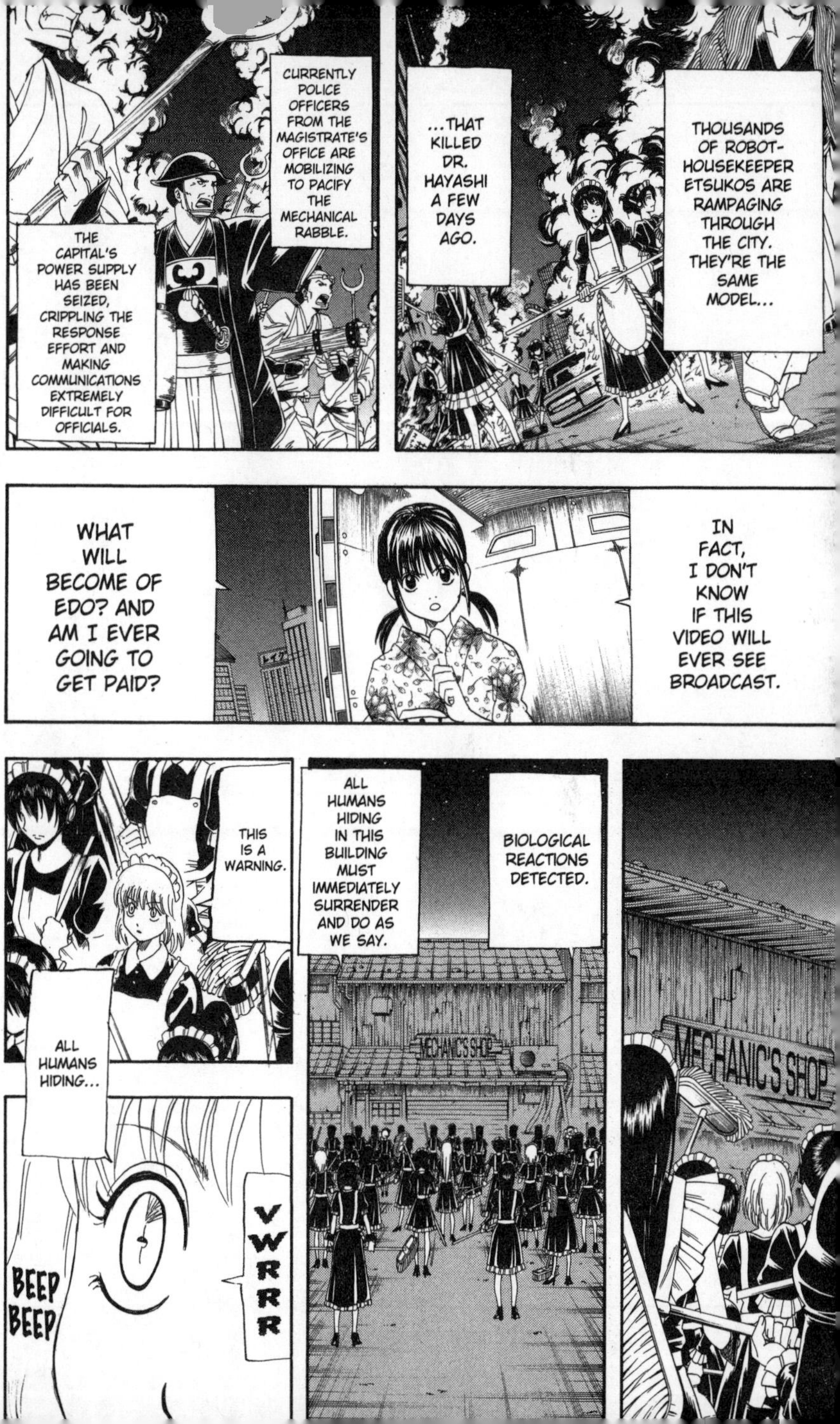
THOUSANDS OF ROBOT-HOUSEKEEPER ETSUKOS ARE RAMPAGING THROUGH THE CITY. THEY'RE THE SAME MODEL...
...THAT KILLED DR. HAYASHI A FEW DAYS AGO.
CURRENTLY POLICE OFFICERS FROM THE MAGISTRATE'S OFFICE ARE MOBILIZING TO PACIFY THE MECHANICAL RABBLE.
THE CAPITAL'S POWER SUPPLY HAS BEEN SEIZED, CRIPPLING THE RESPONSE EFFORT AND MAKING COMMUNICATIONS EXTREMELY DIFFICULT FOR OFFICIALS.
IN FACT, I DON'T KNOW IF THIS VIDEO WILL EVER SEE BROADCAST.
WHAT WILL BECOME OF EDO? AND AM I EVER GOING TO GET PAID?
MECHANIC'S SHOP
BIOLOGICAL REACTIONS DETECTED.
ALL HUMANS HIDING IN THIS BUILDING MUST IMMEDIATELY SURRENDER AND DO AS WE SAY.
MECHANIC'S SHOP
THIS IS A WARNING.
ALL HUMANS HIDING...
VWRRR
BEEP BEEP

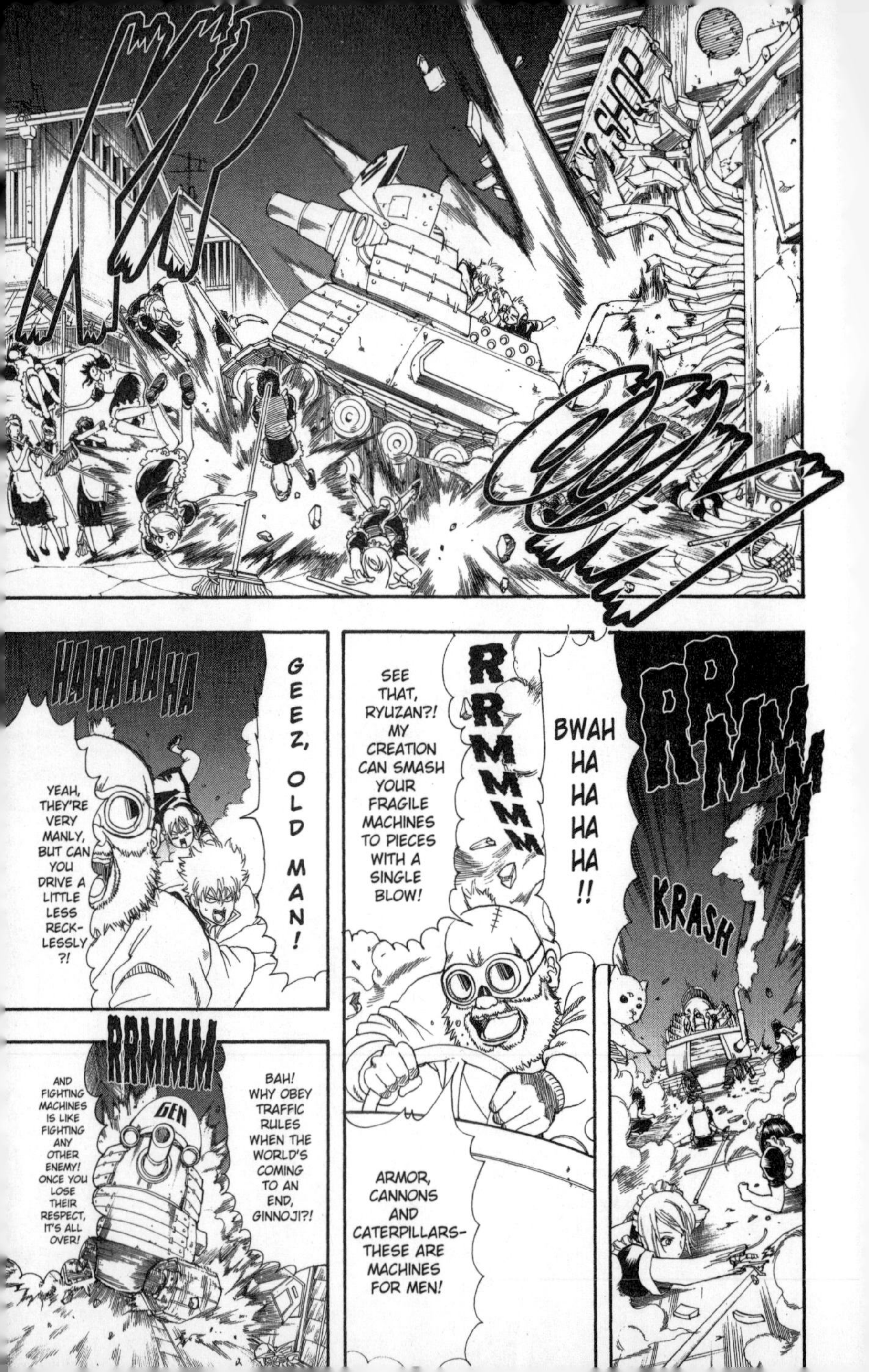
RRMMMMM
KRASH
RRRMMMM
SEE THAT, RYUZAN?! MY CREATION CAN SMASH YOUR FRAGILE MACHINES TO PIECES WITH A SINGLE BLOW!
BWAH HA HA HA HA!!
ARMOR, CANNONS AND CATERPILLARS- THESE ARE MACHINES FOR MEN!
HA HA HA HA HA
GEEZ, OLD MAN!
YEAH, THEY'RE VERY MANLY, BUT CAN YOU DRIVE A LITTLE LESS RECK-LESSLY?!
RRMMMM
GEN
BAH! WHY OBEY TRAFFIC RULES WHEN THE WORLD'S COMING TO AN END, GINNOJI?!
AND FIGHTING MACHINES IS LIKE FIGHTING ANY OTHER ENEMY! ONCE YOU LOSE THEIR RESPECT, IT'S ALL OVER!

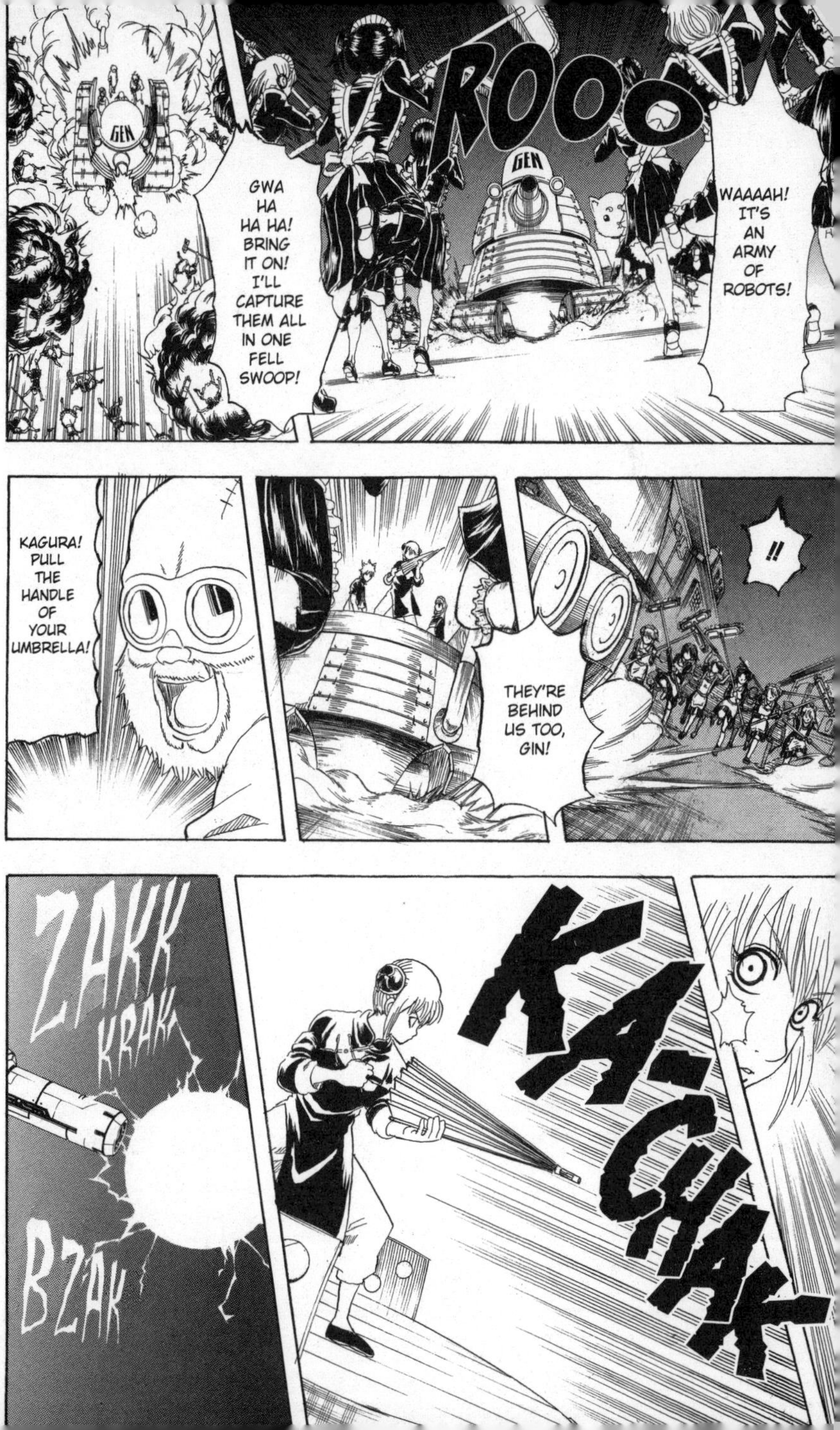
ROOO
WAAAAH! IT'S AN ARMY OF ROBOTS!
GWA HA HA HA! BRING IT ON! I'LL CAPTURE THEM ALL IN ONE FELL SWOOP!
!!
THEY'RE BEHIND US TOO, GIN!
KAGURA! PULL THE HANDLE OF YOUR UMBRELLA!
KA-CHAK
ZAKK
KRAK
BZAK

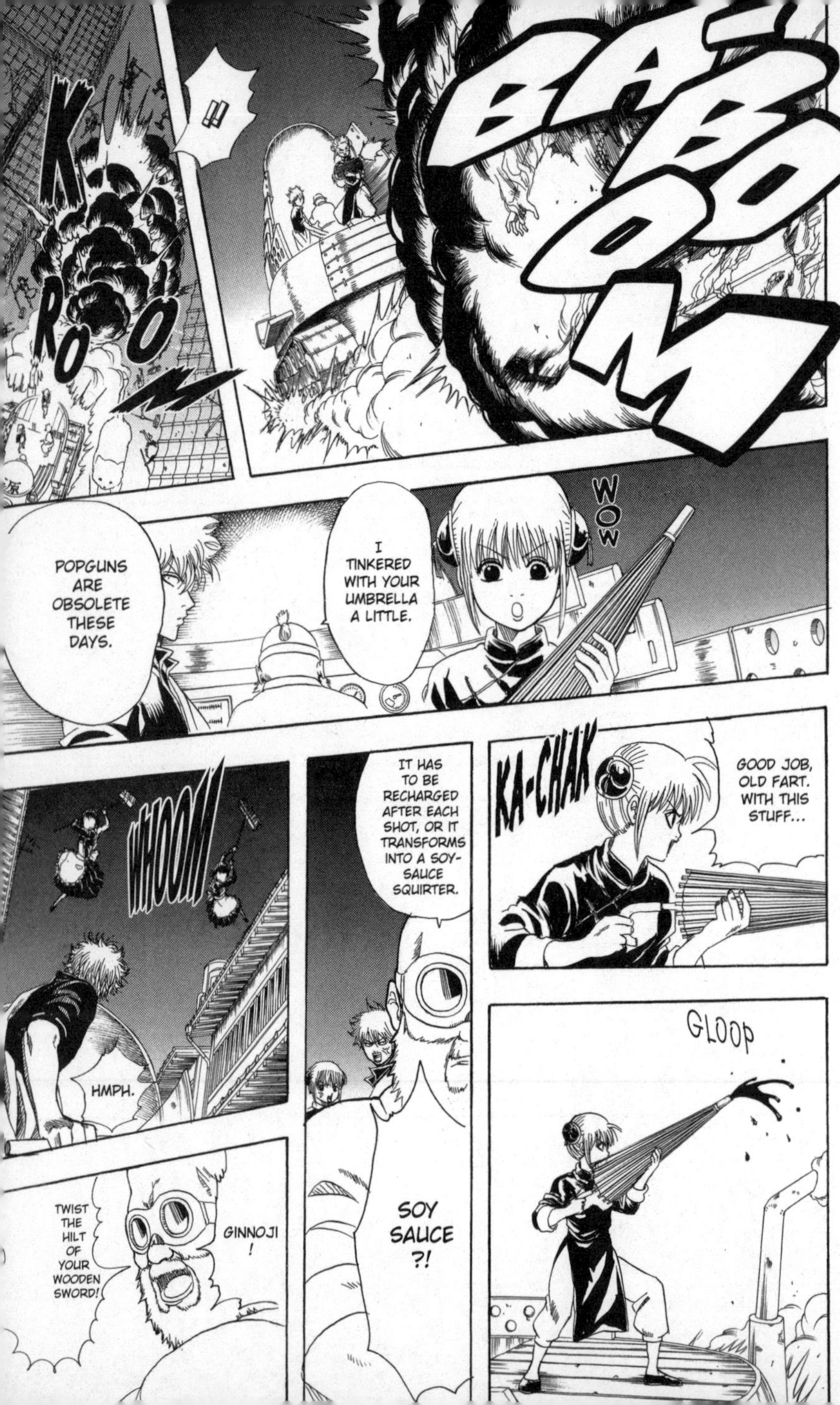
BA-BOOM
!!
KROOO
WOW
I TINKERED WITH YOUR UMBRELLA A LITTLE.
POPGUNS ARE OBSOLETE THESE DAYS.
KA-CHAK
GOOD JOB, OLD FART. WITH THIS STUFF...
GLOOP
IT HAS TO BE RECHARGED AFTER EACH SHOT, OR IT TRANSFORMS INTO A SOY-SAUCE SQUIRTER.
SOY SAUCE ?!
WHOOM
HMPH.
GINNOJI !
TWIST THE HILT OF YOUR WOODEN SWORD!

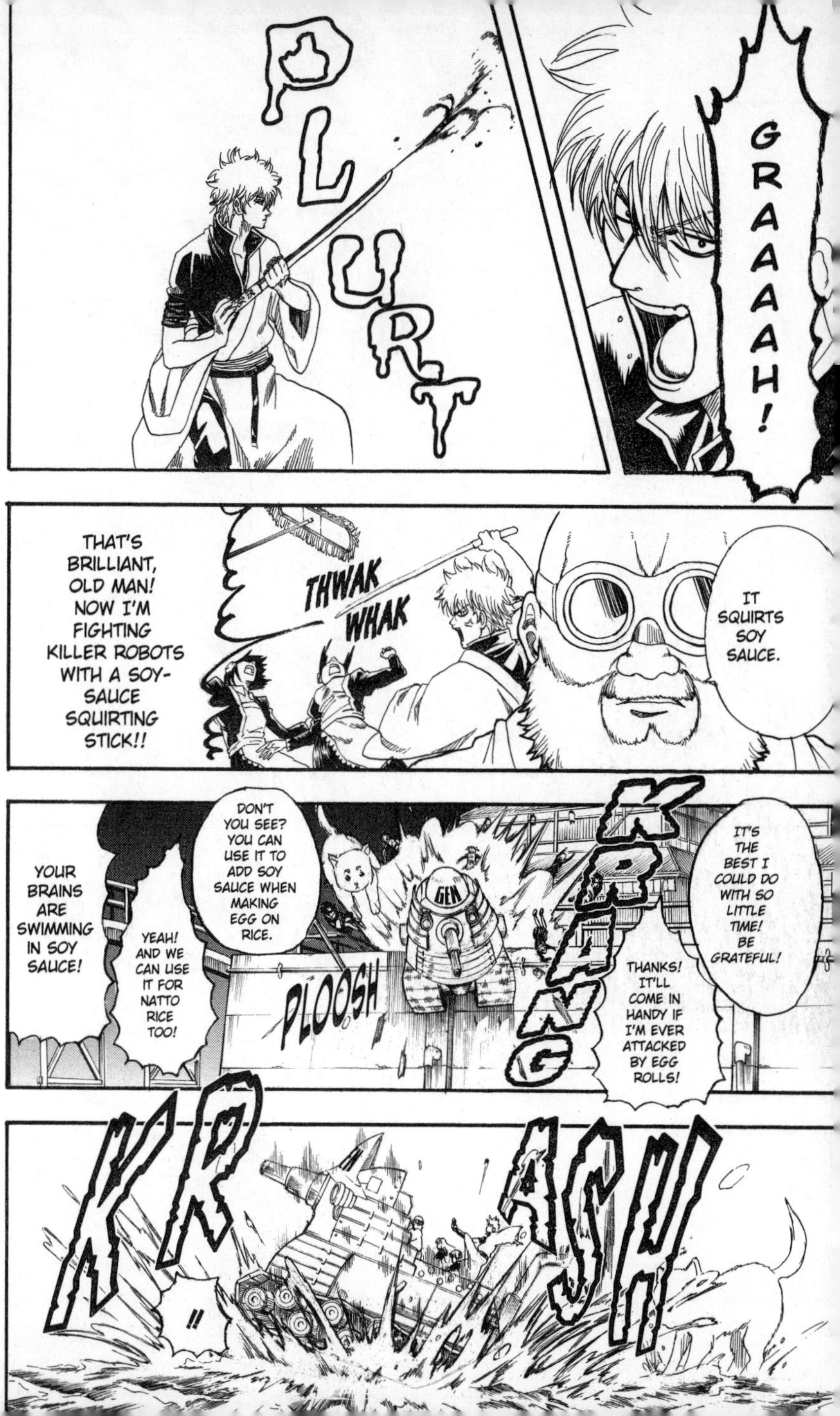
GRAAAAH!
PLURT
IT SQUIRTS SOY SAUCE.
THWAK
WHAK
THAT'S BRILLIANT, OLD MAN! NOW I'M FIGHTING KILLER ROBOTS WITH A SOY-SAUCE SQUIRTING STICK!!
IT'S THE BEST I COULD DO WITH SO LITTLE TIME! BE GRATEFUL!
KRANG
THANKS! IT'LL COME IN HANDY IF I'M EVER ATTACKED BY EGG ROLLS!
GEN
DON'T YOU SEE? YOU CAN USE IT TO ADD SOY SAUCE WHEN MAKING EGG ON RICE.
PLOOSH
YEAH! AND WE CAN USE IT FOR NATTO RICE TOO!
YOUR BRAINS ARE SWIMMING IN SOY SAUCE!
KRASH
!!

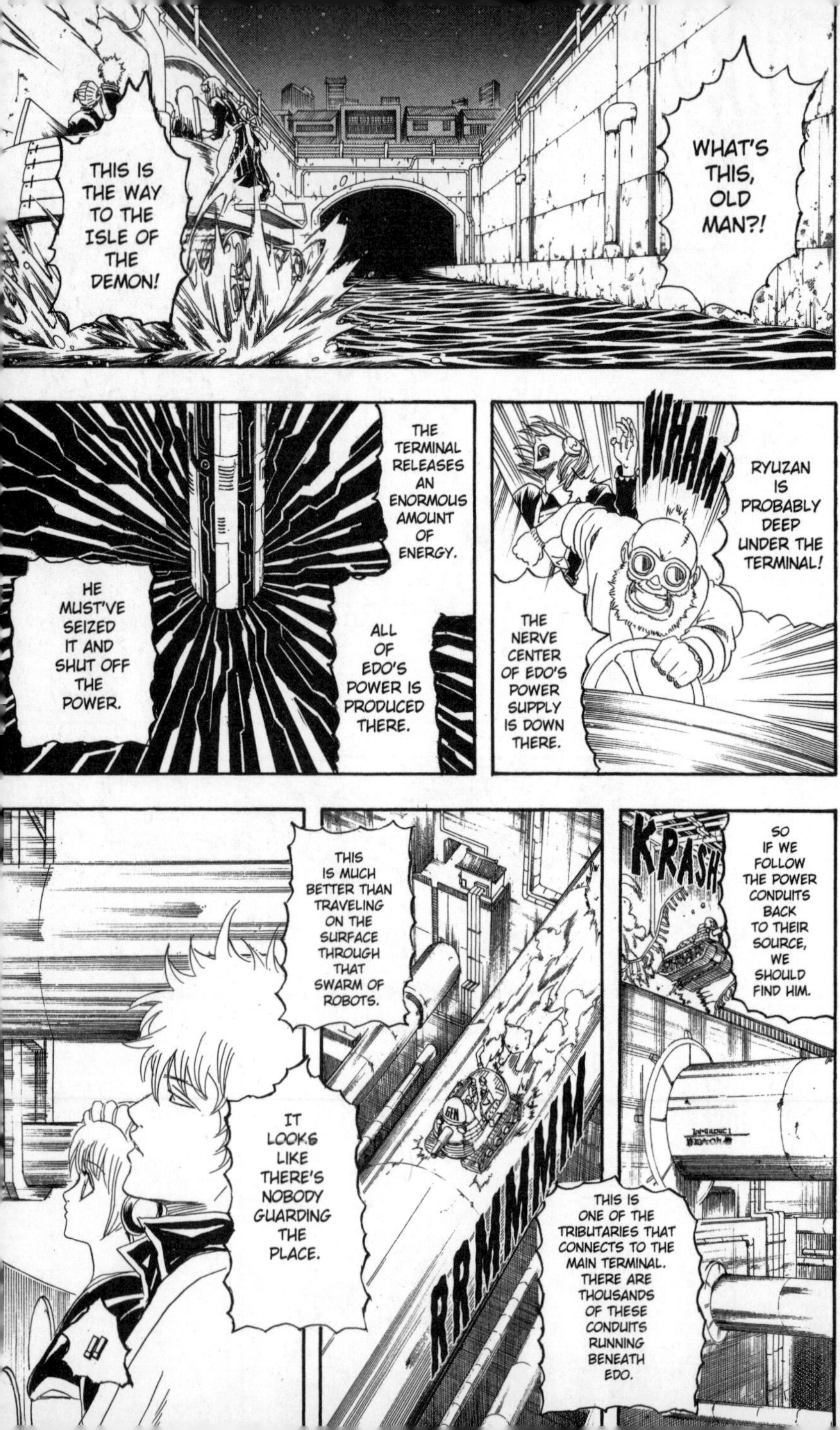
WHAT'S THIS, OLD MAN?!
THIS IS THE WAY TO THE ISLE OF THE DEMON!
WHAM
RYUZAN IS PROBABLY DEEP UNDER THE TERMINAL!
THE NERVE CENTER OF EDO'S POWER SUPPLY IS DOWN THERE.
THE TERMINAL RELEASES AN ENORMOUS AMOUNT OF ENERGY.
ALL OF EDO'S POWER IS PRODUCED THERE.
HE MUST'VE SEIZED IT AND SHUT OFF THE POWER.
KRASH
SO IF WE FOLLOW THE POWER CONDUITS BACK TO THEIR SOURCE, WE SHOULD FIND HIM.
THIS IS ONE OF THE TRIBUTARIES THAT CONNECTS TO THE MAIN TERMINAL. THERE ARE THOUSANDS OF THESE CONDUITS RUNNING BENEATH EDO.
THIS IS MUCH BETTER THAN TRAVELING ON THE SURFACE THROUGH THAT SWARM OF ROBOTS.
RRMMMMM
IT LOOKS LIKE THERE'S NOBODY GUARDING THE PLACE.

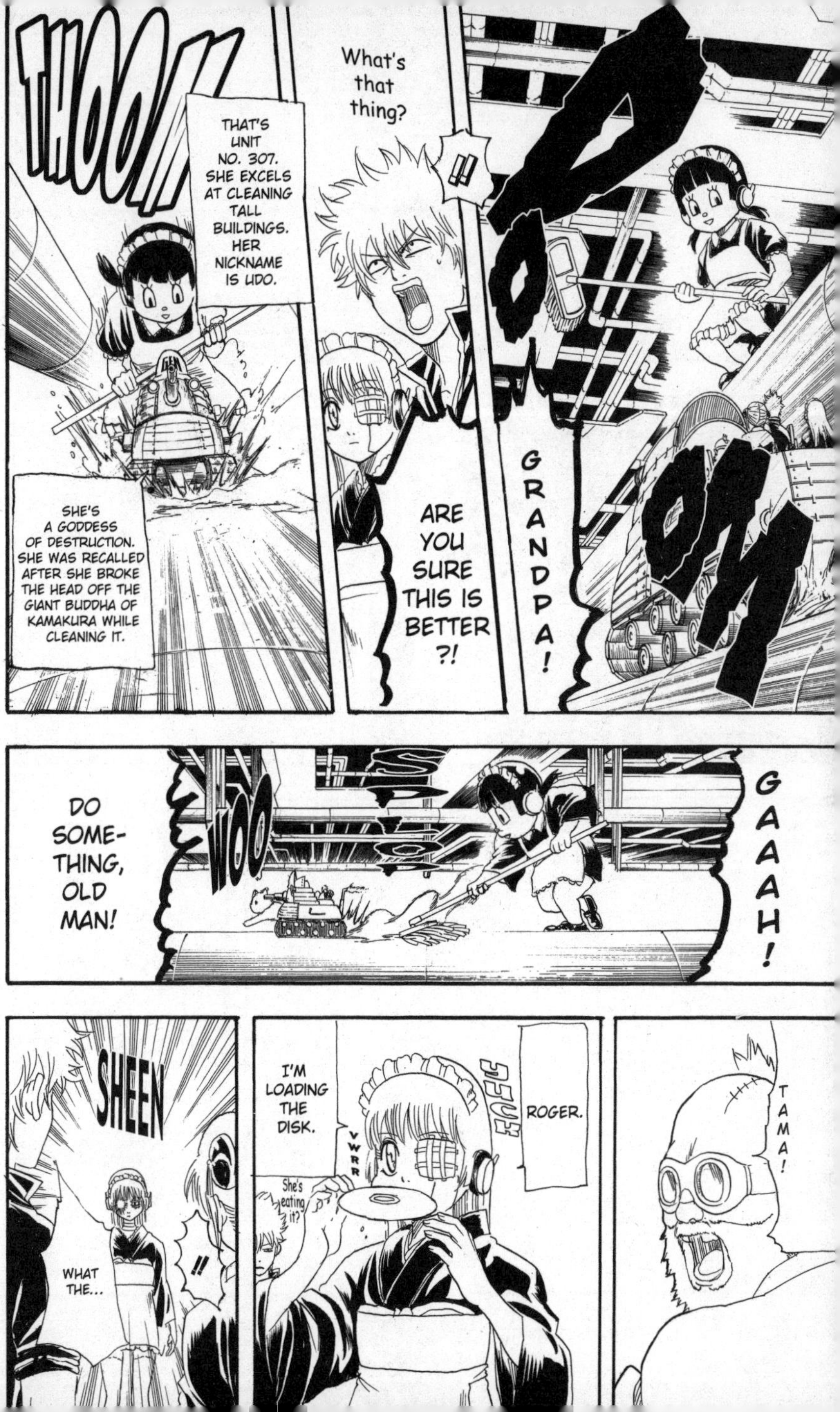
GRANDPA!
What's that thing?
!!
ARE YOU SURE THIS IS BETTER?!
THOOM
THAT'S UNIT NO. 307. SHE EXCELS AT CLEANING TALL BUILDINGS. HER NICKNAME IS UDO.
SHE'S A GODDESS OF DESTRUCTION. SHE WAS RECALLED AFTER SHE BROKE THE HEAD OFF THE GIANT BUDDHA OF KAMAKURA WHILE CLEANING IT.
GAAAAH!
WOO
DO SOME-THING, OLD MAN!
TAMA!
ROGER.
I'M LOADING THE DISK.
VWRR
She's eating it?
SHEEN
!!
WHAT THE...

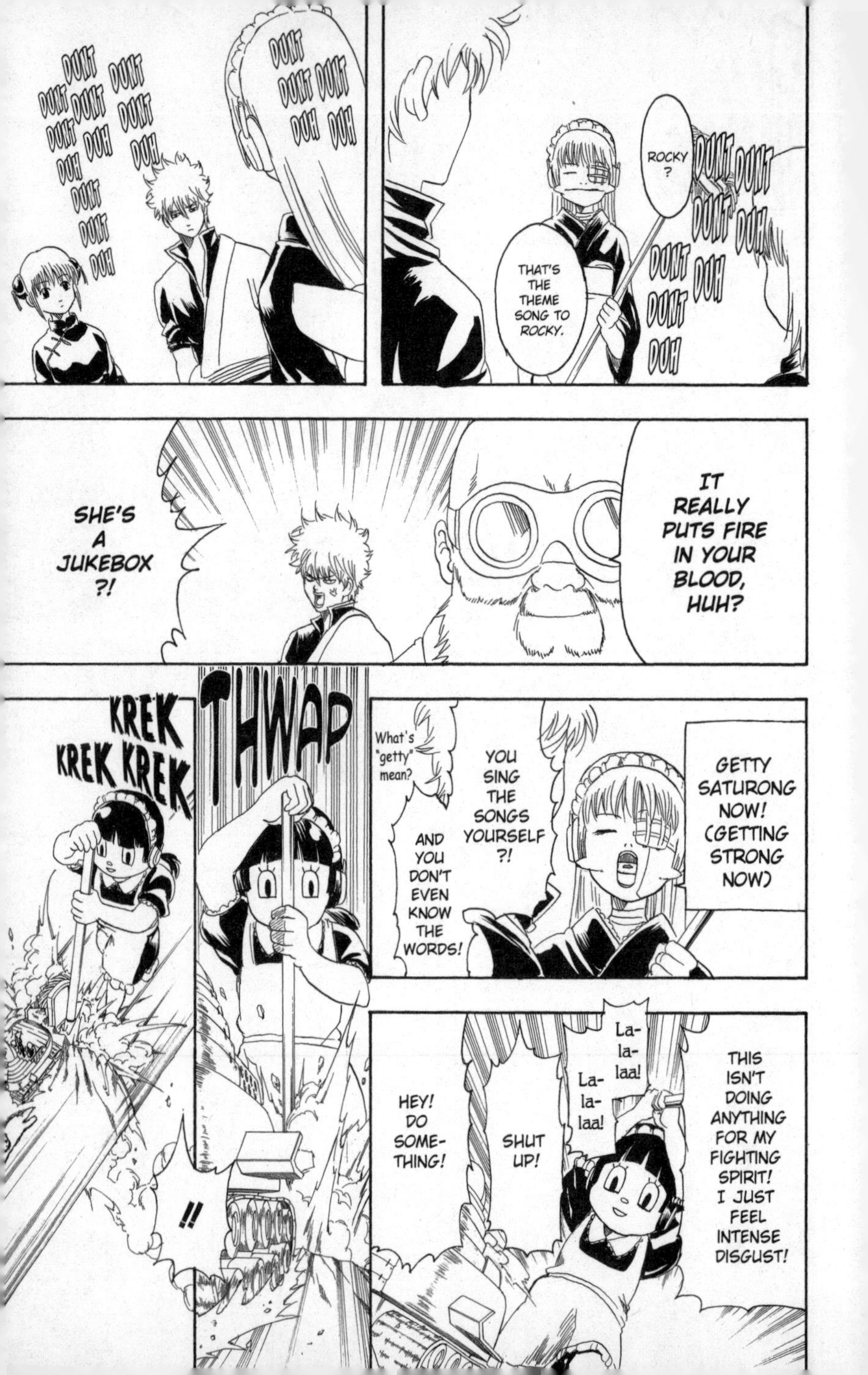
DUNT DUNT DUNT DUNT DUH DUNT DUNT DUH
ROCKY?
THAT'S THE THEME SONG TO ROCKY.
DUNT DUNT DUNT DUNT DUH DUH
DUNT DUNT DUNT DUNT DUH DUNT DUNT DUH
DUNT DUNT DUNT DUH DUNT DUNT DUH
IT REALLY PUTS FIRE IN YOUR BLOOD, HUH?
SHE'S A JUKEBOX?!
GETTY SATURONG NOW! (GETTING STRONG NOW)
YOU SING THE SONGS YOURSELF?!
AND YOU DON'T EVEN KNOW THE WORDS!
What's "getty" mean?
THIS ISN'T DOING ANYTHING FOR MY FIGHTING SPIRIT! I JUST FEEL INTENSE DISGUST!
La-la-laa!
La-la-laa!
SHUT UP!
HEY! DO SOMETHING!
THWAP
KREK KREK KREK
!!

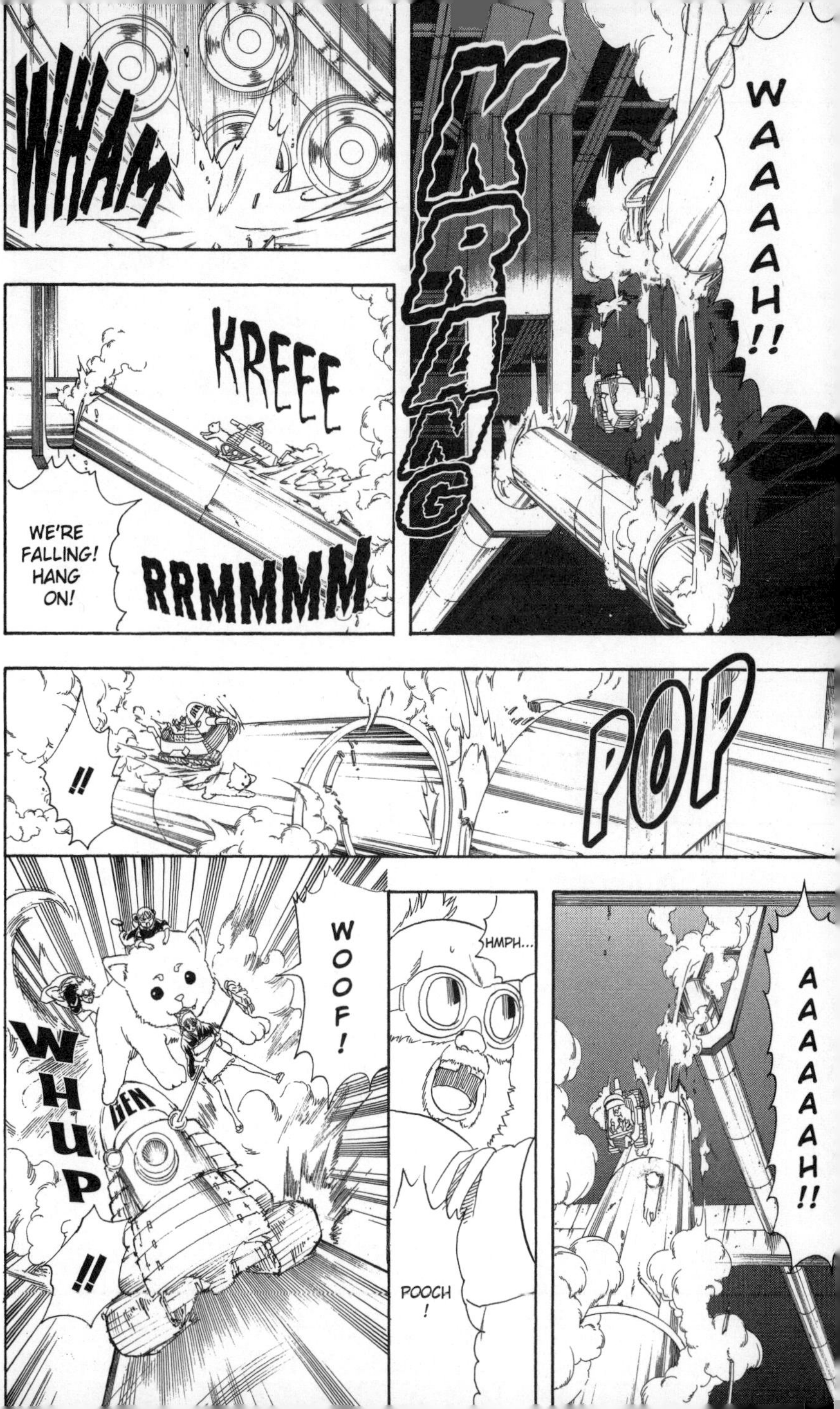
KRANG
WAAAAAH!!
WHAM
KREEE
WE'RE FALLING! HANG ON!
RRMMMM
POP
!!
AAAAAAAH!!
HMPH...
POOCH!
WOOF!
WHUP!!

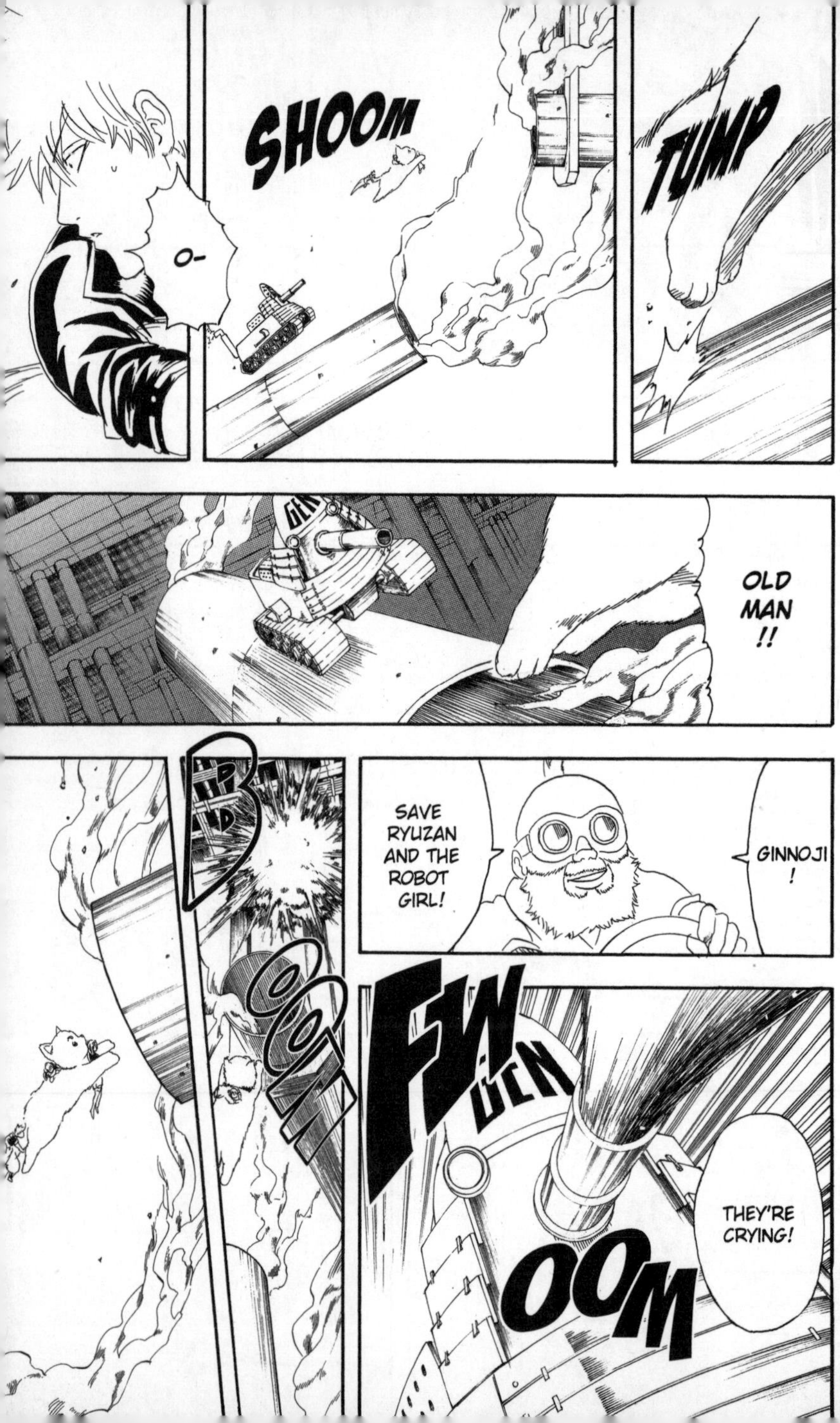
TUMP
SHOOM
O-
OLD MAN !!
GINNOJI !
SAVE RYUZAN AND THE ROBOT GIRL!
FWOOM
THEY'RE CRYING!
BOOOOM

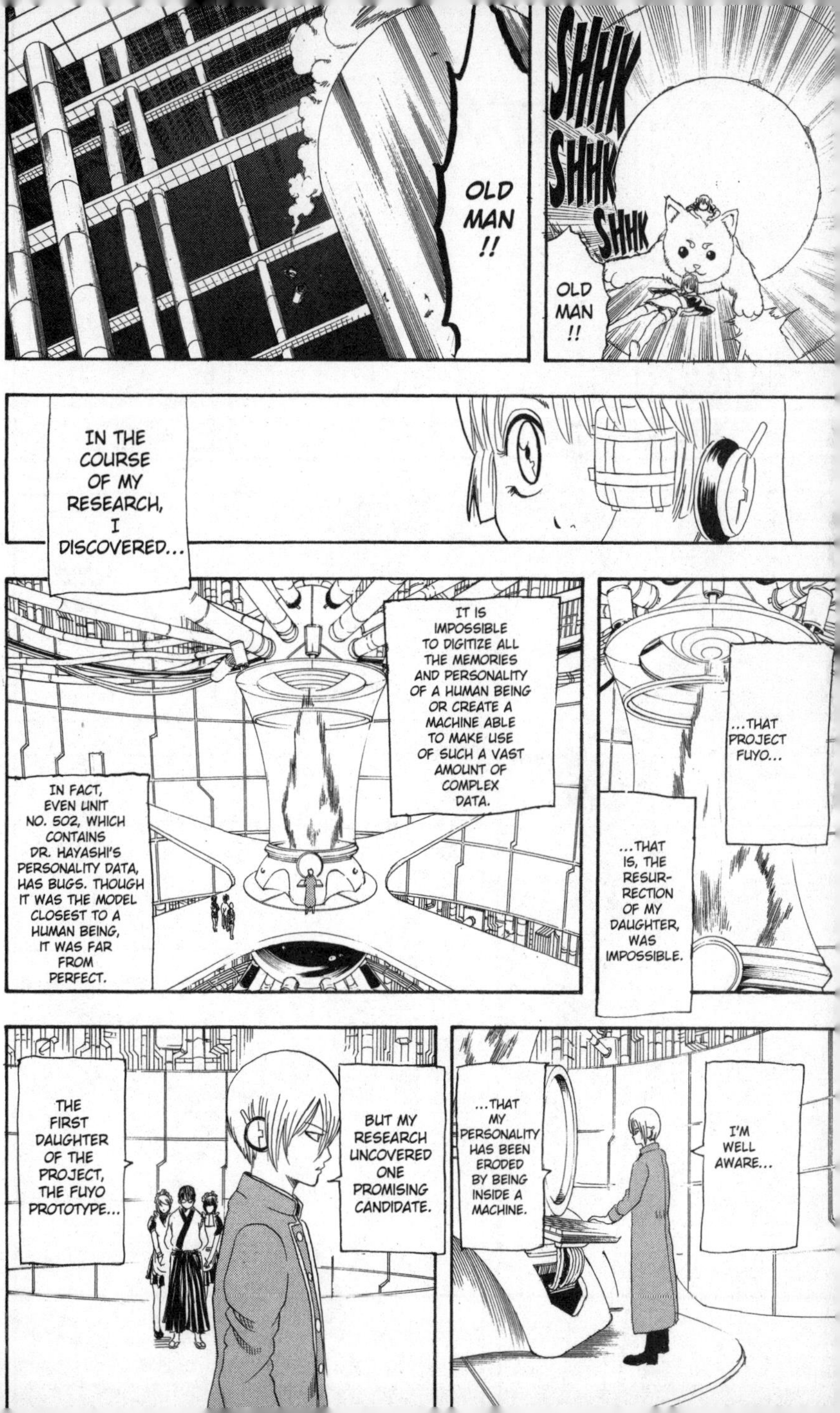
SHHK
SHHK
SHHK
OLD MAN !!
OLD MAN !!
IN THE COURSE OF MY RESEARCH, I DISCOVERED...
...THAT PROJECT FUYO...
...THAT IS, THE RESUR-RECTION OF MY DAUGHTER, WAS IMPOSSIBLE.
IT IS IMPOSSIBLE TO DIGITIZE ALL THE MEMORIES AND PERSONALITY OF A HUMAN BEING OR CREATE A MACHINE ABLE TO MAKE USE OF SUCH A VAST AMOUNT OF COMPLEX DATA.
IN FACT, EVEN UNIT NO. 502, WHICH CONTAINS DR. HAYASHI'S PERSONALITY DATA, HAS BUGS. THOUGH IT WAS THE MODEL CLOSEST TO A HUMAN BEING, IT WAS FAR FROM PERFECT.
I'M WELL AWARE...
...THAT MY PERSONALITY HAS BEEN ERODED BY BEING INSIDE A MACHINE.
BUT MY RESEARCH UNCOVERED ONE PROMISING CANDIDATE.
THE FIRST DAUGHTER OF THE PROJECT, THE FUYO PROTOTYPE...

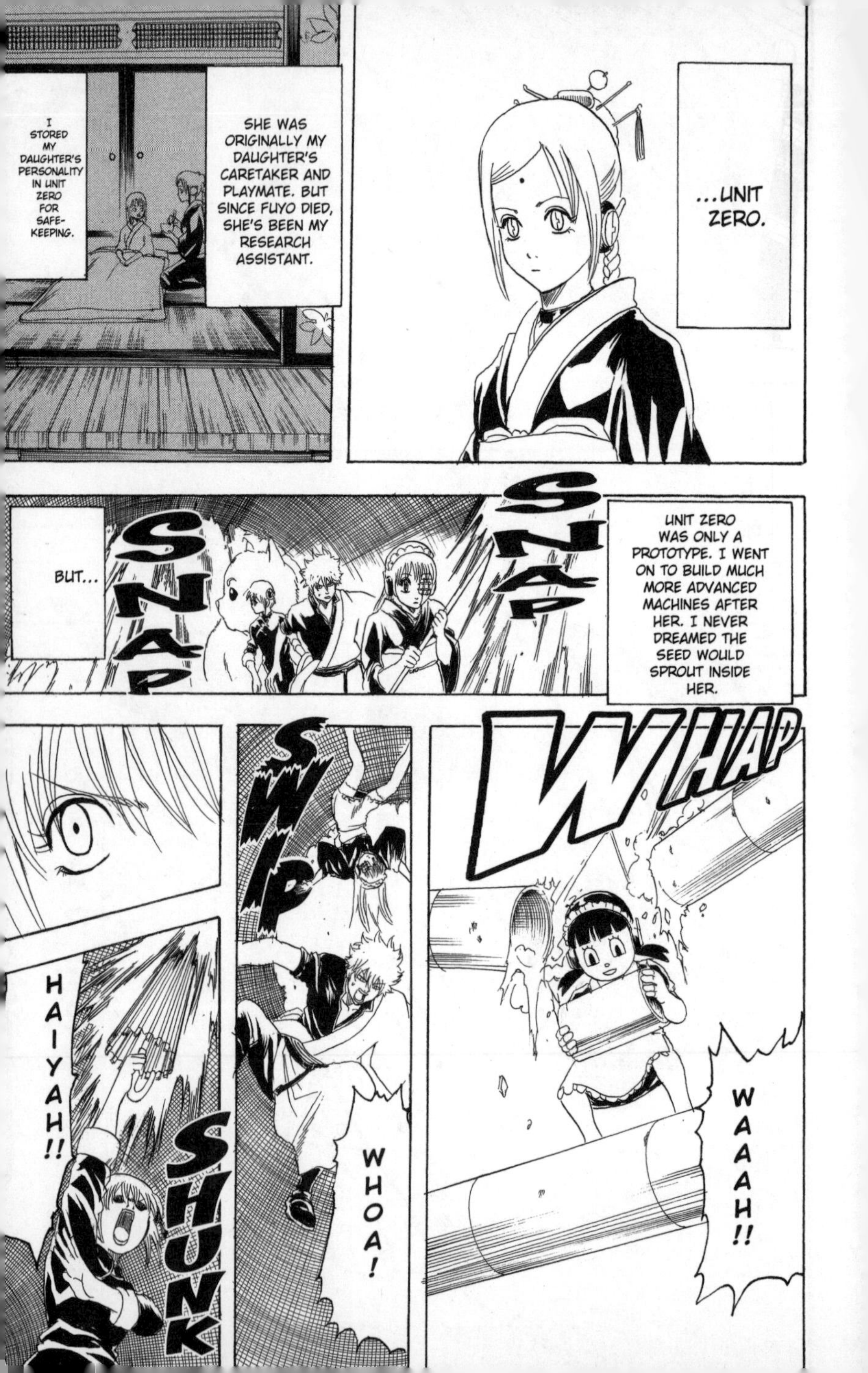
...UNIT ZERO.
SHE WAS ORIGINALLY MY DAUGHTER'S CARETAKER AND PLAYMATE. BUT SINCE FUYO DIED, SHE'S BEEN MY RESEARCH ASSISTANT.
I STORED MY DAUGHTER'S PERSONALITY IN UNIT ZERO FOR SAFE-KEEPING.
UNIT ZERO WAS ONLY A PROTOTYPE. I WENT ON TO BUILD MUCH MORE ADVANCED MACHINES AFTER HER. I NEVER DREAMED THE SEED WOULD SPROUT INSIDE HER.
SNAP
SNAP
BUT...
WHAP
WAAAAH!!
SWIP
WHOA!
HAIYAH!!
SHUNK

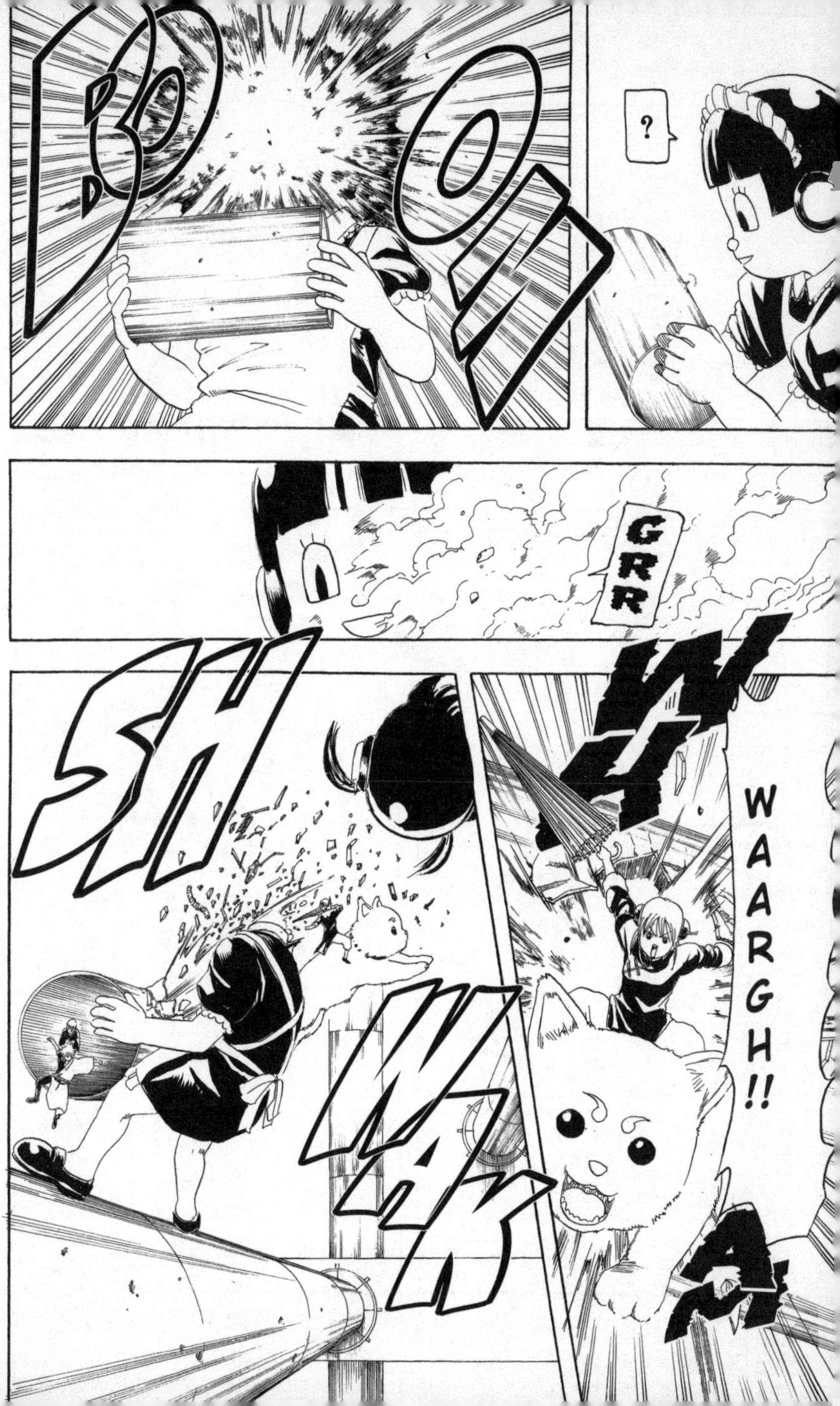
?
BOOM
GRR
WAARGH!!

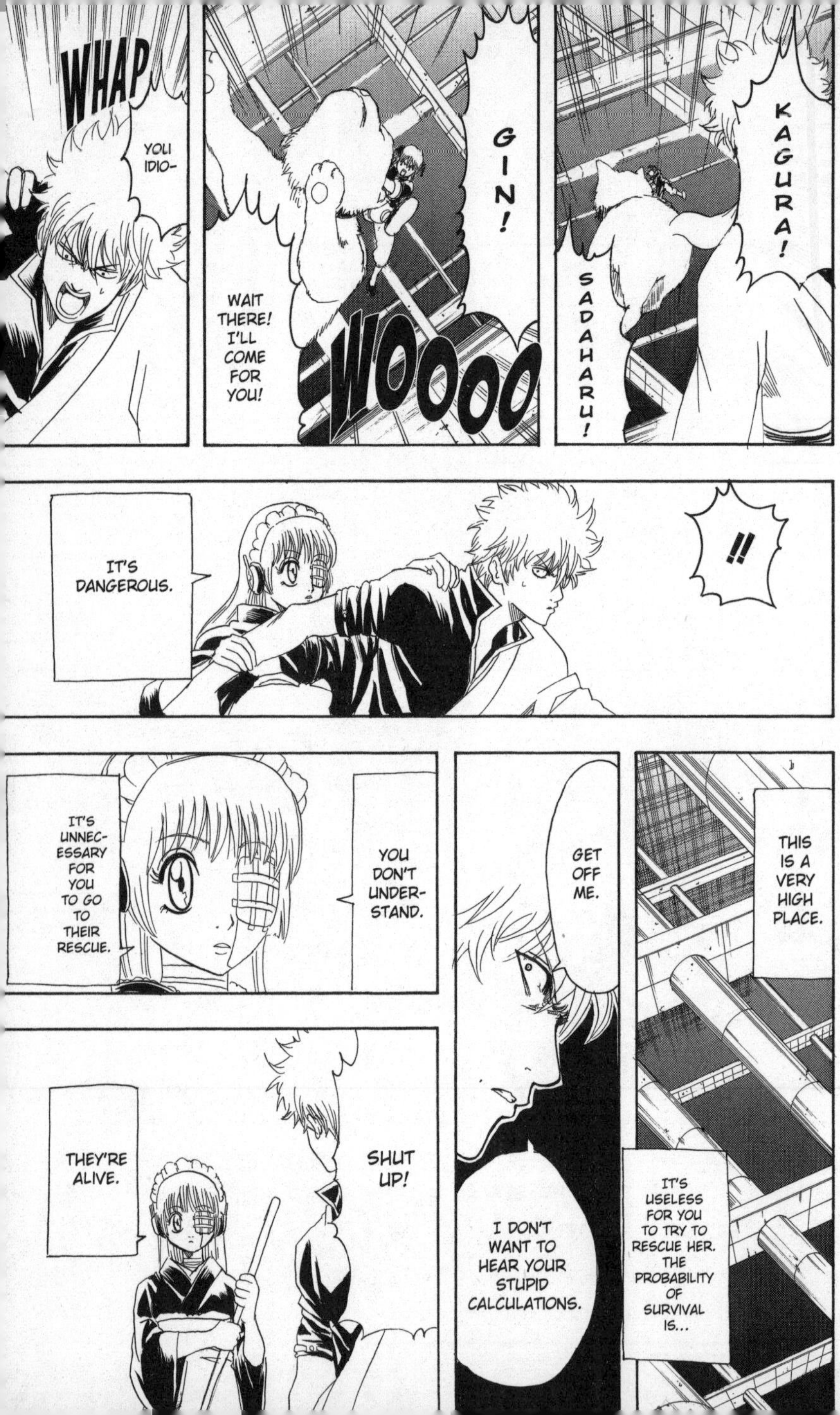
KAGURA!
SADAHARU!
GIN!
WAIT THERE! I'LL COME FOR YOU!
WOOOO
WHAP
YOU IDIO-
!!
IT'S DANGEROUS.
THIS IS A VERY HIGH PLACE.
IT'S USELESS FOR YOU TO TRY TO RESCUE HER. THE PROBABILITY OF SURVIVAL IS...
GET OFF ME.
I DON'T WANT TO HEAR YOUR STUPID CALCULATIONS.
YOU DON'T UNDER-STAND.
IT'S UNNEC-ESSARY FOR YOU TO GO TO THEIR RESCUE.
SHUT UP!
THEY'RE ALIVE.

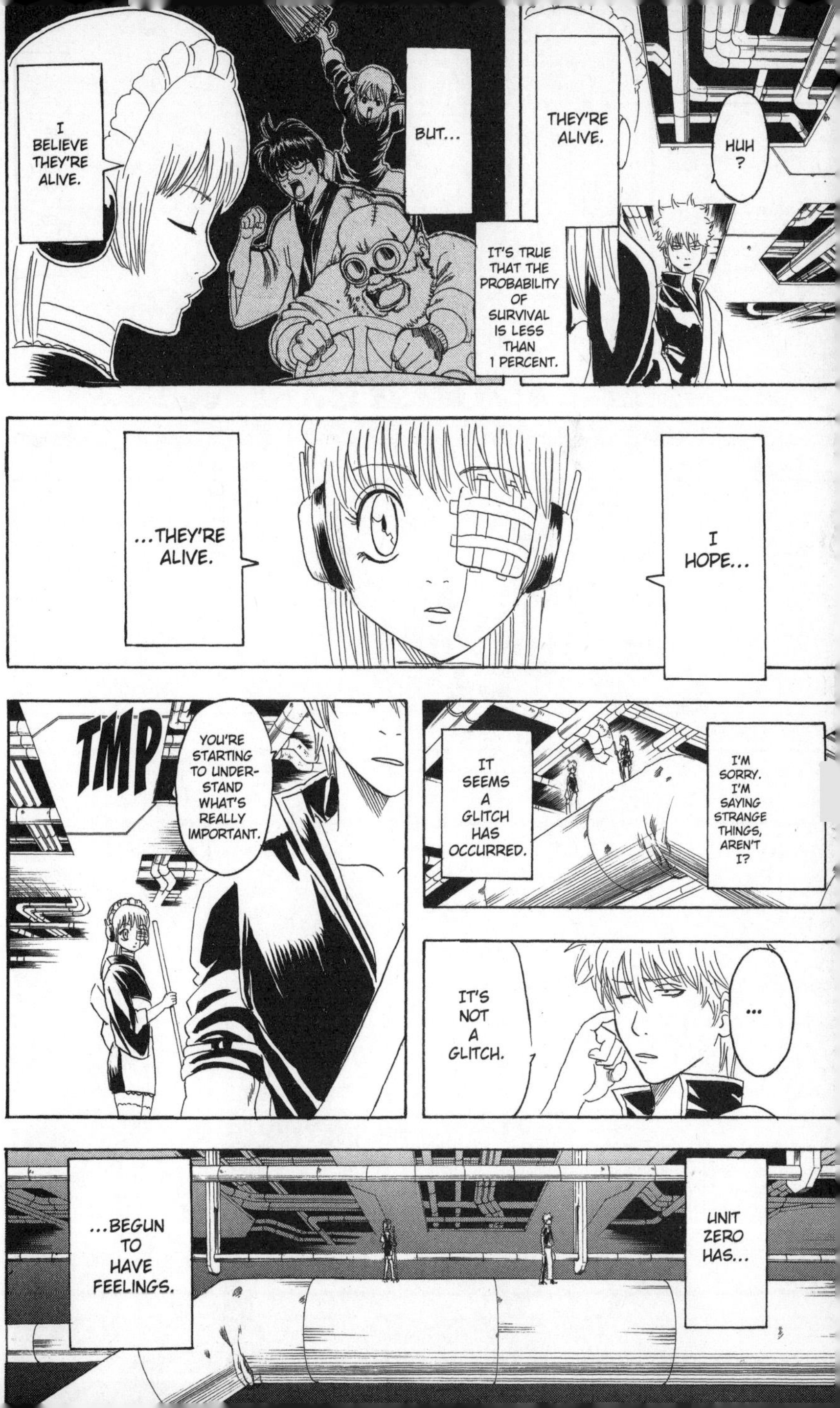
HUH?
THEY'RE ALIVE.
IT'S TRUE THAT THE PROBABILITY OF SURVIVAL IS LESS THAN 1 PERCENT.
BUT...
I BELIEVE THEY'RE ALIVE.
I HOPE...
...THEY'RE ALIVE.
I'M SORRY. I'M SAYING STRANGE THINGS, AREN'T I?
IT SEEMS A GLITCH HAS OCCURRED.
...
IT'S NOT A GLITCH.
YOU'RE STARTING TO UNDER-STAND WHAT'S REALLY IMPORTANT.
TMP
UNIT ZERO HAS...
...BEGUN TO HAVE FEELINGS.

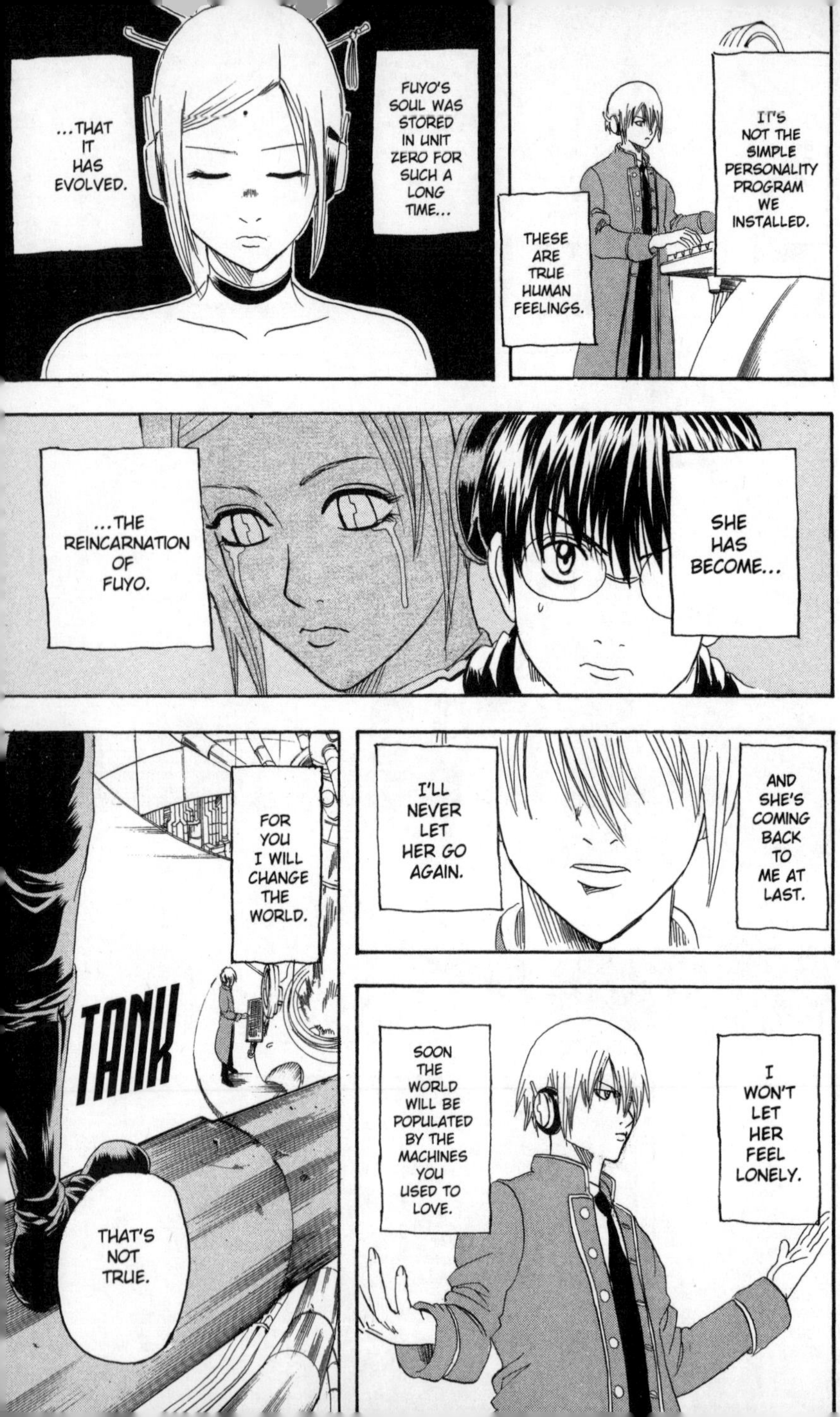
IT'S NOT THE SIMPLE PERSONALITY PROGRAM WE INSTALLED.
THESE ARE TRUE HUMAN FEELINGS.
FUYO'S SOUL WAS STORED IN UNIT ZERO FOR SUCH A LONG TIME...
...THAT IT HAS EVOLVED.
SHE HAS BECOME...
...THE REINCARNATION OF FUYO.
AND SHE'S COMING BACK TO ME AT LAST.
I'LL NEVER LET HER GO AGAIN.
I WON'T LET HER FEEL LONELY.
SOON THE WORLD WILL BE POPULATED BY THE MACHINES YOU USED TO LOVE.
FOR YOU I WILL CHANGE THE WORLD.
TANK
THAT'S NOT TRUE.

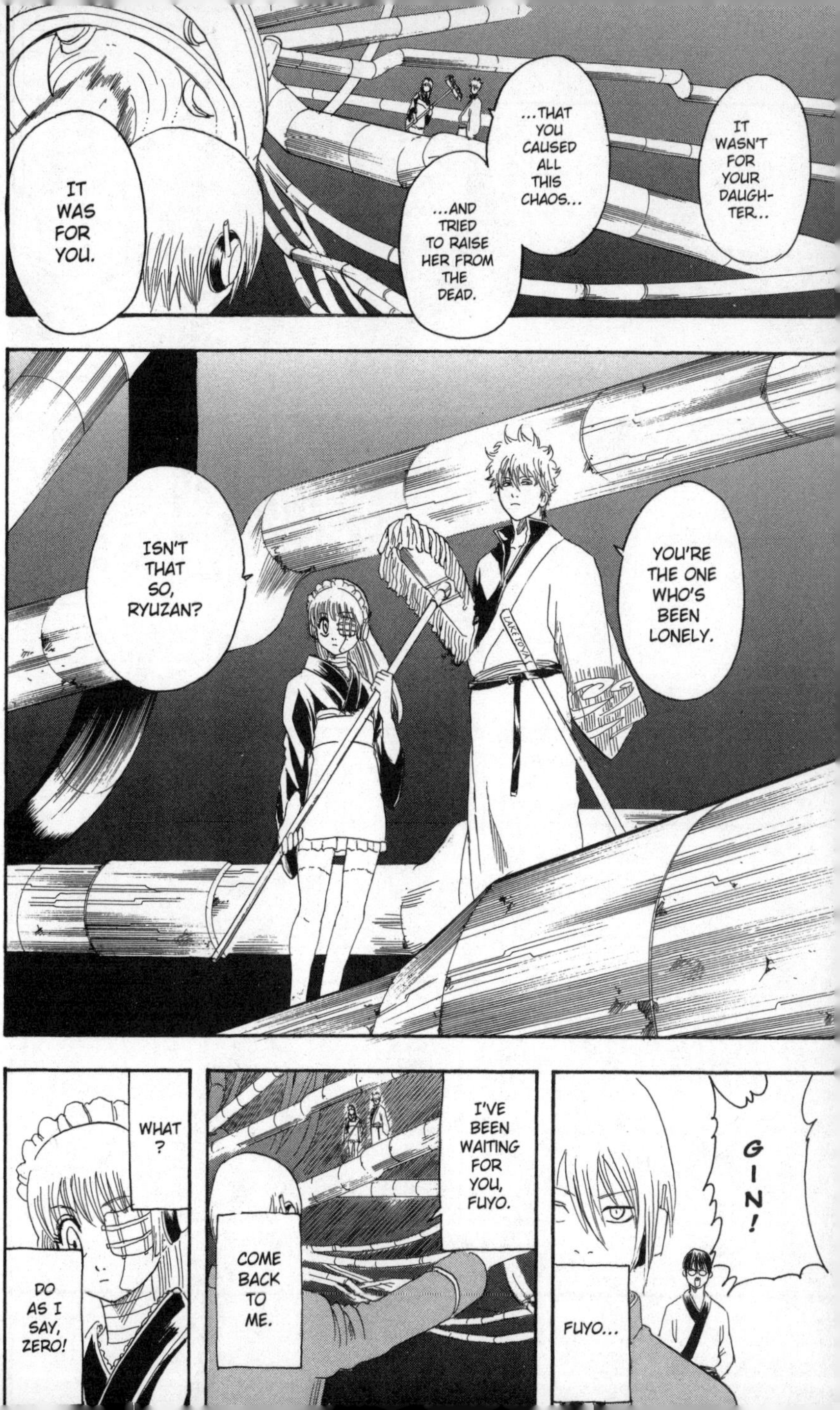
IT WASN'T FOR YOUR DAUGHTER...
...THAT YOU CAUSED ALL THIS CHAOS...
...AND TRIED TO RAISE HER FROM THE DEAD.
IT WAS FOR YOU.
YOU'RE THE ONE WHO'S BEEN LONELY.
LAKE TOYA
ISN'T THAT SO, RYUZAN?
GIN!
FUYO...
I'VE BEEN WAITING FOR YOU, FUYO.
COME BACK TO ME.
WHAT?
DO AS I SAY, ZERO!

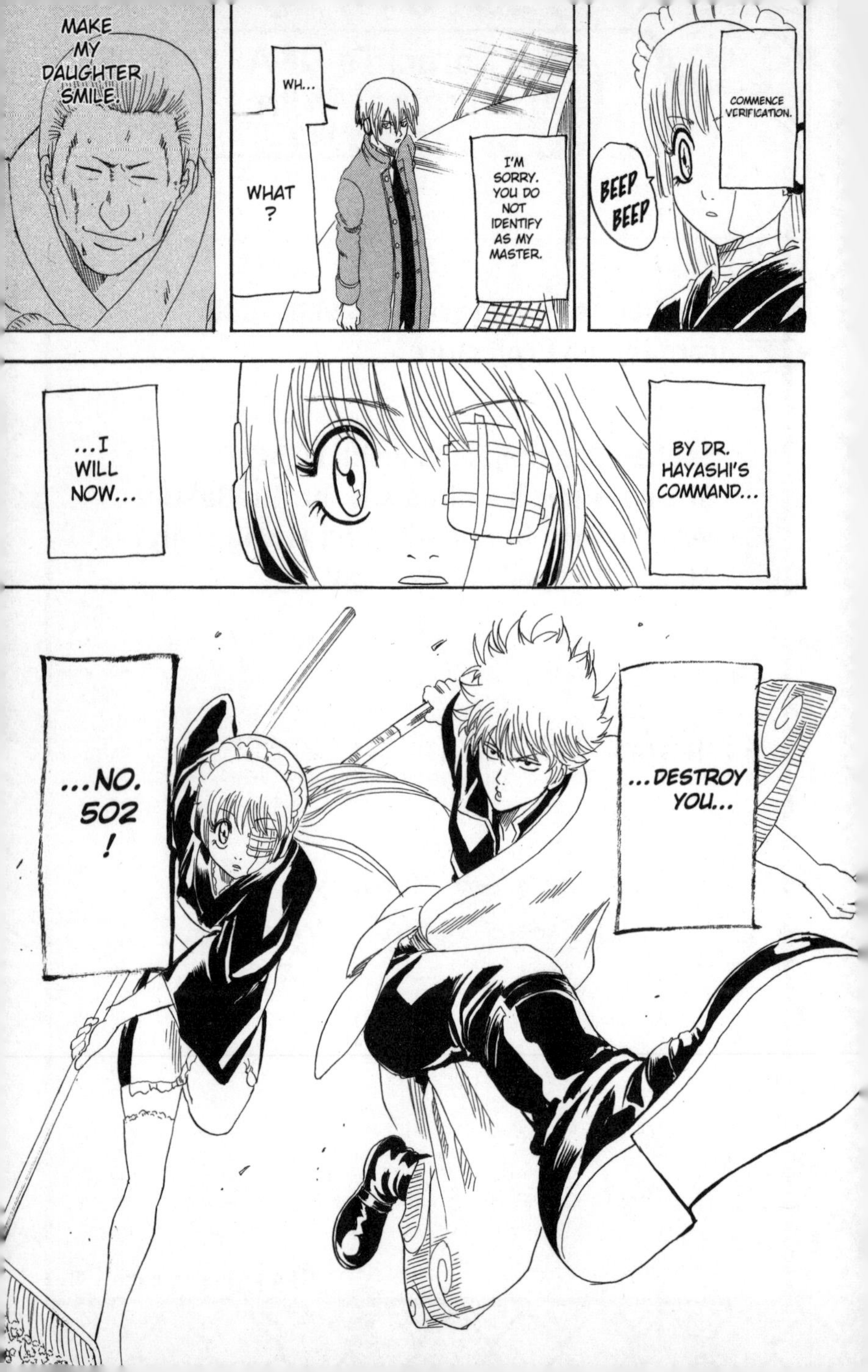
COMMENCE VERIFICATION.
BEEP BEEP
I'M SORRY. YOU DO NOT IDENTIFY AS MY MASTER.
WH...
WHAT ?
MAKE MY DAUGHTER SMILE.
BY DR. HAYASHI'S COMMAND...
...I WILL NOW...
...DESTROY YOU...
...NO. 502 !

Sorachi's Q&A
Hanging with the Readers #52

<Question from Mayoraa & Sweet Tooth Samurai from Hyogo Prefecture>

Sachan is a ninja assassin, right?
She says she's a ninja spy for the Bakufu
government, but how strong is she realy?
Also, did I spell "realy" right?

<Answer>

You spelled it wrong.
Sachan is really strong.

(Q&A #53 is on page 130)

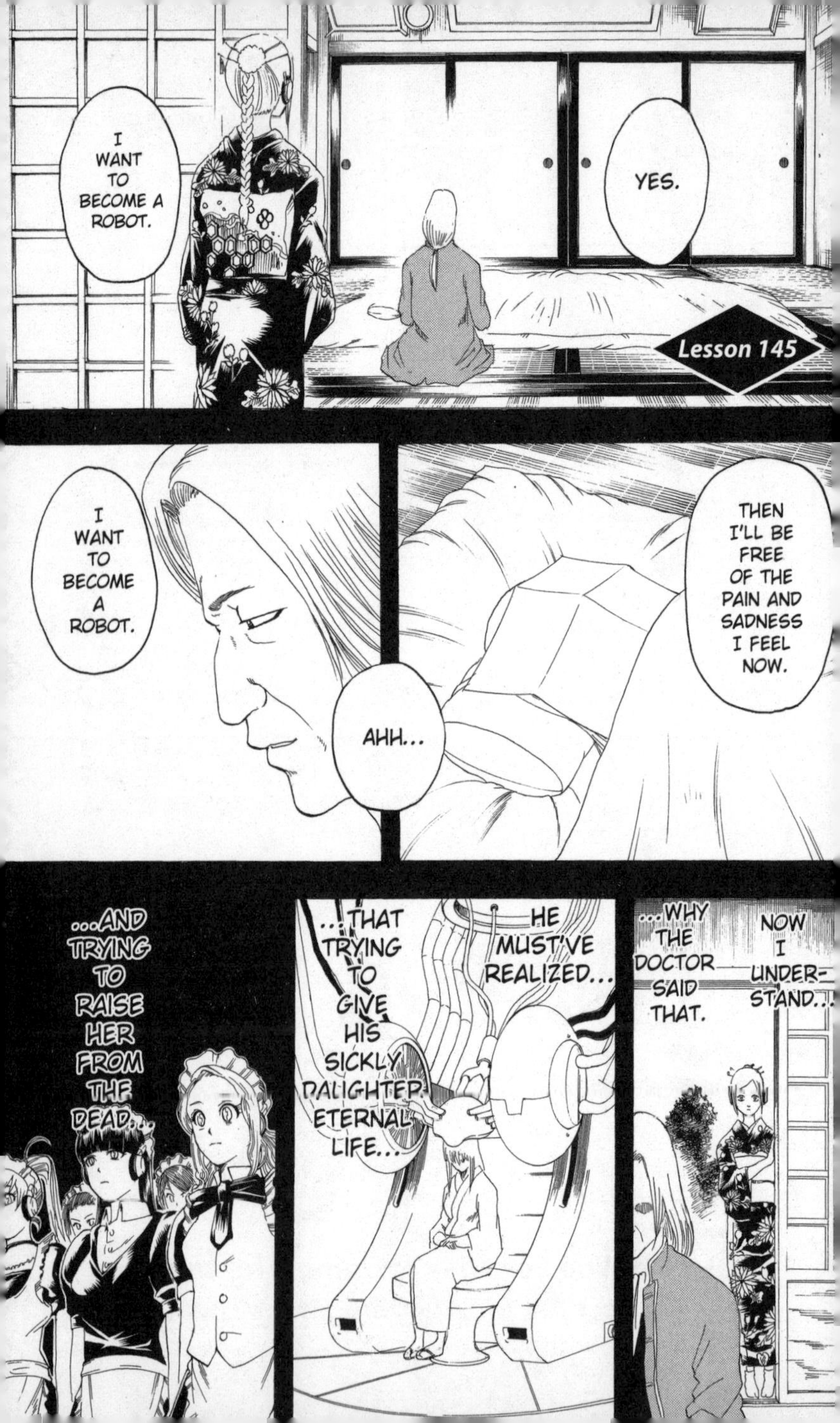
YES.
I WANT TO BECOME A ROBOT.
Lesson 145
THEN I'LL BE FREE OF THE PAIN AND SADNESS I FEEL NOW.
I WANT TO BECOME A ROBOT.
AHH...
NOW I UNDER-STAND...
...WHY THE DOCTOR SAID THAT.
HE MUST'VE REALIZED...
...THAT TRYING TO GIVE HIS SICKLY DAUGHTER ETERNAL LIFE...
...AND TRYING TO RAISE HER FROM THE DEAD...

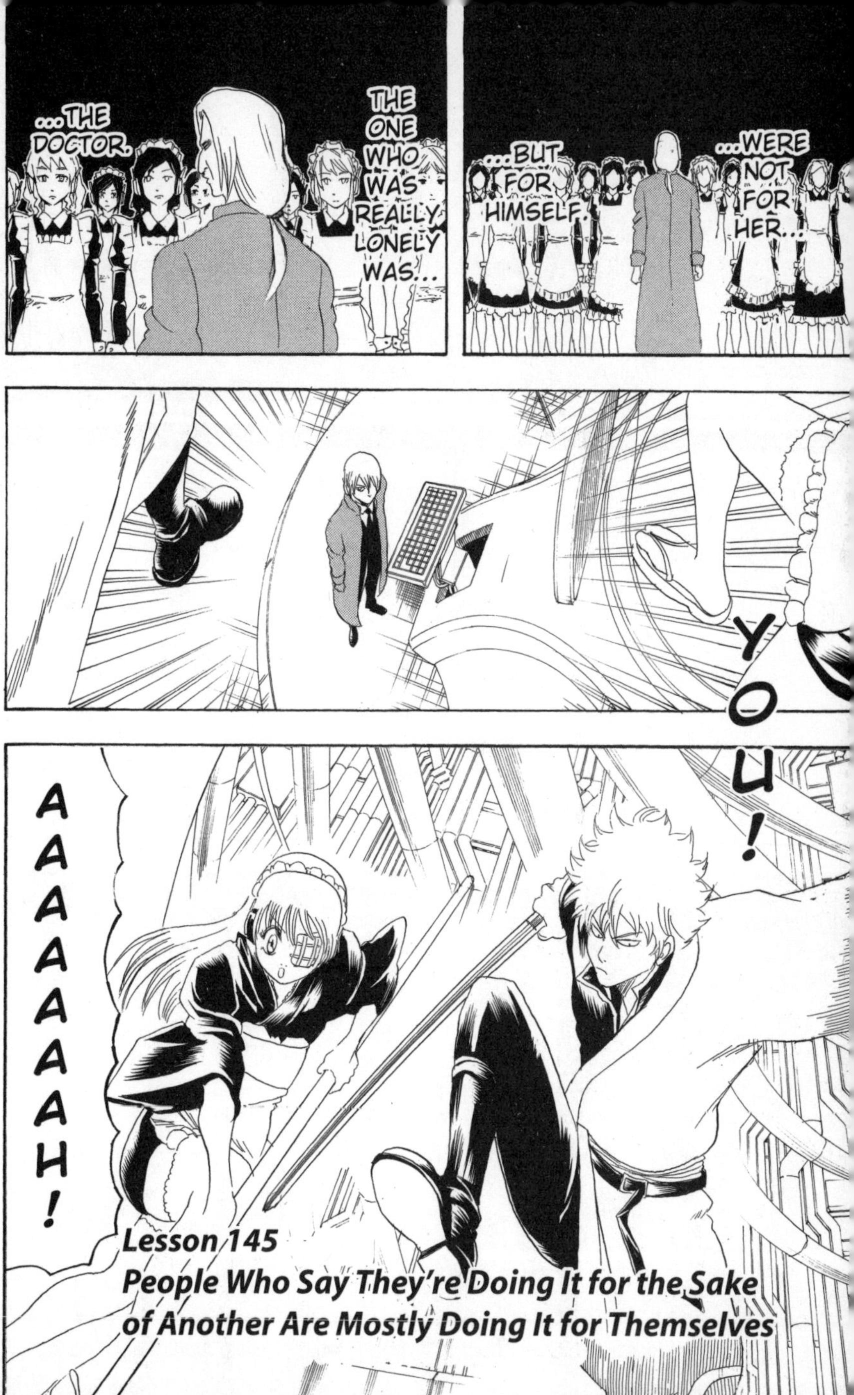
...WERE NOT FOR HER...
...BUT FOR HIMSELF.
THE ONE WHO WAS REALLY LONELY WAS...
...THE DOCTOR.
YOU!
AAAAAAAAAH!

Lesson 145
People Who Say They're Doing It for the Sake of Another Are Mostly Doing It for Themselves

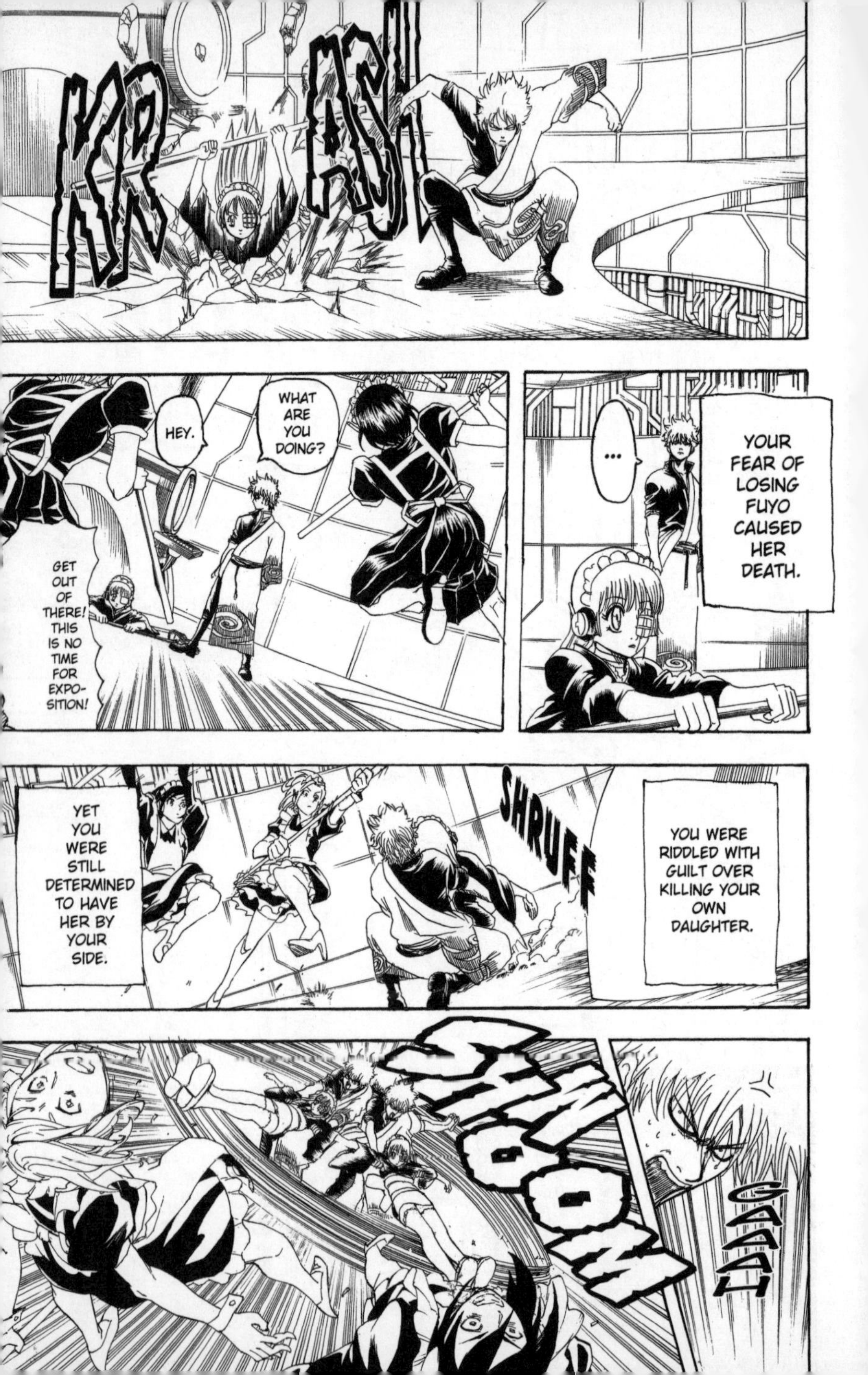
KRASH
...
YOUR FEAR OF LOSING FUYO CAUSED HER DEATH.
WHAT ARE YOU DOING?
HEY.
GET OUT OF THERE! THIS IS NO TIME FOR EXPOSITION!
YOU WERE RIDDLED WITH GUILT OVER KILLING YOUR OWN DAUGHTER.
SHRUFF
YET YOU WERE STILL DETERMINED TO HAVE HER BY YOUR SIDE.
GAAAH
SHWOOM

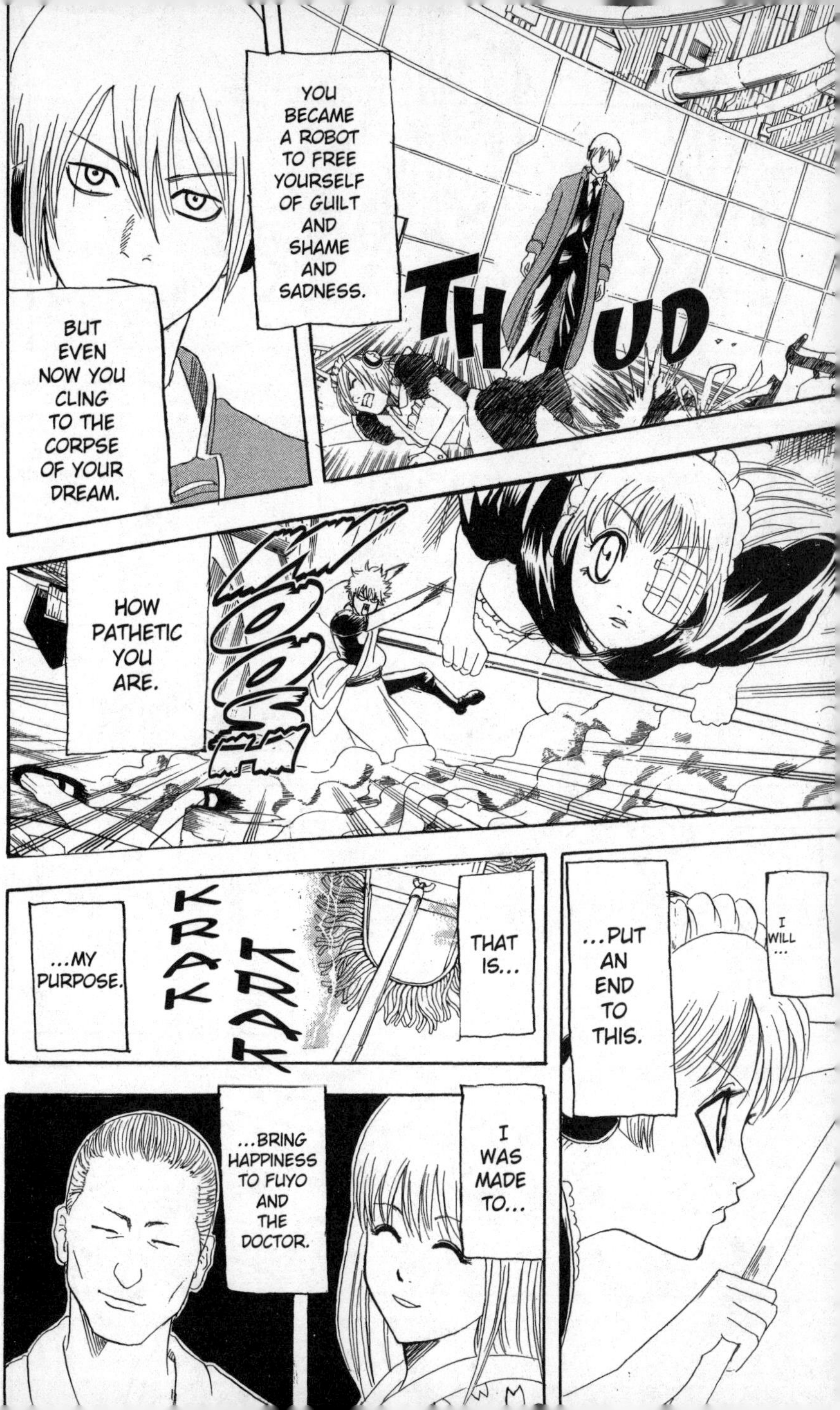
THUD
YOU BECAME A ROBOT TO FREE YOURSELF OF GUILT AND SHAME AND SADNESS.
BUT EVEN NOW YOU CLING TO THE CORPSE OF YOUR DREAM.
HOW PATHETIC YOU ARE.
WHOOSH
I WILL...
...PUT AN END TO THIS.
THAT IS...
KRAK KRAK
...MY PURPOSE.
I WAS MADE TO...
...BRING HAPPINESS TO FUYO AND THE DOCTOR.

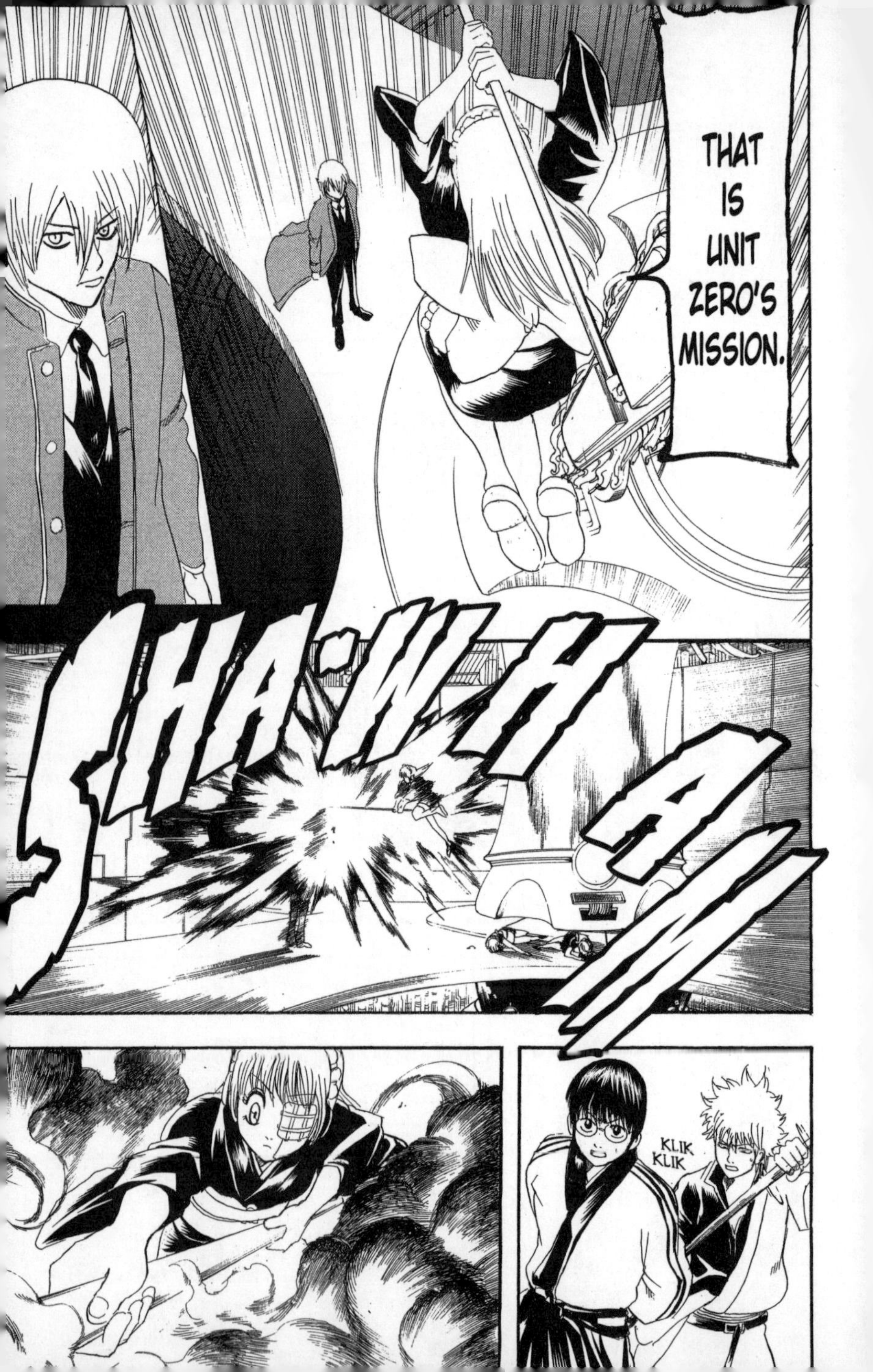
THAT IS UNIT ZERO'S MISSION.
SHA-WHAA!!
KLIK KLIK

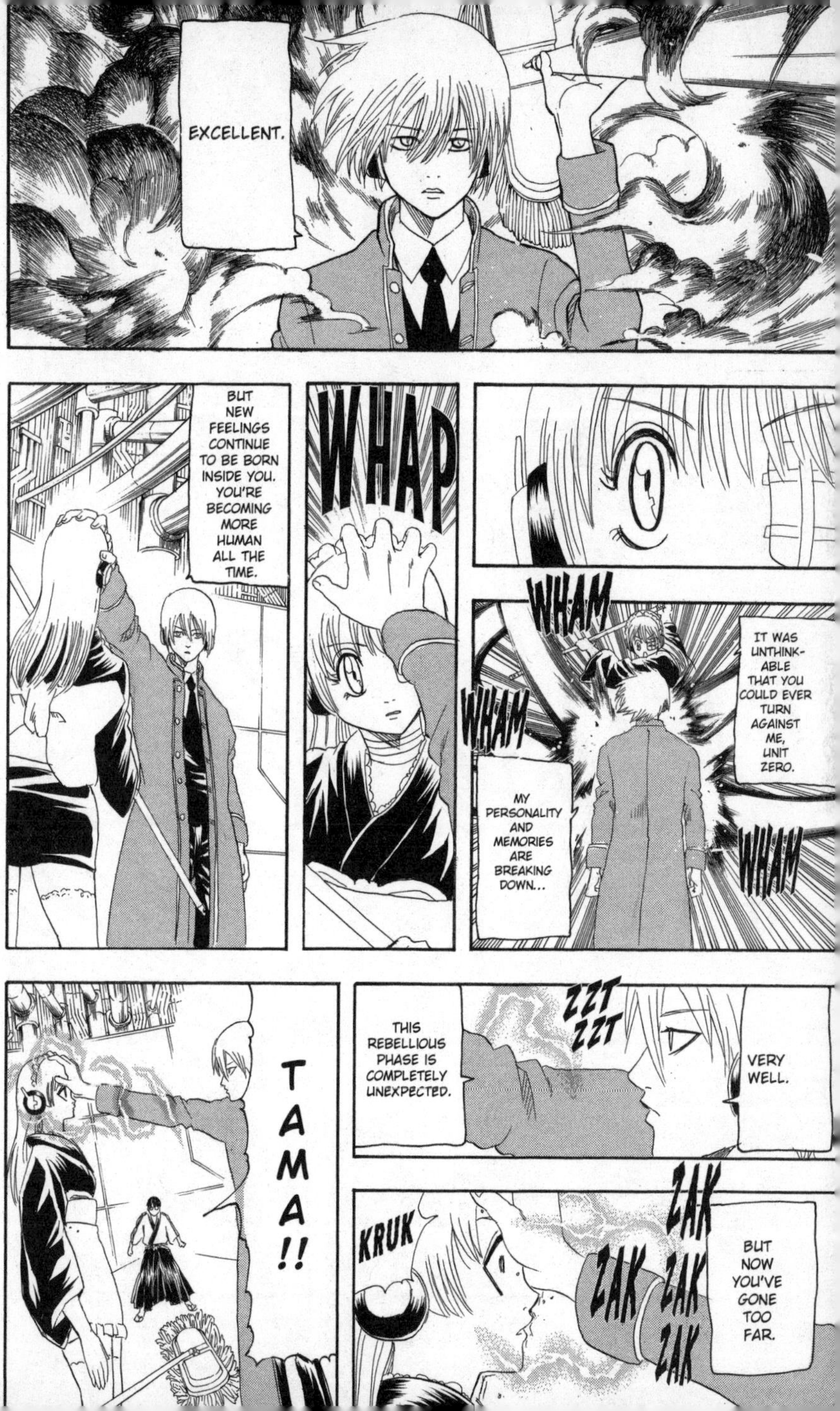
EXCELLENT.
WHAM
WHAM
IT WAS UNTHINKABLE THAT YOU COULD EVER TURN AGAINST ME, UNIT ZERO.
MY PERSONALITY AND MEMORIES ARE BREAKING DOWN...
WHAM
WHAP
BUT NEW FEELINGS CONTINUE TO BE BORN INSIDE YOU. YOU'RE BECOMING MORE HUMAN ALL THE TIME.
ZZT ZZT
VERY WELL.
THIS REBELLIOUS PHASE IS COMPLETELY UNEXPECTED.
ZAK ZAK ZAK ZAK ZAK
BUT NOW YOU'VE GONE TOO FAR.
KRUK
TAMA!!

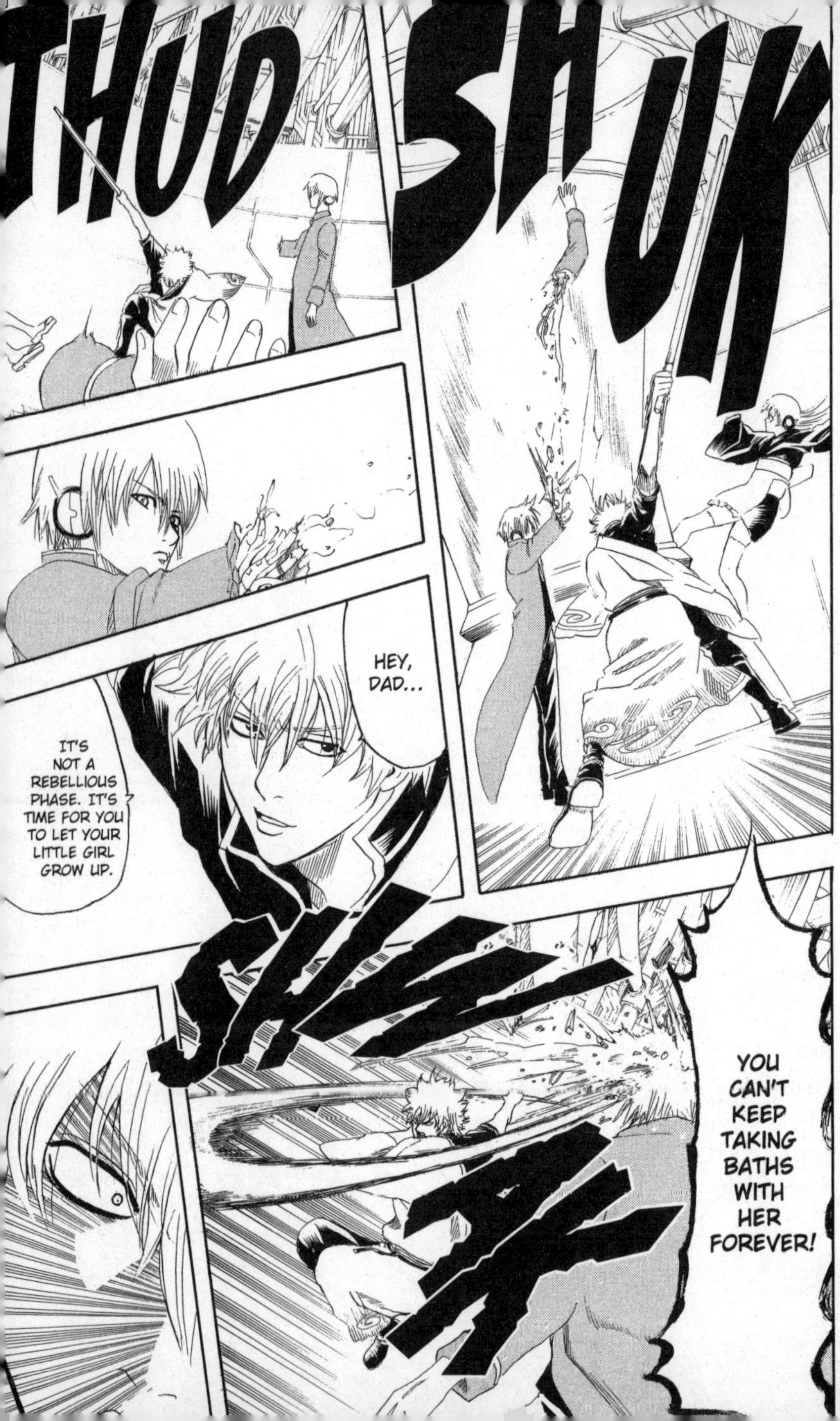
SHUK
THUD
HEY, DAD...
IT'S NOT A REBELLIOUS PHASE. IT'S TIME FOR YOU TO LET YOUR LITTLE GIRL GROW UP.
YOU CAN'T KEEP TAKING BATHS WITH HER FOREVER!
SHW

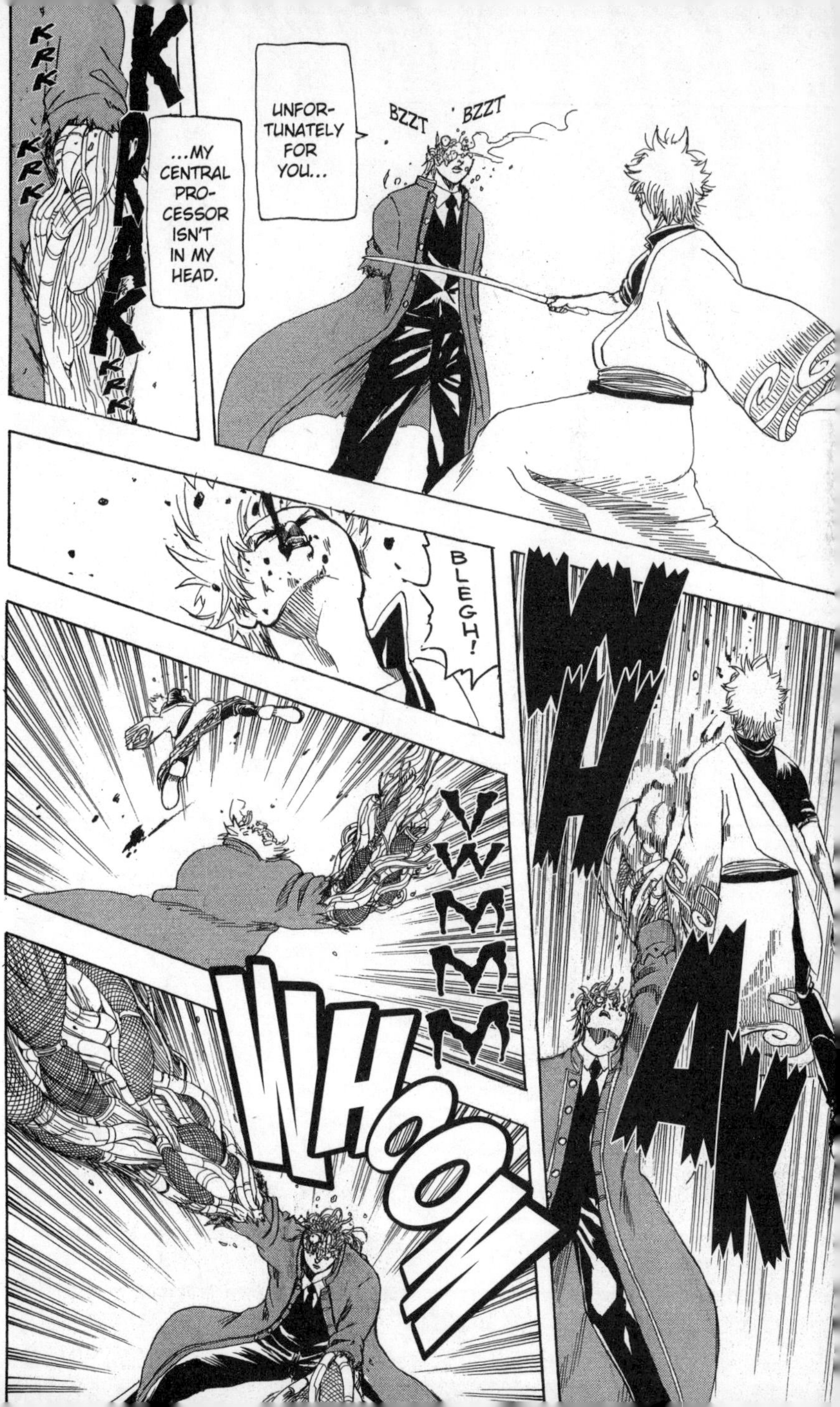
BZZT
BZZT
UNFOR-TUNATELY FOR YOU...
...MY CENTRAL PRO-CESSOR ISN'T IN MY HEAD.
KRAK
KRK KRK
KRK KRK
WHAK
BLEGH!
VWMMM
WHOOOM

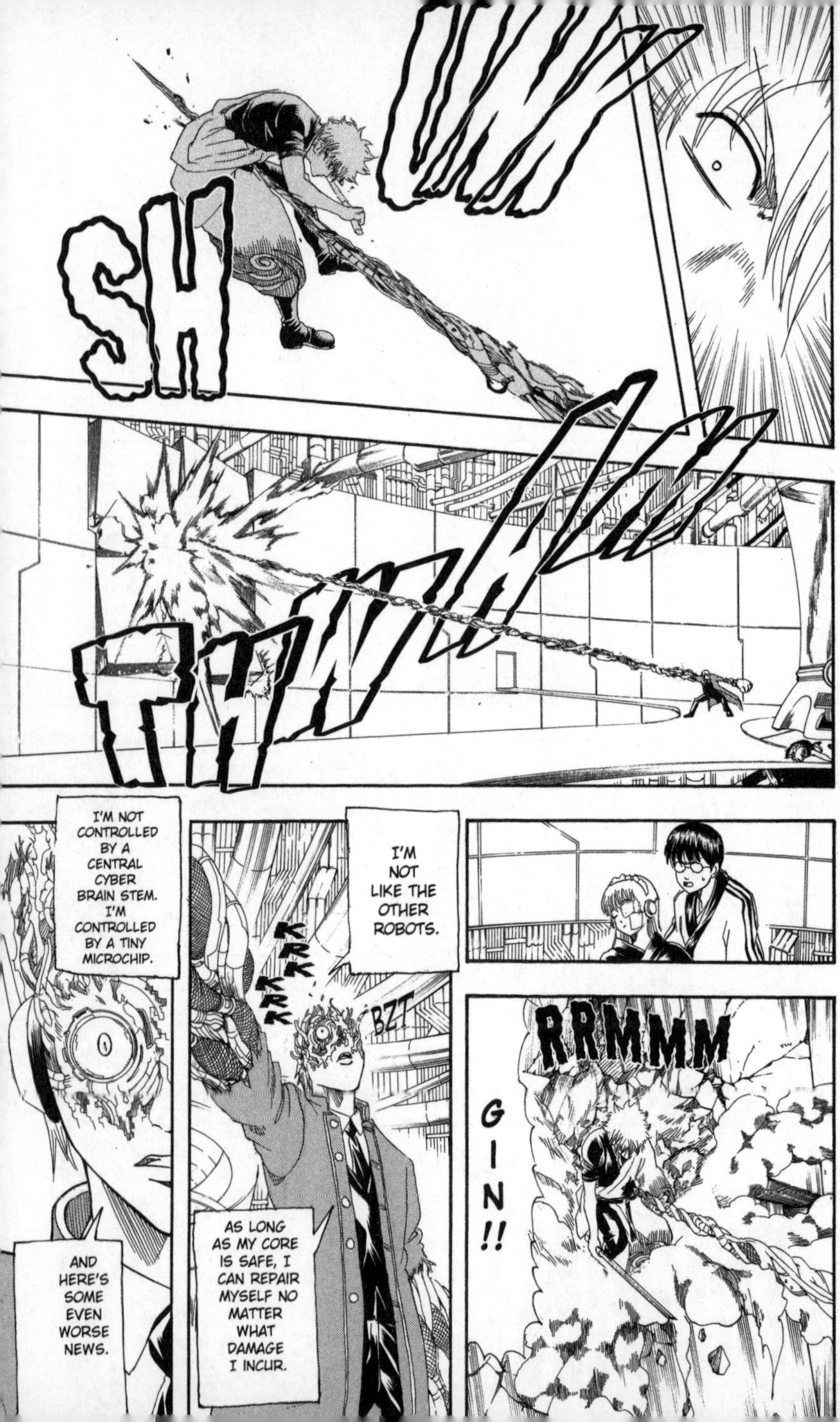
SH
RRMMM
GIN!!
I'M NOT LIKE THE OTHER ROBOTS.
KRK KRK KRK
BZT
AS LONG AS MY CORE IS SAFE, I CAN REPAIR MYSELF NO MATTER WHAT DAMAGE I INCUR.
I'M NOT CONTROLLED BY A CENTRAL CYBER BRAIN STEM. I'M CONTROLLED BY A TINY MICROCHIP.
AND HERE'S SOME EVEN WORSE NEWS.

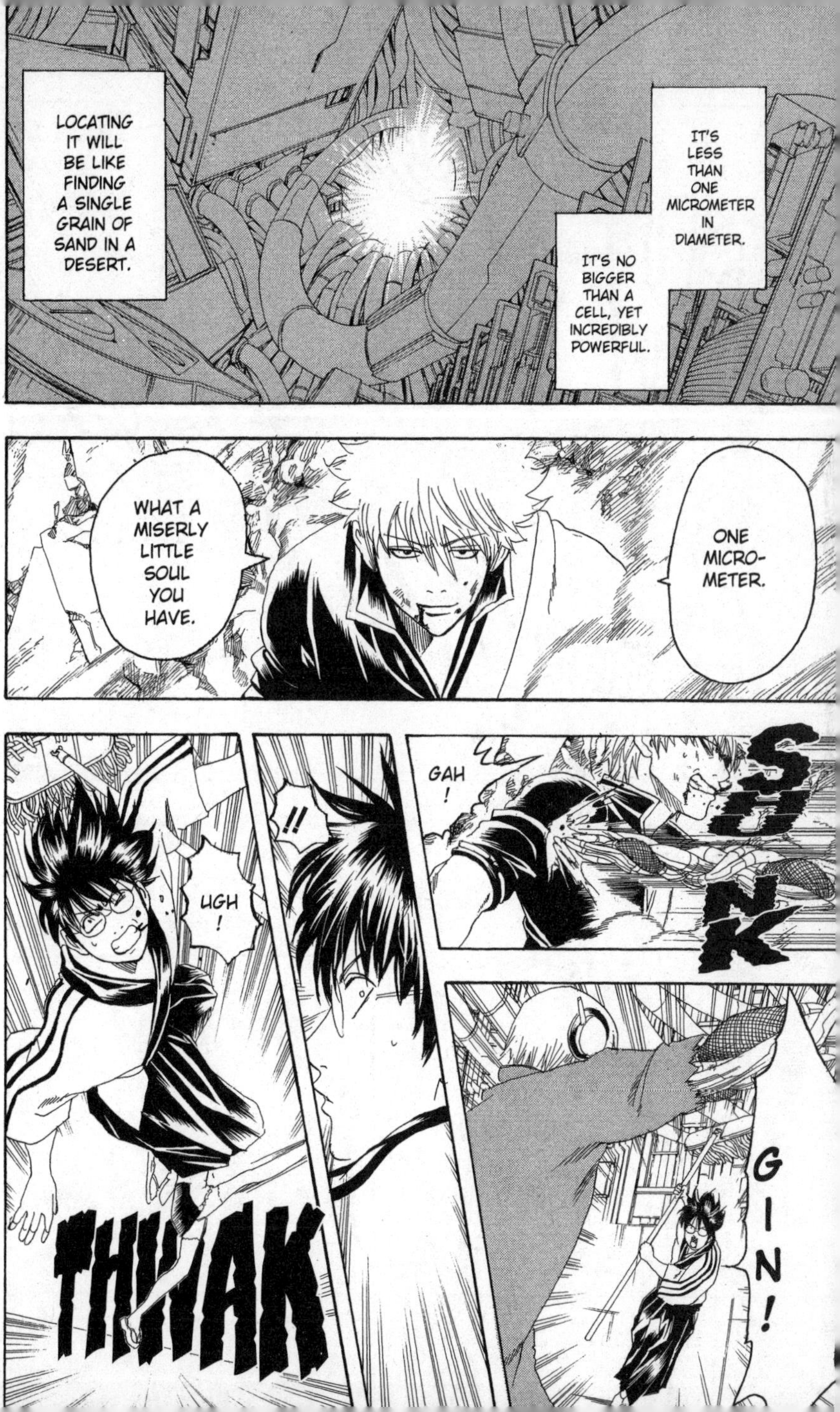
IT'S LESS THAN ONE MICROMETER IN DIAMETER.
IT'S NO BIGGER THAN A CELL, YET INCREDIBLY POWERFUL.
LOCATING IT WILL BE LIKE FINDING A SINGLE GRAIN OF SAND IN A DESERT.
ONE MICRO-METER.
WHAT A MISERLY LITTLE SOUL YOU HAVE.
SUNK
GAH!
GIN!
!!
UGH!
THWAK

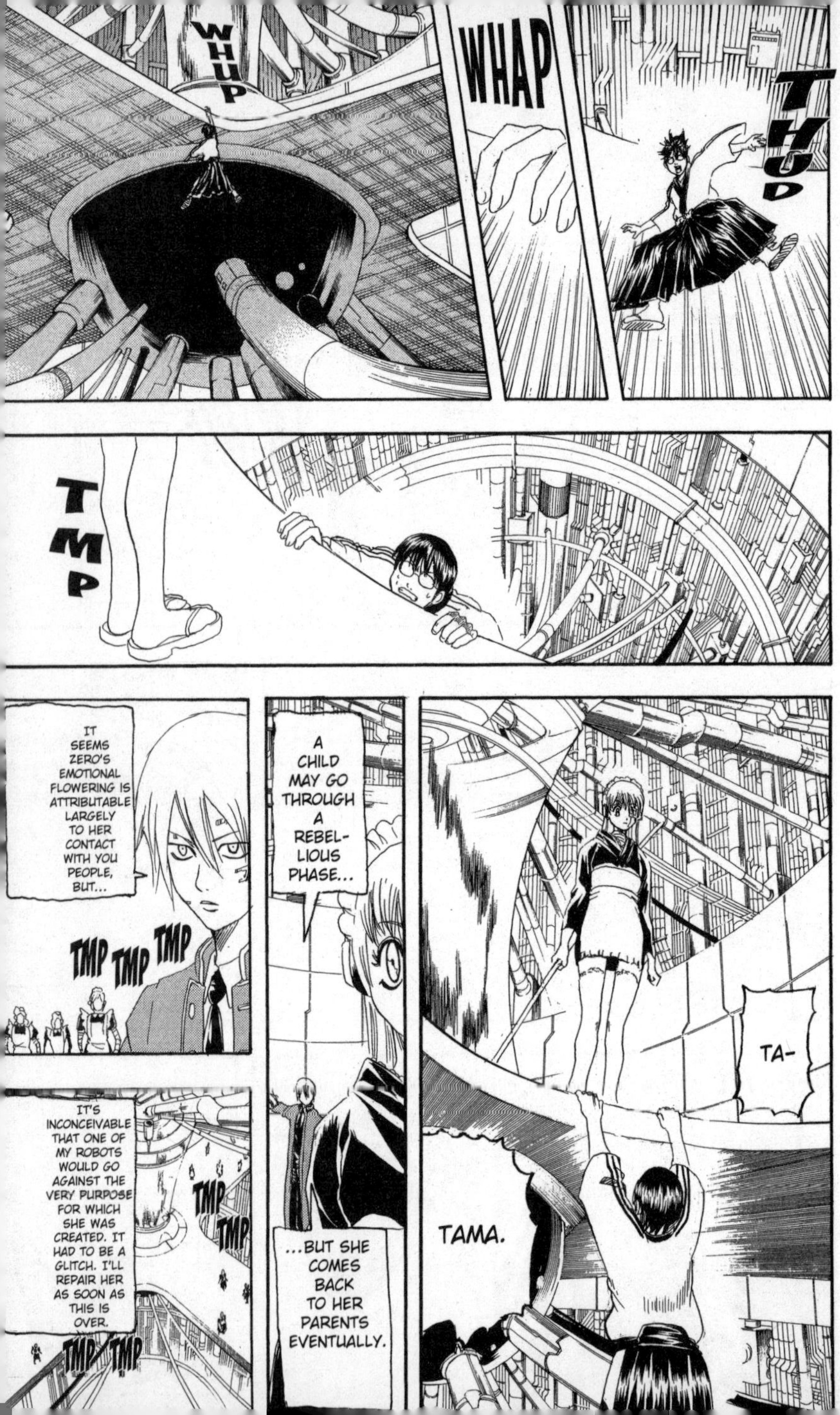
THUD
WHAP
WHUP
TMP
TA-
TAMA.
A CHILD MAY GO THROUGH A REBEL-LIOUS PHASE...
...BUT SHE COMES BACK TO HER PARENTS EVENTUALLY.
IT SEEMS ZERO'S EMOTIONAL FLOWERING IS ATTRIBUTABLE LARGELY TO HER CONTACT WITH YOU PEOPLE, BUT...
TMP TMP TMP
IT'S INCONCEIVABLE THAT ONE OF MY ROBOTS WOULD GO AGAINST THE VERY PURPOSE FOR WHICH SHE WAS CREATED. IT HAD TO BE A GLITCH. I'LL REPAIR HER AS SOON AS THIS IS OVER.
TMP TMP
TMP TMP

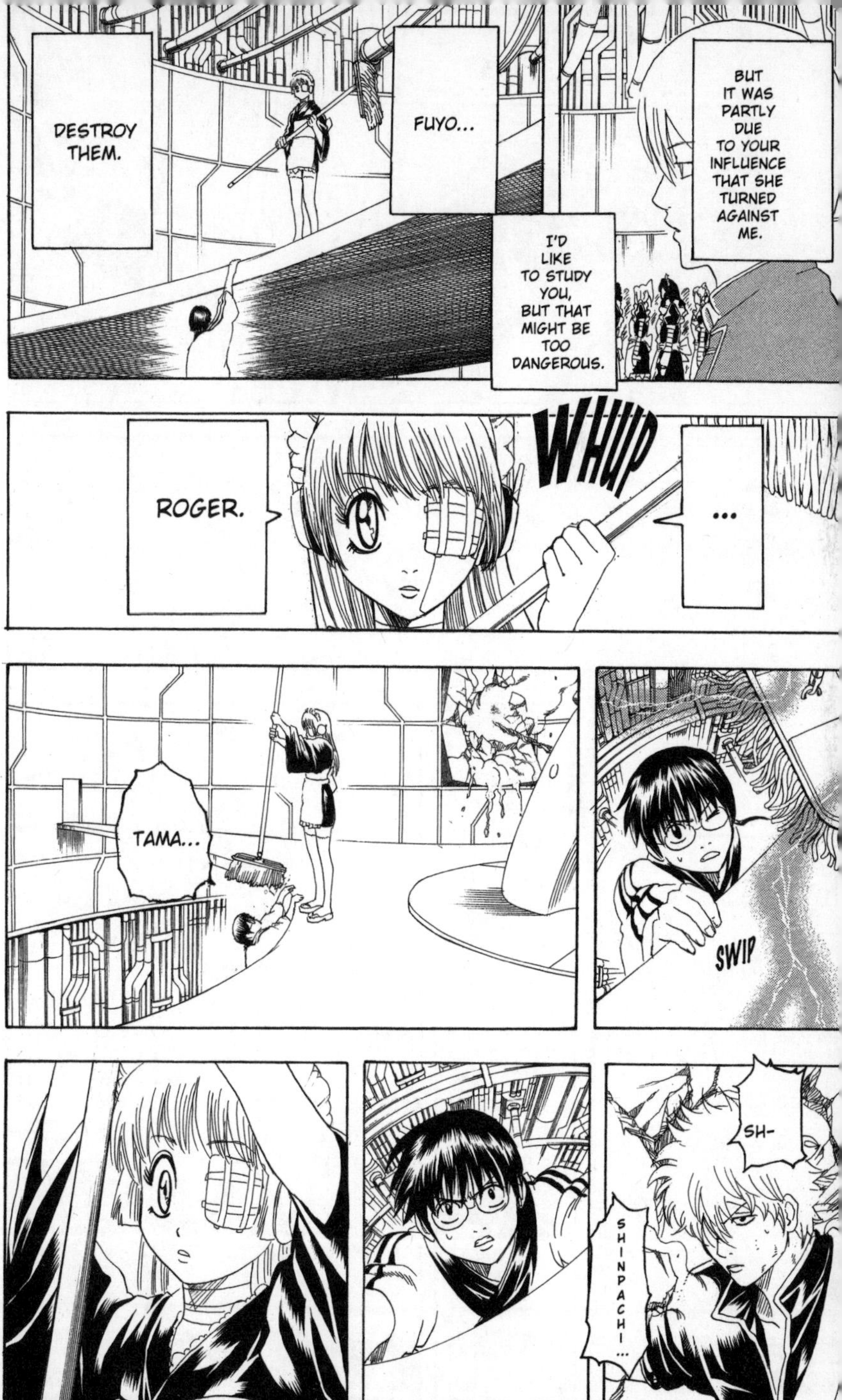
BUT IT WAS PARTLY DUE TO YOUR INFLUENCE THAT SHE TURNED AGAINST ME.
I'D LIKE TO STUDY YOU, BUT THAT MIGHT BE TOO DANGEROUS.
FUYO...
DESTROY THEM.
...
WHUP
ROGER.
SWIP
TAMA...
SH-
SHINPACHI...

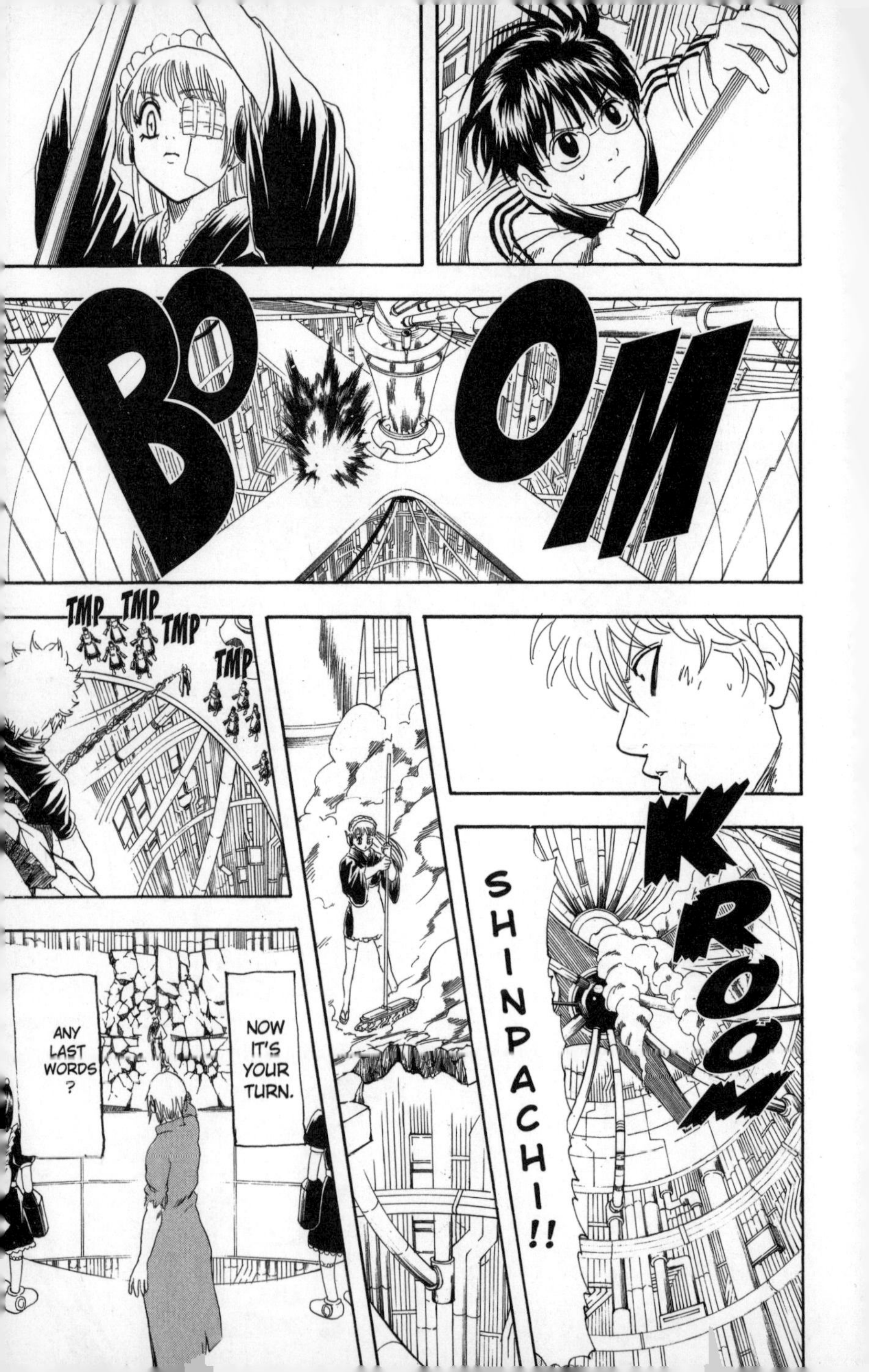
BOOM
KRROOM
SHINPACHI!!
TMP TMP TMP TMP
NOW IT'S YOUR TURN.
ANY LAST WORDS?

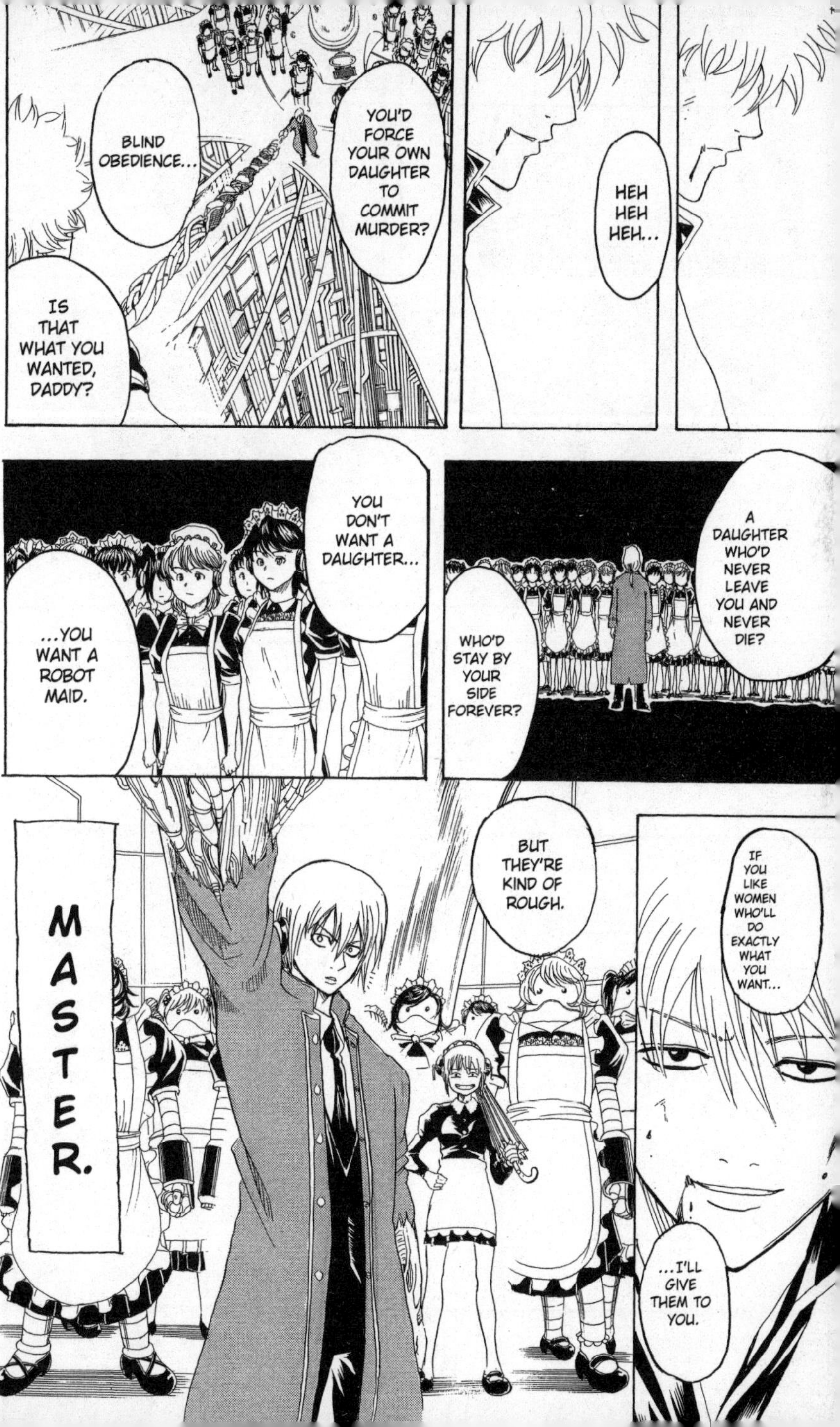
HEH HEH HEH...
YOU'D FORCE YOUR OWN DAUGHTER TO COMMIT MURDER?
BLIND OBEDIENCE...
IS THAT WHAT YOU WANTED, DADDY?
A DAUGHTER WHO'D NEVER LEAVE YOU AND NEVER DIE?
WHO'D STAY BY YOUR SIDE FOREVER?
YOU DON'T WANT A DAUGHTER...
...YOU WANT A ROBOT MAID.
IF YOU LIKE WOMEN WHO'LL DO EXACTLY WHAT YOU WANT...
...I'LL GIVE THEM TO YOU.
BUT THEY'RE KIND OF ROUGH.
MASTER.

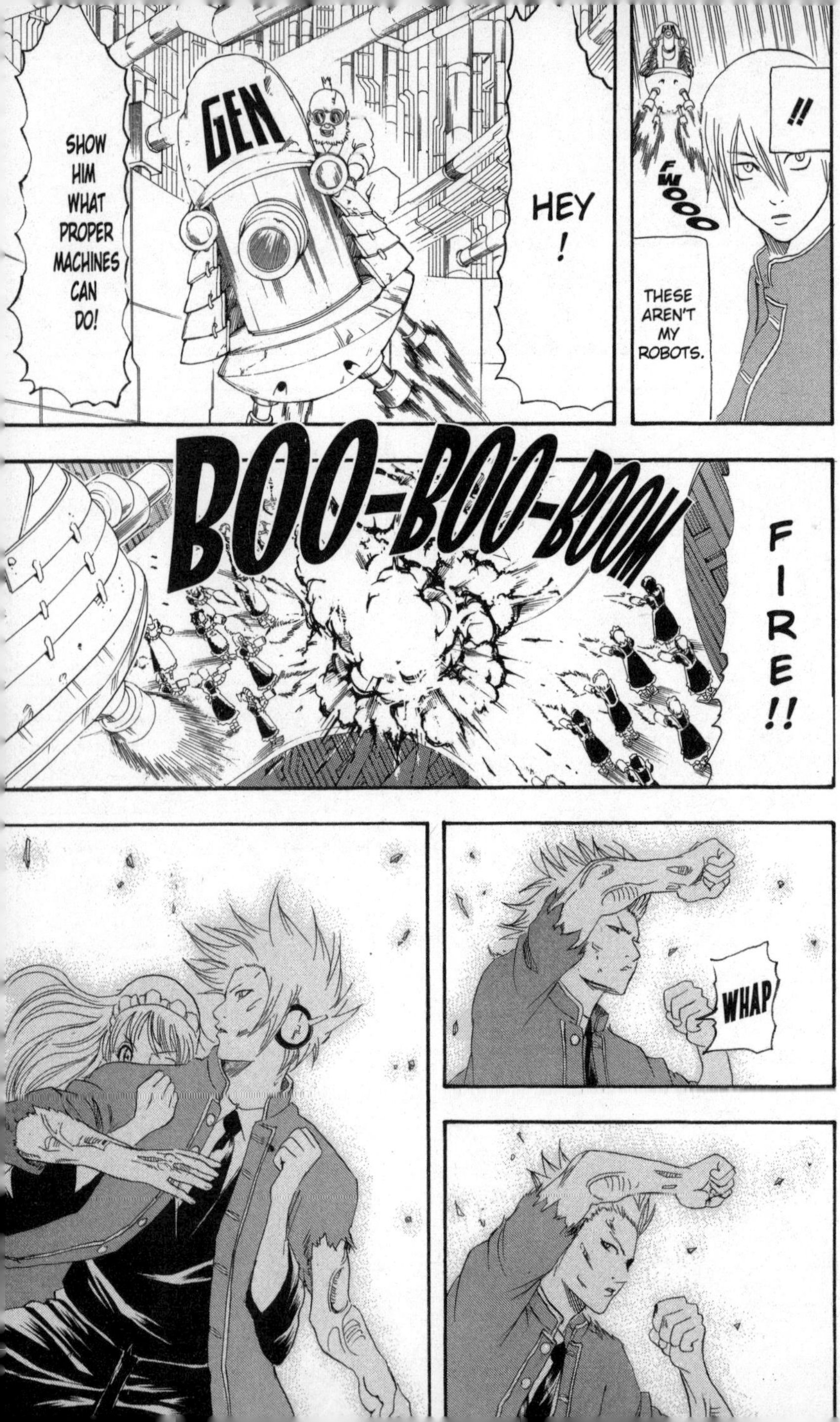
!!
FWOOO
THESE AREN'T MY ROBOTS.
HEY!
SHOW HIM WHAT PROPER MACHINES CAN DO!
GEN
FIRE!!
BOO-BOO-BOOM
WHAP

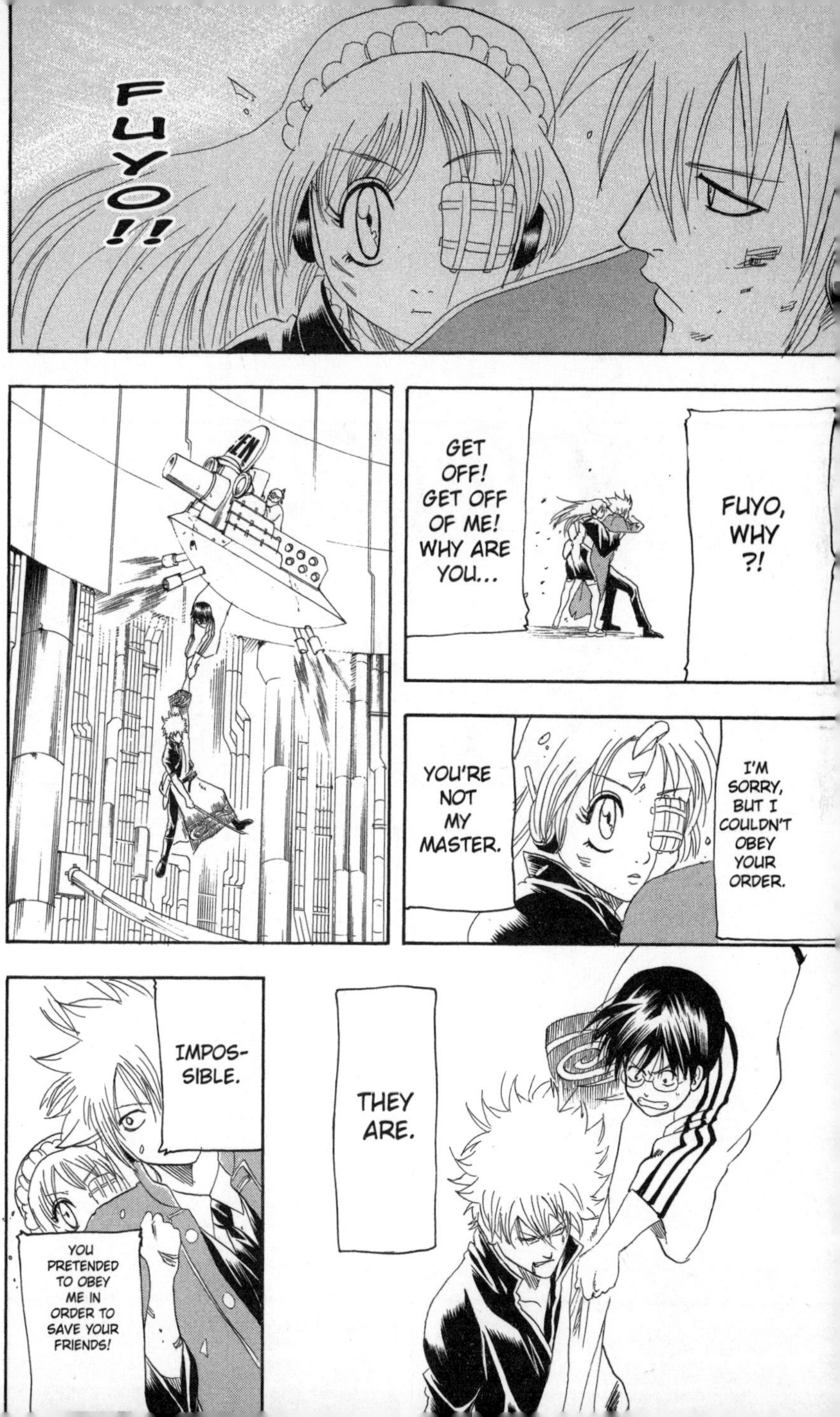
FUYO!!
FUYO, WHY?!
GET OFF! GET OFF OF ME! WHY ARE YOU...
I'M SORRY, BUT I COULDN'T OBEY YOUR ORDER.
YOU'RE NOT MY MASTER.
THEY ARE.
IMPOS-SIBLE.
YOU PRETENDED TO OBEY ME IN ORDER TO SAVE YOUR FRIENDS!

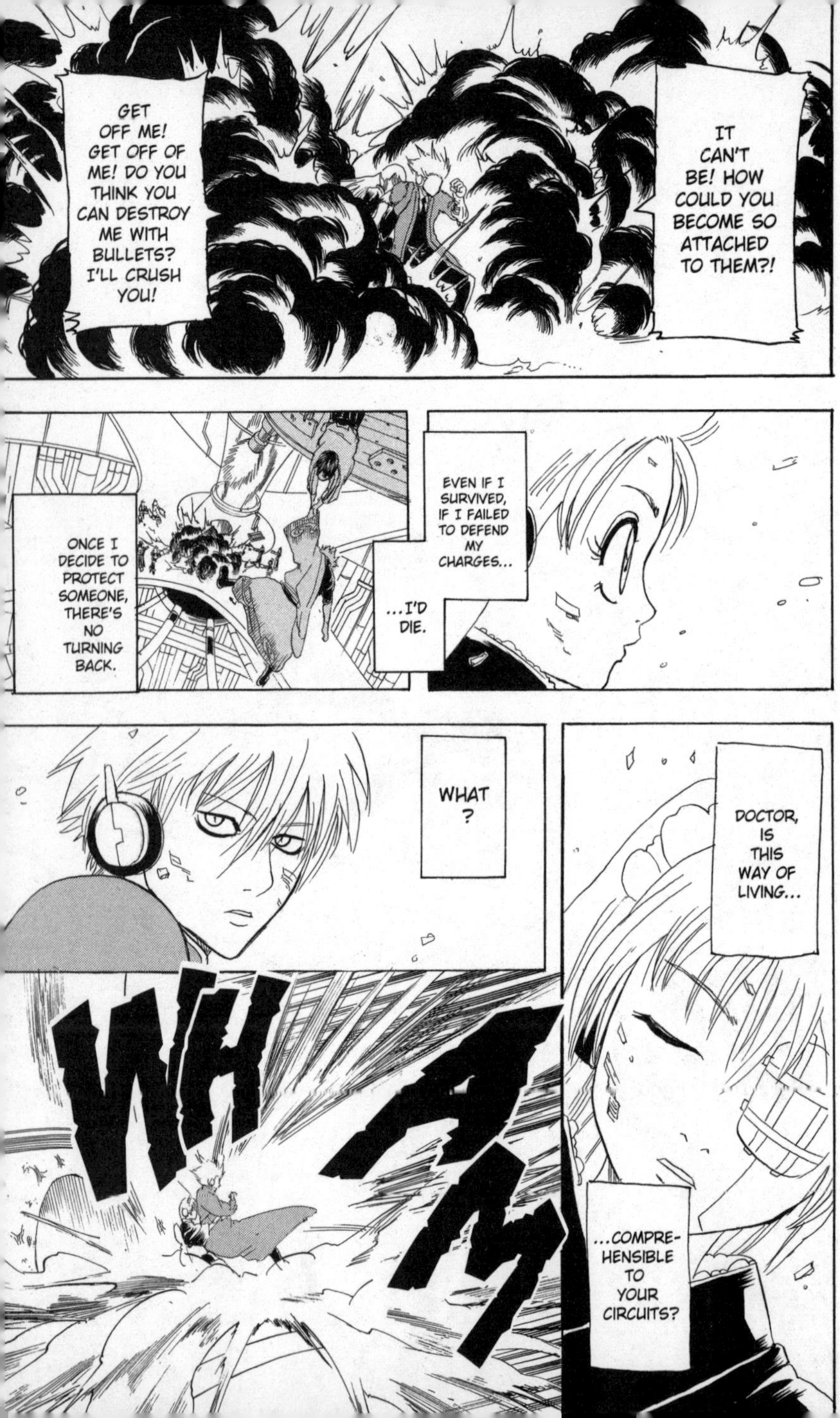
IT CAN'T BE! HOW COULD YOU BECOME SO ATTACHED TO THEM?!
GET OFF ME! GET OFF OF ME! DO YOU THINK YOU CAN DESTROY ME WITH BULLETS? I'LL CRUSH YOU!
EVEN IF I SURVIVED, IF I FAILED TO DEFEND MY CHARGES...
...I'D DIE.
ONCE I DECIDE TO PROTECT SOMEONE, THERE'S NO TURNING BACK.
DOCTOR, IS THIS WAY OF LIVING...
...COMPREHENSIBLE TO YOUR CIRCUITS?
WHAT?
WHAM

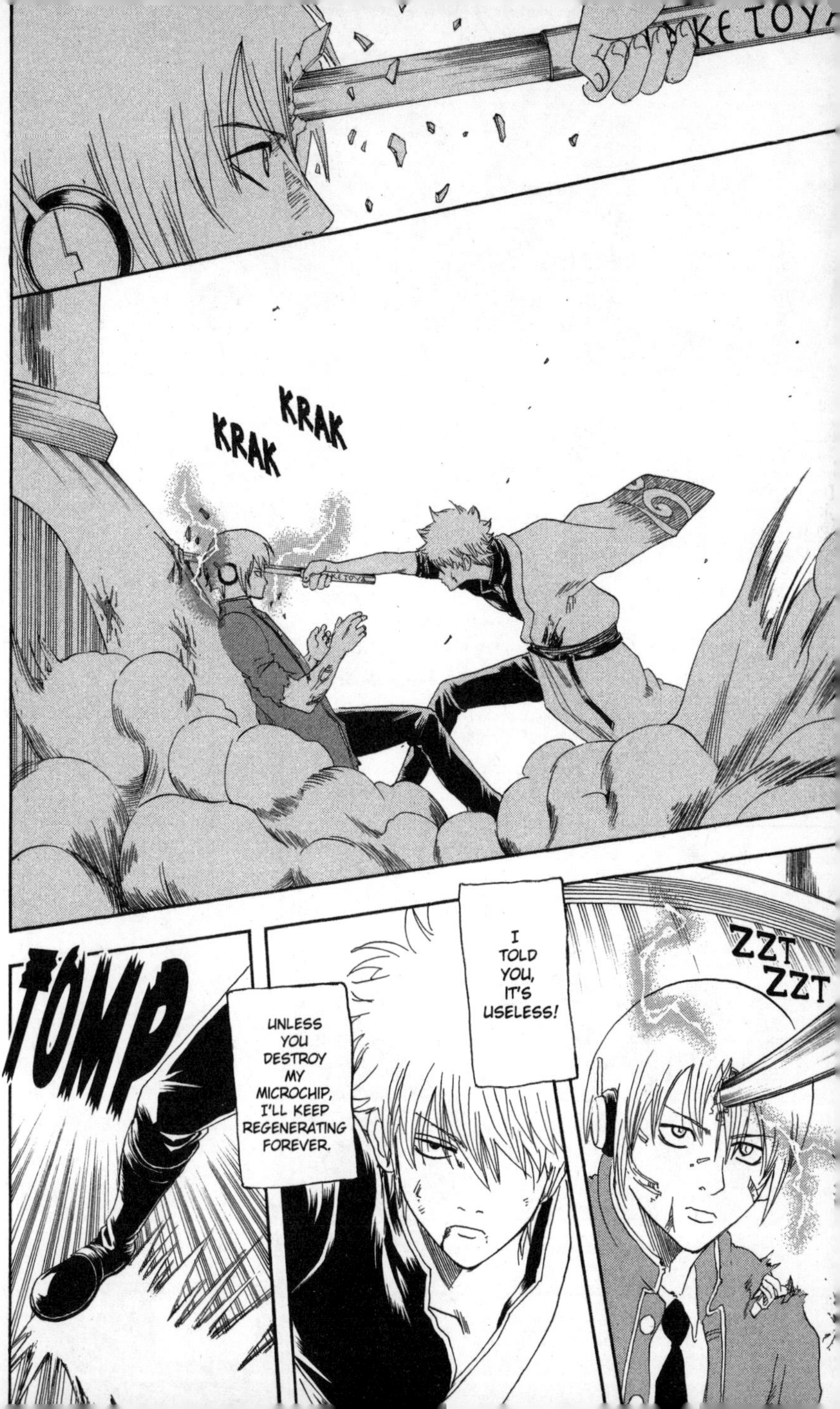
KRAK
KRAK
ZZT
ZZT
I TOLD YOU, IT'S USELESS!
UNLESS YOU DESTROY MY MICROCHIP, I'LL KEEP REGENERATING FOREVER.
TOMP

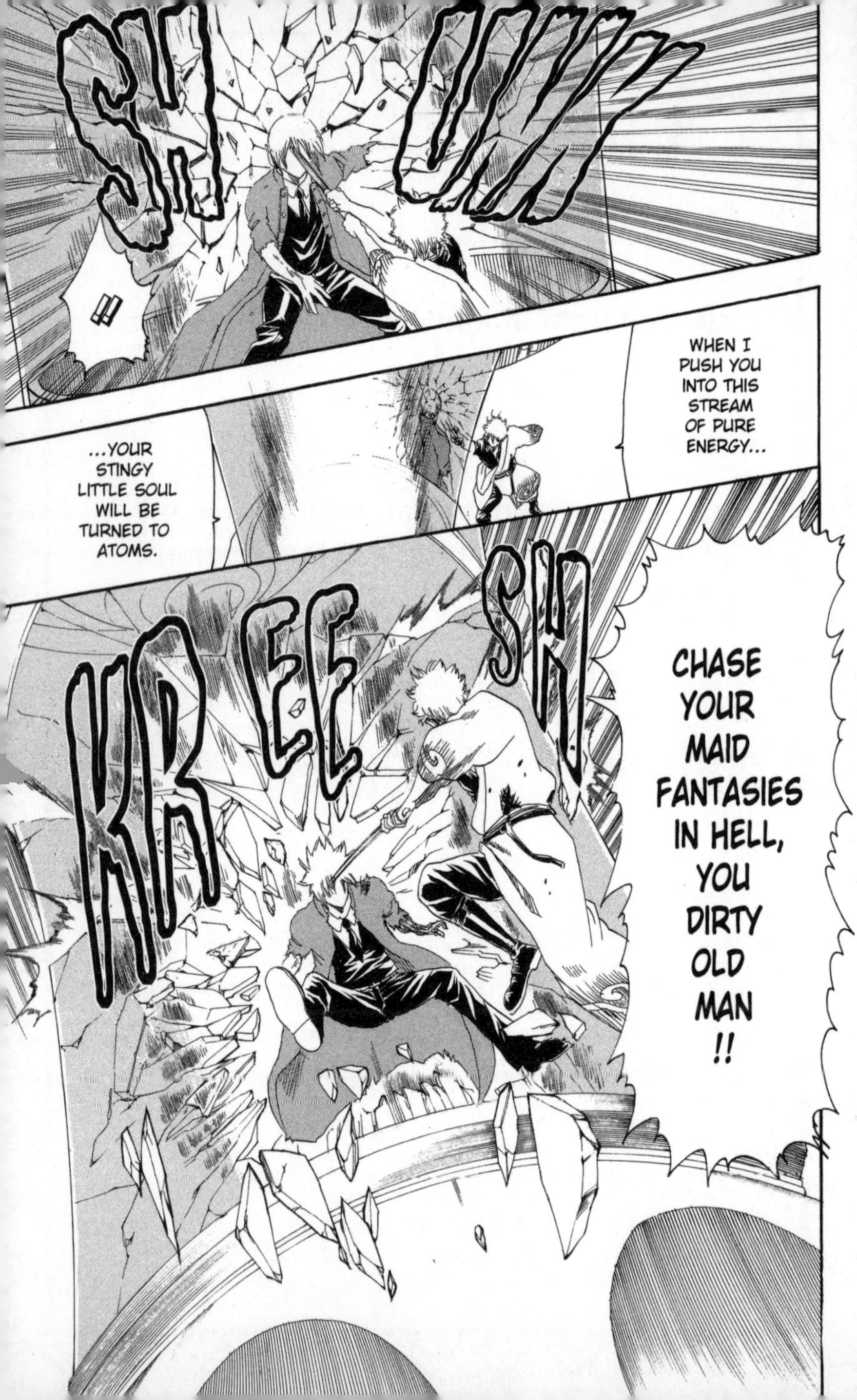
SHOOM
!!
WHEN I PUSH YOU INTO THIS STREAM OF PURE ENERGY...
...YOUR STINGY LITTLE SOUL WILL BE TURNED TO ATOMS.
KREESH
CHASE YOUR MAID FANTASIES IN HELL, YOU DIRTY OLD MAN!!

Sorachi's Q&A
Hanging with the Readers #53

<Question from Orange Kagawa Prefecture>

Hello, Sorachi Sensei. Let me ask you a question right off the bat. Aren't there any foreigners in *Gin Tama*? Are the Japanese the only people left on Earth?

<Answer>

They aren't the only people, but only Edo has a really big space terminal, so it is the main center of trade for the Amanto. Think of Edo as the doorway to the Earth.

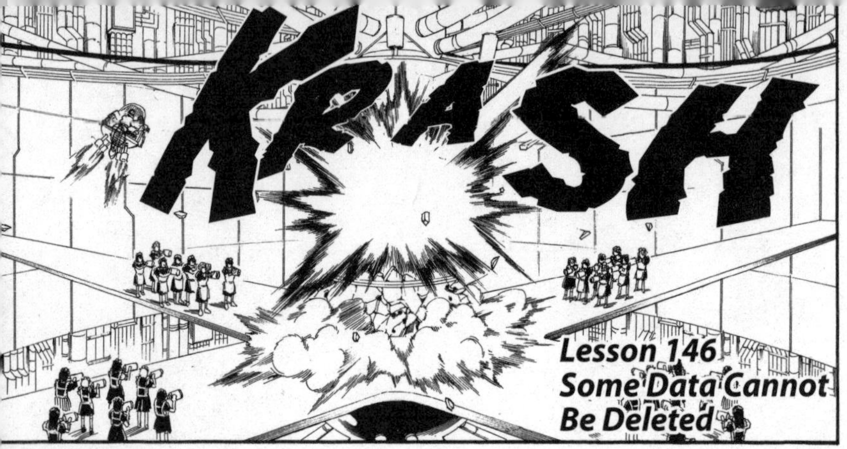
KRASH

Lesson 146
Some Data Cannot Be Deleted

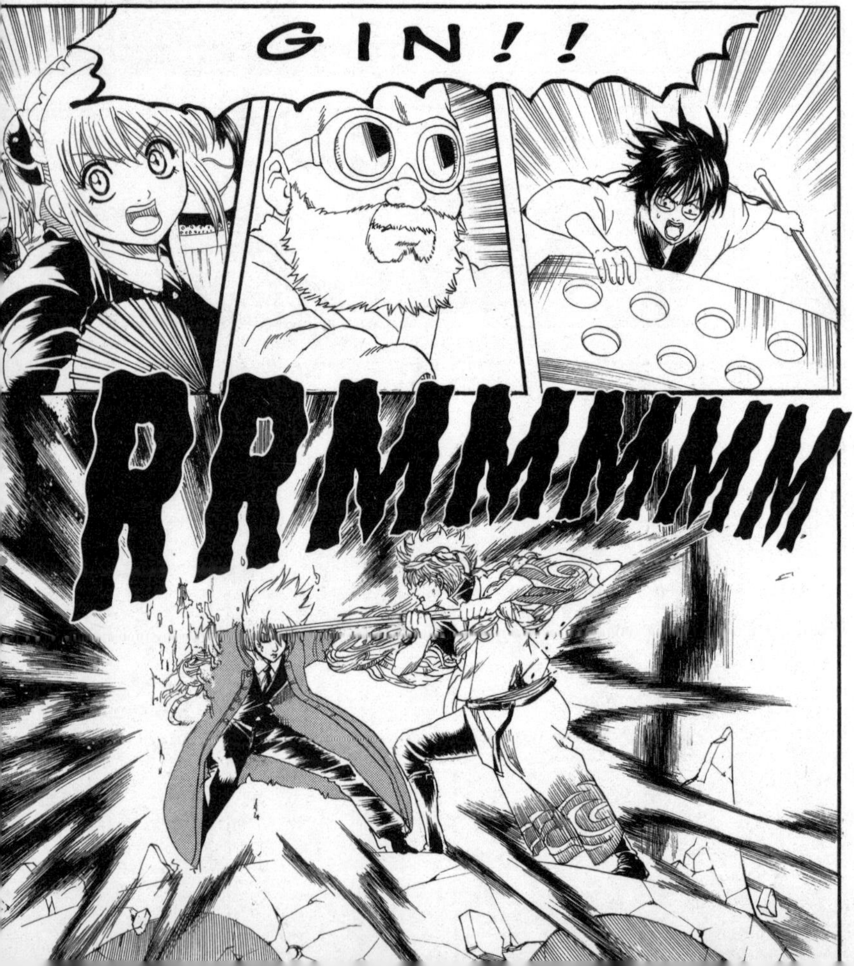
GIN!!
RRMMMMM

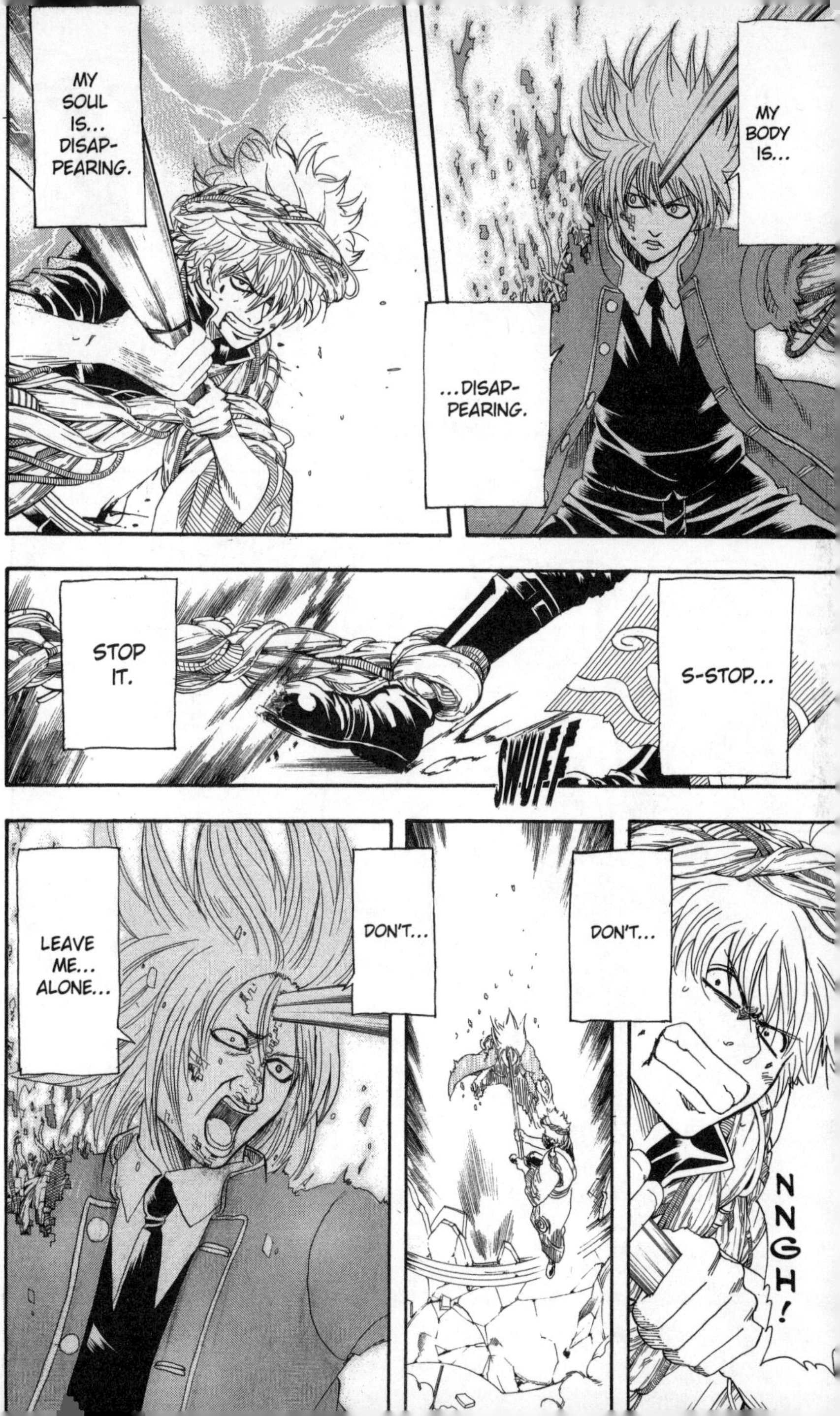
MY BODY IS...
...DISAP-PEARING.
MY SOUL IS... DISAP-PEARING.
S-STOP...
SWUFF
STOP IT.
DON'T...
NNGH!
DON'T...
LEAVE ME... ALONE...

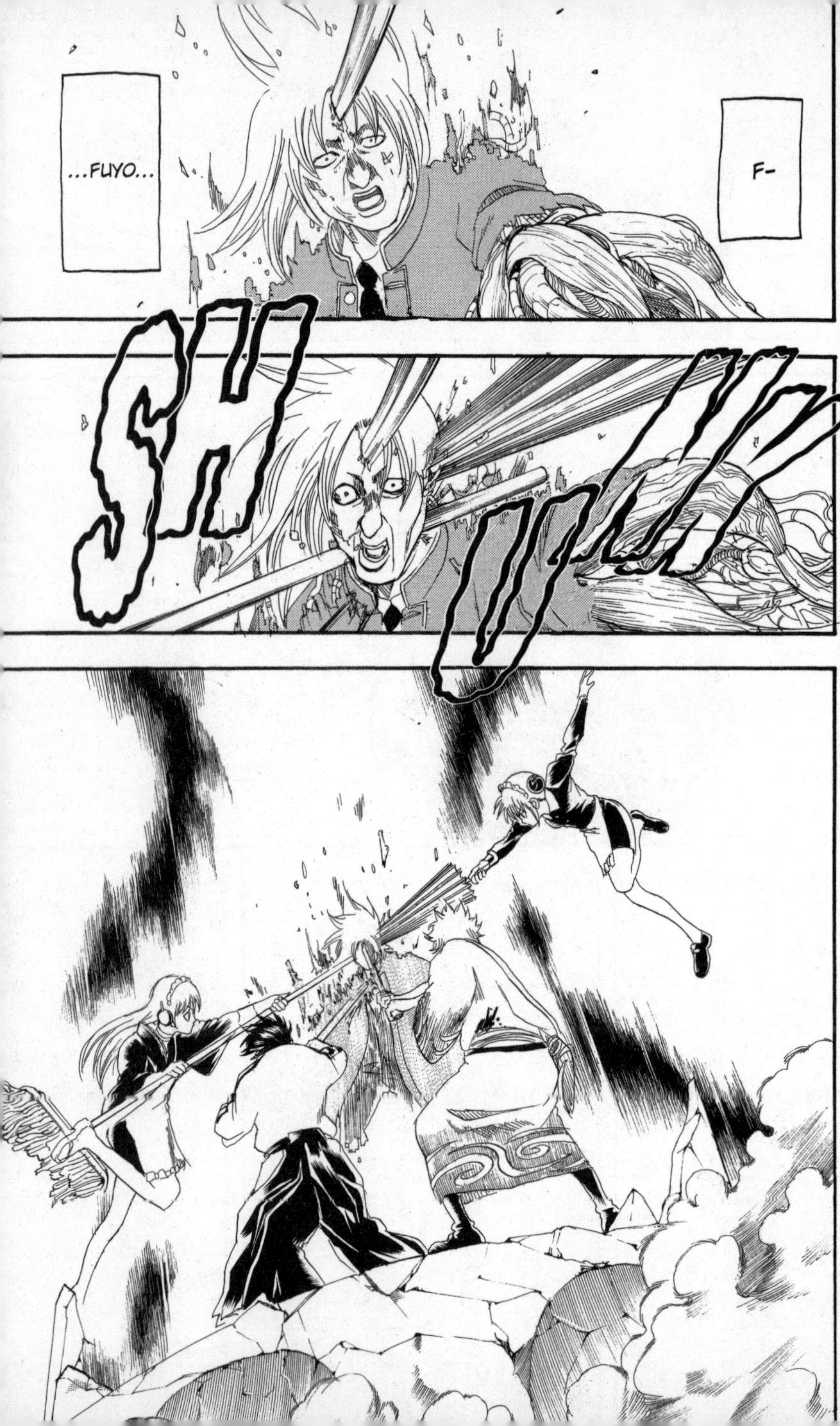
F-
...FUYO...
SHUNK

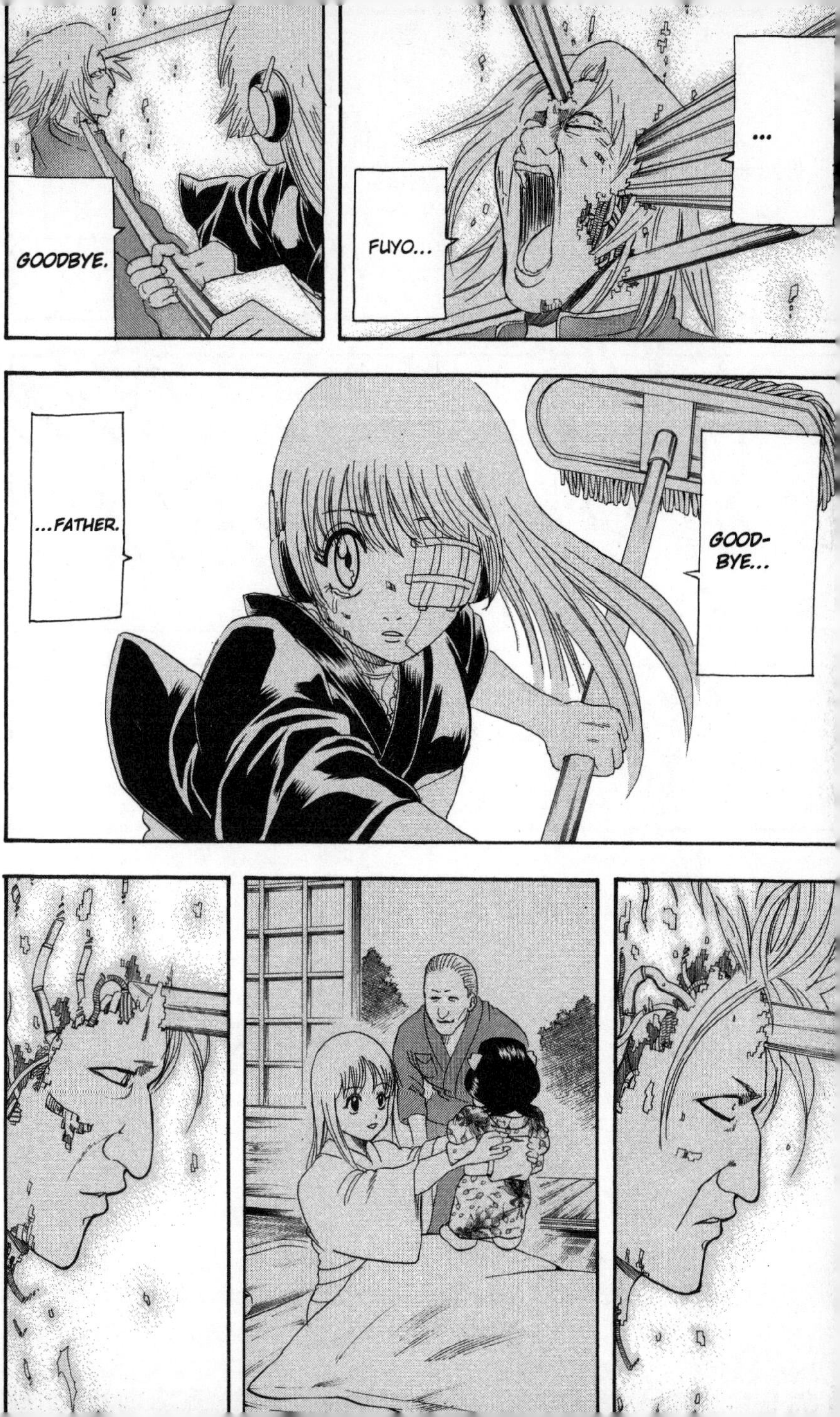
...
FUYO...
GOODBYE.
GOOD-BYE...
...FATHER.

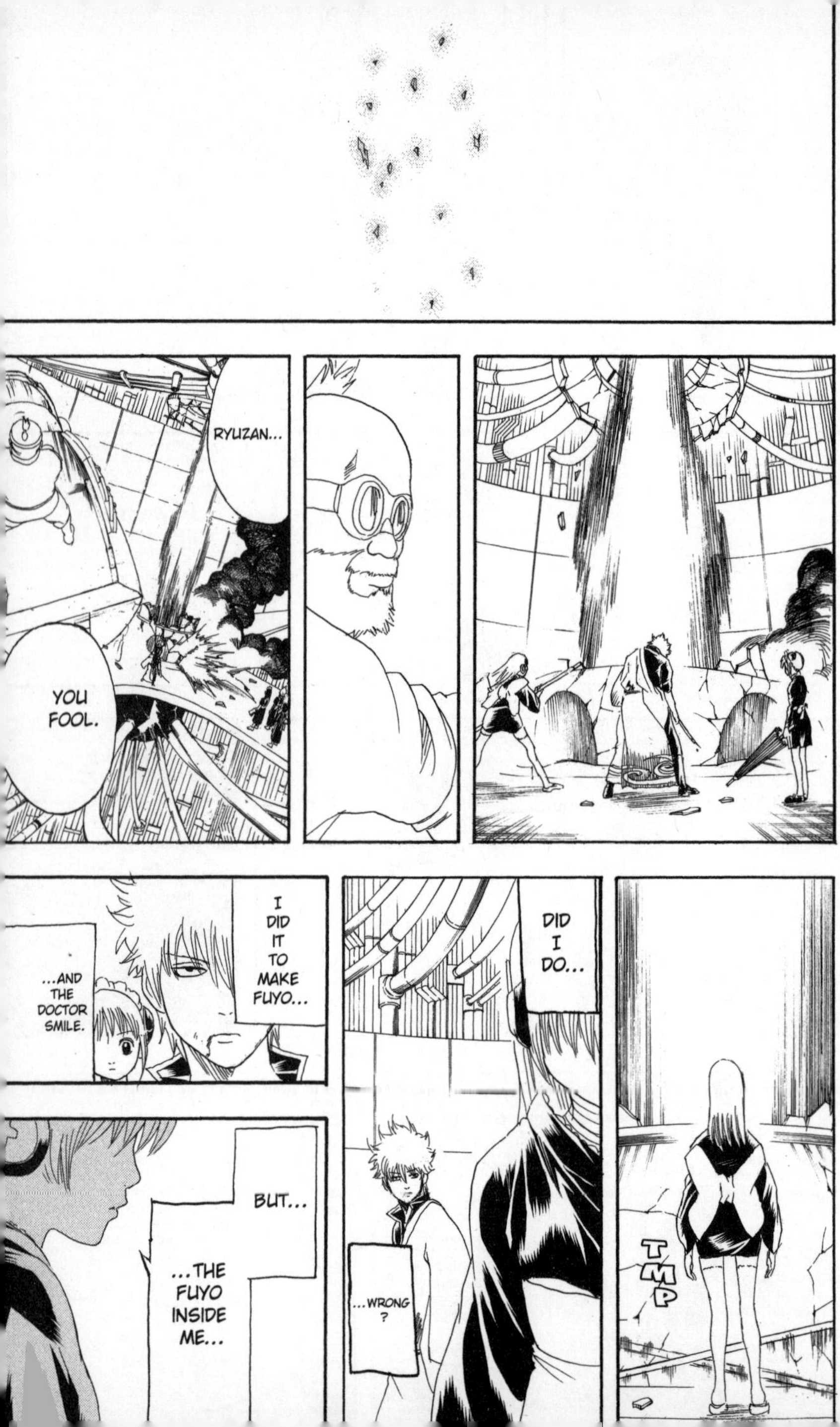
RYUZAN...
YOU FOOL.
I DID IT TO MAKE FUYO...
...AND THE DOCTOR SMILE.
BUT...
...THE FUYO INSIDE ME...
DID I DO...
...WRONG?
TMP

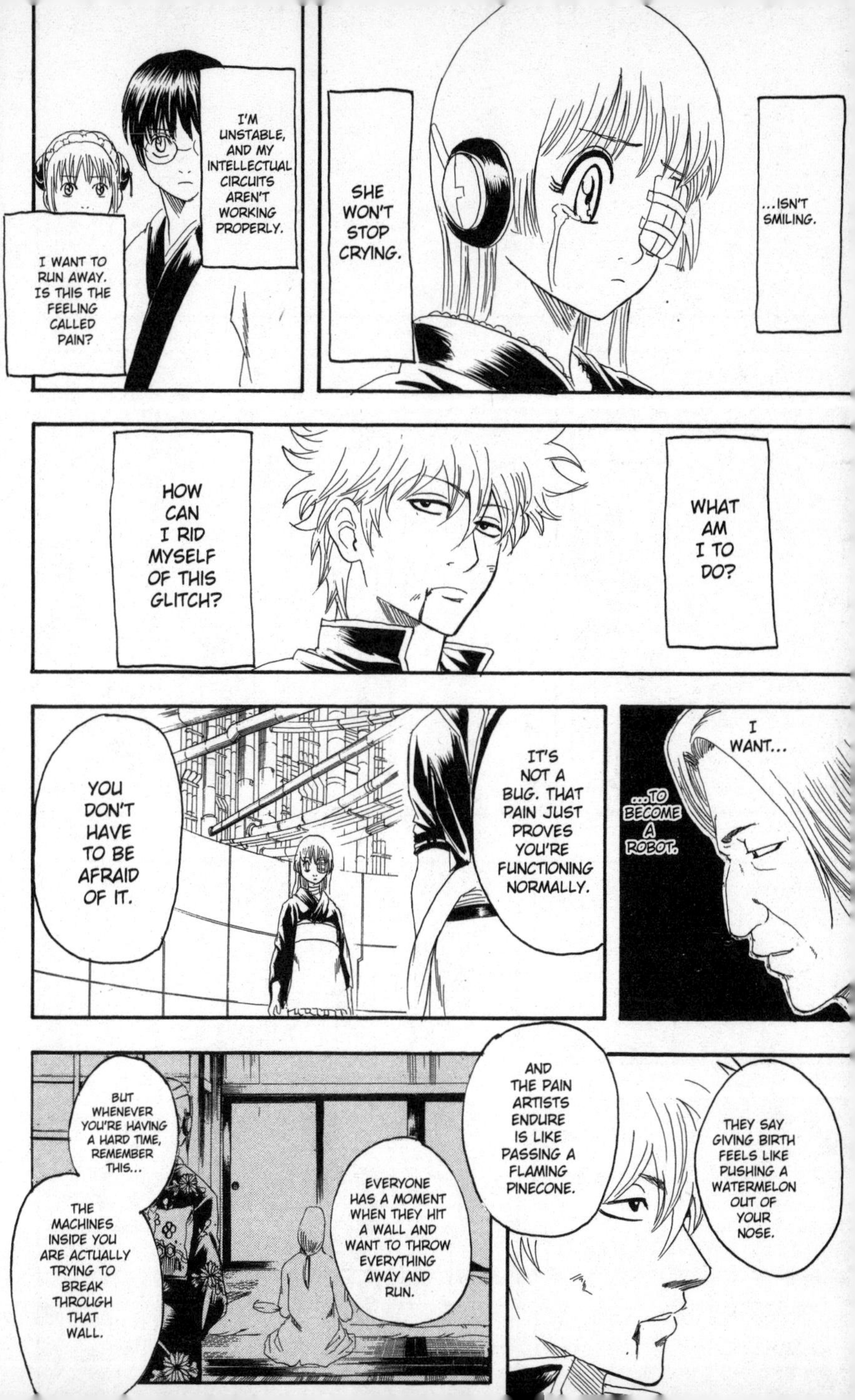
...ISN'T SMILING.
SHE WON'T STOP CRYING.
I'M UNSTABLE, AND MY INTELLECTUAL CIRCUITS AREN'T WORKING PROPERLY.
I WANT TO RUN AWAY. IS THIS THE FEELING CALLED PAIN?
WHAT AM I TO DO?
HOW CAN I RID MYSELF OF THIS GLITCH?
I WANT...
...TO BECOME A ROBOT.
IT'S NOT A BUG. THAT PAIN JUST PROVES YOU'RE FUNCTIONING NORMALLY.
YOU DON'T HAVE TO BE AFRAID OF IT.
THEY SAY GIVING BIRTH FEELS LIKE PUSHING A WATERMELON OUT OF YOUR NOSE.
AND THE PAIN ARTISTS ENDURE IS LIKE PASSING A FLAMING PINECONE.
EVERYONE HAS A MOMENT WHEN THEY HIT A WALL AND WANT TO THROW EVERYTHING AWAY AND RUN.
BUT WHENEVER YOU'RE HAVING A HARD TIME, REMEMBER THIS...
THE MACHINES INSIDE YOU ARE ACTUALLY TRYING TO BREAK THROUGH THAT WALL.

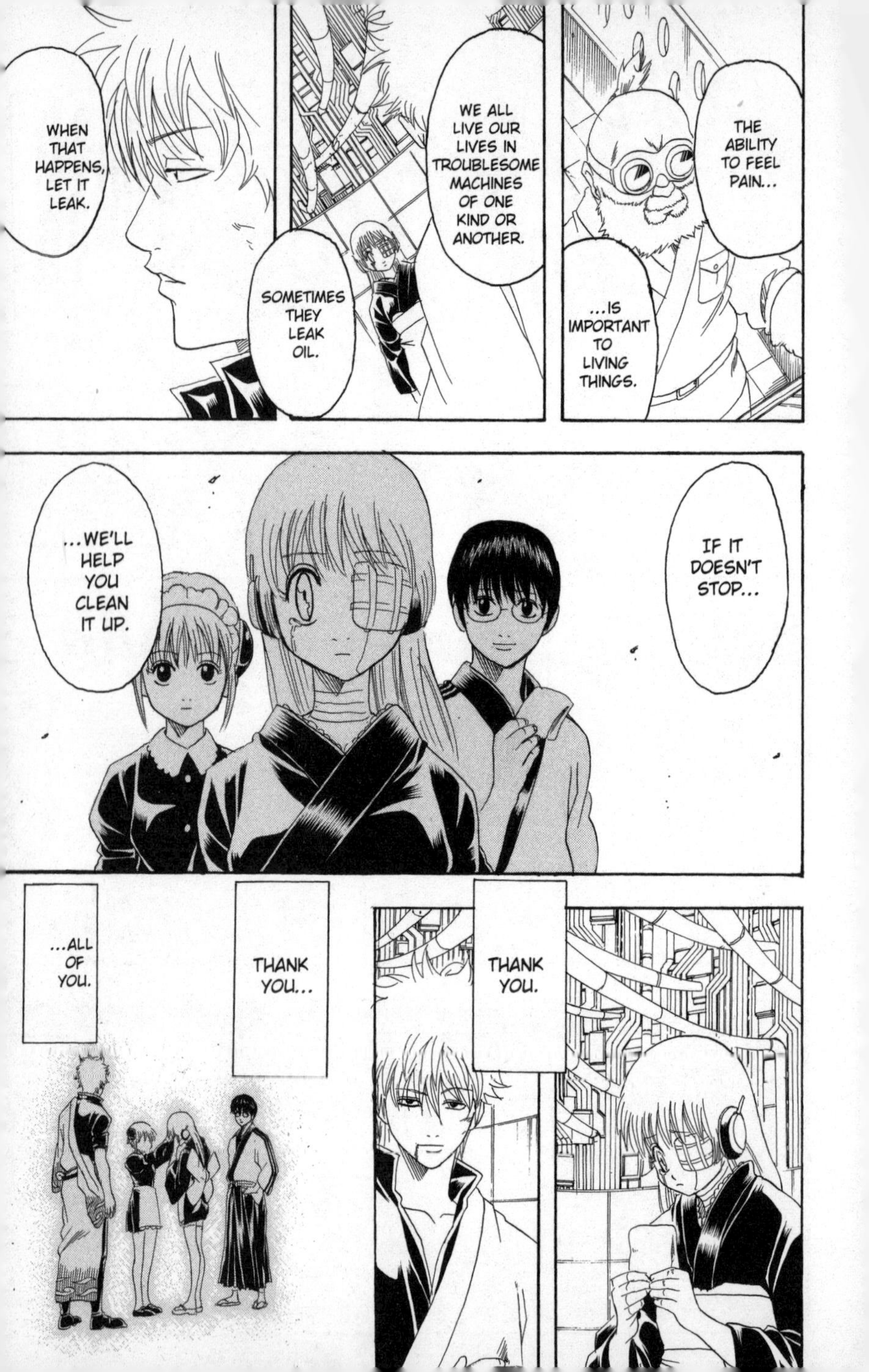
THE ABILITY TO FEEL PAIN...
...IS IMPORTANT TO LIVING THINGS.
WE ALL LIVE OUR LIVES IN TROUBLESOME MACHINES OF ONE KIND OR ANOTHER.
SOMETIMES THEY LEAK OIL.
WHEN THAT HAPPENS, LET IT LEAK.
IF IT DOESN'T STOP...
...WE'LL HELP YOU CLEAN IT UP.
THANK YOU.
THANK YOU...
...ALL OF YOU.

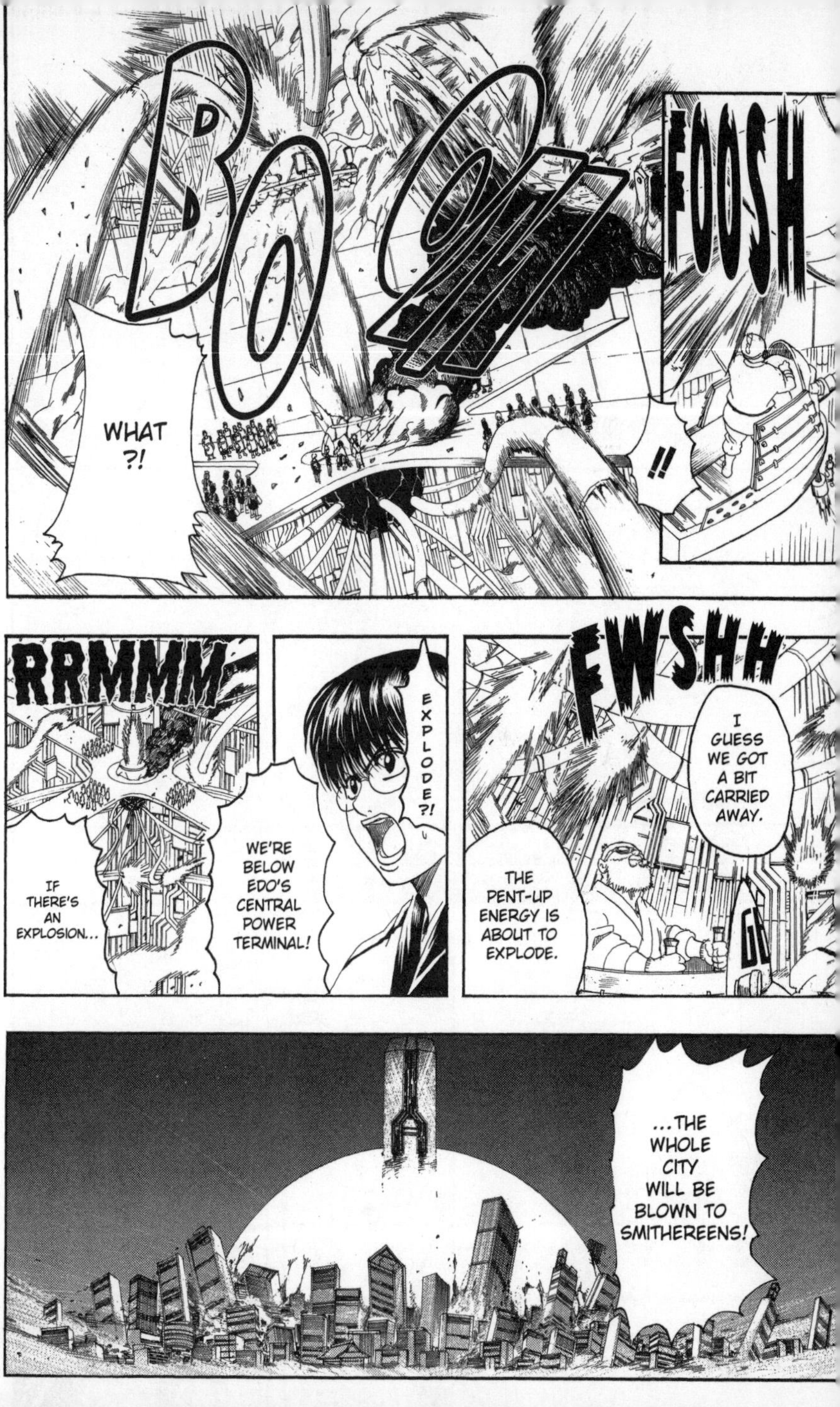
FOOSH
!!
BOOM
WHAT ?!
FWSHH
I GUESS WE GOT A BIT CARRIED AWAY.
THE PENT-UP ENERGY IS ABOUT TO EXPLODE.
EXPLODE?!
WE'RE BELOW EDO'S CENTRAL POWER TERMINAL!
RRMMM
IF THERE'S AN EXPLOSION...
...THE WHOLE CITY WILL BE BLOWN TO SMITHEREENS!

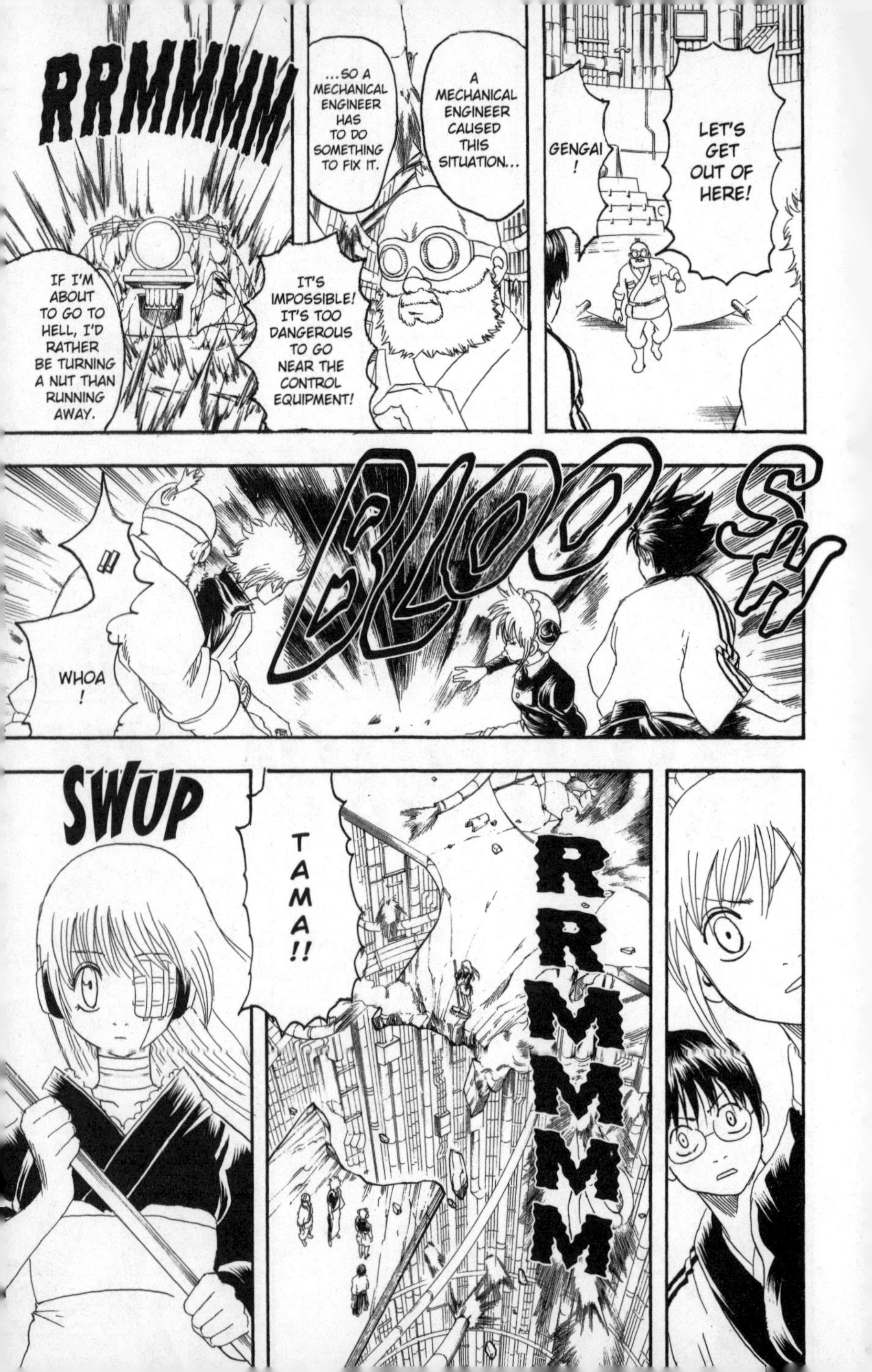
LET'S GET OUT OF HERE!
GENGAI!
A MECHANICAL ENGINEER CAUSED THIS SITUATION...
...SO A MECHANICAL ENGINEER HAS TO DO SOMETHING TO FIX IT.
IT'S IMPOSSIBLE! IT'S TOO DANGEROUS TO GO NEAR THE CONTROL EQUIPMENT!
RRMMMM
IF I'M ABOUT TO GO TO HELL, I'D RATHER BE TURNING A NUT THAN RUNNING AWAY.
BLOOOSH
!!
WHOA!
RRMMMM
TAMA!!
SWUP

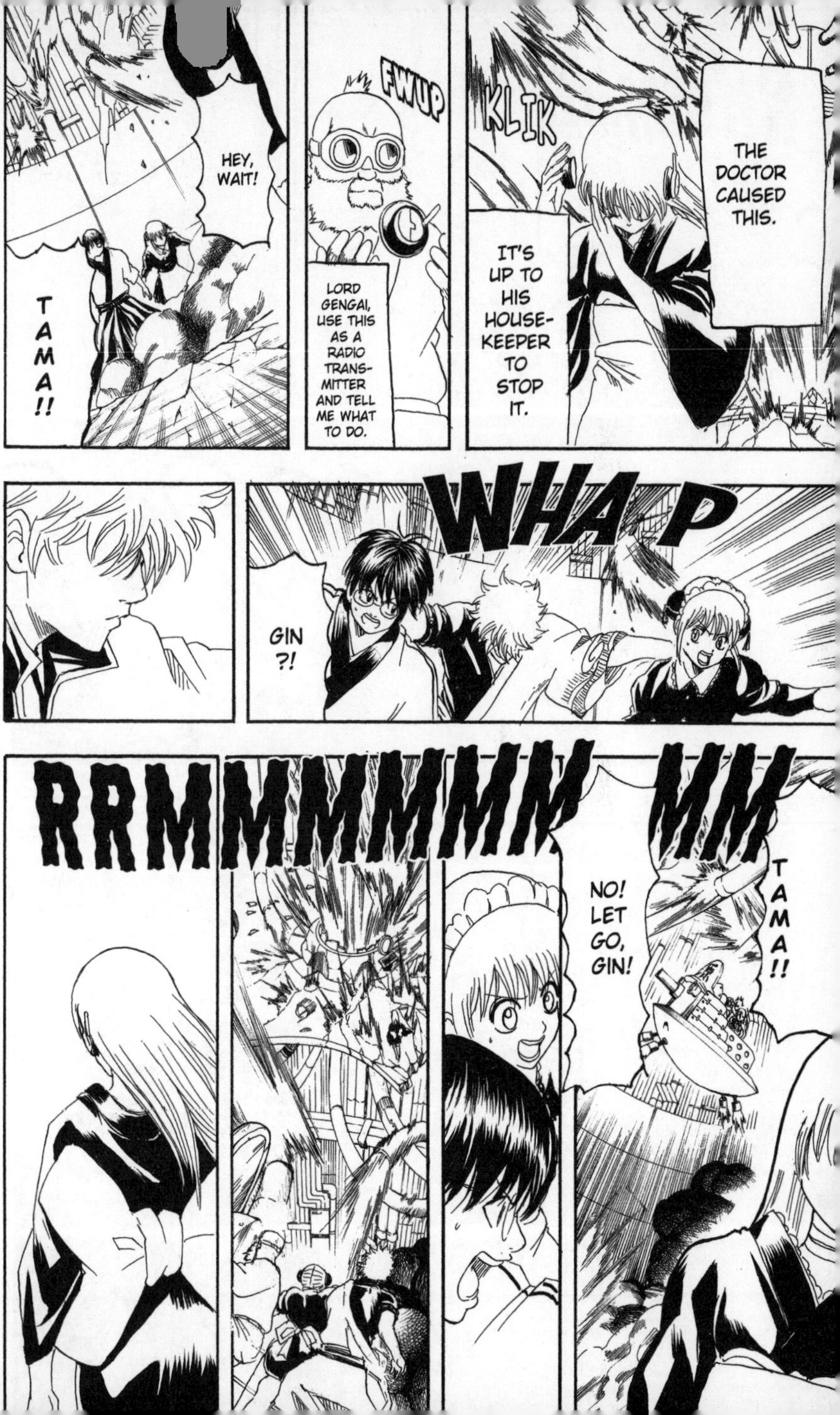
THE DOCTOR CAUSED THIS.
KLIK
IT'S UP TO HIS HOUSEKEEPER TO STOP IT.
FWUP
LORD GENGAI, USE THIS AS A RADIO TRANSMITTER AND TELL ME WHAT TO DO.
HEY, WAIT!
TAMA!!
WHAP
GIN?!
RRMMMMMMM MM
TAMA!!
NO! LET GO, GIN!

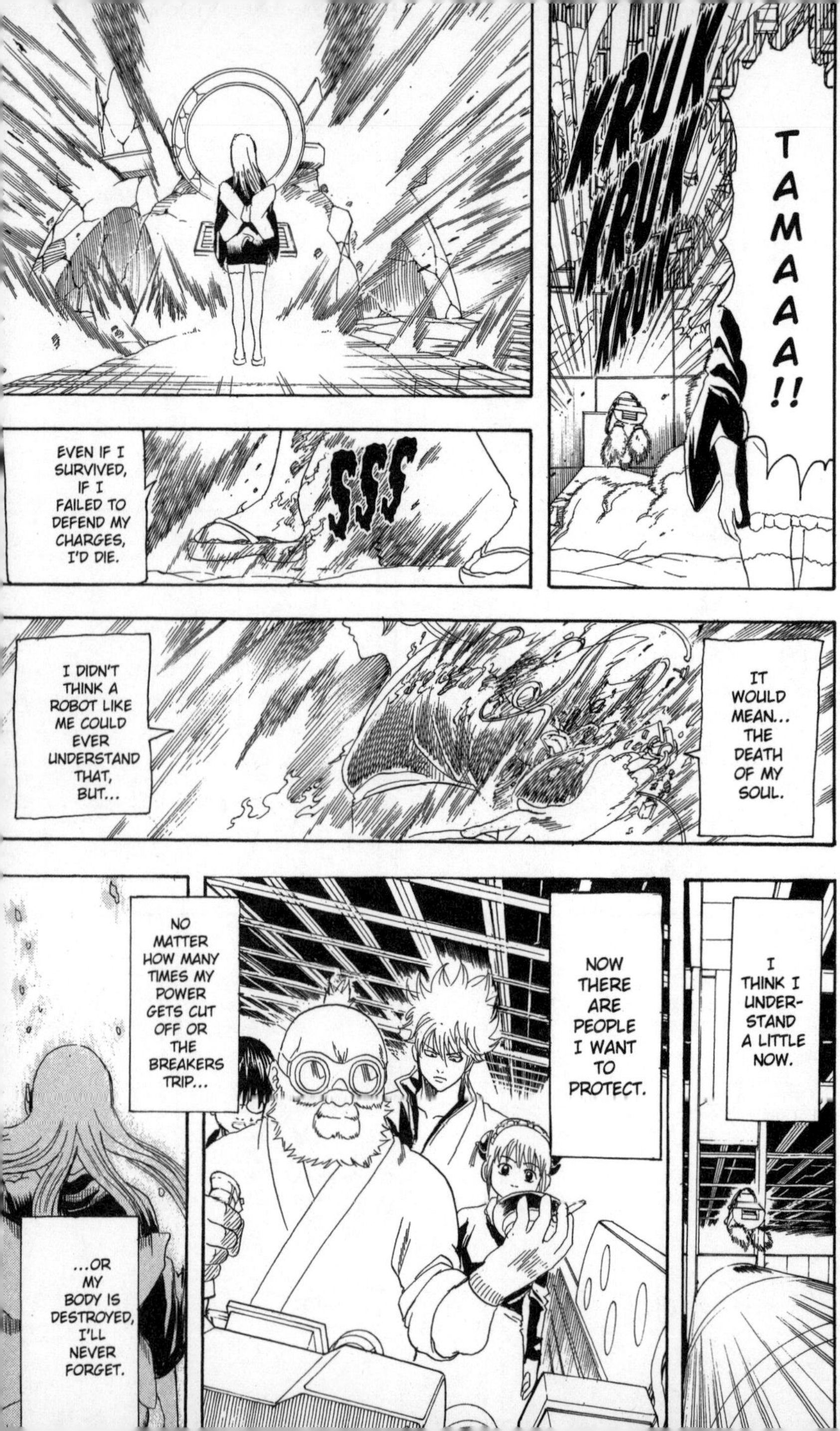
KRUK KRUK KRUK
TAMAAAA!!
EVEN IF I SURVIVED, IF I FAILED TO DEFEND MY CHARGES, I'D DIE.
SSS
IT WOULD MEAN... THE DEATH OF MY SOUL.
I DIDN'T THINK A ROBOT LIKE ME COULD EVER UNDERSTAND THAT, BUT...
I THINK I UNDER-STAND A LITTLE NOW.
NOW THERE ARE PEOPLE I WANT TO PROTECT.
NO MATTER HOW MANY TIMES MY POWER GETS CUT OFF OR THE BREAKERS TRIP...
...OR MY BODY IS DESTROYED, I'LL NEVER FORGET.

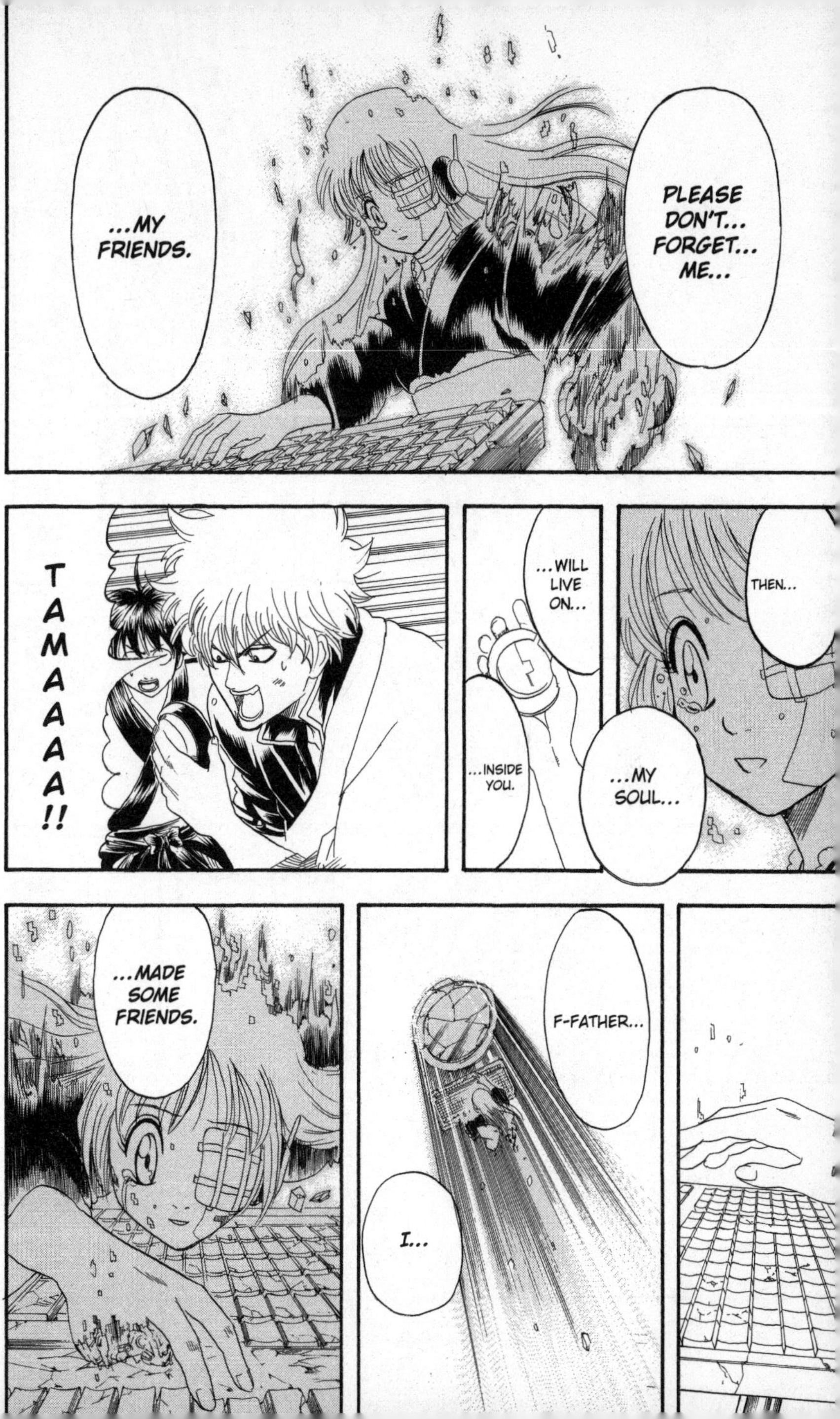
PLEASE DON'T... FORGET... ME...
...MY FRIENDS.
THEN...
...MY SOUL...
...WILL LIVE ON...
...INSIDE YOU.
TAMAAAAAA!!
F-FATHER...
I...
...MADE SOME FRIENDS.

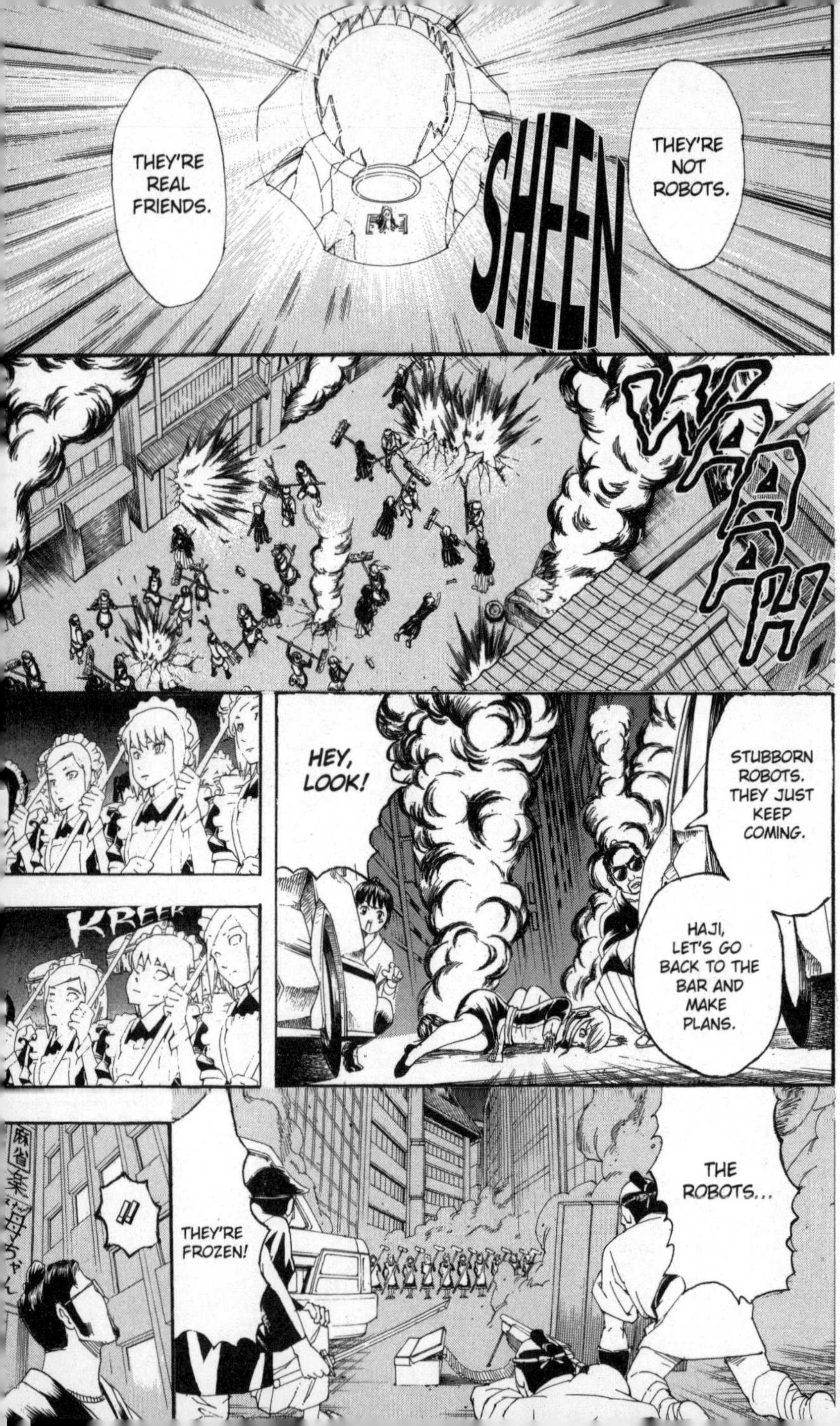
THEY'RE NOT ROBOTS.
SHEEN
THEY'RE REAL FRIENDS.
WAAAH
STUBBORN ROBOTS. THEY JUST KEEP COMING.
HAJI, LET'S GO BACK TO THE BAR AND MAKE PLANS.
HEY, LOOK!
KREE
THE ROBOTS...
!!
THEY'RE FROZEN!

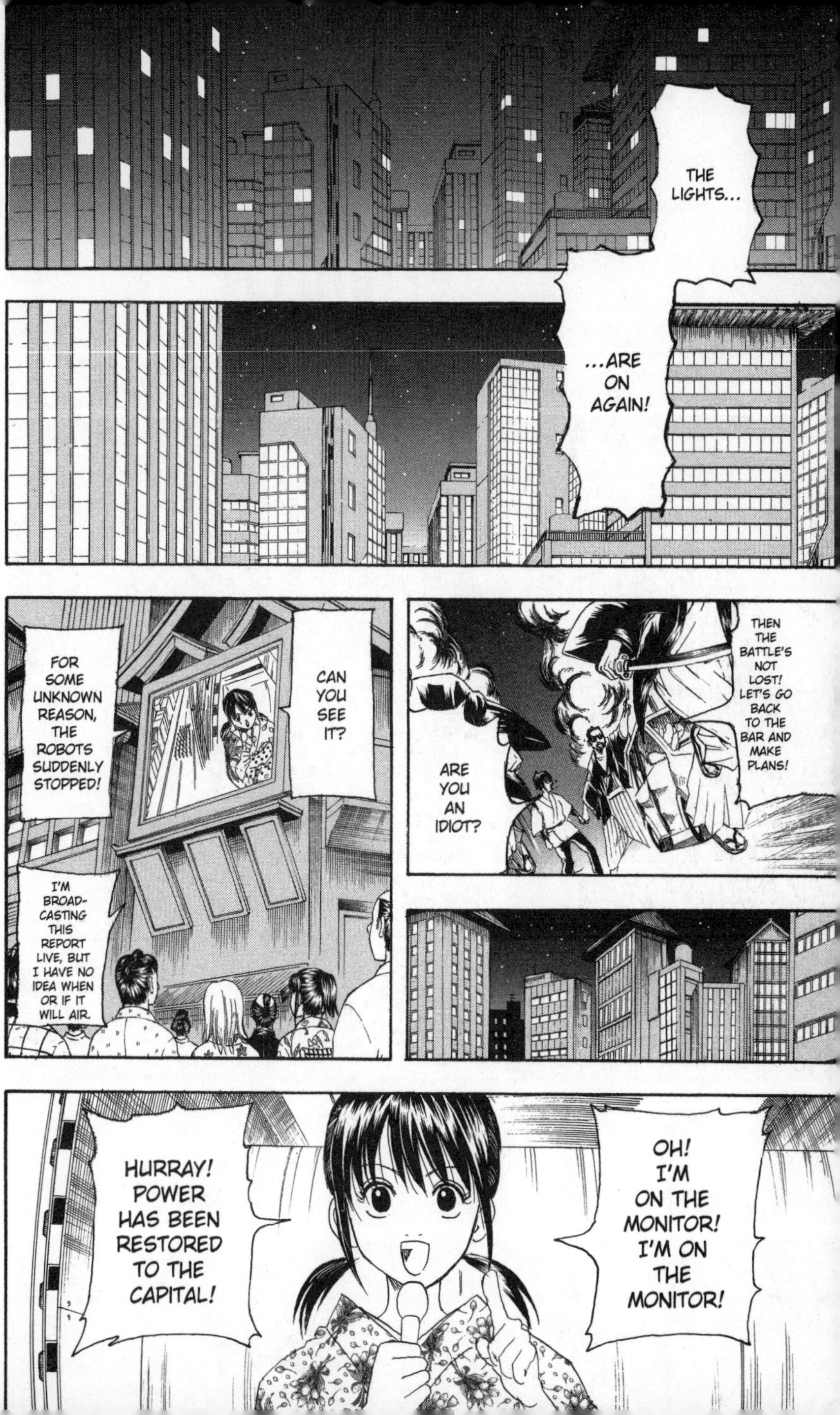
THE LIGHTS...
...ARE ON AGAIN!
THEN THE BATTLE'S NOT LOST! LET'S GO BACK TO THE BAR AND MAKE PLANS!
ARE YOU AN IDIOT?
CAN YOU SEE IT?
FOR SOME UNKNOWN REASON, THE ROBOTS SUDDENLY STOPPED!
I'M BROAD-CASTING THIS REPORT LIVE, BUT I HAVE NO IDEA WHEN OR IF IT WILL AIR.
OH! I'M ON THE MONITOR! I'M ON THE MONITOR!
HURRAY! POWER HAS BEEN RESTORED TO THE CAPITAL!

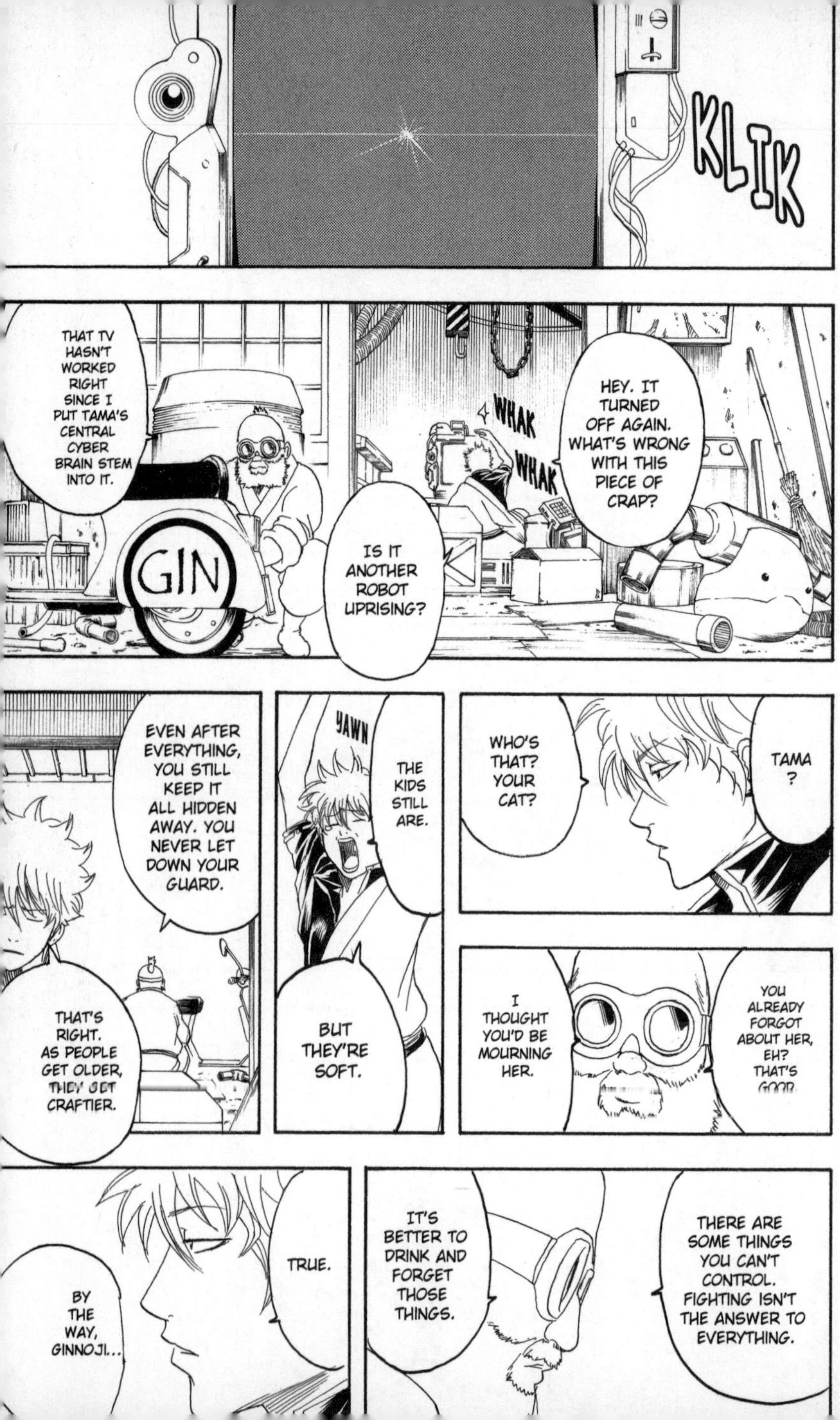
KLIK
HEY. IT TURNED OFF AGAIN. WHAT'S WRONG WITH THIS PIECE OF CRAP?
WHAK WHAK
IS IT ANOTHER ROBOT UPRISING?
THAT TV HASN'T WORKED RIGHT SINCE I PUT TAMA'S CENTRAL CYBER BRAIN STEM INTO IT.
GIN
TAMA?
WHO'S THAT? YOUR CAT?
YOU ALREADY FORGOT ABOUT HER, EH? THAT'S GOOD.
I THOUGHT YOU'D BE MOURNING HER.
YAWN
THE KIDS STILL ARE.
BUT THEY'RE SOFT.
EVEN AFTER EVERYTHING, YOU STILL KEEP IT ALL HIDDEN AWAY. YOU NEVER LET DOWN YOUR GUARD.
THAT'S RIGHT. AS PEOPLE GET OLDER, THEY GET CRAFTIER.
THERE ARE SOME THINGS YOU CAN'T CONTROL. FIGHTING ISN'T THE ANSWER TO EVERYTHING.
IT'S BETTER TO DRINK AND FORGET THOSE THINGS.
TRUE.
BY THE WAY, GINNOJI...

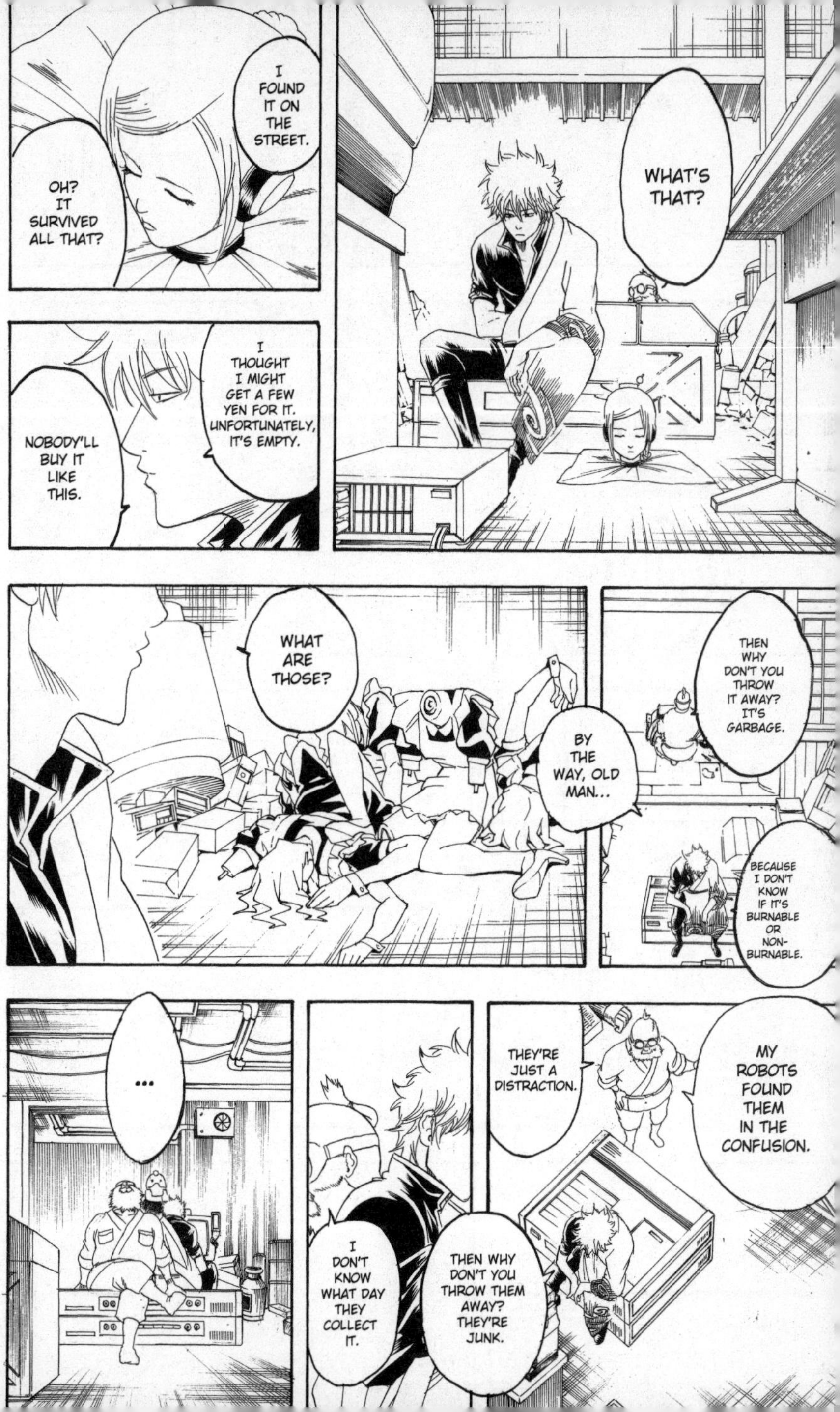
WHAT'S THAT?
I FOUND IT ON THE STREET.
OH? IT SURVIVED ALL THAT?
I THOUGHT I MIGHT GET A FEW YEN FOR IT. UNFORTUNATELY, IT'S EMPTY.
NOBODY'LL BUY IT LIKE THIS.
THEN WHY DON'T YOU THROW IT AWAY? IT'S GARBAGE.
BECAUSE I DON'T KNOW IF IT'S BURNABLE OR NON-BURNABLE.
BY THE WAY, OLD MAN...
WHAT ARE THOSE?
MY ROBOTS FOUND THEM IN THE CONFUSION.
THEY'RE JUST A DISTRACTION.
THEN WHY DON'T YOU THROW THEM AWAY? THEY'RE JUNK.
I DON'T KNOW WHAT DAY THEY COLLECT IT.
...

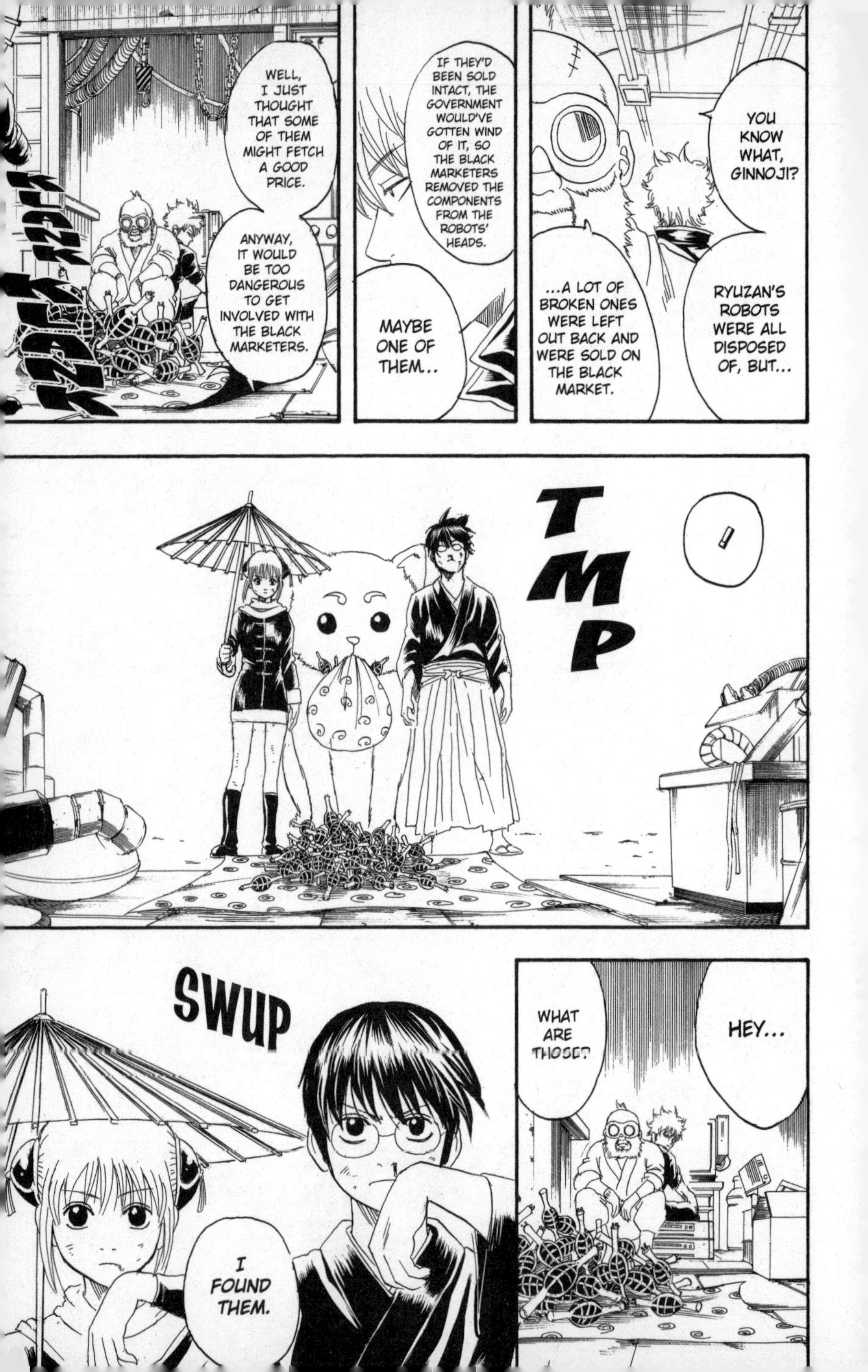

YOU KNOW WHAT, GINNOJI?
RYUZAN'S ROBOTS WERE ALL DISPOSED OF, BUT...
...A LOT OF BROKEN ONES WERE LEFT OUT BACK AND WERE SOLD ON THE BLACK MARKET.
IF THEY'D BEEN SOLD INTACT, THE GOVERNMENT WOULD'VE GOTTEN WIND OF IT, SO THE BLACK MARKETERS REMOVED THE COMPONENTS FROM THE ROBOTS' HEADS.
MAYBE ONE OF THEM...
WELL, I JUST THOUGHT THAT SOME OF THEM MIGHT FETCH A GOOD PRICE.
ANYWAY, IT WOULD BE TOO DANGEROUS TO GET INVOLVED WITH THE BLACK MARKETERS.
!
TMP
HEY...
WHAT ARE THOSE?
SWUP
I FOUND THEM.

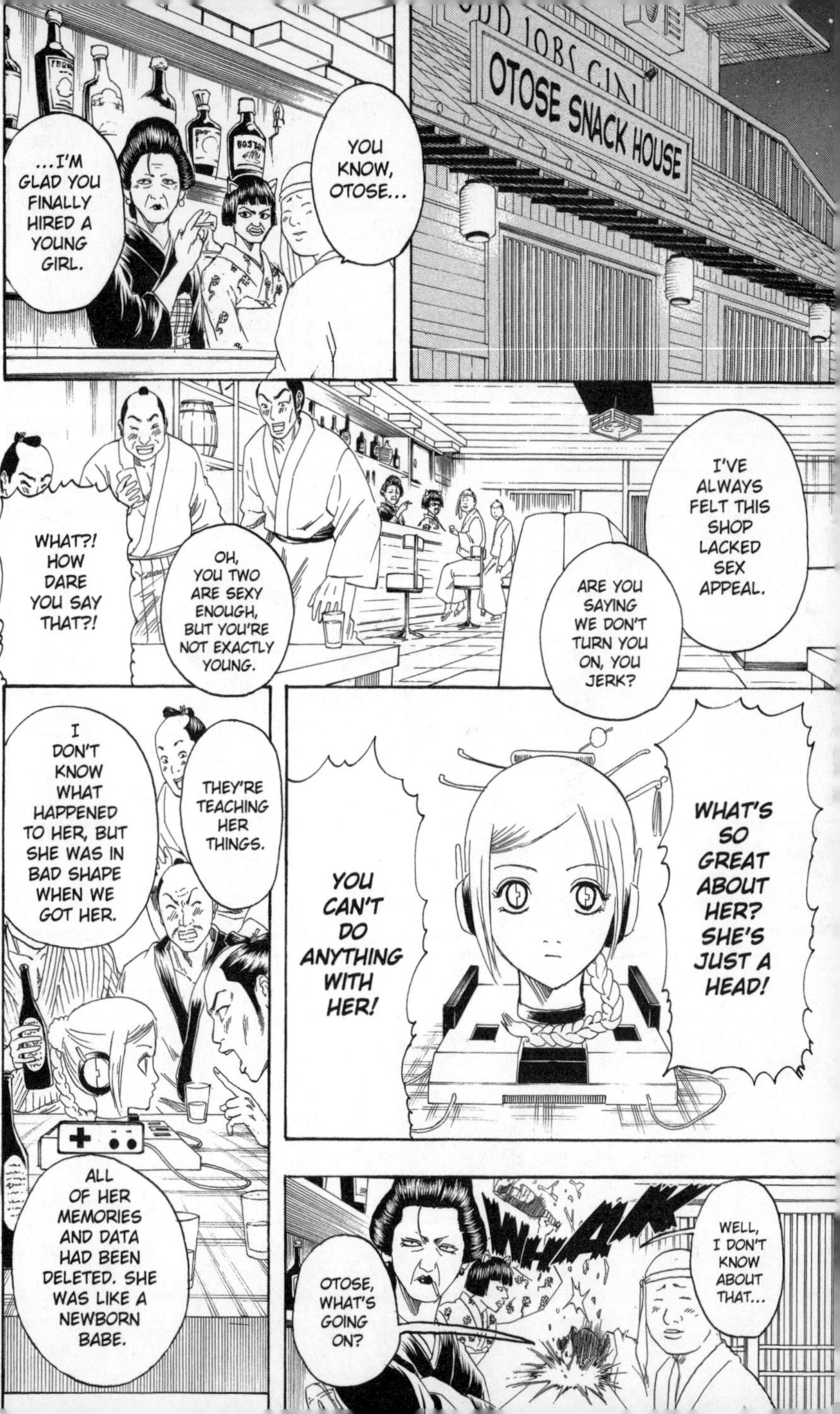
OTOSE SNACK HOUSE
YOU KNOW, OTOSE...
...I'M GLAD YOU FINALLY HIRED A YOUNG GIRL.
I'VE ALWAYS FELT THIS SHOP LACKED SEX APPEAL.
ARE YOU SAYING WE DON'T TURN YOU ON, YOU JERK?
OH, YOU TWO ARE SEXY ENOUGH, BUT YOU'RE NOT EXACTLY YOUNG.
WHAT?! HOW DARE YOU SAY THAT?!
WHAT'S SO GREAT ABOUT HER? SHE'S JUST A HEAD!
YOU CAN'T DO ANYTHING WITH HER!
WELL, I DON'T KNOW ABOUT THAT...
WHAK
OTOSE, WHAT'S GOING ON?
THEY'RE TEACHING HER THINGS.
I DON'T KNOW WHAT HAPPENED TO HER, BUT SHE WAS IN BAD SHAPE WHEN WE GOT HER.
ALL OF HER MEMORIES AND DATA HAD BEEN DELETED. SHE WAS LIKE A NEWBORN BABE.

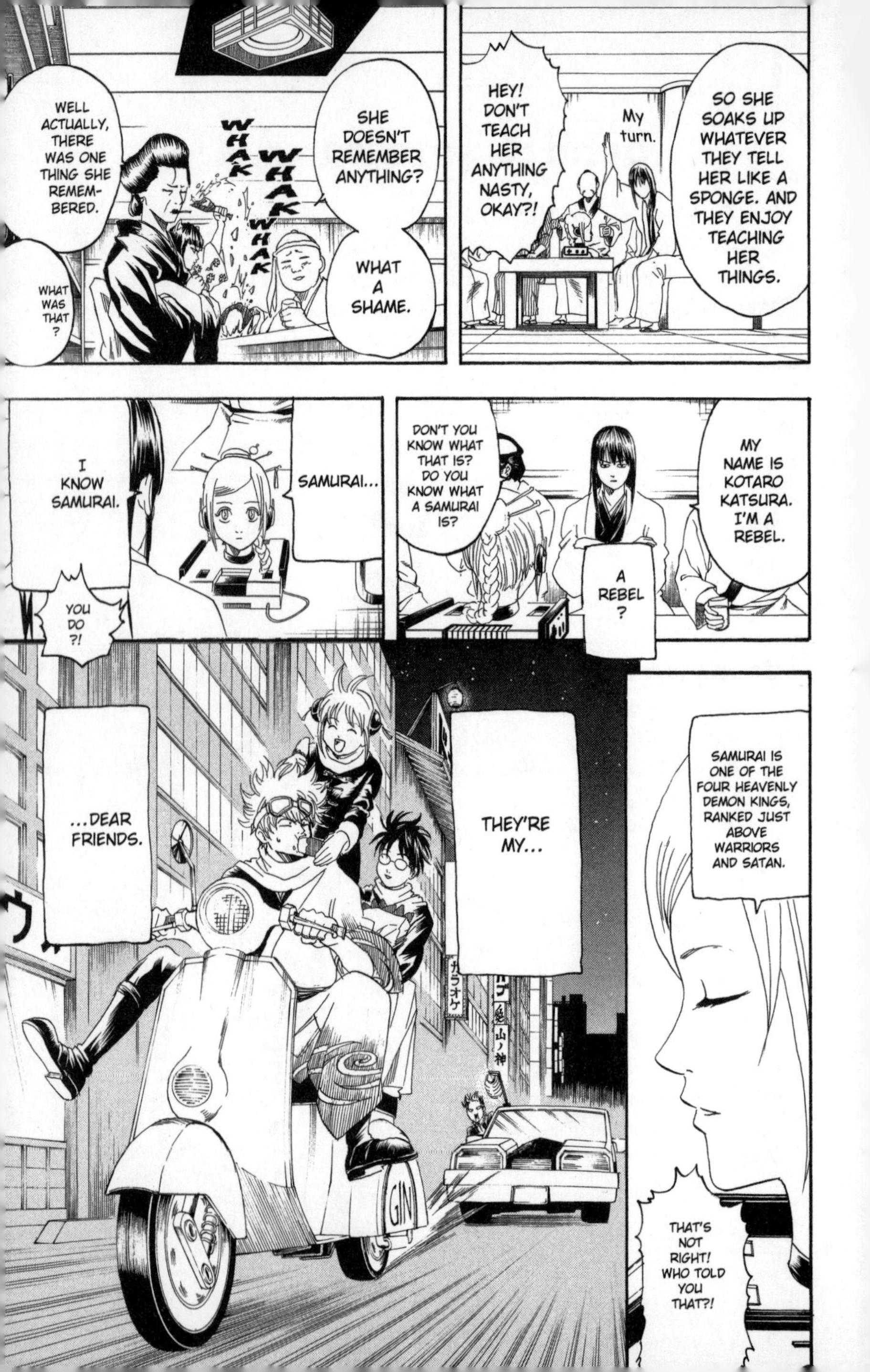
SO SHE SOAKS UP WHATEVER THEY TELL HER LIKE A SPONGE. AND THEY ENJOY TEACHING HER THINGS.
My turn.
HEY! DON'T TEACH HER ANYTHING NASTY, OKAY?!
SHE DOESN'T REMEMBER ANYTHING?
WHAT A SHAME.
WHAK WHAK WHAK WHAK
WELL ACTUALLY, THERE WAS ONE THING SHE REMEMBERED.
WHAT WAS THAT?
MY NAME IS KOTARO KATSURA. I'M A REBEL.
A REBEL?
DON'T YOU KNOW WHAT THAT IS? DO YOU KNOW WHAT A SAMURAI IS?
SAMURAI...
I KNOW SAMURAI.
YOU DO?!
SAMURAI IS ONE OF THE FOUR HEAVENLY DEMON KINGS, RANKED JUST ABOVE WARRIORS AND SATAN.
THAT'S NOT RIGHT! WHO TOLD YOU THAT?!
THEY'RE MY...
...DEAR FRIENDS.
カラオケ
GIN

Send us your Fan Art!

We'd like to give you, our loyal *Gin Tama* readers, a chance to show off your artistic talents! Send us your drawings of the Yorozuya crew or your other favorite characters from *Gin Tama*! If they're good enough to impress Granny Otose (which ain't easy), you just might see them in the pages of future VIZ Media volumes of *Gin Tama*!

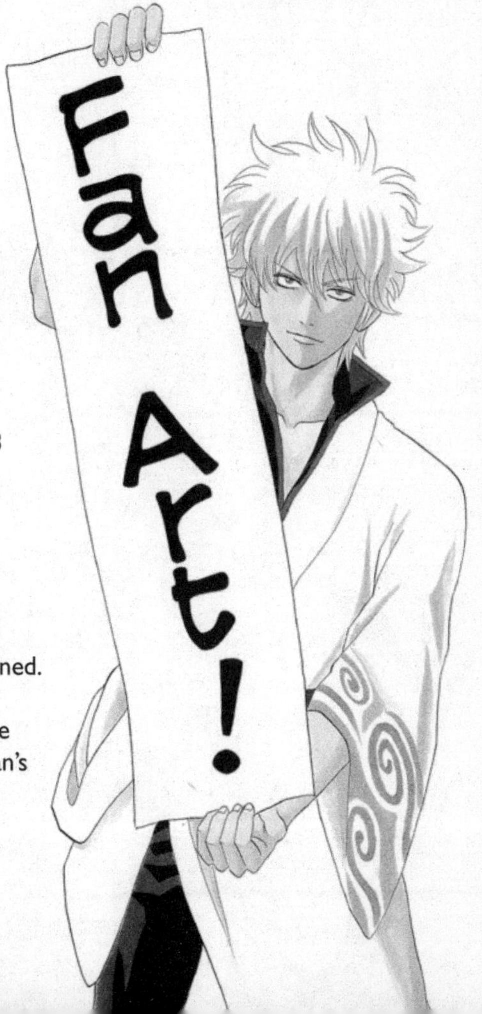
Fan Art!

Send your fan art to:

VIZ Media
Attn: Jann Jones, Editor
295 Bay St.
San Francisco, CA 94133

Be sure to include the signed release form available here:
http://www.shonenjump.com/fanart/Fan_Art_Release.pdf
Submissions will not be returned.
Submissions without a signed release form will be fed to the Amanto sea lions at Fisherman's Wharf…

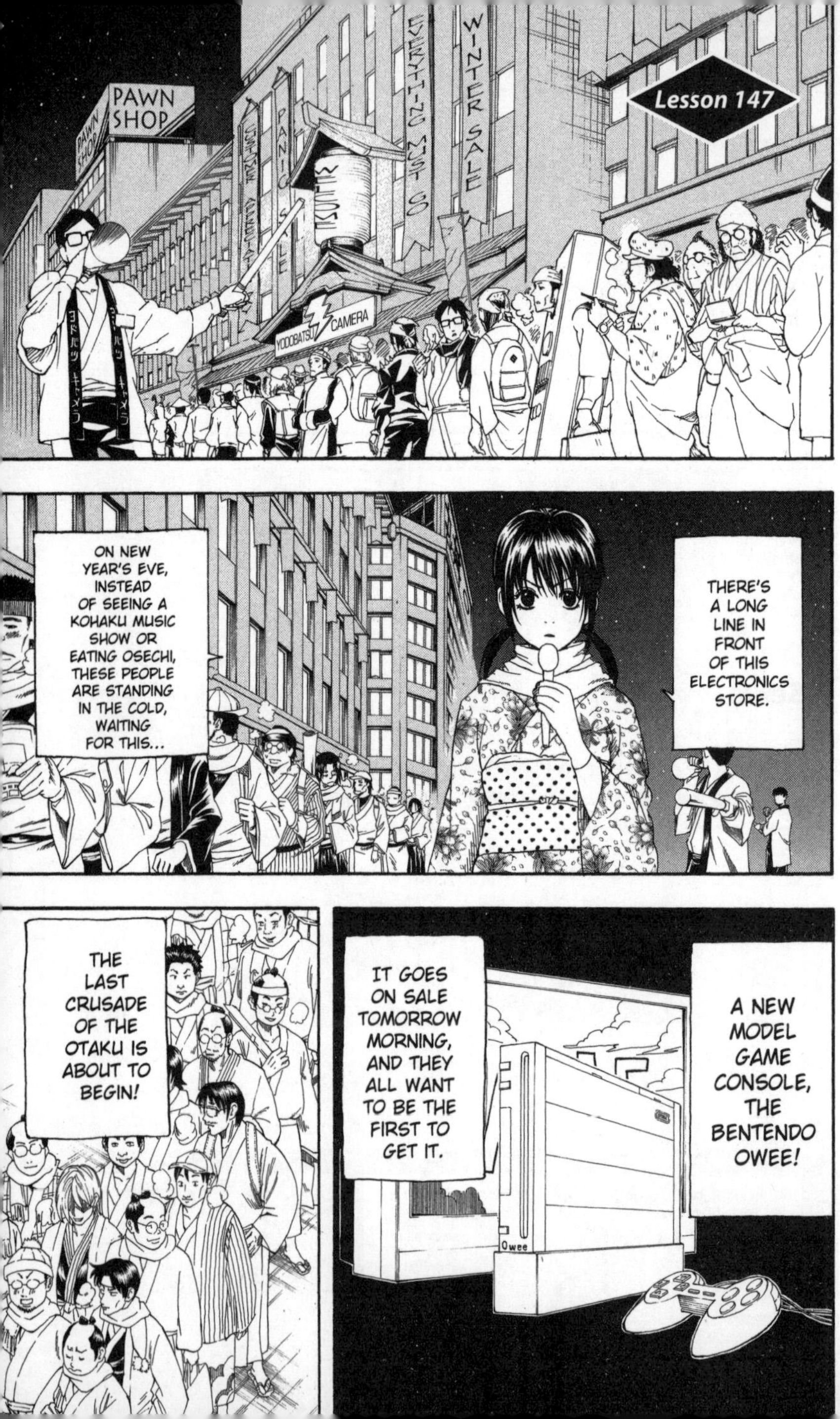
Lesson 147
WINTER SALE
PAWN SHOP
YODOBATSU CAMERA
THERE'S A LONG LINE IN FRONT OF THIS ELECTRONICS STORE.
ON NEW YEAR'S EVE, INSTEAD OF SEEING A KOHAKU MUSIC SHOW OR EATING OSECHI, THESE PEOPLE ARE STANDING IN THE COLD, WAITING FOR THIS...
A NEW MODEL GAME CONSOLE, THE BENTENDO OWEE!
IT GOES ON SALE TOMORROW MORNING, AND THEY ALL WANT TO BE THE FIRST TO GET IT.
Owee
THE LAST CRUSADE OF THE OTAKU IS ABOUT TO BEGIN!

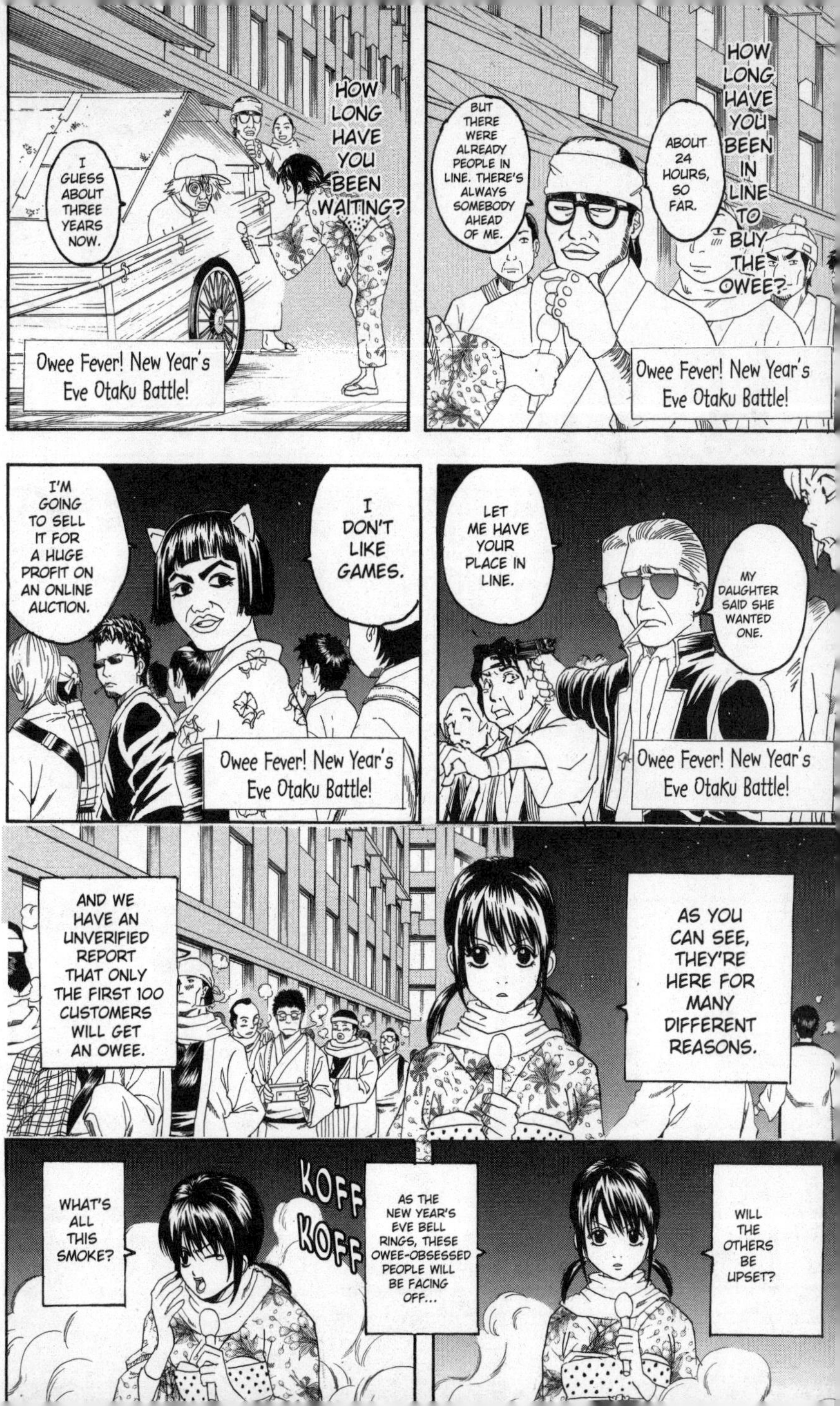
HOW LONG HAVE YOU BEEN IN LINE TO BUY THE OWEE?
ABOUT 24 HOURS, SO FAR.
BUT THERE WERE ALREADY PEOPLE IN LINE. THERE'S ALWAYS SOMEBODY AHEAD OF ME.
Owee Fever! New Year's Eve Otaku Battle!
HOW LONG HAVE YOU BEEN WAITING?
I GUESS ABOUT THREE YEARS NOW.
Owee Fever! New Year's Eve Otaku Battle!
MY DAUGHTER SAID SHE WANTED ONE.
LET ME HAVE YOUR PLACE IN LINE.
Owee Fever! New Year's Eve Otaku Battle!
I DON'T LIKE GAMES.
I'M GOING TO SELL IT FOR A HUGE PROFIT ON AN ONLINE AUCTION.
Owee Fever! New Year's Eve Otaku Battle!
AS YOU CAN SEE, THEY'RE HERE FOR MANY DIFFERENT REASONS.
AND WE HAVE AN UNVERIFIED REPORT THAT ONLY THE FIRST 100 CUSTOMERS WILL GET AN OWEE.
WILL THE OTHERS BE UPSET?
AS THE NEW YEAR'S EVE BELL RINGS, THESE OWEE-OBSESSED PEOPLE WILL BE FACING OFF...
KOFF KOFF
WHAT'S ALL THIS SMOKE?

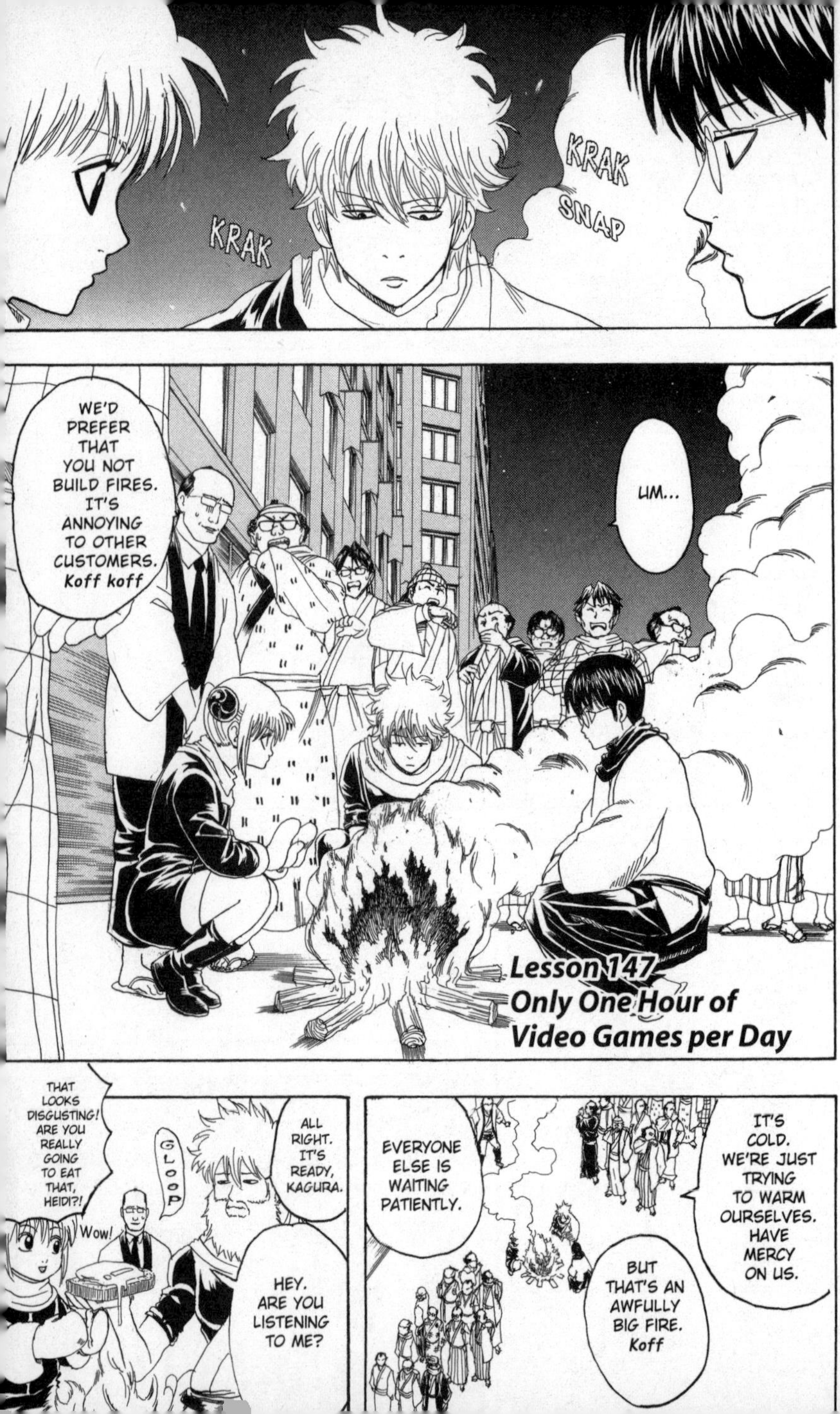
KRAK
SNAP
KRAK
UM...
WE'D PREFER THAT YOU NOT BUILD FIRES. IT'S ANNOYING TO OTHER CUSTOMERS. *Koff koff*
Lesson 147
Only One Hour of Video Games per Day
IT'S COLD. WE'RE JUST TRYING TO WARM OURSELVES. HAVE MERCY ON US.
EVERYONE ELSE IS WAITING PATIENTLY.
BUT THAT'S AN AWFULLY BIG FIRE. *Koff*
ALL RIGHT. IT'S READY, KAGURA.
GLOOP
HEY. ARE YOU LISTENING TO ME?
THAT LOOKS DISGUSTING! ARE YOU REALLY GOING TO EAT THAT, HEIDI?!
Wow!

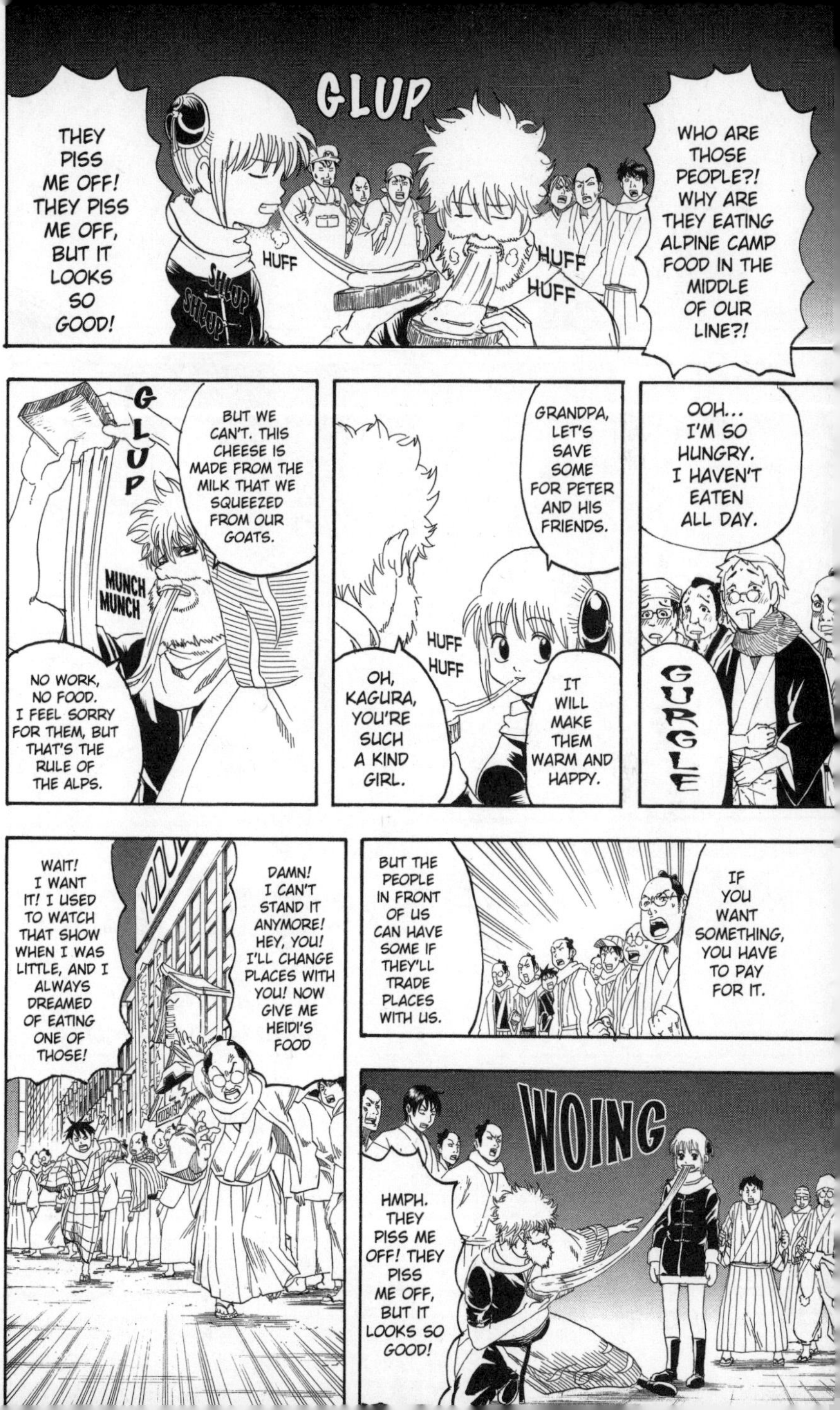
WHO ARE THOSE PEOPLE?! WHY ARE THEY EATING ALPINE CAMP FOOD IN THE MIDDLE OF OUR LINE?!
GLUP
HUFF
HUFF
THEY PISS ME OFF! THEY PISS ME OFF, BUT IT LOOKS SO GOOD!
HUFF
SHLUP
SHLUP
OOH... I'M SO HUNGRY. I HAVEN'T EATEN ALL DAY.
GURGLE
GRANDPA, LET'S SAVE SOME FOR PETER AND HIS FRIENDS.
IT WILL MAKE THEM WARM AND HAPPY.
HUFF
HUFF
OH, KAGURA, YOU'RE SUCH A KIND GIRL.
BUT WE CAN'T. THIS CHEESE IS MADE FROM THE MILK THAT WE SQUEEZED FROM OUR GOATS.
GLUP
MUNCH
MUNCH
NO WORK, NO FOOD. I FEEL SORRY FOR THEM, BUT THAT'S THE RULE OF THE ALPS.
IF YOU WANT SOMETHING, YOU HAVE TO PAY FOR IT.
BUT THE PEOPLE IN FRONT OF US CAN HAVE SOME IF THEY'LL TRADE PLACES WITH US.
WOING
HMPH. THEY PISS ME OFF! THEY PISS ME OFF, BUT IT LOOKS SO GOOD!
DAMN! I CAN'T STAND IT ANYMORE! HEY, YOU! I'LL CHANGE PLACES WITH YOU! NOW GIVE ME HEIDI'S FOOD
WAIT! I WANT IT! I USED TO WATCH THAT SHOW WHEN I WAS LITTLE, AND I ALWAYS DREAMED OF EATING ONE OF THOSE!

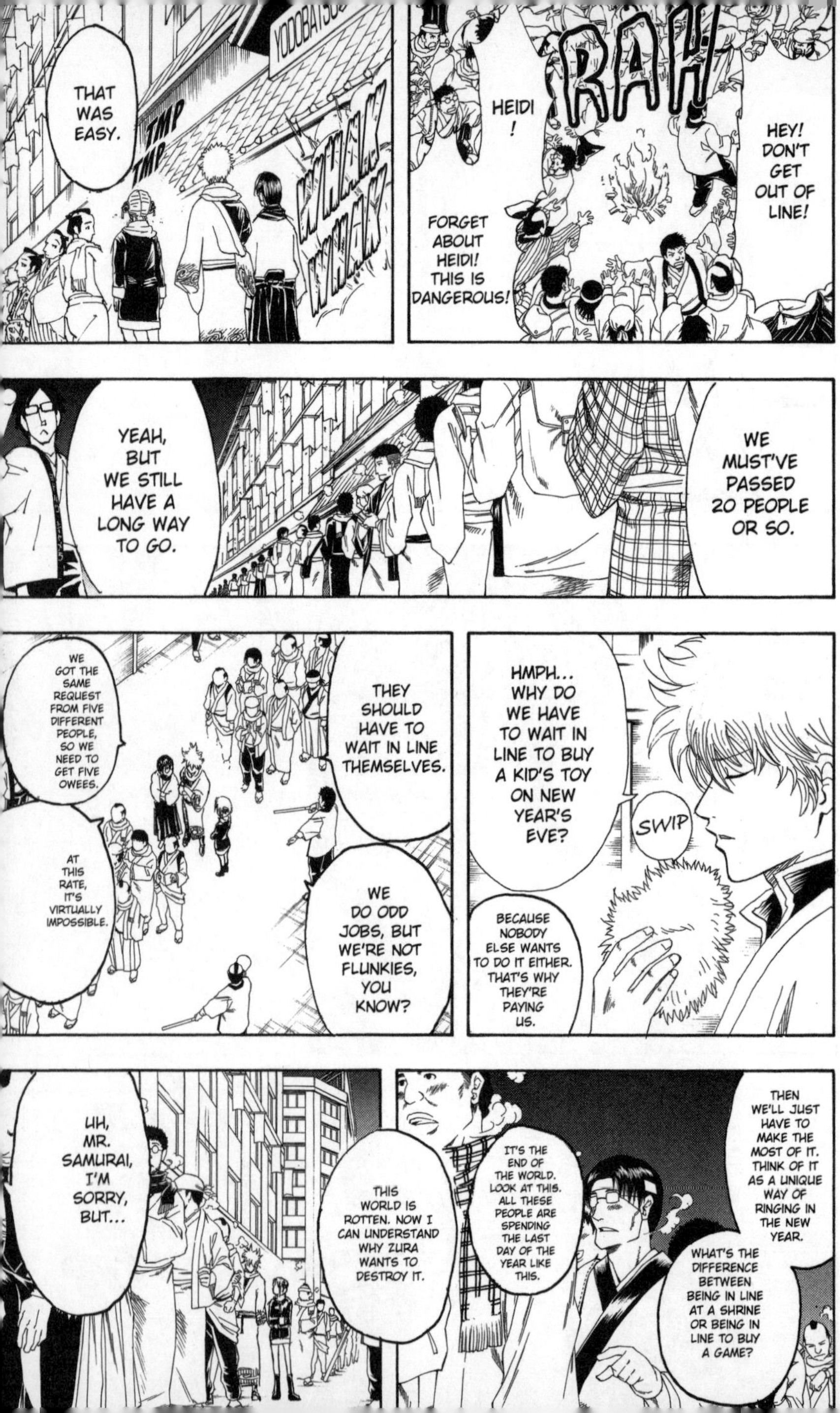
RAH
HEY! DON'T GET OUT OF LINE!
HEIDI!
FORGET ABOUT HEIDI! THIS IS DANGEROUS!
YODOBATSU
WHAK WHAK
TMP TMP
THAT WAS EASY.
WE MUST'VE PASSED 20 PEOPLE OR SO.
YEAH, BUT WE STILL HAVE A LONG WAY TO GO.
HMPH... WHY DO WE HAVE TO WAIT IN LINE TO BUY A KID'S TOY ON NEW YEAR'S EVE?
SWIP
BECAUSE NOBODY ELSE WANTS TO DO IT EITHER. THAT'S WHY THEY'RE PAYING US.
THEY SHOULD HAVE TO WAIT IN LINE THEMSELVES.
WE DO ODD JOBS, BUT WE'RE NOT FLUNKIES, YOU KNOW?
WE GOT THE SAME REQUEST FROM FIVE DIFFERENT PEOPLE, SO WE NEED TO GET FIVE OWEES.
AT THIS RATE, IT'S VIRTUALLY IMPOSSIBLE.
THEN WE'LL JUST HAVE TO MAKE THE MOST OF IT. THINK OF IT AS A UNIQUE WAY OF RINGING IN THE NEW YEAR.
WHAT'S THE DIFFERENCE BETWEEN BEING IN LINE AT A SHRINE OR BEING IN LINE TO BUY A GAME?
IT'S THE END OF THE WORLD. LOOK AT THIS. ALL THESE PEOPLE ARE SPENDING THE LAST DAY OF THE YEAR LIKE THIS.
THIS WORLD IS ROTTEN. NOW I CAN UNDERSTAND WHY ZURA WANTS TO DESTROY IT.
UH, MR. SAMURAI, I'M SORRY, BUT...

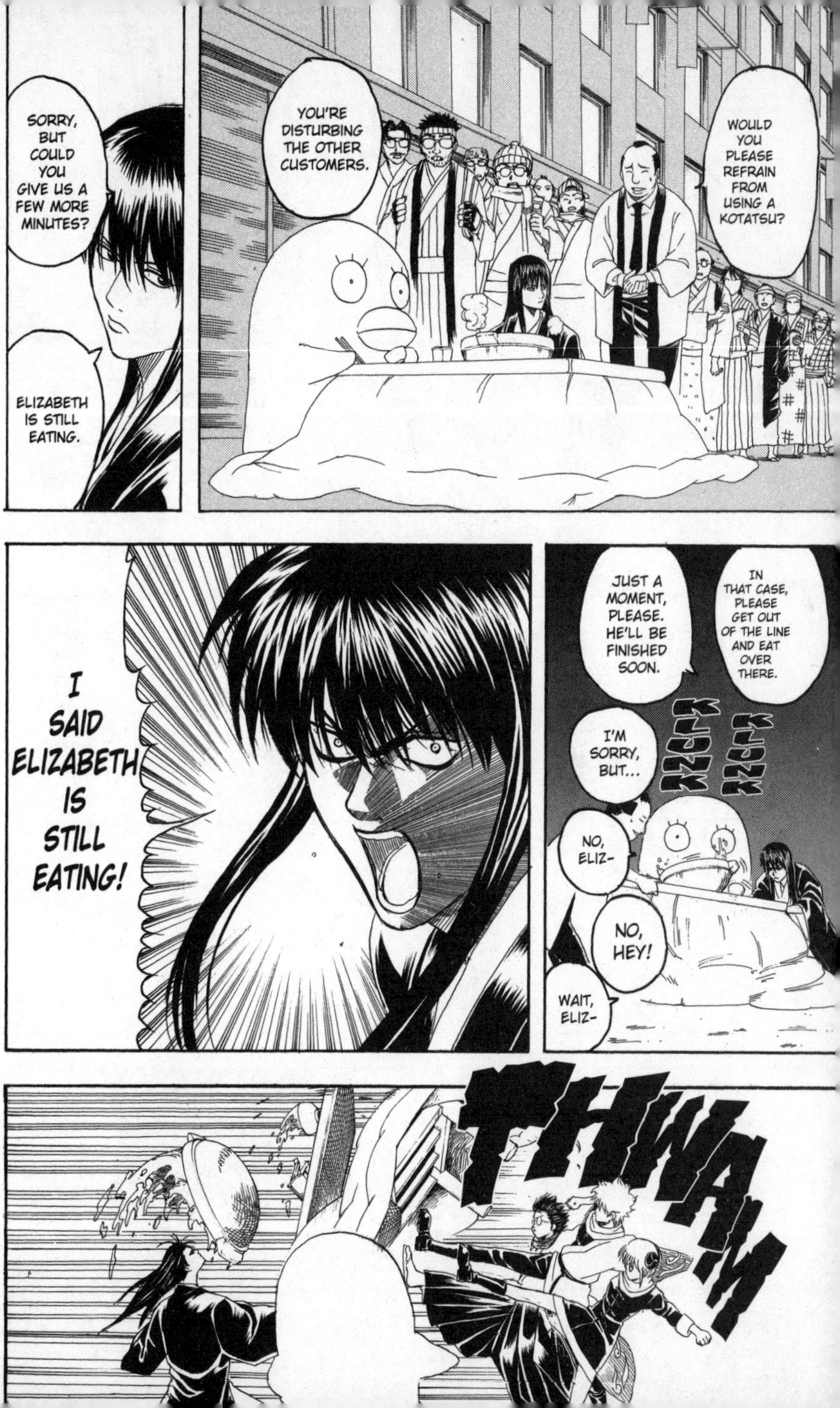
WOULD YOU PLEASE REFRAIN FROM USING A KOTATSU?
YOU'RE DISTURBING THE OTHER CUSTOMERS.
SORRY, BUT COULD YOU GIVE US A FEW MORE MINUTES?
ELIZABETH IS STILL EATING.
IN THAT CASE, PLEASE GET OUT OF THE LINE AND EAT OVER THERE.
JUST A MOMENT, PLEASE. HE'LL BE FINISHED SOON.
KLUNK KLUNK
I'M SORRY, BUT...
NO, ELIZ-
NO, HEY!
WAIT, ELIZ-
I SAID ELIZABETH IS STILL EATING!
THWAM

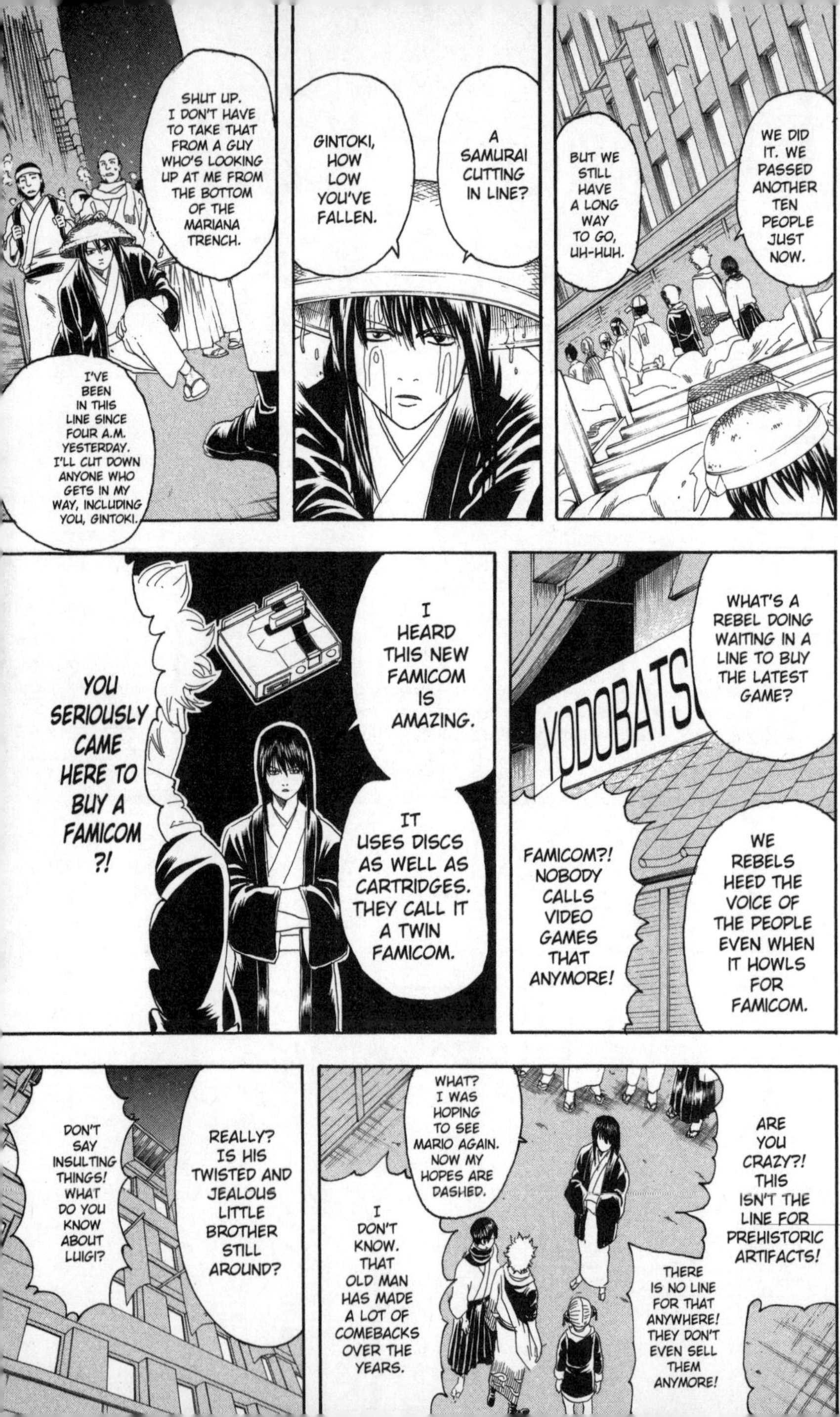
WE DID IT. WE PASSED ANOTHER TEN PEOPLE JUST NOW.
BUT WE STILL HAVE A LONG WAY TO GO, UH-HUH.
A SAMURAI CUTTING IN LINE?
GINTOKI, HOW LOW YOU'VE FALLEN.
SHUT UP. I DON'T HAVE TO TAKE THAT FROM A GUY WHO'S LOOKING UP AT ME FROM THE BOTTOM OF THE MARIANA TRENCH.
I'VE BEEN IN THIS LINE SINCE FOUR A.M. YESTERDAY. I'LL CUT DOWN ANYONE WHO GETS IN MY WAY, INCLUDING YOU, GINTOKI.
WHAT'S A REBEL DOING WAITING IN A LINE TO BUY THE LATEST GAME?
YODOBATS
WE REBELS HEED THE VOICE OF THE PEOPLE EVEN WHEN IT HOWLS FOR FAMICOM.
FAMICOM?! NOBODY CALLS VIDEO GAMES THAT ANYMORE!
I HEARD THIS NEW FAMICOM IS AMAZING.
IT USES DISCS AS WELL AS CARTRIDGES. THEY CALL IT A TWIN FAMICOM.
YOU SERIOUSLY CAME HERE TO BUY A FAMICOM ?!
ARE YOU CRAZY?! THIS ISN'T THE LINE FOR PREHISTORIC ARTIFACTS!
WHAT? I WAS HOPING TO SEE MARIO AGAIN. NOW MY HOPES ARE DASHED.
THERE IS NO LINE FOR THAT ANYWHERE! THEY DON'T EVEN SELL THEM ANYMORE!
I DON'T KNOW. THAT OLD MAN HAS MADE A LOT OF COMEBACKS OVER THE YEARS.
REALLY? IS HIS TWISTED AND JEALOUS LITTLE BROTHER STILL AROUND?
DON'T SAY INSULTING THINGS! WHAT DO YOU KNOW ABOUT LUIGI?

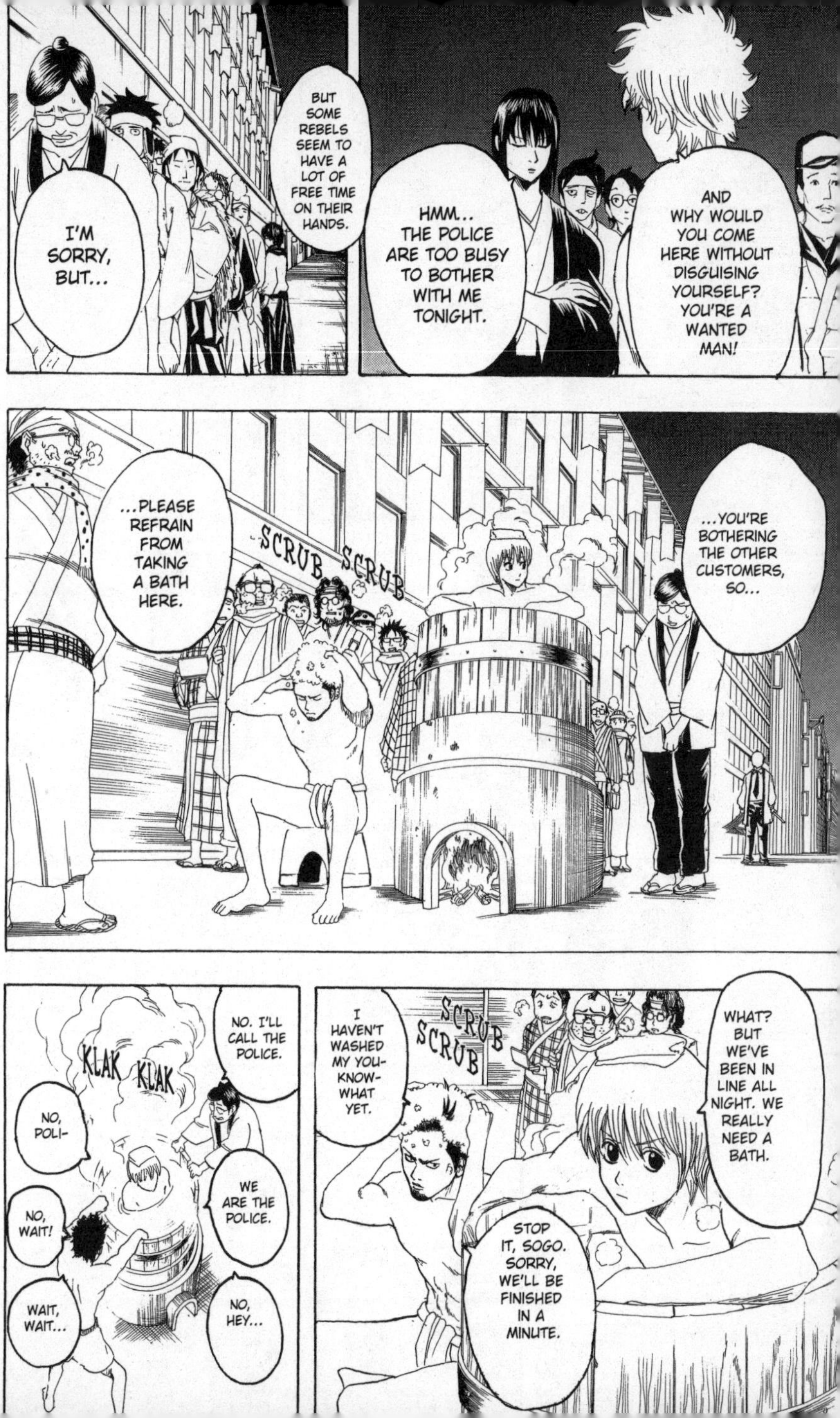
AND WHY WOULD YOU COME HERE WITHOUT DISGUISING YOURSELF? YOU'RE A WANTED MAN!
HMM... THE POLICE ARE TOO BUSY TO BOTHER WITH ME TONIGHT.
BUT SOME REBELS SEEM TO HAVE A LOT OF FREE TIME ON THEIR HANDS.
I'M SORRY, BUT...
...YOU'RE BOTHERING THE OTHER CUSTOMERS, SO...
SCRUB SCRUB
...PLEASE REFRAIN FROM TAKING A BATH HERE.
WHAT? BUT WE'VE BEEN IN LINE ALL NIGHT. WE REALLY NEED A BATH.
SCRUB SCRUB
I HAVEN'T WASHED MY YOU-KNOW-WHAT YET.
STOP IT, SOGO. SORRY, WE'LL BE FINISHED IN A MINUTE.
NO. I'LL CALL THE POLICE.
KLAK KLAK
NO, POLI-
WE ARE THE POLICE.
NO, WAIT!
NO, HEY...
WAIT, WAIT...

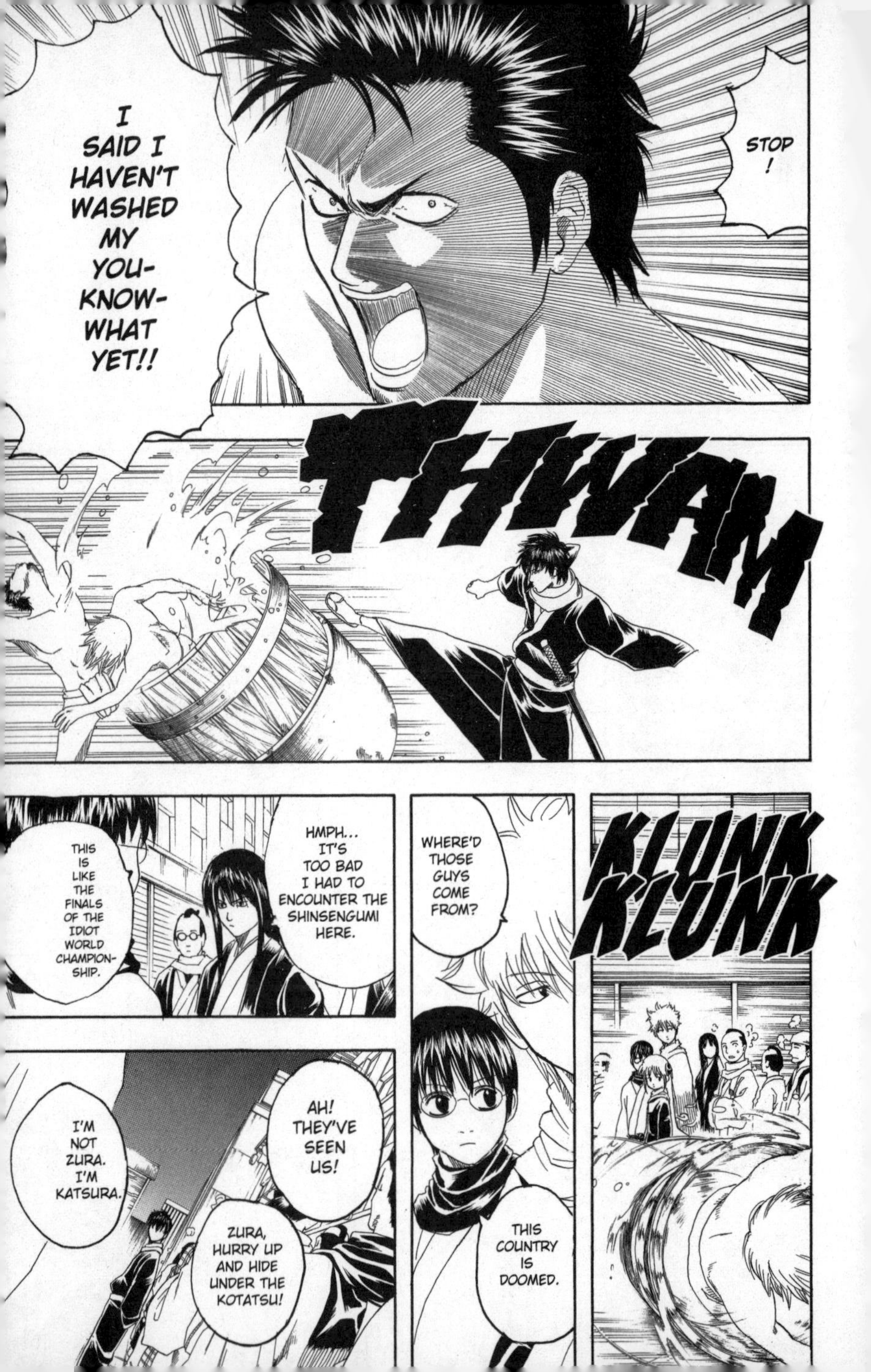
STOP!
I SAID I HAVEN'T WASHED MY YOU-KNOW-WHAT YET!!
THWAM
KLUNK KLUNK
WHERE'D THOSE GUYS COME FROM?
THIS COUNTRY IS DOOMED.
HMPH... IT'S TOO BAD I HAD TO ENCOUNTER THE SHINSENGUMI HERE.
THIS IS LIKE THE FINALS OF THE IDIOT WORLD CHAMPION-SHIP.
AH! THEY'VE SEEN US!
ZURA, HURRY UP AND HIDE UNDER THE KOTATSU!
I'M NOT ZURA. I'M KATSURA.

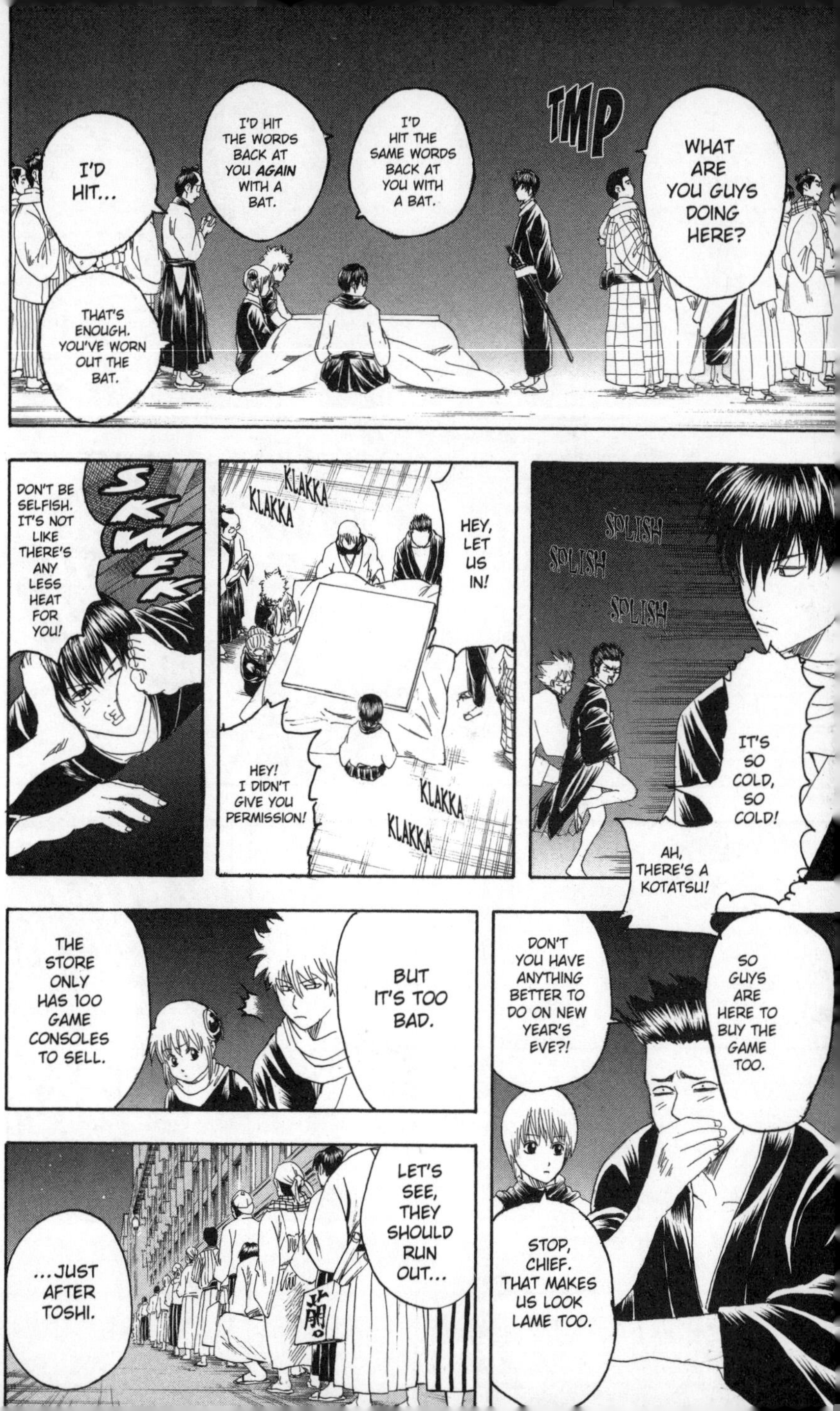
WHAT ARE YOU GUYS DOING HERE?
TMP
I'D HIT THE SAME WORDS BACK AT YOU WITH A BAT.
I'D HIT THE WORDS BACK AT YOU **AGAIN** WITH A BAT.
I'D HIT...
THAT'S ENOUGH. YOU'VE WORN OUT THE BAT.
SPLISH
SPLISH
SPLISH
IT'S SO COLD, SO COLD!
AH, THERE'S A KOTATSU!
KLAKKA
KLAKKA
HEY, LET US IN!
KLAKKA
KLAKKA
HEY! I DIDN'T GIVE YOU PERMISSION!
SKWEEK
DON'T BE SELFISH. IT'S NOT LIKE THERE'S ANY LESS HEAT FOR YOU!
SO GUYS ARE HERE TO BUY THE GAME TOO.
DON'T YOU HAVE ANYTHING BETTER TO DO ON NEW YEAR'S EVE?!
STOP, CHIEF. THAT MAKES US LOOK LAME TOO.
BUT IT'S TOO BAD.
THE STORE ONLY HAS 100 GAME CONSOLES TO SELL.
LET'S SEE, THEY SHOULD RUN OUT...
...JUST AFTER TOSHI.

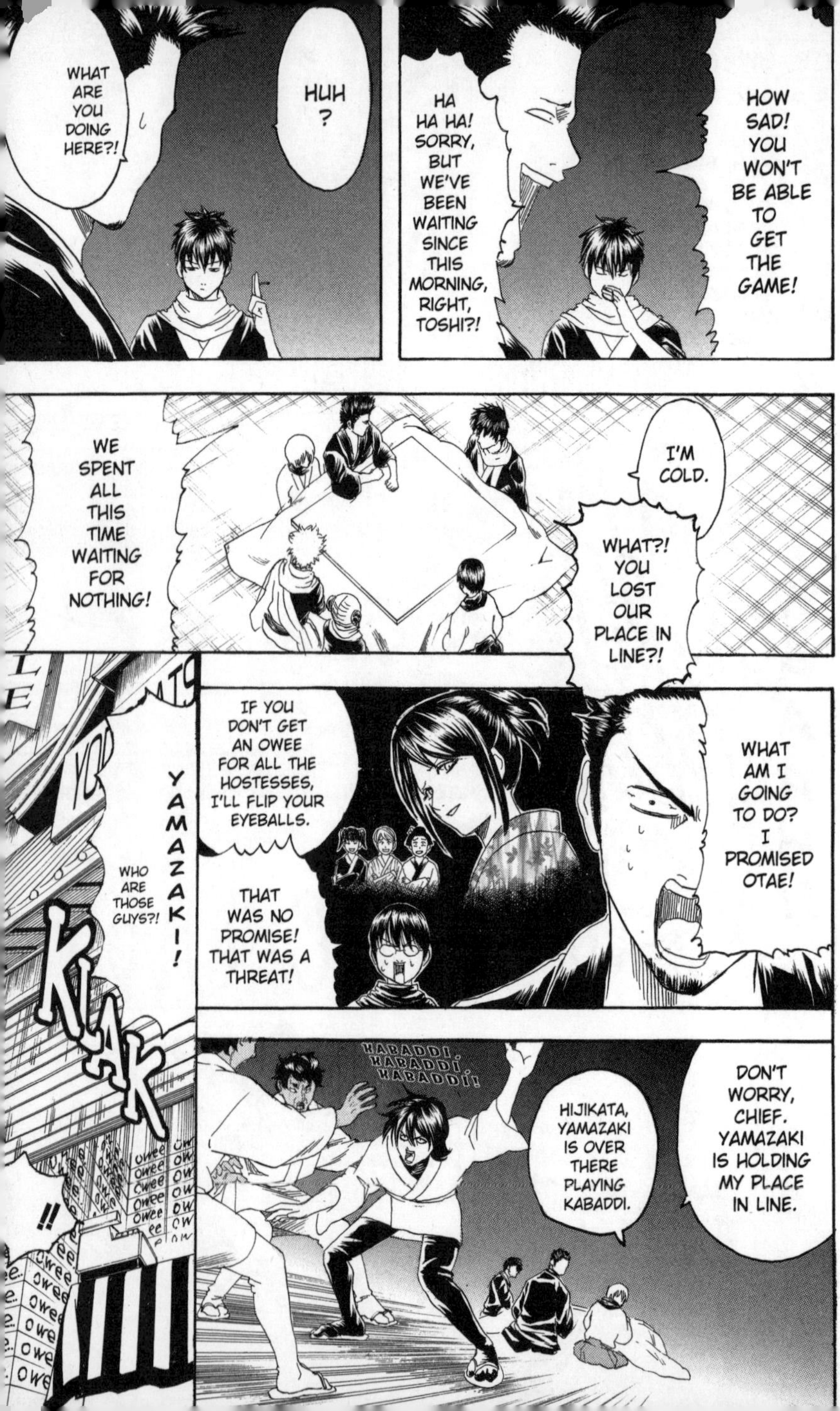
HOW SAD! YOU WON'T BE ABLE TO GET THE GAME!
HA HA HA! SORRY, BUT WE'VE BEEN WAITING SINCE THIS MORNING, RIGHT, TOSHI?!
HUH?
WHAT ARE YOU DOING HERE?!
I'M COLD.
WHAT?! YOU LOST OUR PLACE IN LINE?!
WE SPENT ALL THIS TIME WAITING FOR NOTHING!
WHAT AM I GOING TO DO? I PROMISED OTAE!
IF YOU DON'T GET AN OWEE FOR ALL THE HOSTESSES, I'LL FLIP YOUR EYEBALLS.
THAT WAS NO PROMISE! THAT WAS A THREAT!
DON'T WORRY, CHIEF. YAMAZAKI IS HOLDING MY PLACE IN LINE.
HIJIKATA, YAMAZAKI IS OVER THERE PLAYING KABADDI.
KABADDI, KABADDI, KABADDI!
YAMAZAKI!
WHO ARE THOSE GUYS?!
KLAK
!!

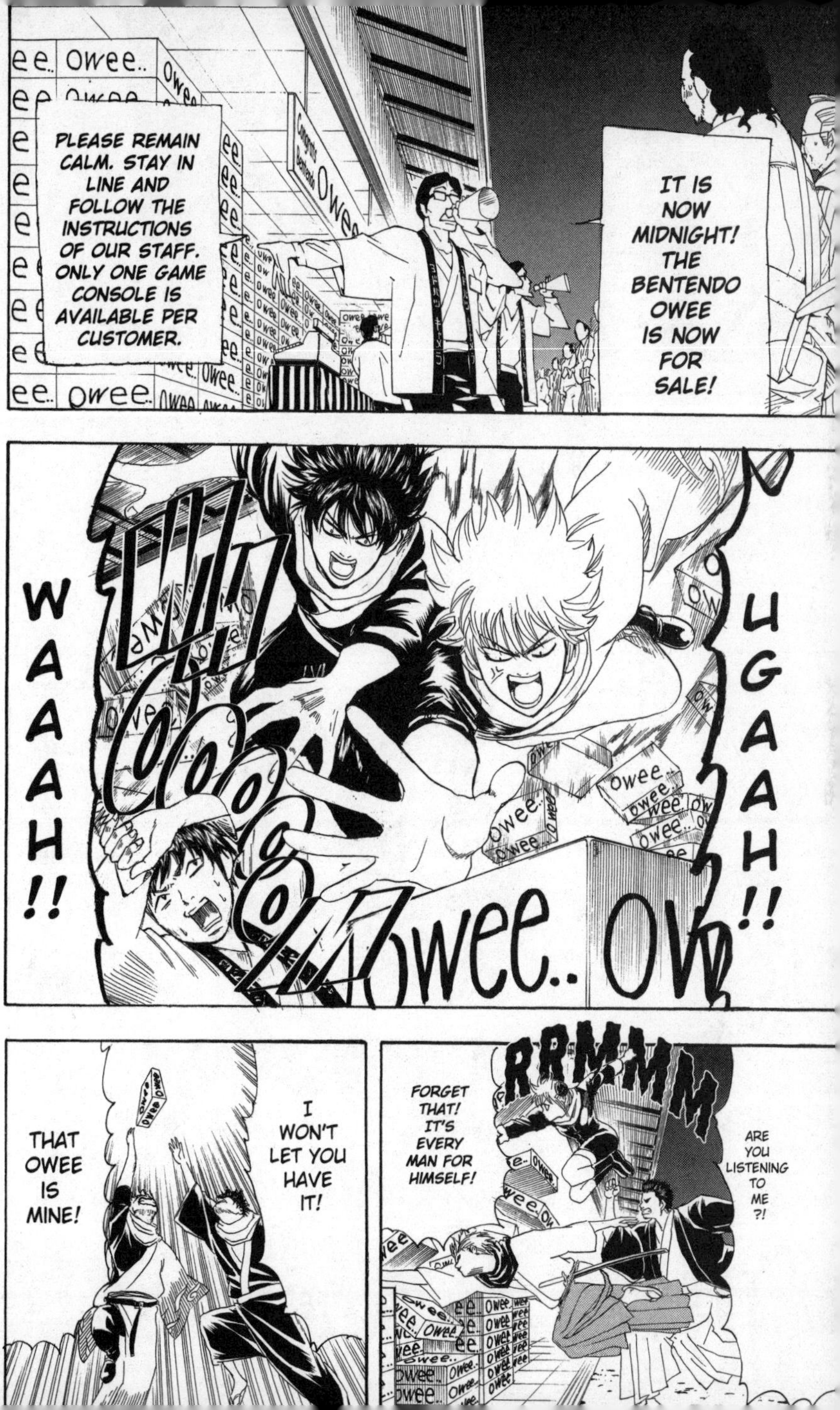

IT IS NOW MIDNIGHT! THE BENTENDO OWEE IS NOW FOR SALE!
PLEASE REMAIN CALM. STAY IN LINE AND FOLLOW THE INSTRUCTIONS OF OUR STAFF. ONLY ONE GAME CONSOLE IS AVAILABLE PER CUSTOMER.
UGAAAH!!
WAAAAH!!
RRMMMM
ARE YOU LISTENING TO ME?!
FORGET THAT! IT'S EVERY MAN FOR HIMSELF!
I WON'T LET YOU HAVE IT!
THAT OWEE IS MINE!

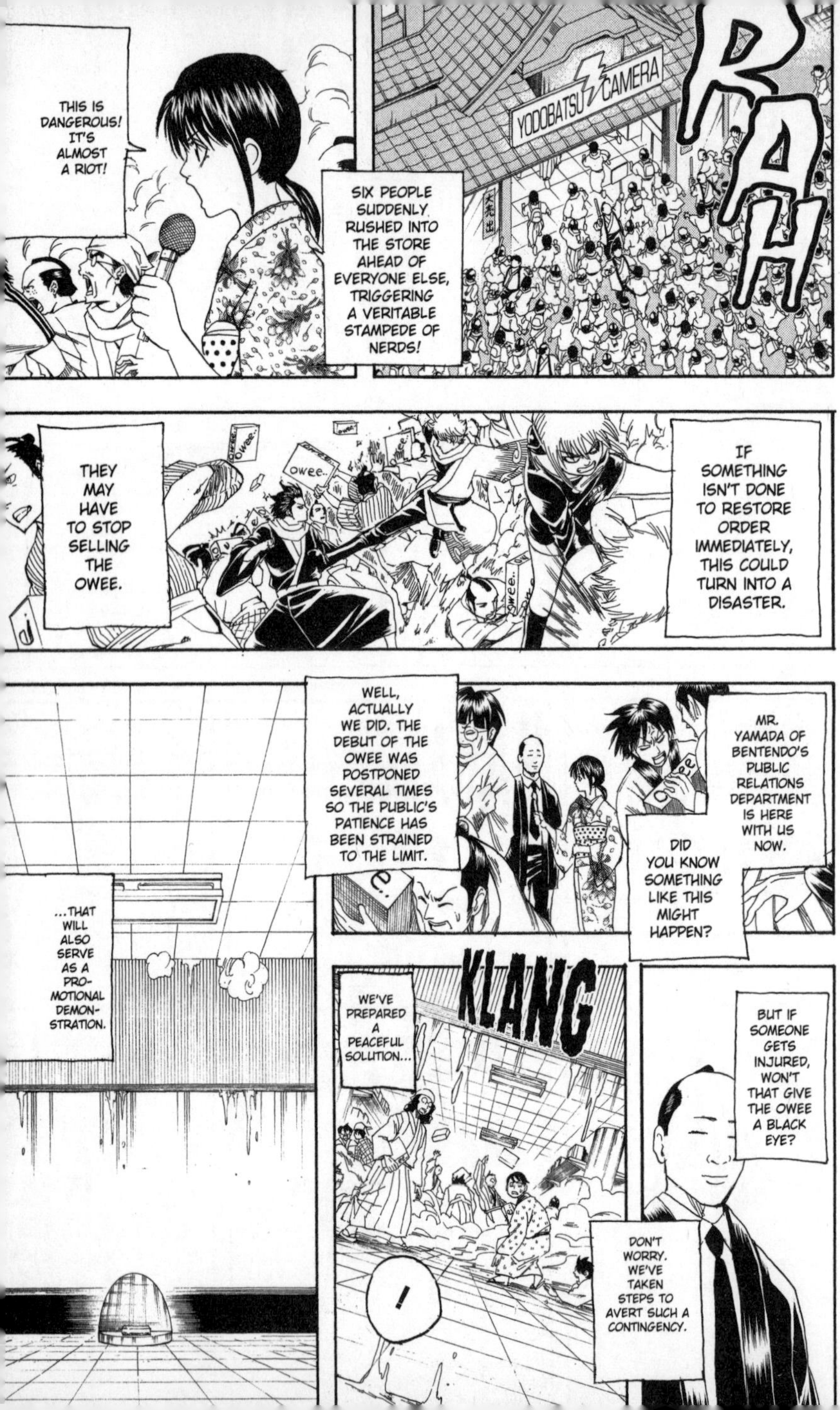
RAH
YODOBATSU CAMERA
SIX PEOPLE SUDDENLY RUSHED INTO THE STORE AHEAD OF EVERYONE ELSE, TRIGGERING A VERITABLE STAMPEDE OF NERDS!
THIS IS DANGEROUS! IT'S ALMOST A RIOT!
IF SOMETHING ISN'T DONE TO RESTORE ORDER IMMEDIATELY, THIS COULD TURN INTO A DISASTER.
THEY MAY HAVE TO STOP SELLING THE OWEE.
MR. YAMADA OF BENTENDO'S PUBLIC RELATIONS DEPARTMENT IS HERE WITH US NOW.
DID YOU KNOW SOMETHING LIKE THIS MIGHT HAPPEN?
WELL, ACTUALLY WE DID. THE DEBUT OF THE OWEE WAS POSTPONED SEVERAL TIMES SO THE PUBLIC'S PATIENCE HAS BEEN STRAINED TO THE LIMIT.
BUT IF SOMEONE GETS INJURED, WON'T THAT GIVE THE OWEE A BLACK EYE?
DON'T WORRY. WE'VE TAKEN STEPS TO AVERT SUCH A CONTINGENCY.
KLANG
WE'VE PREPARED A PEACEFUL SOLUTION...
!
...THAT WILL ALSO SERVE AS A PROMOTIONAL DEMONSTRATION.

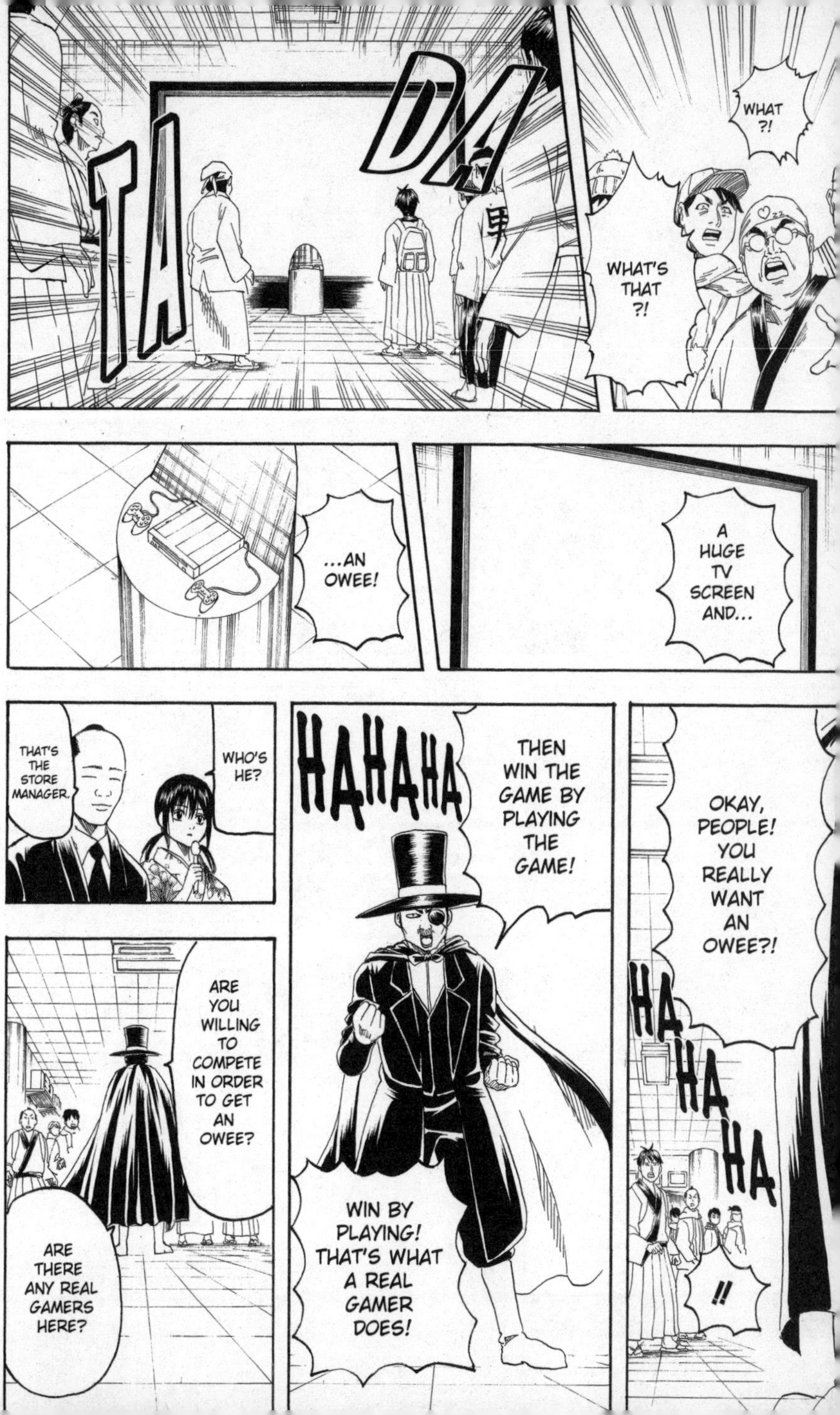
WHAT ?!
WHAT'S THAT ?!
TA DA
A HUGE TV SCREEN AND...
...AN OWEE!
OKAY, PEOPLE! YOU REALLY WANT AN OWEE?!
HA HA HA HA
!!
HAHAHA
THEN WIN THE GAME BY PLAYING THE GAME!
WIN BY PLAYING! THAT'S WHAT A REAL GAMER DOES!
WHO'S HE?
THAT'S THE STORE MANAGER.
ARE YOU WILLING TO COMPETE IN ORDER TO GET AN OWEE?
ARE THERE ANY REAL GAMERS HERE?

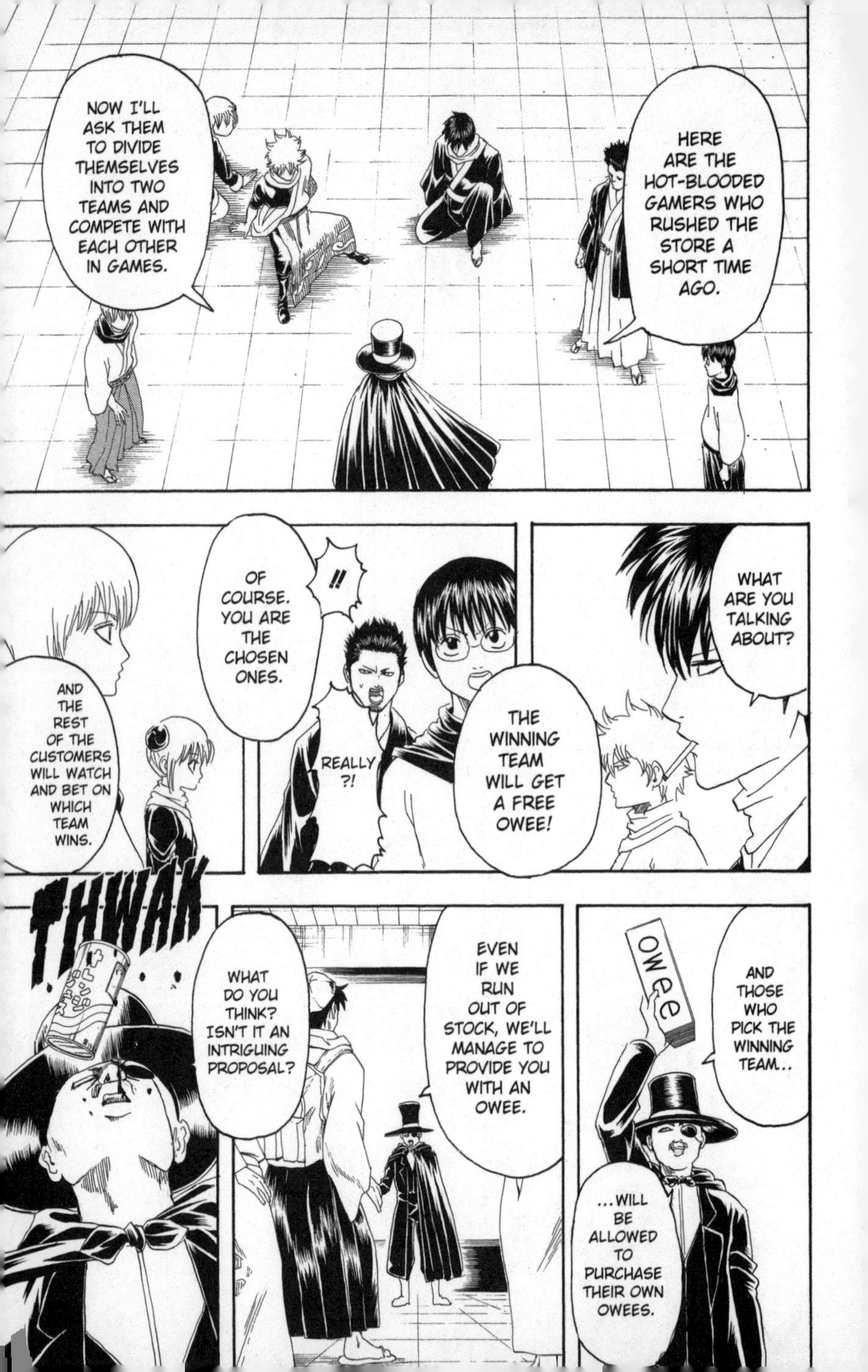
HERE ARE THE HOT-BLOODED GAMERS WHO RUSHED THE STORE A SHORT TIME AGO.
NOW I'LL ASK THEM TO DIVIDE THEMSELVES INTO TWO TEAMS AND COMPETE WITH EACH OTHER IN GAMES.
WHAT ARE YOU TALKING ABOUT?
THE WINNING TEAM WILL GET A FREE OWEE!
!!
REALLY?!
OF COURSE. YOU ARE THE CHOSEN ONES.
AND THE REST OF THE CUSTOMERS WILL WATCH AND BET ON WHICH TEAM WINS.
OWee
AND THOSE WHO PICK THE WINNING TEAM...
...WILL BE ALLOWED TO PURCHASE THEIR OWN OWEES.
EVEN IF WE RUN OUT OF STOCK, WE'LL MANAGE TO PROVIDE YOU WITH AN OWEE.
WHAT DO YOU THINK? ISN'T IT AN INTRIGUING PROPOSAL?
THWAK

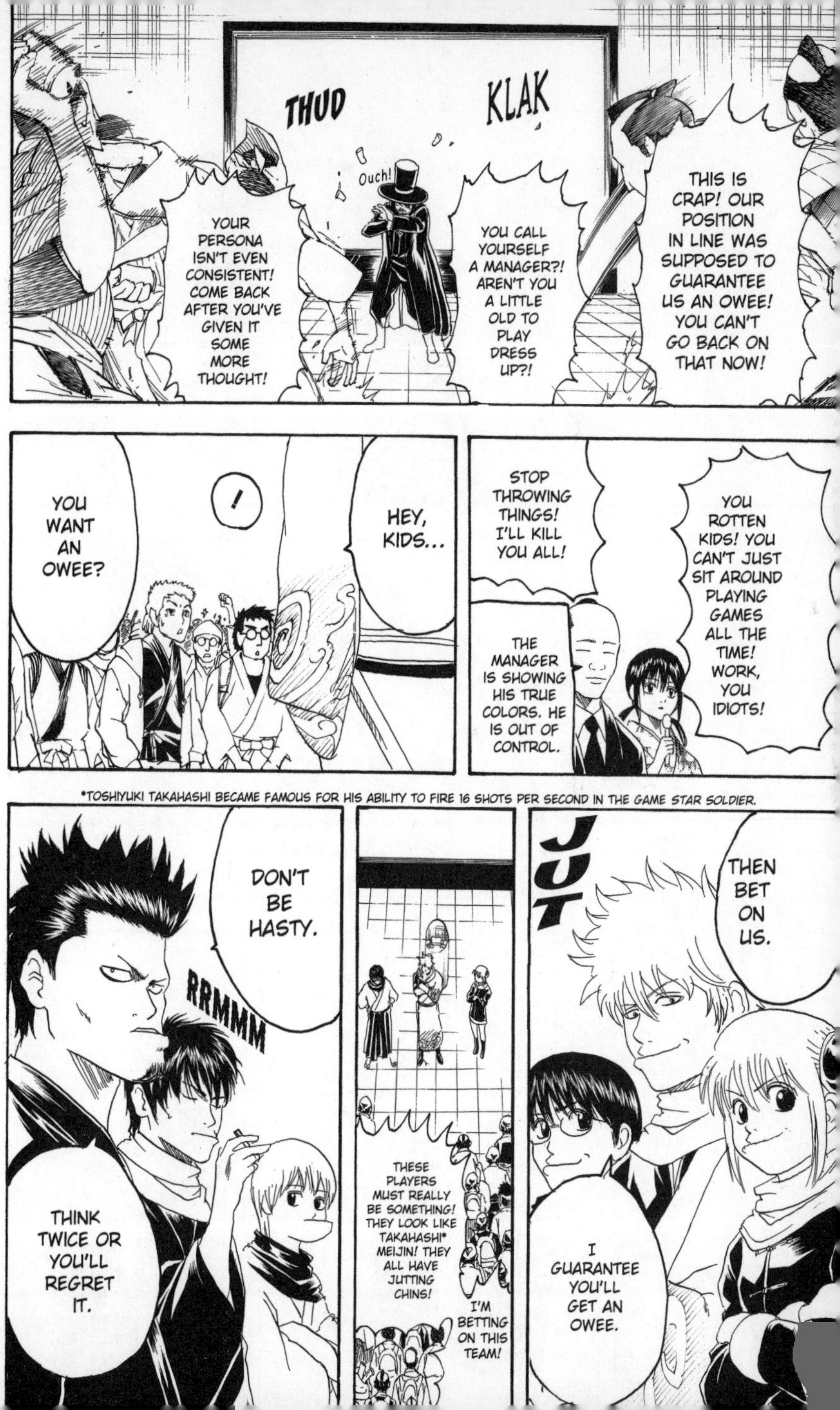
THIS IS CRAP! OUR POSITION IN LINE WAS SUPPOSED TO GUARANTEE US AN OWEE! YOU CAN'T GO BACK ON THAT NOW!
YOU CALL YOURSELF A MANAGER?! AREN'T YOU A LITTLE OLD TO PLAY DRESS UP?!
KLAK
Ouch!
THUD
YOUR PERSONA ISN'T EVEN CONSISTENT! COME BACK AFTER YOU'VE GIVEN IT SOME MORE THOUGHT!
YOU ROTTEN KIDS! YOU CAN'T JUST SIT AROUND PLAYING GAMES ALL THE TIME! WORK, YOU IDIOTS!
STOP THROWING THINGS! I'LL KILL YOU ALL!
THE MANAGER IS SHOWING HIS TRUE COLORS. HE IS OUT OF CONTROL.
HEY, KIDS...
!
YOU WANT AN OWEE?
THEN BET ON US.
JUT
I GUARANTEE YOU'LL GET AN OWEE.
THESE PLAYERS MUST REALLY BE SOMETHING! THEY LOOK LIKE TAKAHASHI* MEIJIN! THEY ALL HAVE JUTTING CHINS!
I'M BETTING ON THIS TEAM!
DON'T BE HASTY.
RRMMMM
THINK TWICE OR YOU'LL REGRET IT.

*TOSHIYUKI TAKAHASHI BECAME FAMOUS FOR HIS ABILITY TO FIRE 16 SHOTS PER SECOND IN THE GAME STAR SOLDIER.

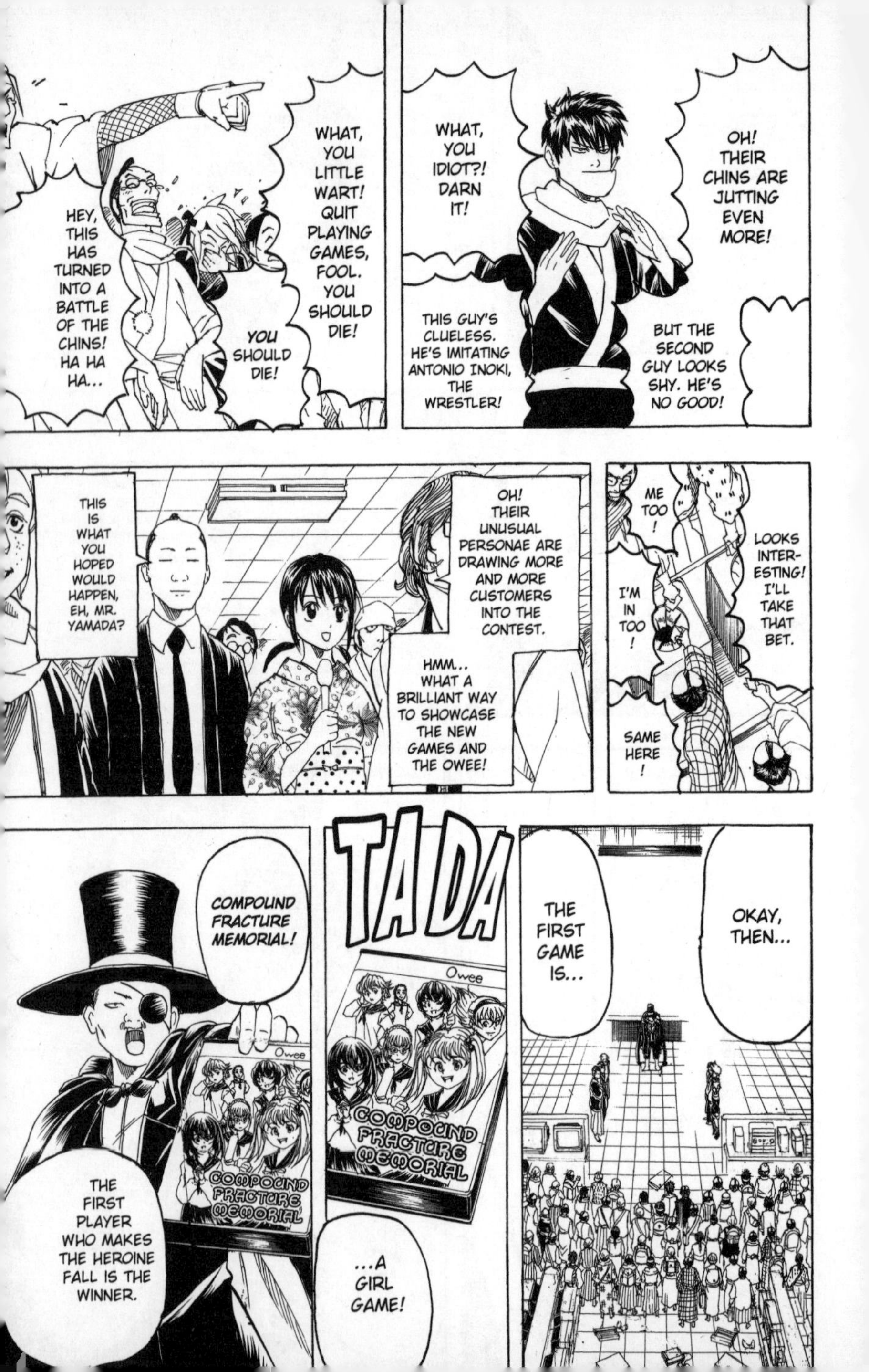
OH! THEIR CHINS ARE JUTTING EVEN MORE!
BUT THE SECOND GUY LOOKS SHY. HE'S NO GOOD!
WHAT, YOU IDIOT?! DARN IT!
THIS GUY'S CLUELESS. HE'S IMITATING ANTONIO INOKI, THE WRESTLER!
WHAT, YOU LITTLE WART! QUIT PLAYING GAMES, FOOL. YOU SHOULD DIE!
YOU SHOULD DIE!
HEY, THIS HAS TURNED INTO A BATTLE OF THE CHINS! HA HA HA...
LOOKS INTERESTING! I'LL TAKE THAT BET.
ME TOO!
I'M IN TOO!
SAME HERE!
OH! THEIR UNUSUAL PERSONAE ARE DRAWING MORE AND MORE CUSTOMERS INTO THE CONTEST.
HMM... WHAT A BRILLIANT WAY TO SHOWCASE THE NEW GAMES AND THE OWEE!
THIS IS WHAT YOU HOPED WOULD HAPPEN, EH, MR. YAMADA?
OKAY, THEN...
THE FIRST GAME IS...
TA DA
Owee
COMPOUND FRACTURE MEMORIAL
...A GIRL GAME!
COMPOUND FRACTURE MEMORIAL!
Owee
COMPOUND FRACTURE MEMORIAL
THE FIRST PLAYER WHO MAKES THE HEROINE FALL IS THE WINNER.

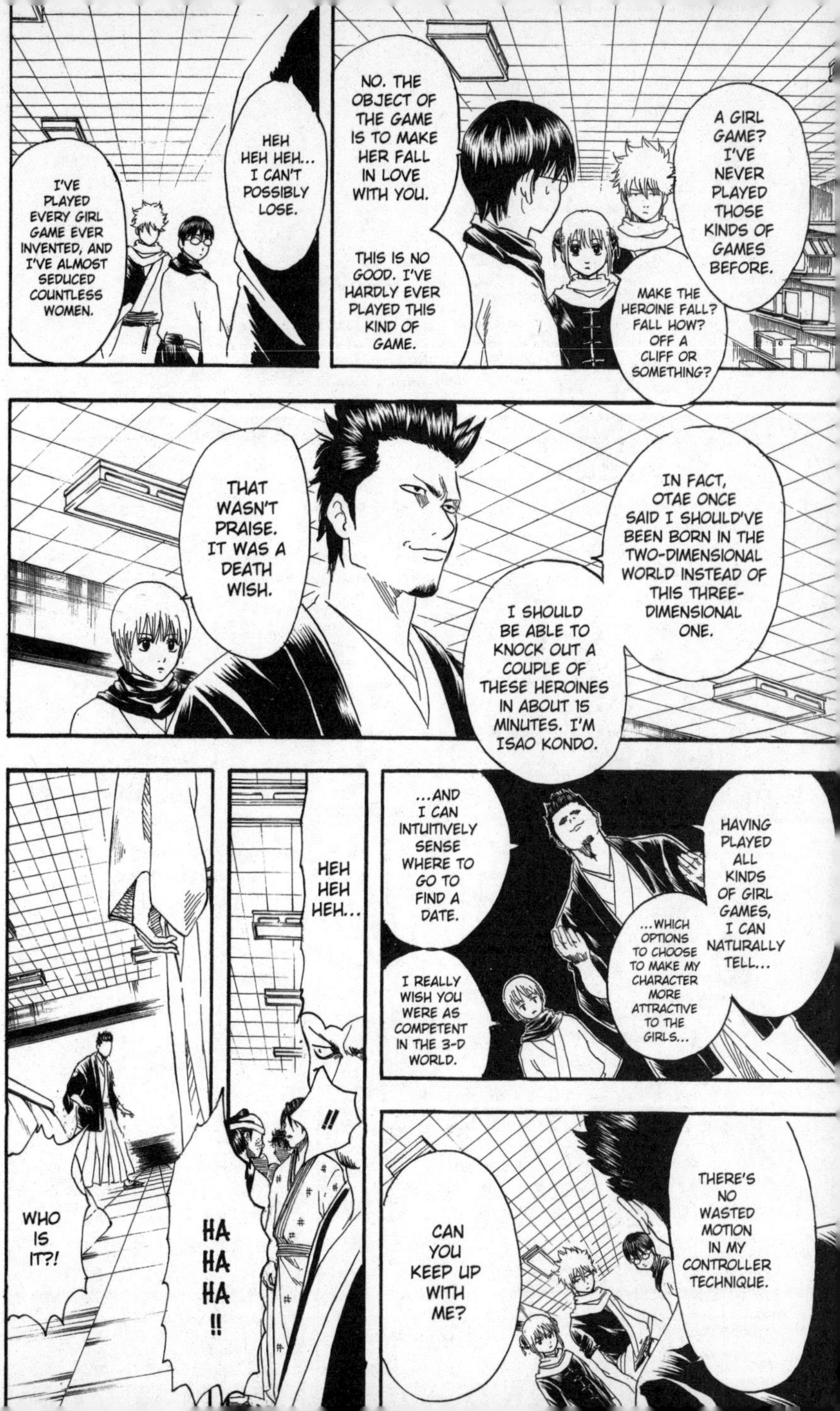
A GIRL GAME? I'VE NEVER PLAYED THOSE KINDS OF GAMES BEFORE.
MAKE THE HEROINE FALL? FALL HOW? OFF A CLIFF OR SOMETHING?
NO. THE OBJECT OF THE GAME IS TO MAKE HER FALL IN LOVE WITH YOU.
THIS IS NO GOOD. I'VE HARDLY EVER PLAYED THIS KIND OF GAME.
HEH HEH HEH... I CAN'T POSSIBLY LOSE.
I'VE PLAYED EVERY GIRL GAME EVER INVENTED, AND I'VE ALMOST SEDUCED COUNTLESS WOMEN.
IN FACT, OTAE ONCE SAID I SHOULD'VE BEEN BORN IN THE TWO-DIMENSIONAL WORLD INSTEAD OF THIS THREE-DIMENSIONAL ONE.
I SHOULD BE ABLE TO KNOCK OUT A COUPLE OF THESE HEROINES IN ABOUT 15 MINUTES. I'M ISAO KONDO.
THAT WASN'T PRAISE. IT WAS A DEATH WISH.
HAVING PLAYED ALL KINDS OF GIRL GAMES, I CAN NATURALLY TELL...
...WHICH OPTIONS TO CHOOSE TO MAKE MY CHARACTER MORE ATTRACTIVE TO THE GIRLS...
...AND I CAN INTUITIVELY SENSE WHERE TO GO TO FIND A DATE.
I REALLY WISH YOU WERE AS COMPETENT IN THE 3-D WORLD.
THERE'S NO WASTED MOTION IN MY CONTROLLER TECHNIQUE.
CAN YOU KEEP UP WITH ME?
HEH HEH HEH...
!!
HA HA HA !!
WHO IS IT?!

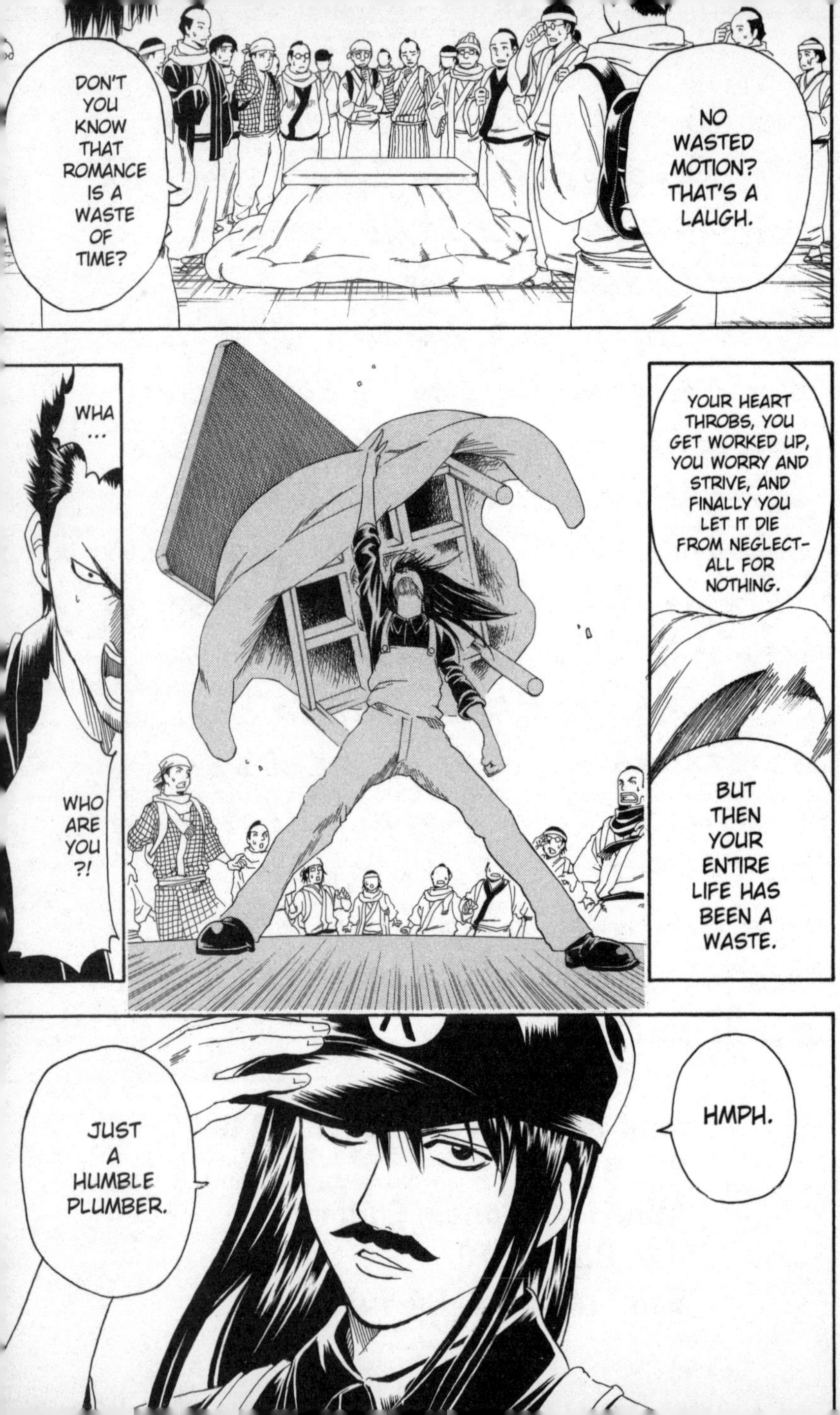
NO WASTED MOTION? THAT'S A LAUGH.
DON'T YOU KNOW THAT ROMANCE IS A WASTE OF TIME?
YOUR HEART THROBS, YOU GET WORKED UP, YOU WORRY AND STRIVE, AND FINALLY YOU LET IT DIE FROM NEGLECT-ALL FOR NOTHING.
BUT THEN YOUR ENTIRE LIFE HAS BEEN A WASTE.
WHA ...
WHO ARE YOU ?!
HMPH.
JUST A HUMBLE PLUMBER.

So this is it for the "Goodbye, Mr. Onishi's Single Life" special volume. But then the wedding hasn't happened yet, and you never know what will happen. It's not uncommon for the bride to back out on the wedding day. I mean, I hope she does run away because that would be hilarious. I hope she runs away as fast as she can. Maybe she'll hear the story about the umbrella and say, "Pink umbrella?! I don't have a pink umbrella!" What will happen to them then? Then again, I'm the one who wrote the story. But I really did see the umbrella, so leave me out of it!

Send your letters and fan art to:
VIZ Media
Attn: Jann Jones, Editor
P.O. Box 77010
San Francisco, CA 94107

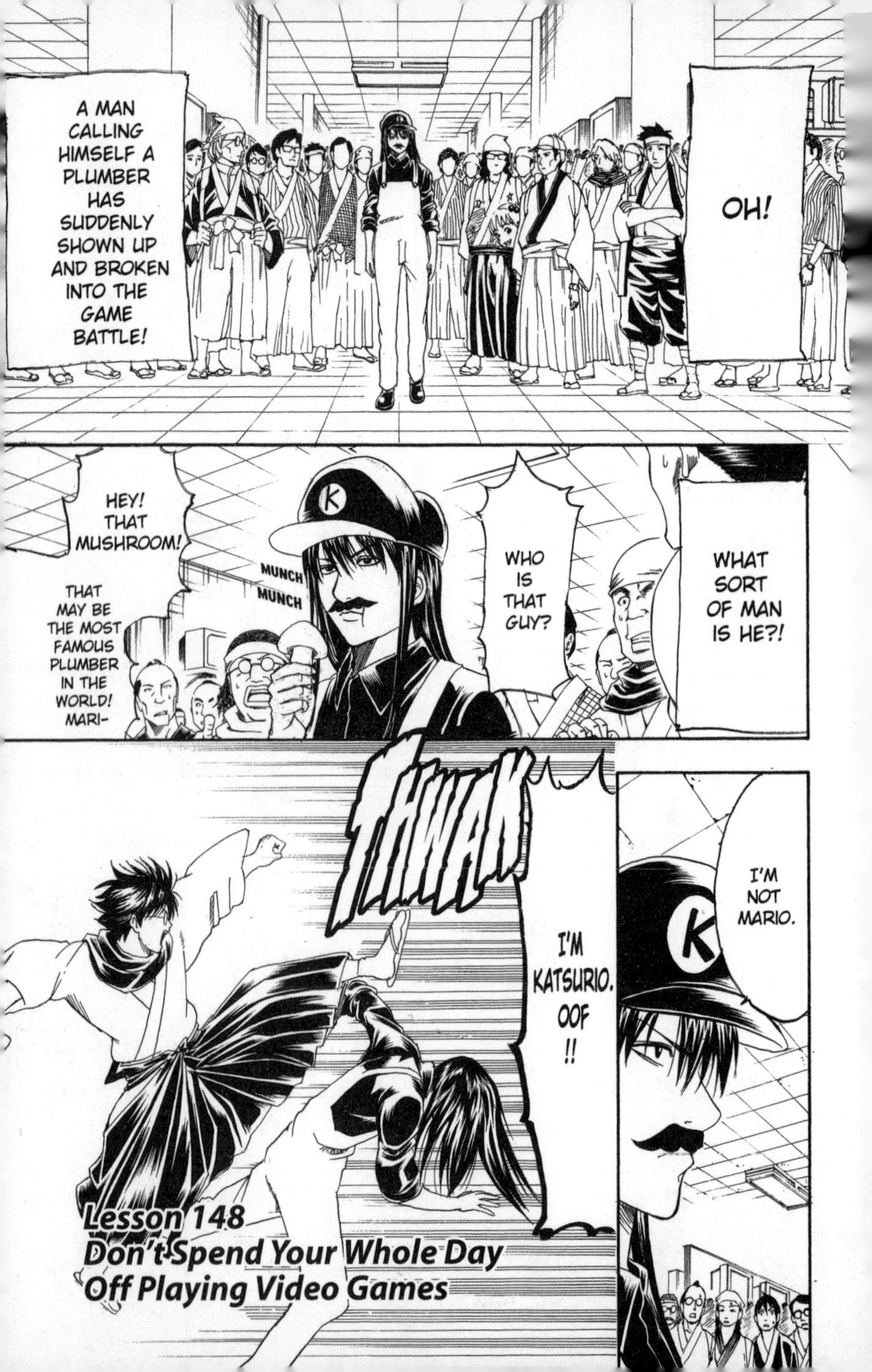
OH!
A MAN CALLING HIMSELF A PLUMBER HAS SUDDENLY SHOWN UP AND BROKEN INTO THE GAME BATTLE!
WHAT SORT OF MAN IS HE?!
WHO IS THAT GUY?
MUNCH MUNCH
HEY! THAT MUSHROOM!
THAT MAY BE THE MOST FAMOUS PLUMBER IN THE WORLD! MARI-
I'M NOT MARIO.
I'M KATSURIO. OOF !!
THWAK
Lesson 148
Don't Spend Your Whole Day Off Playing Video Games

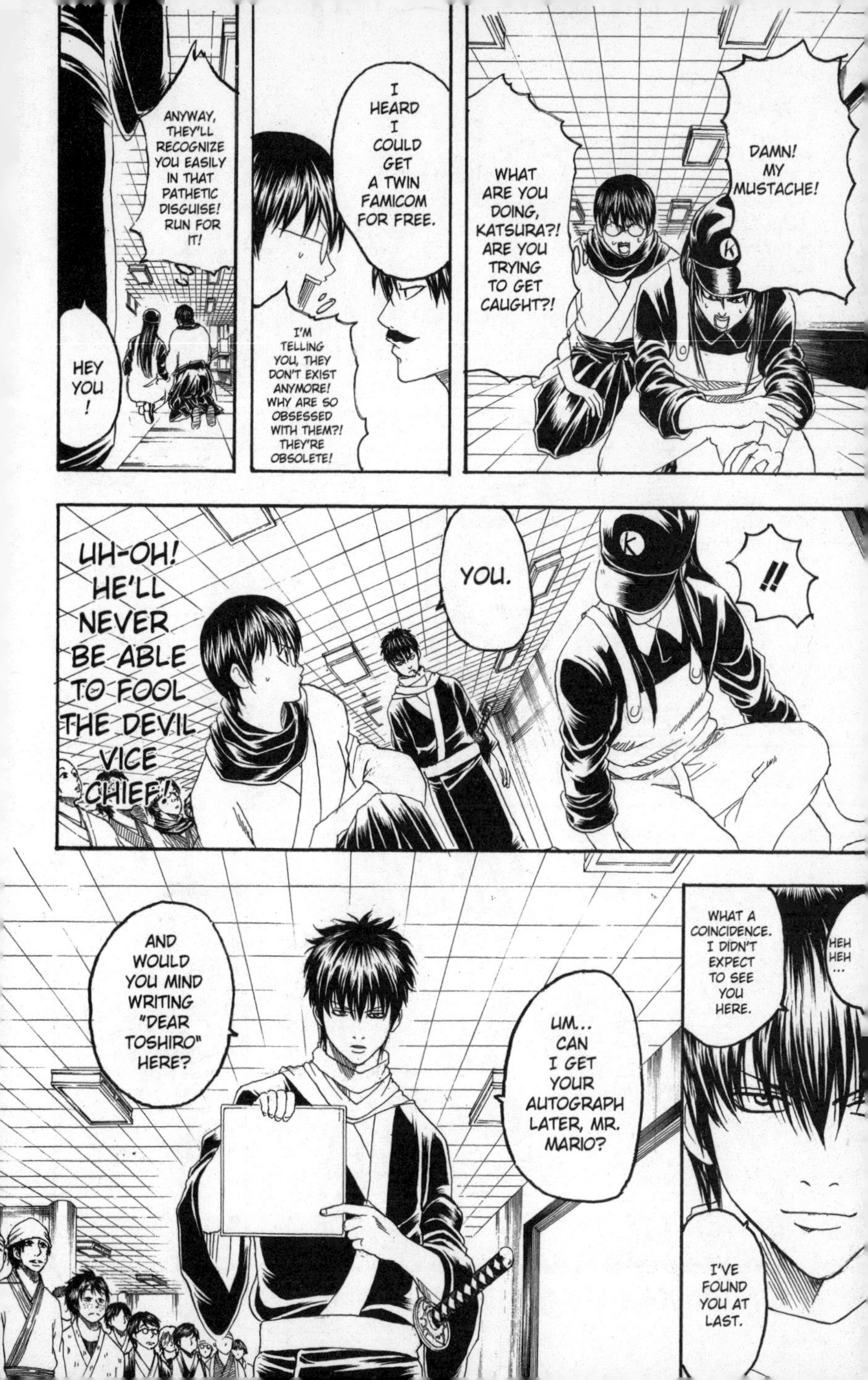
DAMN! MY MUSTACHE!
WHAT ARE YOU DOING, KATSURA?! ARE YOU TRYING TO GET CAUGHT?!
I HEARD I COULD GET A TWIN FAMICOM FOR FREE.
I'M TELLING YOU, THEY DON'T EXIST ANYMORE! WHY ARE SO OBSESSED WITH THEM?! THEY'RE OBSOLETE!
ANYWAY, THEY'LL RECOGNIZE YOU EASILY IN THAT PATHETIC DISGUISE! RUN FOR IT!
HEY YOU!
!!
YOU.
UH-OH! HE'LL NEVER BE ABLE TO FOOL THE DEVIL VICE CHIEF!
HEH HEH...
WHAT A COINCIDENCE. I DIDN'T EXPECT TO SEE YOU HERE.
I'VE FOUND YOU AT LAST.
UM... CAN I GET YOUR AUTOGRAPH LATER, MR. MARIO?
AND WOULD YOU MIND WRITING "DEAR TOSHIRO" HERE?

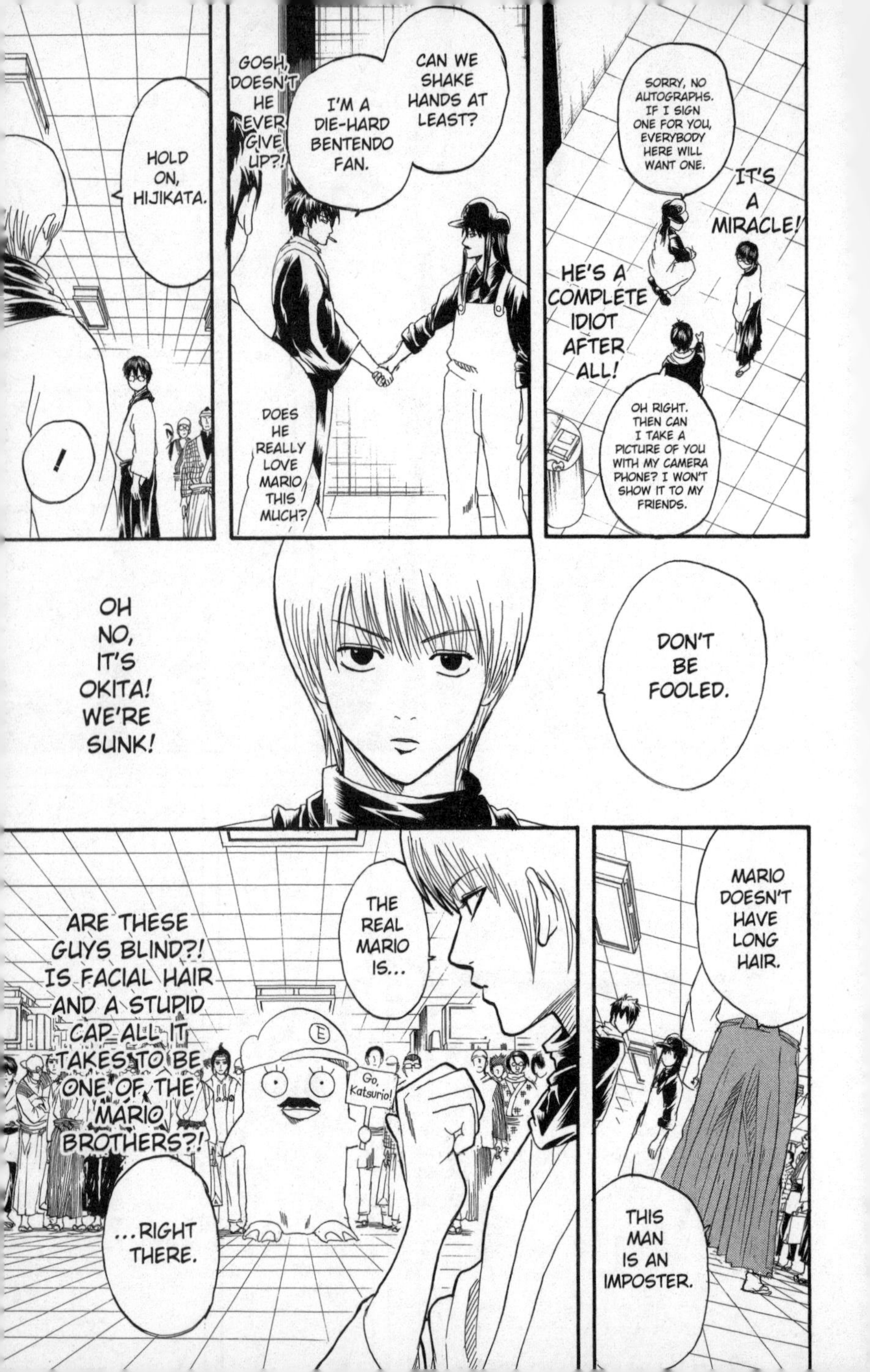
SORRY, NO AUTOGRAPHS. IF I SIGN ONE FOR YOU, EVERYBODY HERE WILL WANT ONE.
IT'S A MIRACLE!
HE'S A COMPLETE IDIOT AFTER ALL!
OH RIGHT. THEN CAN I TAKE A PICTURE OF YOU WITH MY CAMERA PHONE? I WON'T SHOW IT TO MY FRIENDS.
CAN WE SHAKE HANDS AT LEAST?
I'M A DIE-HARD BENTENDO FAN.
GOSH, DOESN'T HE EVER GIVE UP?!
DOES HE REALLY LOVE MARIO THIS MUCH?
HOLD ON, HIJIKATA.
!
DON'T BE FOOLED.
OH NO, IT'S OKITA! WE'RE SUNK!
MARIO DOESN'T HAVE LONG HAIR.
THIS MAN IS AN IMPOSTER.
THE REAL MARIO IS...
ARE THESE GUYS BLIND?! IS FACIAL HAIR AND A STUPID CAP ALL IT TAKES TO BE ONE OF THE MARIO BROTHERS?!
Go, Katsurio!
...RIGHT THERE.

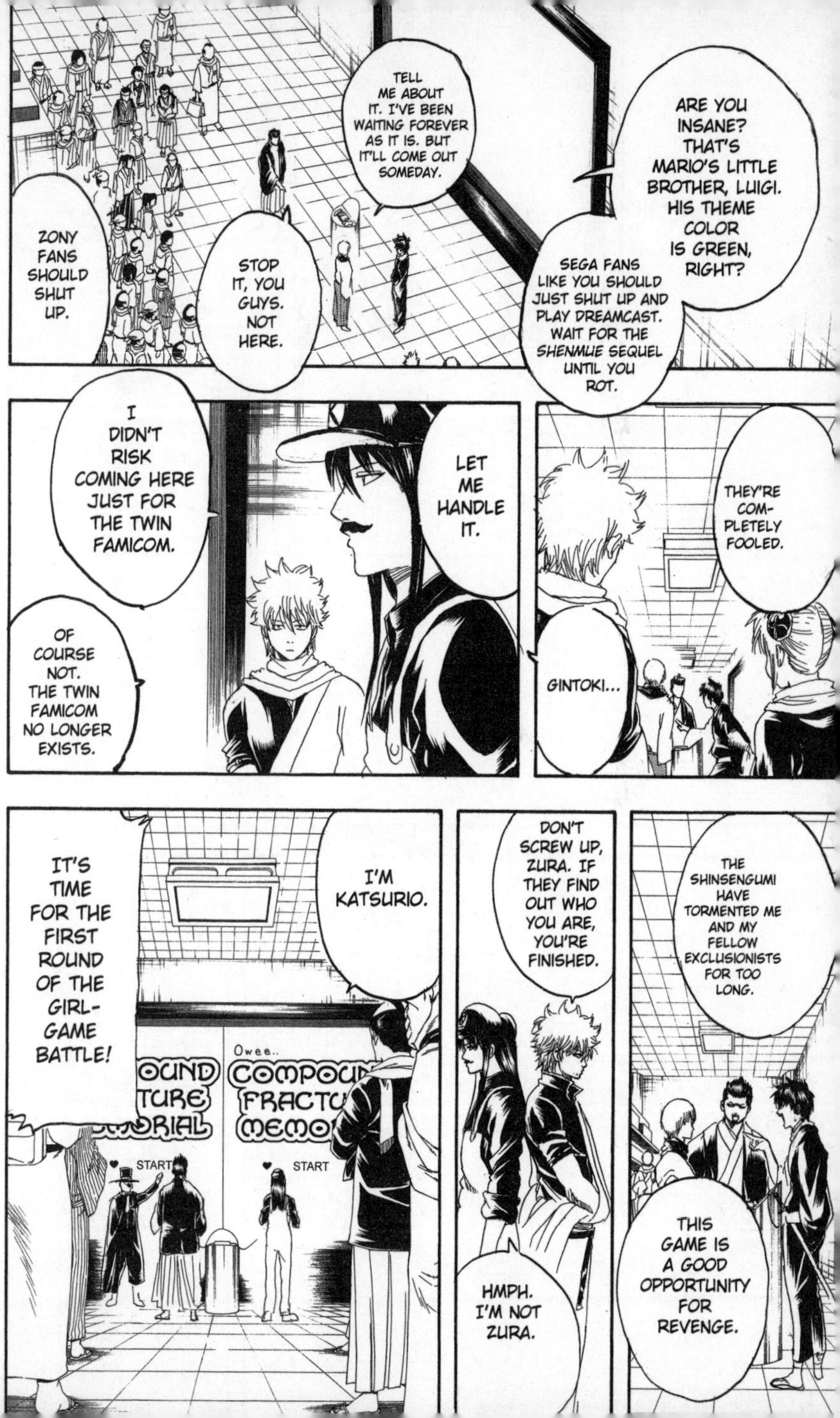
ARE YOU INSANE? THAT'S MARIO'S LITTLE BROTHER, LUIGI. HIS THEME COLOR IS GREEN, RIGHT?
TELL ME ABOUT IT. I'VE BEEN WAITING FOREVER AS IT IS. BUT IT'LL COME OUT SOMEDAY.
SEGA FANS LIKE YOU SHOULD JUST SHUT UP AND PLAY DREAMCAST. WAIT FOR THE SHENMUE SEQUEL UNTIL YOU ROT.
STOP IT, YOU GUYS. NOT HERE.
ZONY FANS SHOULD SHUT UP.
THEY'RE COMPLETELY FOOLED.
GINTOKI...
LET ME HANDLE IT.
I DIDN'T RISK COMING HERE JUST FOR THE TWIN FAMICOM.
OF COURSE NOT. THE TWIN FAMICOM NO LONGER EXISTS.
THE SHINSENGUMI HAVE TORMENTED ME AND MY FELLOW EXCLUSIONISTS FOR TOO LONG.
THIS GAME IS A GOOD OPPORTUNITY FOR REVENGE.
DON'T SCREW UP, ZURA. IF THEY FIND OUT WHO YOU ARE, YOU'RE FINISHED.
HMPH. I'M NOT ZURA.
I'M KATSURIO.
IT'S TIME FOR THE FIRST ROUND OF THE GIRL-GAME BATTLE!
Owee..
START
START

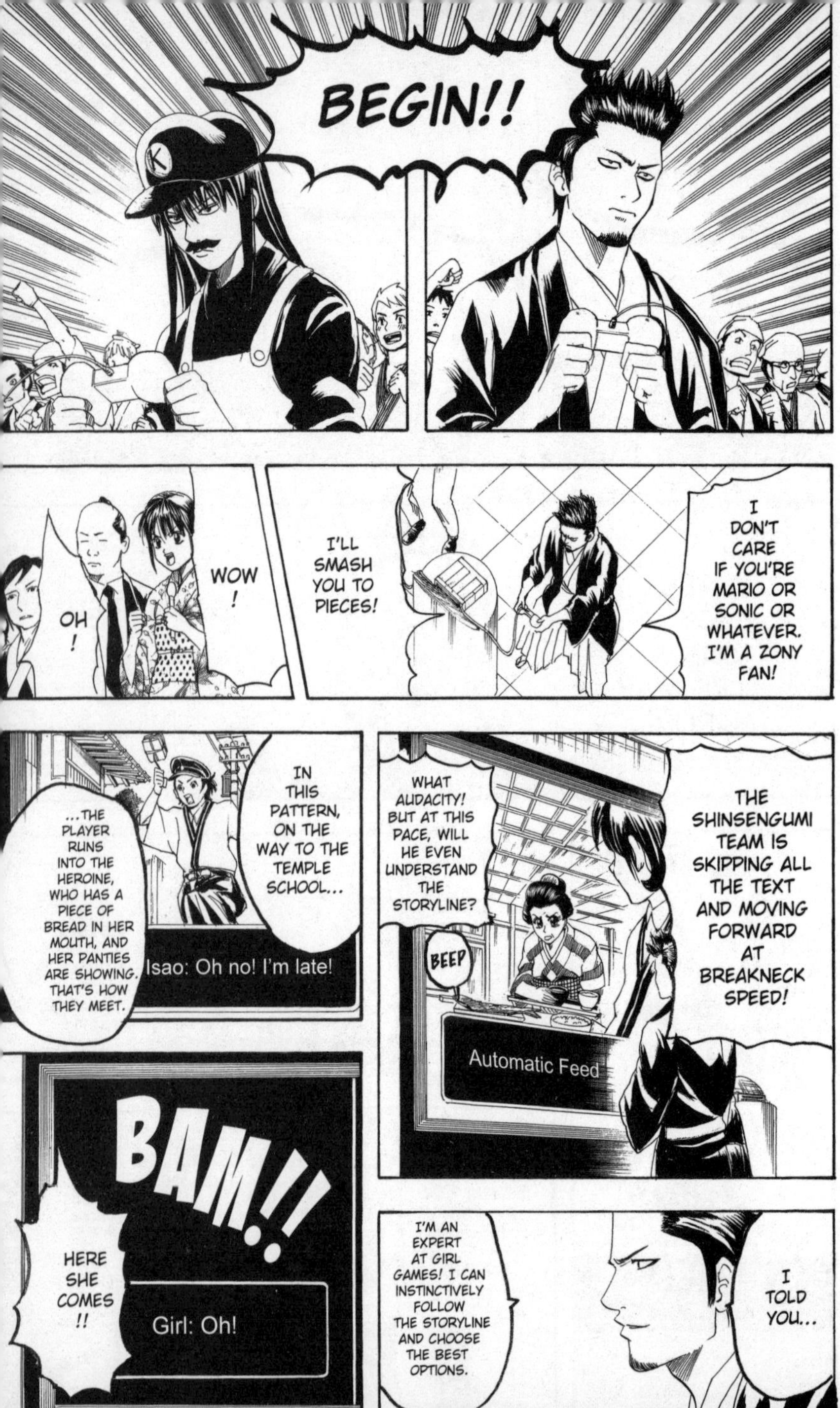
BEGIN!!
I DON'T CARE IF YOU'RE MARIO OR SONIC OR WHATEVER. I'M A ZONY FAN!
I'LL SMASH YOU TO PIECES!
WOW!
OH!
THE SHINSENGUMI TEAM IS SKIPPING ALL THE TEXT AND MOVING FORWARD AT BREAKNECK SPEED!
WHAT AUDACITY! BUT AT THIS PACE, WILL HE EVEN UNDERSTAND THE STORYLINE?
BEEP
Automatic Feed
IN THIS PATTERN, ON THE WAY TO THE TEMPLE SCHOOL...
...THE PLAYER RUNS INTO THE HEROINE, WHO HAS A PIECE OF BREAD IN HER MOUTH, AND HER PANTIES ARE SHOWING. THAT'S HOW THEY MEET.
Isao: Oh no! I'm late!
BAM!!
HERE SHE COMES!!
Girl: Oh!
I TOLD YOU...
I'M AN EXPERT AT GIRL GAMES! I CAN INSTINCTIVELY FOLLOW THE STORYLINE AND CHOOSE THE BEST OPTIONS.

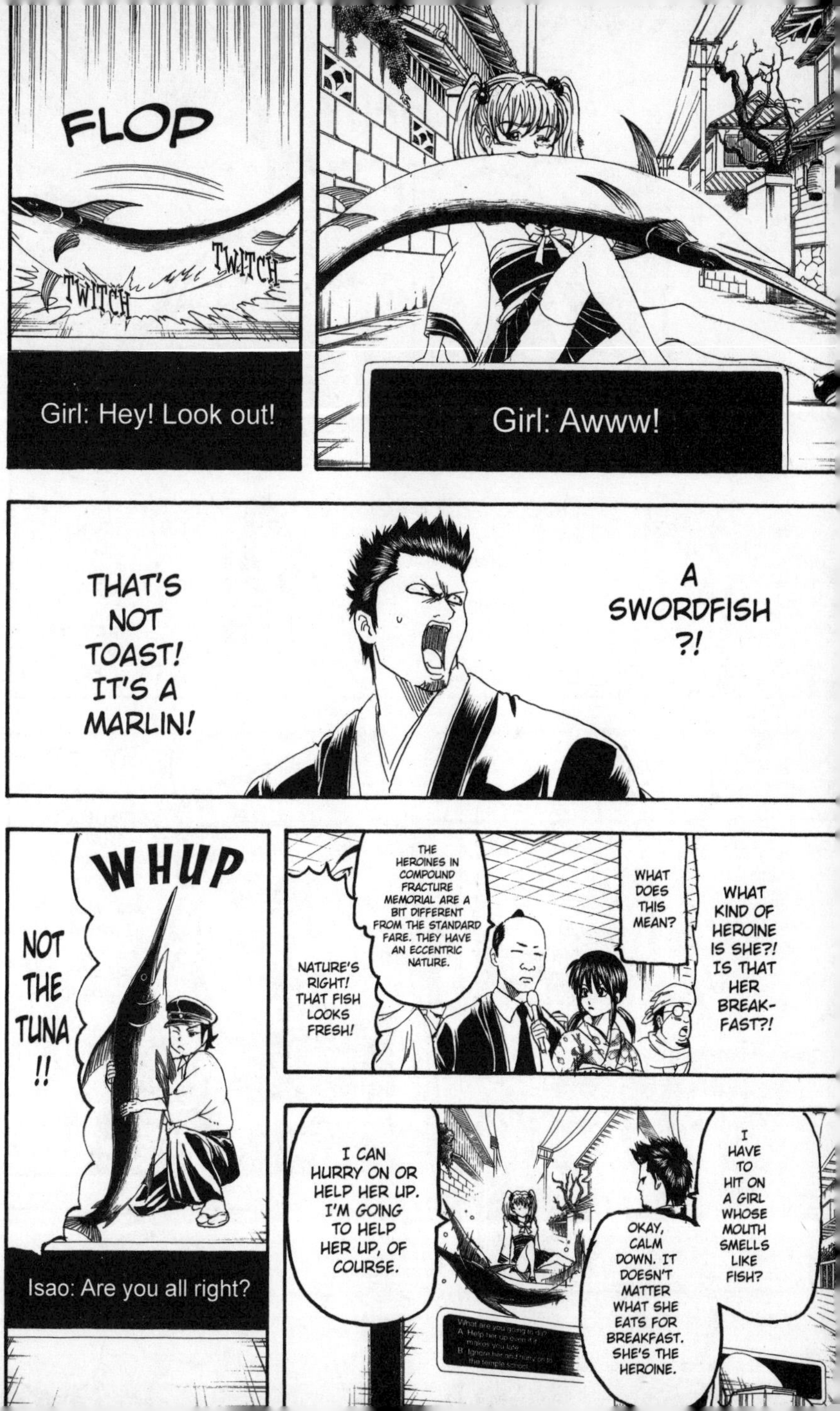
Girl: Awww!
FLOP
TWITCH
TWITCH
Girl: Hey! Look out!
A SWORDFISH?!
THAT'S NOT TOAST! IT'S A MARLIN!
WHAT KIND OF HEROINE IS SHE?! IS THAT HER BREAK-FAST?!
WHAT DOES THIS MEAN?
THE HEROINES IN COMPOUND FRACTURE MEMORIAL ARE A BIT DIFFERENT FROM THE STANDARD FARE. THEY HAVE AN ECCENTRIC NATURE.
NATURE'S RIGHT! THAT FISH LOOKS FRESH!
I HAVE TO HIT ON A GIRL WHOSE MOUTH SMELLS LIKE FISH?
OKAY, CALM DOWN. IT DOESN'T MATTER WHAT SHE EATS FOR BREAKFAST. SHE'S THE HEROINE.
I CAN HURRY ON OR HELP HER UP. I'M GOING TO HELP HER UP, OF COURSE.
What are you going to do?
A Help her up even if it makes you late
B Ignore her and hurry on to the temple school
WHUP
NOT THE TUNA!!
Isao: Are you all right?

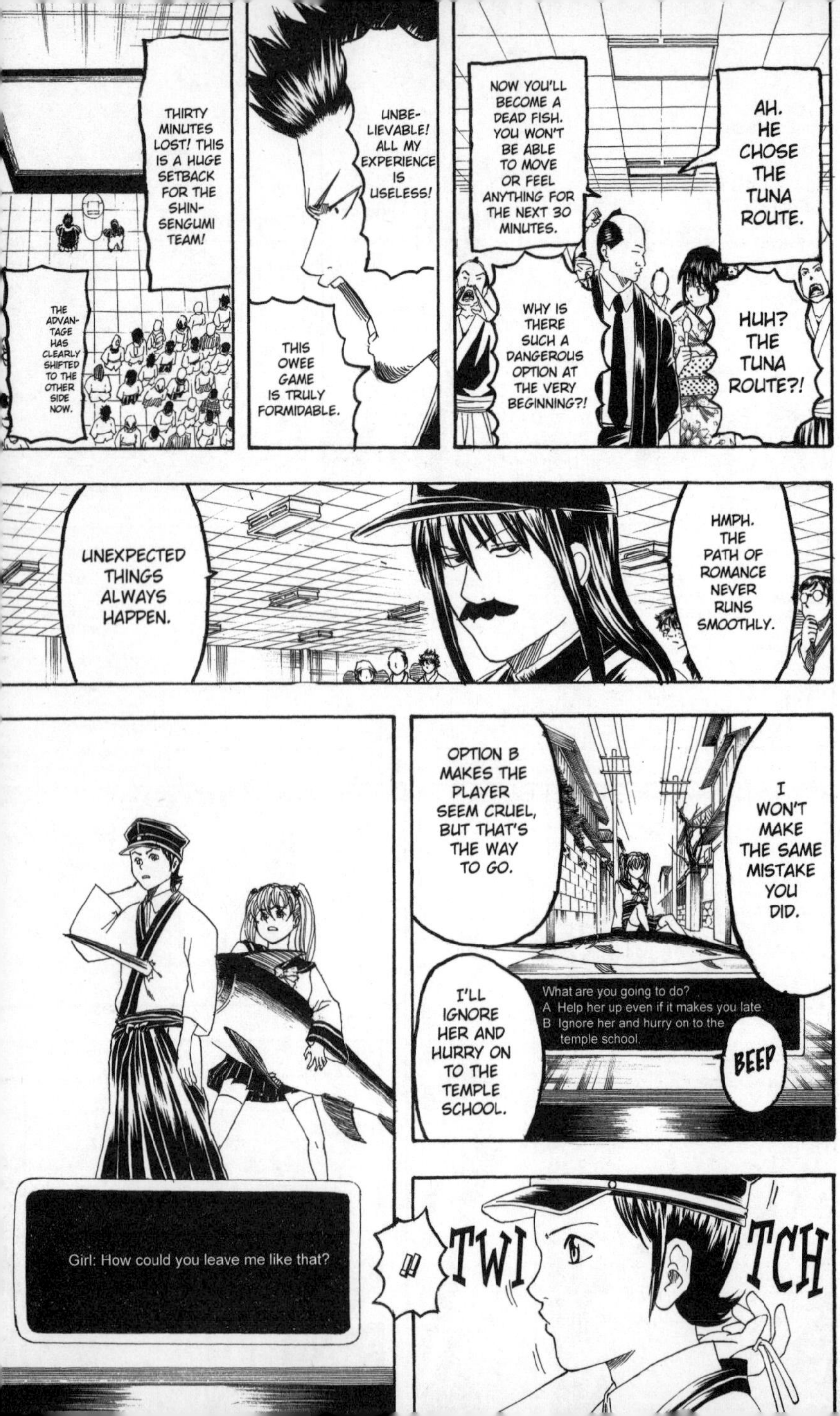
AH. HE CHOSE THE TUNA ROUTE.
NOW YOU'LL BECOME A DEAD FISH. YOU WON'T BE ABLE TO MOVE OR FEEL ANYTHING FOR THE NEXT 30 MINUTES.
HUH? THE TUNA ROUTE?!
WHY IS THERE SUCH A DANGEROUS OPTION AT THE VERY BEGINNING?!
UNBE-LIEVABLE! ALL MY EXPERIENCE IS USELESS!
THIS OWEE GAME IS TRULY FORMIDABLE.
THIRTY MINUTES LOST! THIS IS A HUGE SETBACK FOR THE SHIN-SENGUMI TEAM!
THE ADVAN-TAGE HAS CLEARLY SHIFTED TO THE OTHER SIDE NOW.
HMPH. THE PATH OF ROMANCE NEVER RUNS SMOOTHLY.
UNEXPECTED THINGS ALWAYS HAPPEN.
I WON'T MAKE THE SAME MISTAKE YOU DID.
OPTION B MAKES THE PLAYER SEEM CRUEL, BUT THAT'S THE WAY TO GO.
What are you going to do?
A Help her up even if it makes you late.
B Ignore her and hurry on to the temple school.
BEEP
I'LL IGNORE HER AND HURRY ON TO THE TEMPLE SCHOOL.
!!
TWI TCH
Girl: How could you leave me like that?

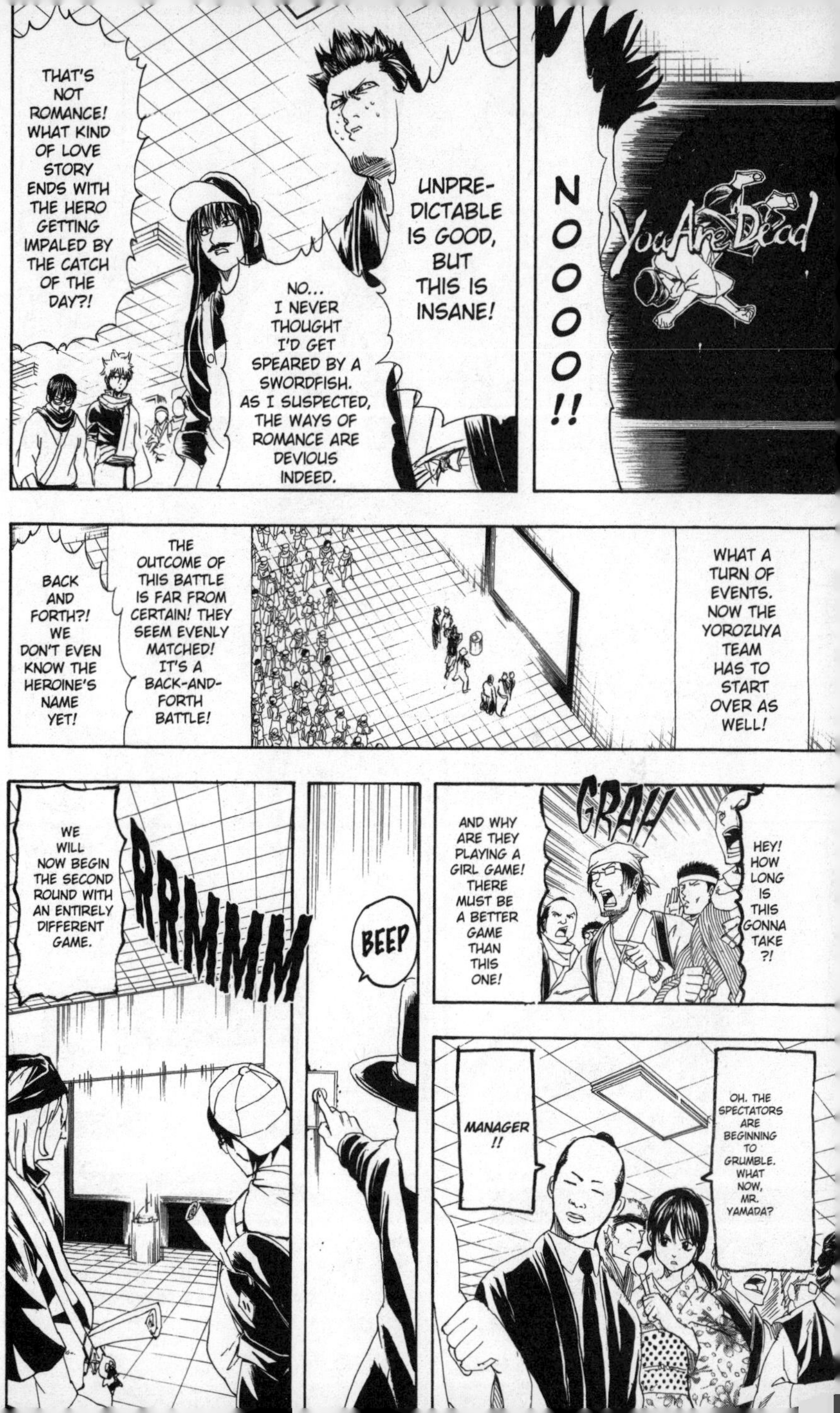
NOOOOO!!
You Are Dead
UNPRE-DICTABLE IS GOOD, BUT THIS IS INSANE!
THAT'S NOT ROMANCE! WHAT KIND OF LOVE STORY ENDS WITH THE HERO GETTING IMPALED BY THE CATCH OF THE DAY?!
NO... I NEVER THOUGHT I'D GET SPEARED BY A SWORDFISH. AS I SUSPECTED, THE WAYS OF ROMANCE ARE DEVIOUS INDEED.
WHAT A TURN OF EVENTS. NOW THE YOROZUYA TEAM HAS TO START OVER AS WELL!
THE OUTCOME OF THIS BATTLE IS FAR FROM CERTAIN! THEY SEEM EVENLY MATCHED! IT'S A BACK-AND-FORTH BATTLE!
BACK AND FORTH?! WE DON'T EVEN KNOW THE HEROINE'S NAME YET!
GRAH
HEY! HOW LONG IS THIS GONNA TAKE?!
AND WHY ARE THEY PLAYING A GIRL GAME! THERE MUST BE A BETTER GAME THAN THIS ONE!
OH. THE SPECTATORS ARE BEGINNING TO GRUMBLE. WHAT NOW, MR. YAMADA?
MANAGER!!
BEEP
RRMMMM
WE WILL NOW BEGIN THE SECOND ROUND WITH AN ENTIRELY DIFFERENT GAME.

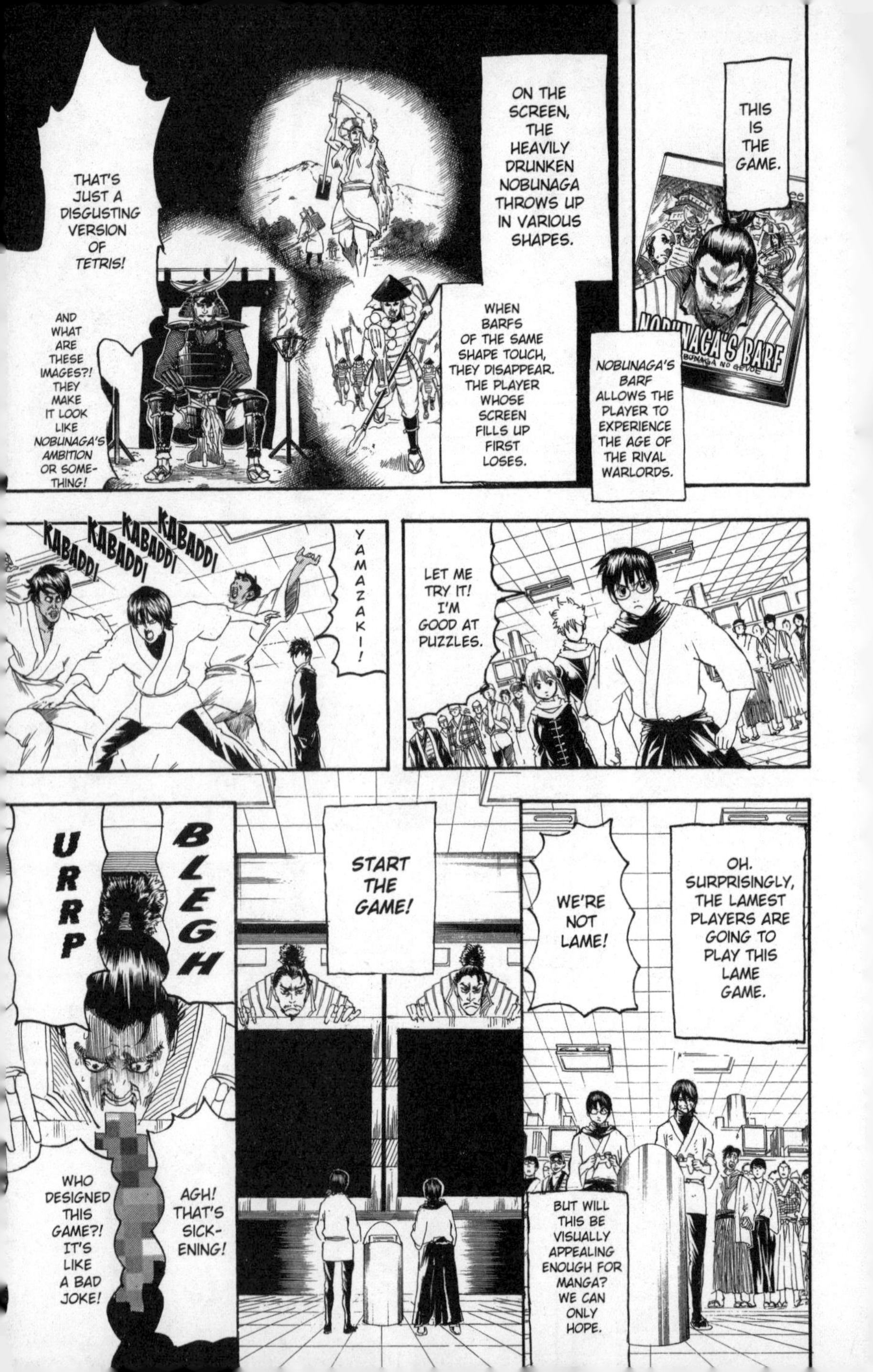
THIS IS THE GAME.
NOBUNAGA'S BARF
NOBUNAGA'S BARF ALLOWS THE PLAYER TO EXPERIENCE THE AGE OF THE RIVAL WARLORDS.
ON THE SCREEN, THE HEAVILY DRUNKEN NOBUNAGA THROWS UP IN VARIOUS SHAPES.
WHEN BARFS OF THE SAME SHAPE TOUCH, THEY DISAPPEAR. THE PLAYER WHOSE SCREEN FILLS UP FIRST LOSES.
THAT'S JUST A DISGUSTING VERSION OF TETRIS!
AND WHAT ARE THESE IMAGES?! THEY MAKE IT LOOK LIKE NOBUNAGA'S AMBITION OR SOME-THING!
LET ME TRY IT! I'M GOOD AT PUZZLES.
YAMAZAKI!
KABADDI
KABADDI
KABADDI
OH. SURPRISINGLY, THE LAMEST PLAYERS ARE GOING TO PLAY THIS LAME GAME.
WE'RE NOT LAME!
BUT WILL THIS BE VISUALLY APPEALING ENOUGH FOR MANGA? WE CAN ONLY HOPE.
START THE GAME!
BLEGH
URRP
AGH! THAT'S SICK-ENING!
WHO DESIGNED THIS GAME?! IT'S LIKE A BAD JOKE!

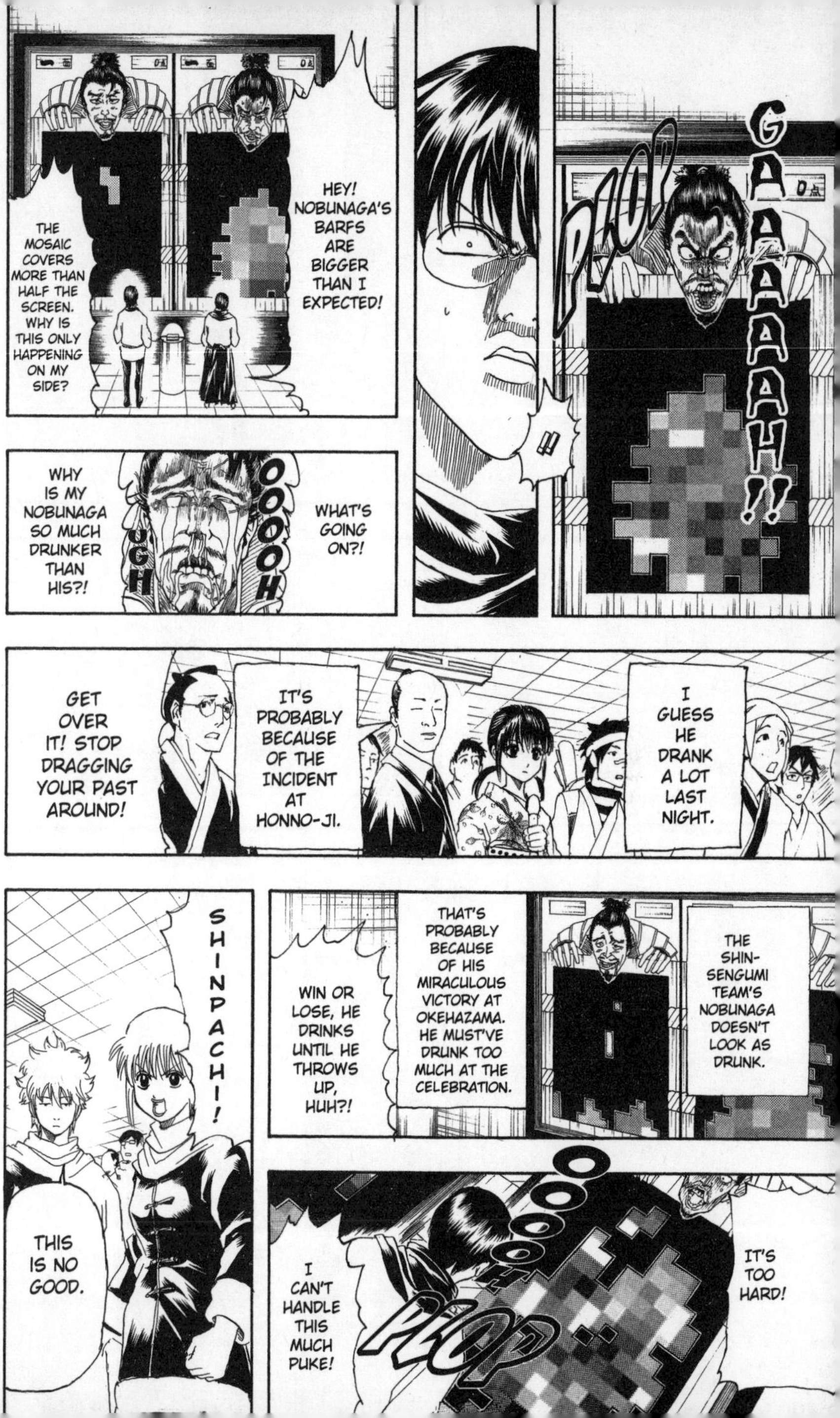
GAAAAAAAH!!
PLOP
!!
HEY! NOBUNAGA'S BARFS ARE BIGGER THAN I EXPECTED!
THE MOSAIC COVERS MORE THAN HALF THE SCREEN. WHY IS THIS ONLY HAPPENING ON MY SIDE?
WHAT'S GOING ON?!
OOOOOH
UGH
WHY IS MY NOBUNAGA SO MUCH DRUNKER THAN HIS?!
I GUESS HE DRANK A LOT LAST NIGHT.
IT'S PROBABLY BECAUSE OF THE INCIDENT AT HONNO-JI.
GET OVER IT! STOP DRAGGING YOUR PAST AROUND!
THE SHIN-SENGUMI TEAM'S NOBUNAGA DOESN'T LOOK AS DRUNK.
THAT'S PROBABLY BECAUSE OF HIS MIRACULOUS VICTORY AT OKEHAZAMA. HE MUST'VE DRUNK TOO MUCH AT THE CELEBRATION.
WIN OR LOSE, HE DRINKS UNTIL HE THROWS UP, HUH?!
IT'S TOO HARD!
OOOOOH
PLOP
I CAN'T HANDLE THIS MUCH PUKE!
SHINPACHI!
THIS IS NO GOOD.

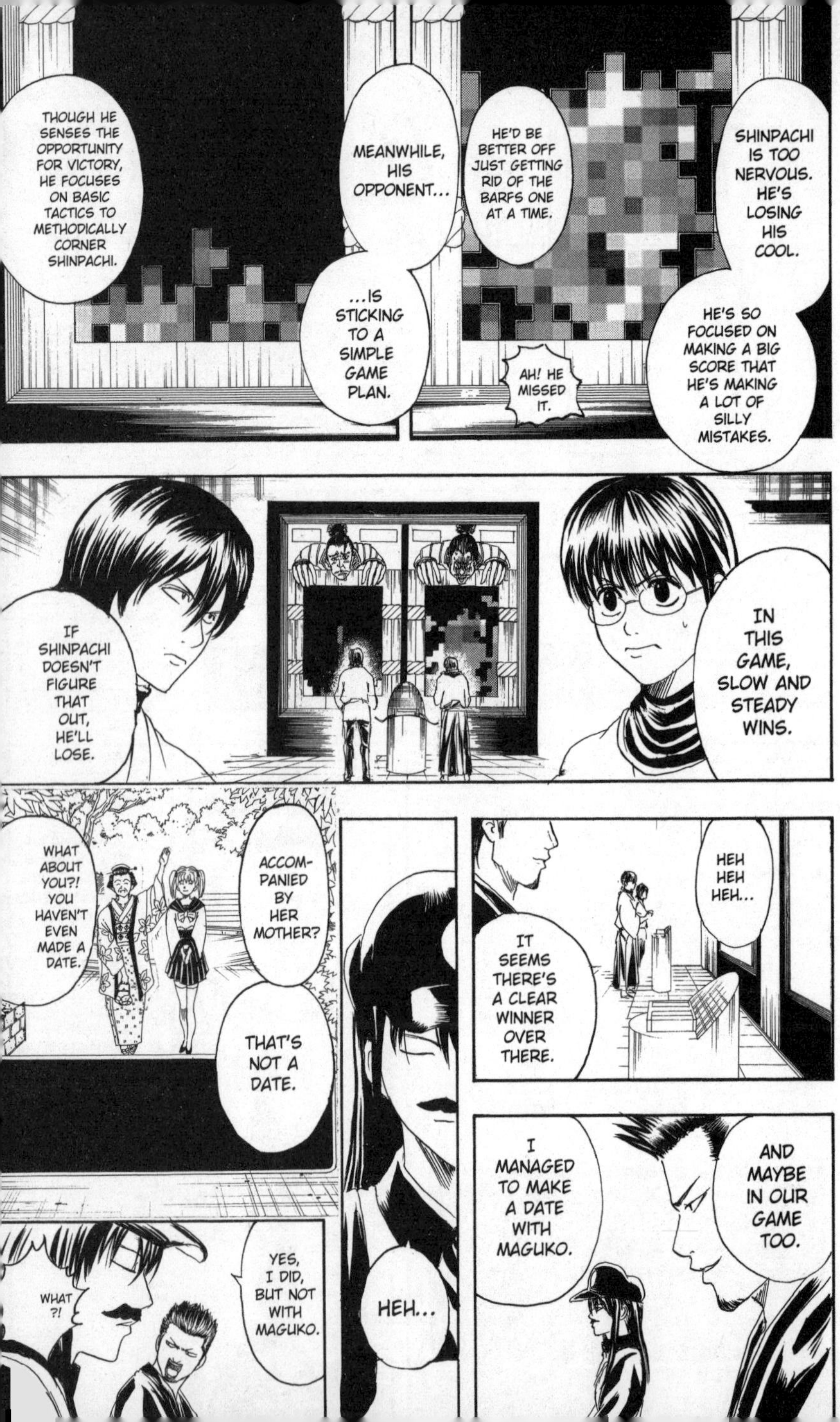

SHINPACHI IS TOO NERVOUS. HE'S LOSING HIS COOL.
HE'D BE BETTER OFF JUST GETTING RID OF THE BARFS ONE AT A TIME.
HE'S SO FOCUSED ON MAKING A BIG SCORE THAT HE'S MAKING A LOT OF SILLY MISTAKES.
AH! HE MISSED IT.
MEANWHILE, HIS OPPONENT...
...IS STICKING TO A SIMPLE GAME PLAN.
THOUGH HE SENSES THE OPPORTUNITY FOR VICTORY, HE FOCUSES ON BASIC TACTICS TO METHODICALLY CORNER SHINPACHI.
IN THIS GAME, SLOW AND STEADY WINS.
IF SHINPACHI DOESN'T FIGURE THAT OUT, HE'LL LOSE.
HEH HEH HEH...
IT SEEMS THERE'S A CLEAR WINNER OVER THERE.
AND MAYBE IN OUR GAME TOO.
I MANAGED TO MAKE A DATE WITH MAGUKO.
HEH...
ACCOM-PANIED BY HER MOTHER?
THAT'S NOT A DATE.
WHAT ABOUT YOU?! YOU HAVEN'T EVEN MADE A DATE.
YES, I DID, BUT NOT WITH MAGUKO.
WHAT ?!

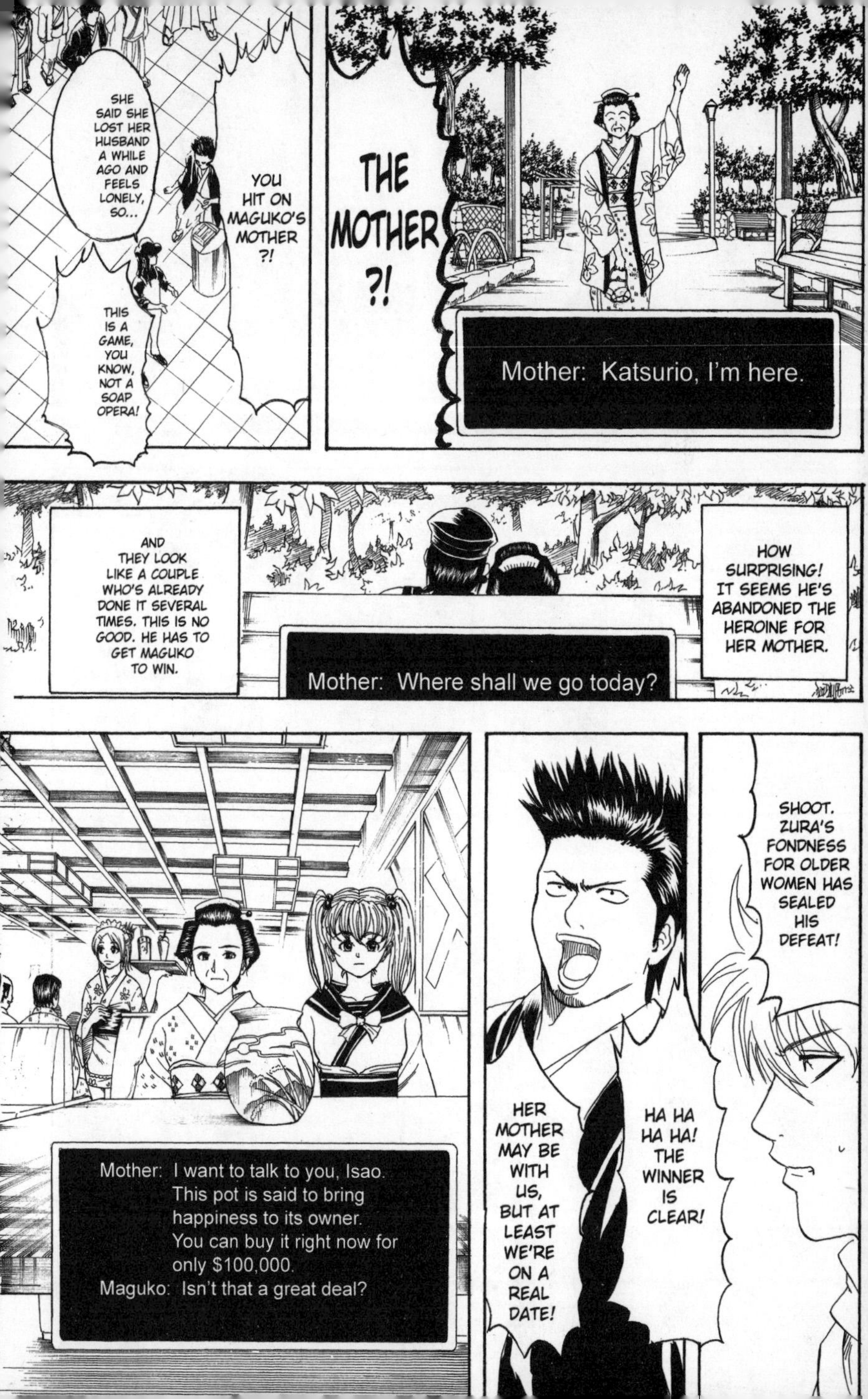
THE MOTHER ?!
Mother: Katsurio, I'm here.
YOU HIT ON MAGUKO'S MOTHER ?!
SHE SAID SHE LOST HER HUSBAND A WHILE AGO AND FEELS LONELY, SO...
THIS IS A GAME, YOU KNOW, NOT A SOAP OPERA!
HOW SURPRISING! IT SEEMS HE'S ABANDONED THE HEROINE FOR HER MOTHER.
Mother: Where shall we go today?
AND THEY LOOK LIKE A COUPLE WHO'S ALREADY DONE IT SEVERAL TIMES. THIS IS NO GOOD. HE HAS TO GET MAGUKO TO WIN.
SHOOT. ZURA'S FONDNESS FOR OLDER WOMEN HAS SEALED HIS DEFEAT!
HA HA HA HA! THE WINNER IS CLEAR!
HER MOTHER MAY BE WITH US, BUT AT LEAST WE'RE ON A REAL DATE!
Mother: I want to talk to you, Isao.
This pot is said to bring happiness to its owner.
You can buy it right now for only $100,000.
Maguko: Isn't that a great deal?

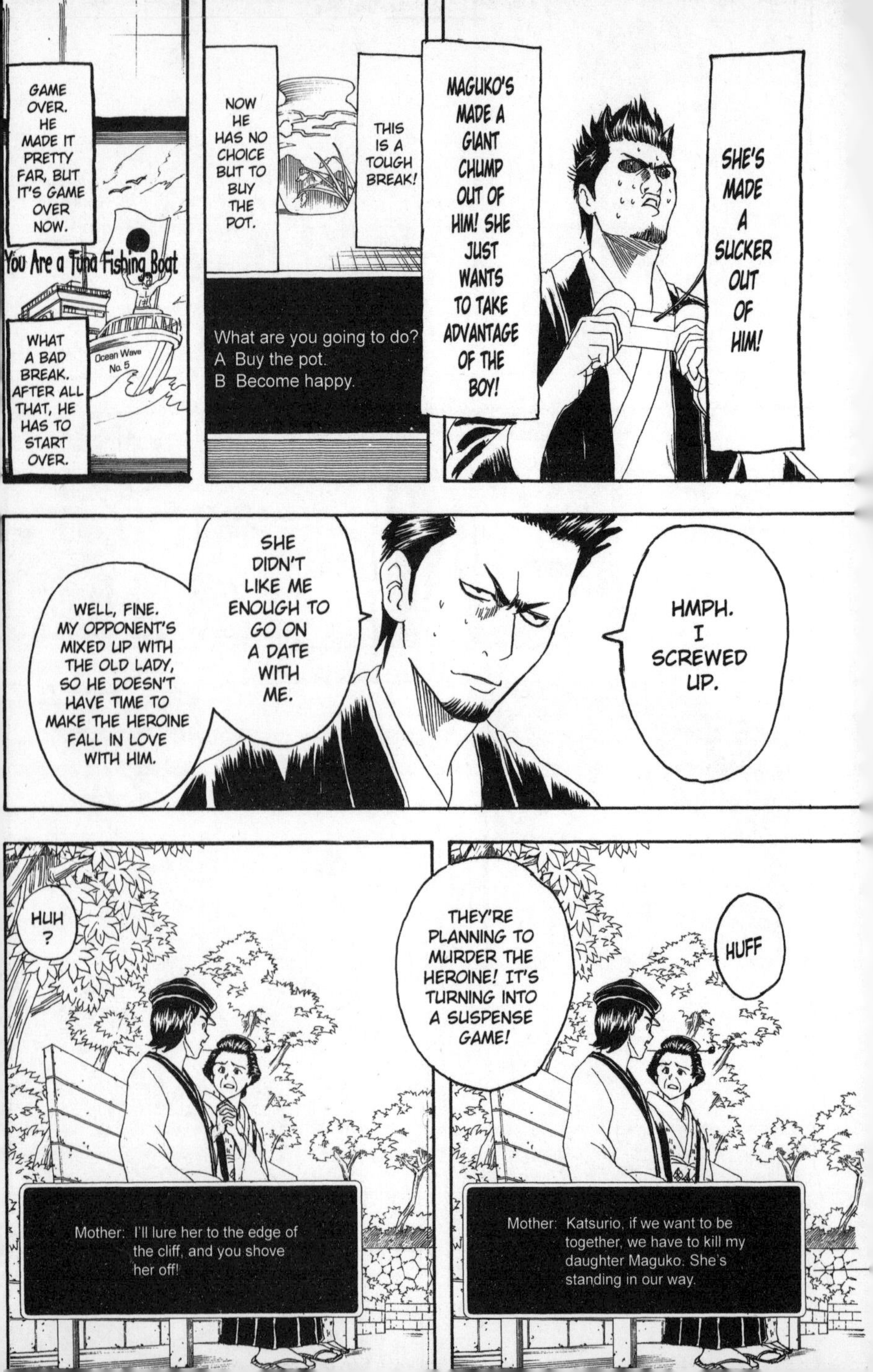
SHE'S MADE A SUCKER OUT OF HIM!
MAGUKO'S MADE A GIANT CHUMP OUT OF HIM! SHE JUST WANTS TO TAKE ADVANTAGE OF THE BOY!
THIS IS A TOUGH BREAK!
NOW HE HAS NO CHOICE BUT TO BUY THE POT.
What are you going to do?
A Buy the pot.
B Become happy.
GAME OVER. HE MADE IT PRETTY FAR, BUT IT'S GAME OVER NOW.
You Are a Tuna Fishing Boat
Ocean Wave No. 5
WHAT A BAD BREAK. AFTER ALL THAT, HE HAS TO START OVER.
HMPH. I SCREWED UP.
SHE DIDN'T LIKE ME ENOUGH TO GO ON A DATE WITH ME.
WELL, FINE. MY OPPONENT'S MIXED UP WITH THE OLD LADY, SO HE DOESN'T HAVE TIME TO MAKE THE HEROINE FALL IN LOVE WITH HIM.
HUFF
THEY'RE PLANNING TO MURDER THE HEROINE! IT'S TURNING INTO A SUSPENSE GAME!
Mother: Katsurio, if we want to be together, we have to kill my daughter Maguko. She's standing in our way.
HUH?
Mother: I'll lure her to the edge of the cliff, and you shove her off!

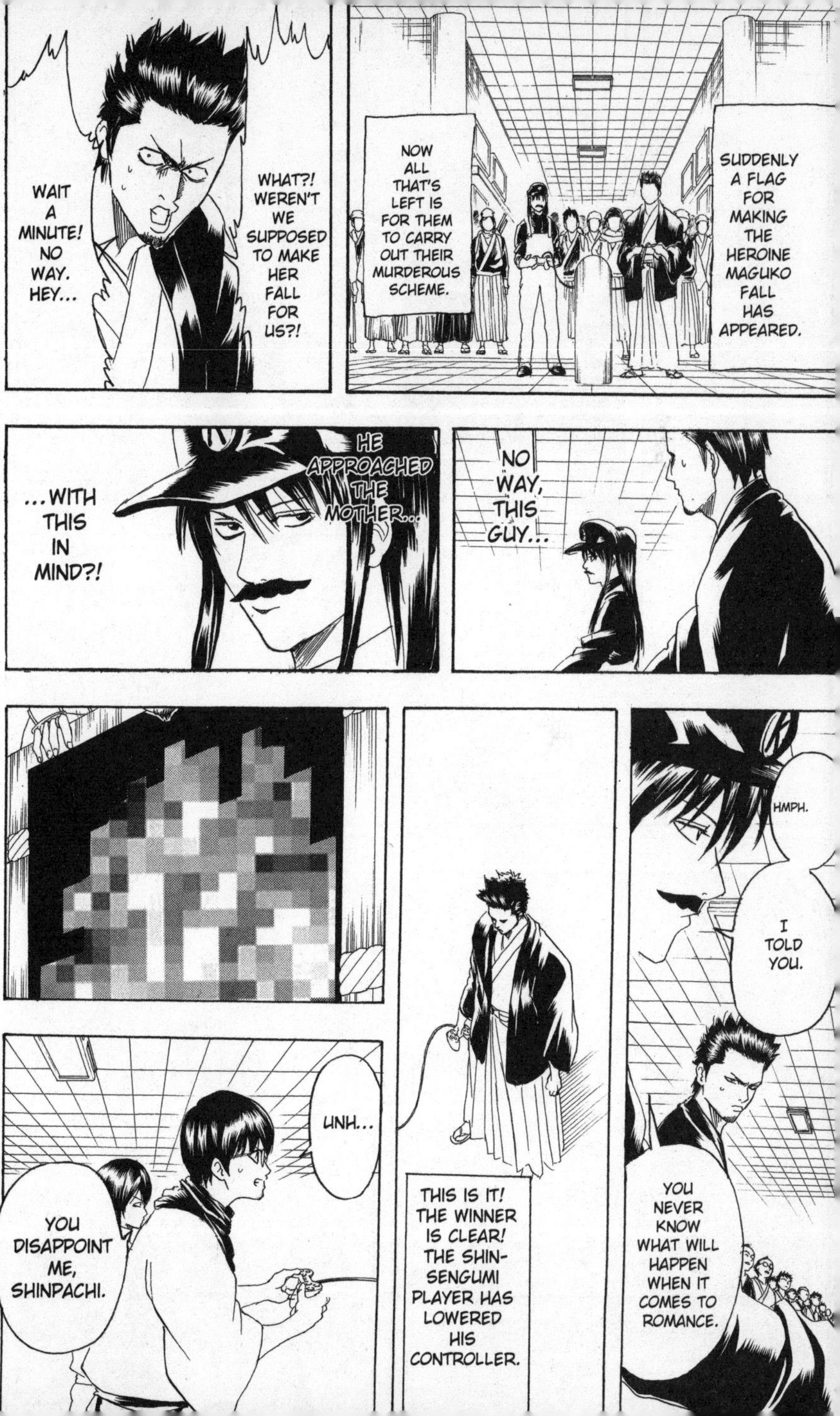
SUDDENLY A FLAG FOR MAKING THE HEROINE MAGUKO FALL HAS APPEARED.
NOW ALL THAT'S LEFT IS FOR THEM TO CARRY OUT THEIR MURDEROUS SCHEME.
WHAT?! WEREN'T WE SUPPOSED TO MAKE HER FALL FOR US?!
WAIT A MINUTE! NO WAY. HEY...
NO WAY, THIS GUY...
HE APPROACHED THE MOTHER...
...WITH THIS IN MIND?!
HMPH.
I TOLD YOU.
YOU NEVER KNOW WHAT WILL HAPPEN WHEN IT COMES TO ROMANCE.
THIS IS IT! THE WINNER IS CLEAR! THE SHIN-SENGUMI PLAYER HAS LOWERED HIS CONTROLLER.
UNH...
YOU DISAPPOINT ME, SHINPACHI.

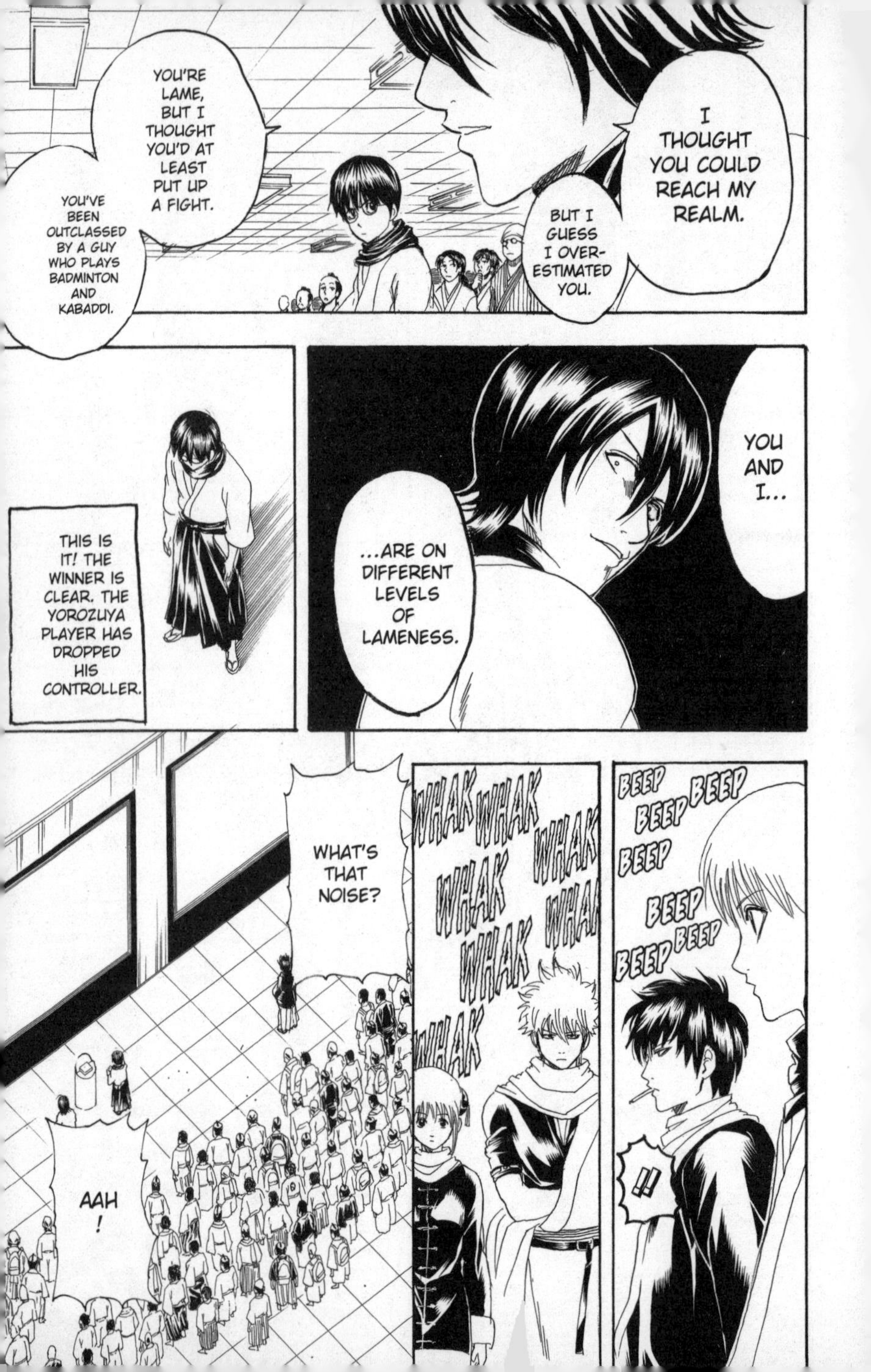
I THOUGHT YOU COULD REACH MY REALM.
BUT I GUESS I OVER-ESTIMATED YOU.
YOU'RE LAME, BUT I THOUGHT YOU'D AT LEAST PUT UP A FIGHT.
YOU'VE BEEN OUTCLASSED BY A GUY WHO PLAYS BADMINTON AND KABADDI.
YOU AND I...
...ARE ON DIFFERENT LEVELS OF LAMENESS.
THIS IS IT! THE WINNER IS CLEAR. THE YOROZUYA PLAYER HAS DROPPED HIS CONTROLLER.
BEEP BEEP BEEP
BEEP
BEEP
BEEP BEEP
!!
WHAK WHAK
WHAK
WHAK
WHAK
WHAK
WHAK
WHAT'S THAT NOISE?
AAH!

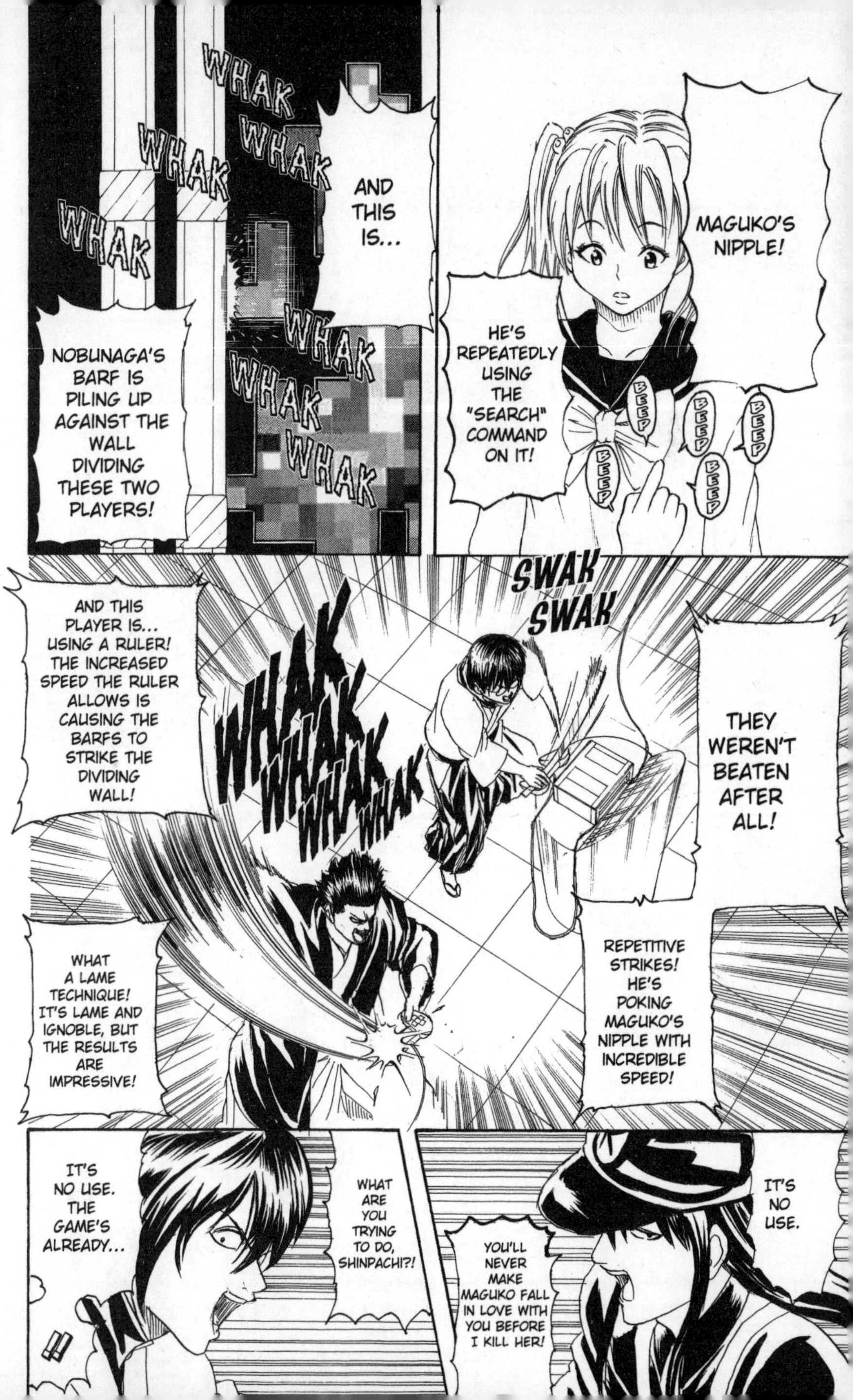
MAGUKO'S NIPPLE!
HE'S REPEATEDLY USING THE "SEARCH" COMMAND ON IT!
BEEP
BEEP
BEEP
BEEP
BEEP
AND THIS IS...
WHAK
WHAK
WHAK
WHAK
WHAK
WHAK
WHAK
NOBUNAGA'S BARF IS PILING UP AGAINST THE WALL DIVIDING THESE TWO PLAYERS!
SWAK
SWAK
THEY WEREN'T BEATEN AFTER ALL!
AND THIS PLAYER IS... USING A RULER! THE INCREASED SPEED THE RULER ALLOWS IS CAUSING THE BARFS TO STRIKE THE DIVIDING WALL!
WHAK WHAK WHAK WHAK
REPETITIVE STRIKES! HE'S POKING MAGUKO'S NIPPLE WITH INCREDIBLE SPEED!
WHAT A LAME TECHNIQUE! IT'S LAME AND IGNOBLE, BUT THE RESULTS ARE IMPRESSIVE!
IT'S NO USE.
YOU'LL NEVER MAKE MAGUKO FALL IN LOVE WITH YOU BEFORE I KILL HER!
WHAT ARE YOU TRYING TO DO, SHINPACHI?!
IT'S NO USE. THE GAME'S ALREADY...
!!

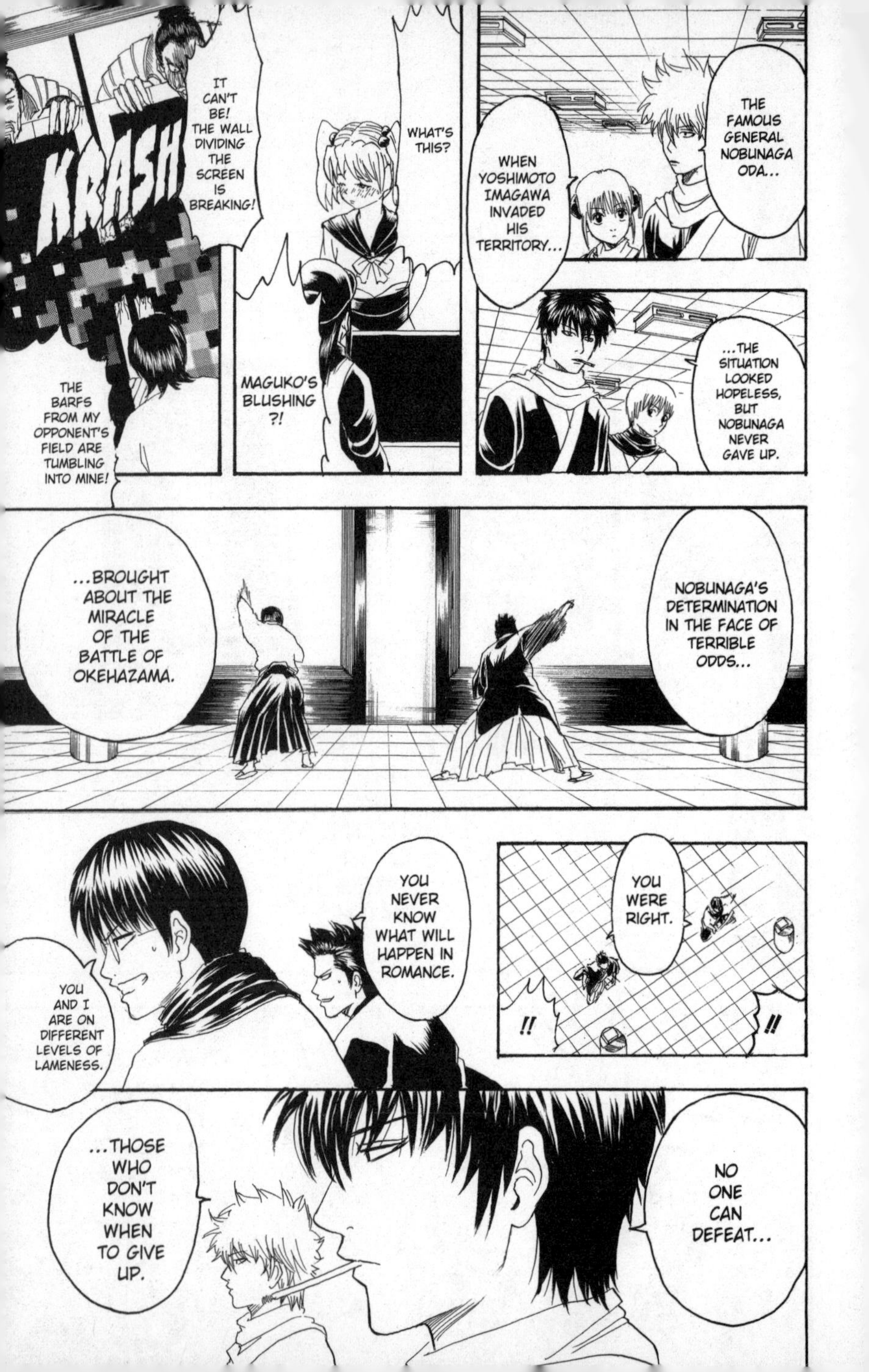
THE FAMOUS GENERAL NOBUNAGA ODA...
WHEN YOSHIMOTO IMAGAWA INVADED HIS TERRITORY...
...THE SITUATION LOOKED HOPELESS, BUT NOBUNAGA NEVER GAVE UP.
WHAT'S THIS?
MAGUKO'S BLUSHING?!
KRASH
IT CAN'T BE! THE WALL DIVIDING THE SCREEN IS BREAKING!
THE BARFS FROM MY OPPONENT'S FIELD ARE TUMBLING INTO MINE!
NOBUNAGA'S DETERMINATION IN THE FACE OF TERRIBLE ODDS...
...BROUGHT ABOUT THE MIRACLE OF THE BATTLE OF OKEHAZAMA.
YOU WERE RIGHT.
!!
!!
YOU NEVER KNOW WHAT WILL HAPPEN IN ROMANCE.
YOU AND I ARE ON DIFFERENT LEVELS OF LAMENESS.
NO ONE CAN DEFEAT...
...THOSE WHO DON'T KNOW WHEN TO GIVE UP.

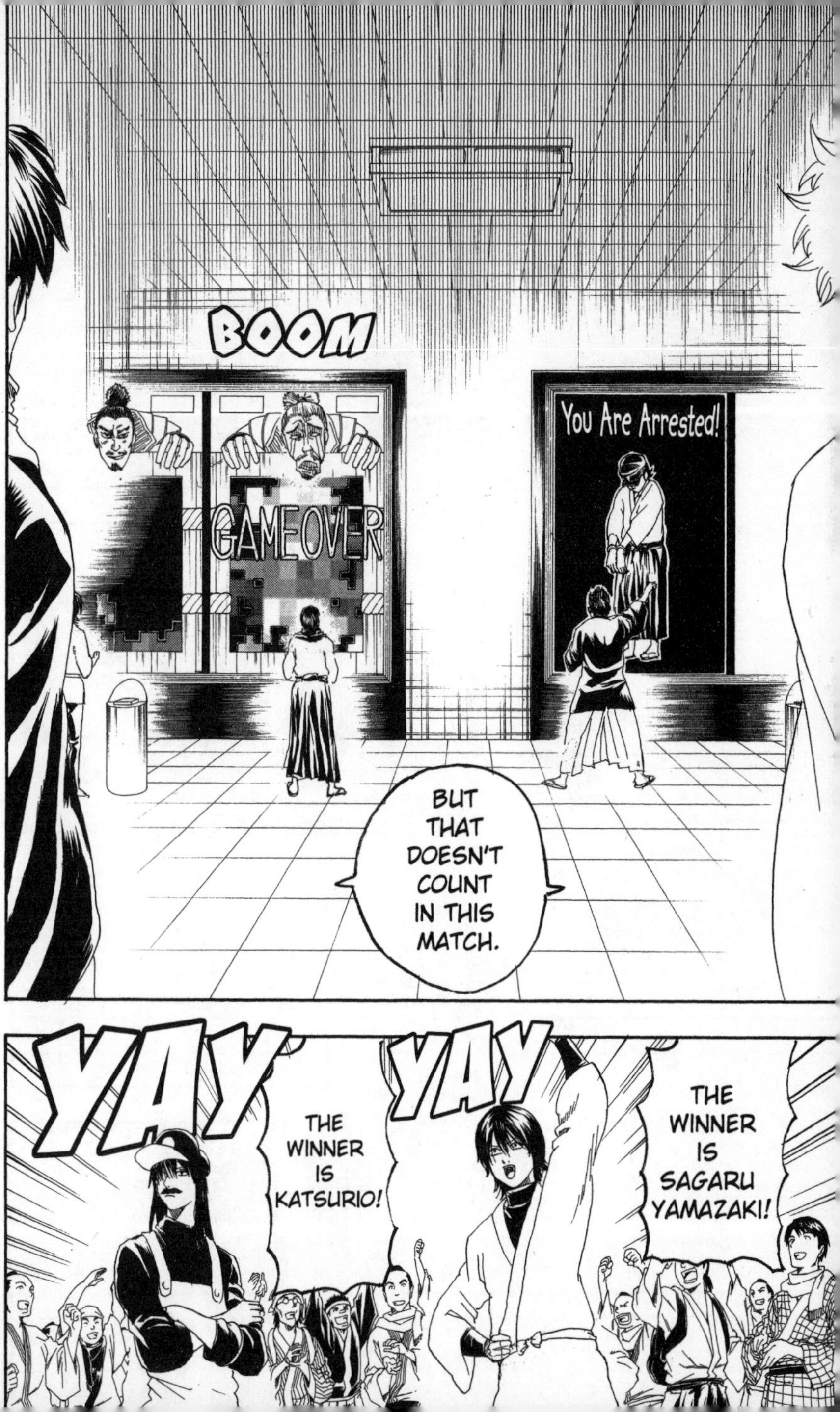
BOOM
GAMEOVER
You Are Arrested!
BUT THAT DOESN'T COUNT IN THIS MATCH.
YAY
THE WINNER IS SAGARU YAMAZAKI!
YAY
THE WINNER IS KATSURIO!

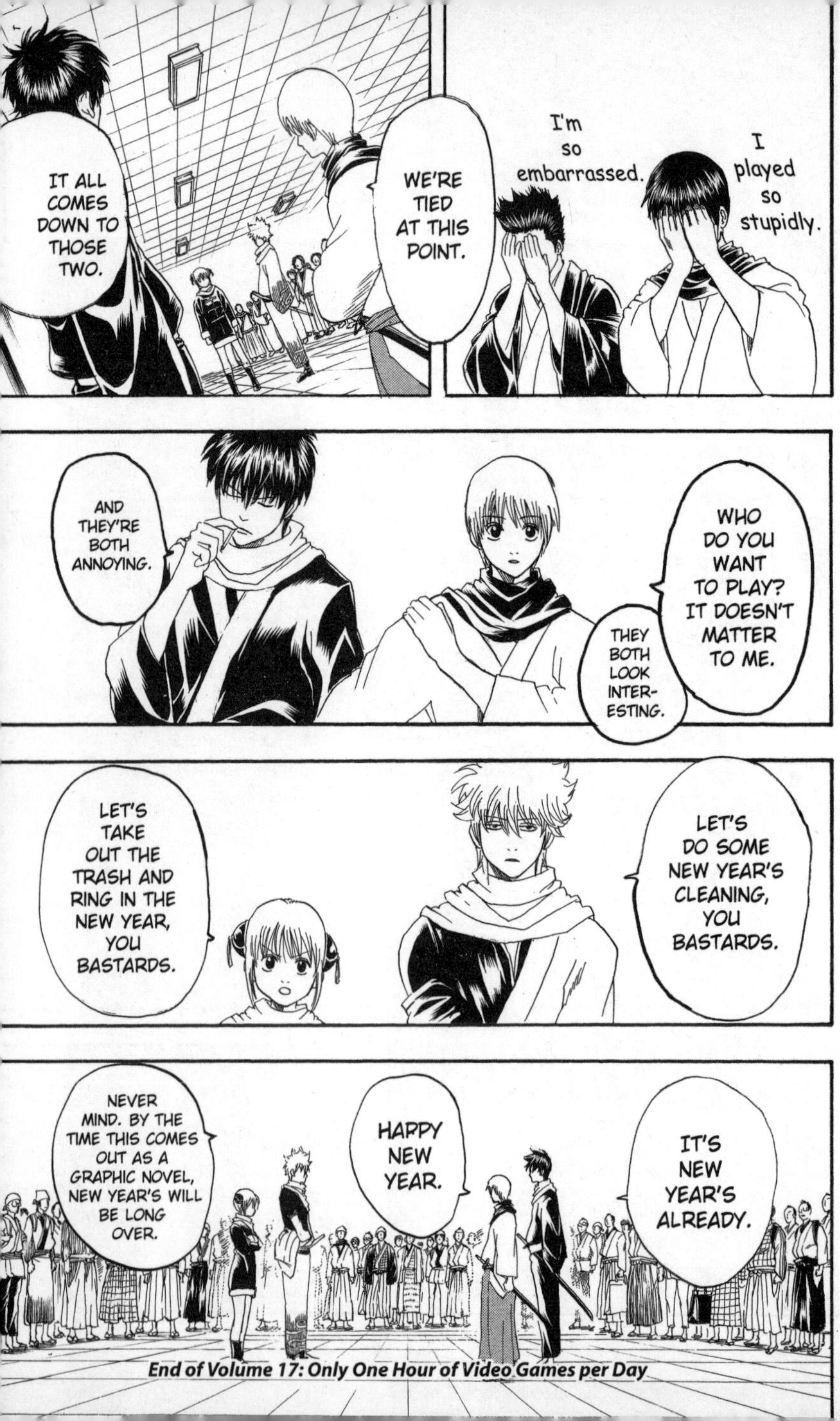
I played so stupidly.
I'm so embarrassed.
WE'RE TIED AT THIS POINT.
IT ALL COMES DOWN TO THOSE TWO.
WHO DO YOU WANT TO PLAY? IT DOESN'T MATTER TO ME.
THEY BOTH LOOK INTER-ESTING.
AND THEY'RE BOTH ANNOYING.
LET'S DO SOME NEW YEAR'S CLEANING, YOU BASTARDS.
LET'S TAKE OUT THE TRASH AND RING IN THE NEW YEAR, YOU BASTARDS.
IT'S NEW YEAR'S ALREADY.
HAPPY NEW YEAR.
NEVER MIND. BY THE TIME THIS COMES OUT AS A GRAPHIC NOVEL, NEW YEAR'S WILL BE LONG OVER.

End of Volume 17: Only One Hour of Video Games per Day

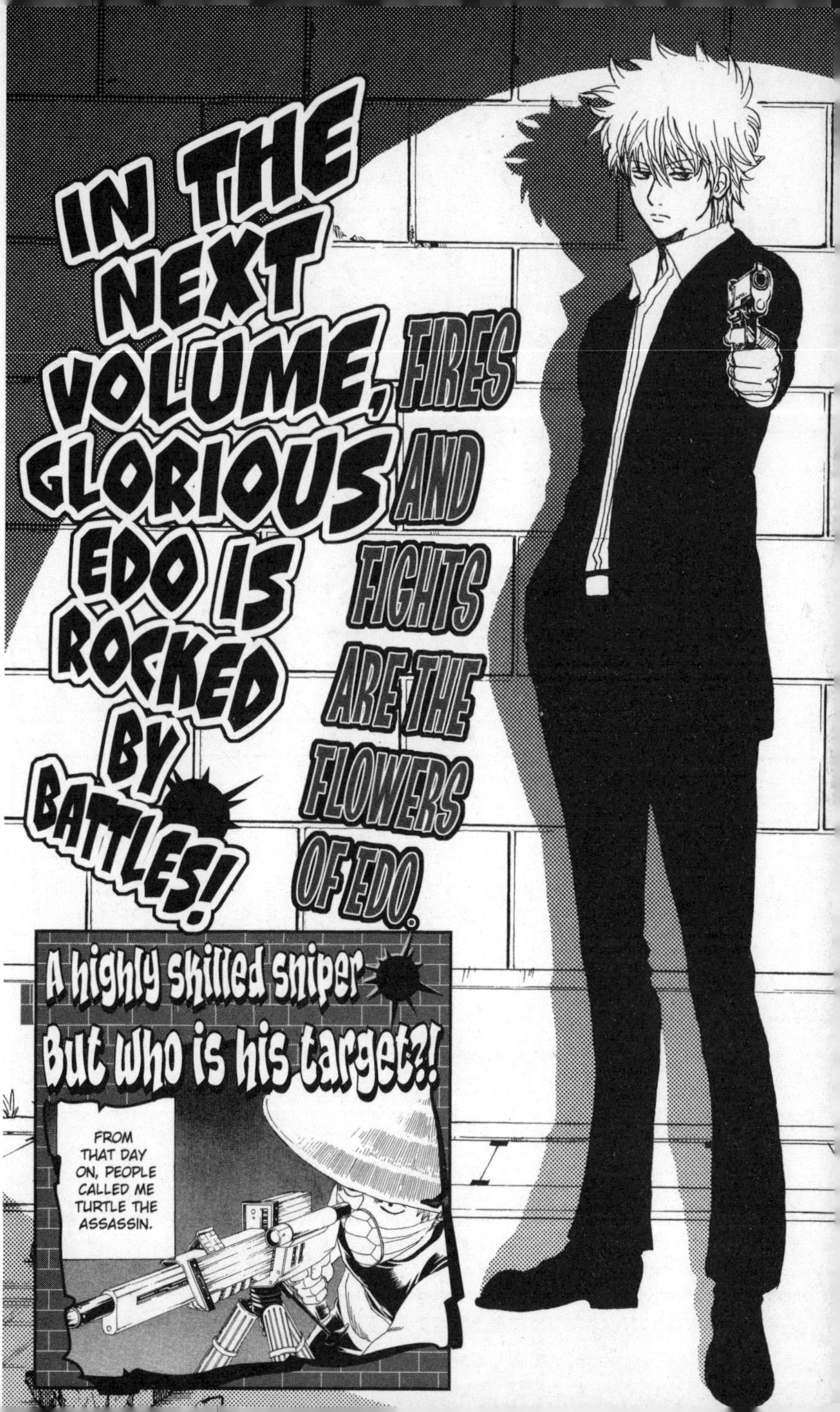
IN THE NEXT VOLUME, GLORIOUS EDO IS ROCKED BY BATTLES!
FIRES AND FIGHTS ARE THE FLOWERS OF EDO.
A highly skilled sniper
But who is his target?!
FROM THAT DAY ON, PEOPLE CALLED ME TURTLE THE ASSASSIN.

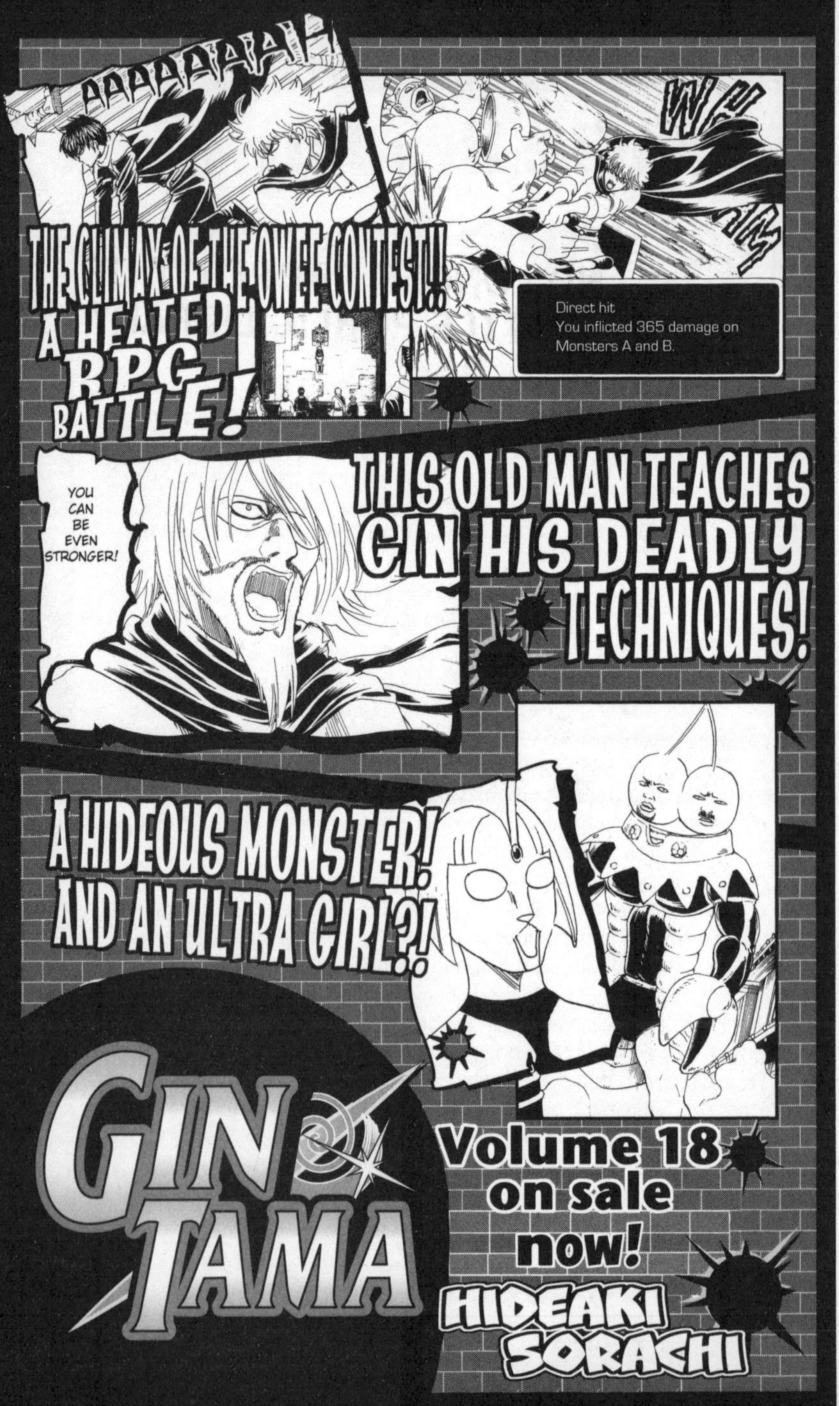
WHAM
AAAAAAAAAH!
THE CLIMAX OF THE OWEE CONTEST!!
A HEATED RPG BATTLE!
Direct hit
You inflicted 365 damage on Monsters A and B.
THIS OLD MAN TEACHES GIN HIS DEADLY TECHNIQUES!
YOU CAN BE EVEN STRONGER!
A HIDEOUS MONSTER! AND AN ULTRA GIRL?!
GIN TAMA
Volume 18 on sale now!
HIDEAKI SORACHI

You're Reading in the Wrong Direction!!

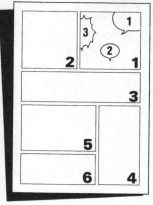

Whoops! Guess what? You're starting at the wrong end of the comic!

…It's true! In keeping with the original Japanese format, **Gin Tama** is meant to be read from right to left, starting in the upper-right corner.

Unlike English, which is read from left to right, Japanese is read from right to left, meaning that action, sound effects and word-balloon order are completely reversed… something which can make readers unfamiliar with Japanese feel pretty backwards themselves. For this reason, manga or Japanese comics published in the U.S. in English have sometimes been published "flopped"—that is, printed in exact reverse order, as though seen from the other side of a mirror.

By flopping pages, U.S. publishers can avoid confusing readers, but the compromise is not without its downside. For one thing, a character in a flopped manga series who once wore in the original Japanese version a T-shirt emblazoned with "M A Y" (as in "the merry month of") now wears one which reads "Y A M"! Additionally, many manga creators in Japan are themselves unhappy with the process, as some feel the mirror-imaging of their art alters their original intentions.

We are proud to bring you Hideaki Sorachi's **Gin Tama** in the original unflopped format. For now, though, turn to the other side of the book and let the wackiness begin…!

–Editor

GIN TAMA VOL. 17
SHONEN JUMP ADVANCED Manga Edition

STORY & ART BY HIDEAKI SORACHI

Translation/Kyoko Shapiro, Honyaku Center Inc.
English Adaptation/Lance Caselman
Touch-up Art & Lettering/Avril Averill
Design/Ronnie Casson
Editor/Jann Jones

Published by VIZ Media, LLC
P.O. Box 77010
San Francisco, CA 94107

10 9 8 7 6 5 4 3 2
First printing, March 2010
Second printing, November 2018

www.viz.com

THE WORLD'S
MOST POPULAR MANGA

www.shonenjump.com

…day's my birthday.
…n't Dad home?

Mom, why?

Just shut up
and eat!

CLINK
CLINK

Hideaki Sorachi

My editor, Mr. Onishi,
is getting married in April.
I cannot ask a man with a family
to come to my place to pick
up manuscripts at 3 a.m.,
so I hereby declare:
I will finish my manuscripts one
hour earlier, at 2 a.m.

Hideaki Sorachi was born on
May 25, 1979, and grew up in
Hokkaido, Japan. His ongoing
series, *GIN TAMA*, became a huge hit when
it began running in the pages of Japan's
Weekly Shonen Jump in 2004. A *GIN
TAMA* animated series followed soon after,
premiering on Japanese TV in April 2006.
Sorachi made his manga debut with the
one-shot story *DANDELION*.